KT-392-941

501
MUST-VISIT
WILD PLACES

501 MUST-VISIT
WILD PLACES

Bounty
BOOKS

An Hachette UK Company
www.hachette.co.uk

First published in Great Britain in 2010 by Bounty Books,
a division of Octopus Publishing Group Ltd
Carmelite House
50 Victoria Embankment
London EC4Y 0DZ
www.octopusbooks.co.uk

This revised edition published in 2017

Copyright © Octopus Publishing Group Limited 2010, 2011, 2013, 2017

All rights reserved. No part of this publication may be reproduced, stored in a retrieval system,
or transmitted, in any form or by any means, electronic, mechanical, photocopying, recording
or otherwise without the prior written permission of the publisher.

ISBN: 978-0-7537-3255-7

A CIP catalogue record is available from the British Library

Printed and bound in China

10 9 8 7 6 5 4 3 2 1

Publisher: Lucy Pessell
Designer: Lisa Layton
Editor: Sarah Vaughan
Assistant Production Manager: Lucy Carter

Notes
For your own safety please note this book is only intended as a guide. Octopus Publishing
Group is not responsible for the actions or precautionary measures taken by readers. Please
check with your government's own foreign travel advice before travelling.

CONTENTS

INTRODUCTION

The dictionary defines the word 'wild' as describing uninhabited and unspoilt regions, and also plants or animals that live independently of humankind. But this evocative word has as many nuances as there are people who use it. For some unapologetic city lovers, a wild place is anywhere more than 30 minutes away from a decent restaurant, warm bath and comfortable bed. At the opposite extreme others feel the 'wildness' of a remote island can be ruined by a distant glimpse of another person. In between are those who simply want to appreciate the breathtaking variety of Nature's bounteous natural wonders. *501 Must-Visit Wild Places* provides an overview of many different types of wild place around the world, with the aim of surprising and satisfying every reader… whatever their definition of 'wild'.

Despite today's booming travel industry and easier access to parts of the world our grandparents had barely heard of, it is practically impossible for any individual to see more than a fraction of Planet Earth in a lifetime. And for reasons of climate and politics, there will forever be wilderness areas that are hard to reach. Always check in advance whether a wild place could also be a dangerous one particularly near borders where there are hostilities or countries where extremists target tourists to try to score crude political points. Take official advice about travel and safety arrangements.

Even when nearer home common sense should prevail when going off the beaten track. Leave information with family or friends about the latest adventure and where you expect to be on certain dates. Take a detailed map, torch, lightweight warm-and-waterproof clothing, water and even a whistle with which to attract attention. More elaborate survival packs may be bought from specialist shops or made up following advice on adventure-travel websites.

It almost seems unfair to single out any of the amazing places featured in this book, but a perfect example of the unexpected is Dasht-e Lut in Iran. One of the hottest places on earth, it is such a hostile environment that no flora or fauna live there. However, it can be seen from settlements in the surrounding hills and is a quite remarkable sight. For most, it is enough just to have seen it from afar. Other extraordinary places are endangered by the number of visitors they attract, putting rare plants, animals and sometimes the landscape itself in jeopardy. It goes without saying (but is still worth repeating) that visitors must behave responsibly to help conserve precious wilderness areas. Observe basic rules such as not lighting fires in tinder-dry forests or digging up plants imagining that just one won't matter. And if advised to stay on tracks do just that. In Jamaica's Cockpit Country, a fascinating region, exploring tempting virgin forest off-trail can lead to disaster. In many places what appears to be solid rock is actually a deceptively thin layer covering deep sinkholes beneath.

Of course, it's not necessary to travel to distant lands to experience the untamed natural world. Some places that appear familiar in daylight – say a local wood – can seem very different in the moonlight when night birds call and badgers, foxes, stoats and weasels go about their business. Nature is full of surprises. A beautiful but sparse hillside in the west of England, grazed by sheep, became an extraordinary wild place in the autumn of 2009 when thousands of poppies in every shade from red to cream appeared spontaneously, having lain dormant throughout living memory. Unusually warm and sunny weather and a local farmer turning over a field to aerate the soil prompted this unexpected reclamation of the land by wild flowers. In a few short weeks they were gone.

Not everyone wants to visit truly wild places, preferring instead to visit the national parks that preserve some of the world's landscapes, animals and plants before returning to civilization for a good night's rest. And some of us have a deep desire to see a specific place or animal during our lifetime. It might be mountain gorillas in Rwanda or Royal Bengal tigers in Nepal, lemurs in Madagascar or the hundreds of thousands of water birds that rest at Lake Ichkeul in Tunisia… perhaps simply the sun setting over the Pacific from a lonely palm-fringed beach in the company of a loved one or true friends. Whatever the dream, it may be possible to make it come true. Hatch a firm plan, start saving and go with an enquiring mind and open heart.

AMERICAS & THE CARIBBEAN

THE YUKON

North America/Canada

DON'T MISS
Mount Logan: second
highest in North America.

YOU SHOULD KNOW

The Klondike Gold Rush that began in the late 1890s was sparked by the discovery of a rich gold deposit in Rabbit Creek – which soon became Bonanza Creek.

The Yukon in the far west is the smallest of Canada's three federal territories, and down from a desolate arctic coast in the north is one of the wildest – and loneliest – places on Earth.

Most of the territory's population of 35,000 live in Whitehorse, but the town is only a staging post for those visiting the wild areas. The territory largely consists of the Yukon River's watershed, a fabulous landscape dotted with snow-capped mountains and long alpine lakes fed by glaciers, often surrounded by a sporadic growth of stunted trees. Elsewhere, dense pine forests surround crystal-clear meltwater lakes. The Yukon supports a fascinating diversity of animals and birds and the whole place comes alive with a brilliant display of wild flowers in summer. Vast areas are completely undeveloped, and much of the Yukon is strictly protected by National Park or other conservation status. To the delight of visitors who want to get away from it all, the destructive hand of man has barely touched this pristine wilderness. That can make exploration difficult or even dangerous, but happily the locals are welcoming and many of them make a good living from helping visitors to enjoy individual access to this unique environment. Every settlement has its own airstrip and outfitter, while guides may be found for numerous rewarding activities ranging from simple backcountry trekking through angling, kayaking, skiing, snowboarding and snowmobiling to exceptional opportunities to observe the varied local wildlife.

WHEN TO GO: Summer (June–August). Adventurous winter visitors can drive the famous Tuktoyaktuk Winter Road along the frozen Mackenzie River's delta channels.

TUKTOYAKTUK AND THE PINGOS

North America/Canada

A visit to the atmospheric Pingo National Landmark on the Arctic Ocean shore of Canada's Northwest Territories is an experience to treasure. Pingos – hydrolaccoliths to the scientifically minded – are amazing domed ice hills in areas of permafrost that have been formed over time by the slow build-up of ice during the long winters. The landmark extends to 16 sq km (6 sq mi) and in addition to large pingos rising from the watery landscape, it contains fine examples of impressive frozen features like massive ice blocks and wedge ice that forms intricate patterns of interlocking tundra polygons.

Before accessing the landmark's unique natural wonders, it is necessary to reach Tuktoyaktuk, located on Kugmallit Bay in the far north. This is an Inuvialuit settlement usually referred to simply as Tuk, and many of the local Inuit people still follow a traditional way of life. But to that may be added thoroughly modern oil and gas industries plus transportation (mainly by tugs and barges). Tuktoyaktuk has around 900 inhabitants, and some of them cater for determined travellers who wish to explore the nearby Pingo National Landmark, just west of town.

CUMBERLAND PENINSULA

North America/Canada

Baffin Island in Nunavut is an outpost of Canada's northland, and the demanding climate ensures that the population consists of no more than 10,000 hardy souls. The island is well known for BASE-jumping, thanks to a profusion of high cliffs, and another ideal destination is the east coast's Cumberland Peninsula, home to Auyuittuq National Park. The latter consists of classic Arctic wilderness, where granite mountains rub jagged shoulders with sweeping glaciers, rugged fjords and polar sea ice. The name means 'land that never melts' in the language of indigenous Inuits, although it remains to be seen whether global warming will change this. This opportunity to experience the majestic beauty of the Arctic is not for the unfit, faint-hearted or budget travellers. It's hard enough to reach the access points – Qikiqtarjuaq on Broughton Island or Pangnirtung –

and registration is required at either park office. Would-be explorers must then attend an orientation session before proceeding to the park with a local guide by boat, snowmobile or dog sled.

WORTH A DETOUR: Take the rare but compelling opportunity to see polar bears in their natural habitat.

GWAII HAANAS NATIONAL PARK

North America/Canada

YOU SHOULD KNOW

This is definitely not a place where nature lovers can turn up and explore unaided.

WORTH A DETOUR:
Ninstints (officially Sgang Gwaay Llanagaay, which translates as 'Red Cod Island Village') – a UNESCO World Heritage Site on Anthony Island at the southern end of Gwaii Haanas that is a former Haida village site complete with a large collection of totems.

This unspoiled archipelago, consisting of 138 of the southernmost Queen Charlotte Islands, is 130 km (80 mi) off the coast of British Columbia. It is well worth the considerable effort needed to reach this magical destination from the mainland. Gwaii Haanas – or to choose a specific destination Gwaii Haanas National Park Reserve and Haida Heritage Site – is home to Canada's indigenous Haida Nation. These indigenous people have maintained a pristine environment protected by sustainable management practices. With the advent of NMCAR (National Marine Conservation Area Reserve) status, the whole of Gwaii Haanas from mountain top to seabed will be protected forever.

The dramatic landscapes of Gwaii Haanas Park range from rugged mountains to deep fjords, alpine meadows to sub-alpine tundra, wetlands to rushing streams, dense forests to beguiling lakes. Within this unique environment distinct flora and fauna have evolved. The local animals – such as a subspecies of black bear larger than its mainland cousin – have been joined by imported species such as beaver, squirrel, racoon and Sitka black-tailed deer. There are great opportunities for wildlife-watching and in addition to four-footed inhabitants there is a thriving bird population. This includes extensive seabird colonies where nesting can be observed along the shorelines between May and September. Bald eagles are a common sight and many different species stop off as they migrate along the Pacific flyway.

Carefully managed tourism is important to the local economy and for those who like to escape from the madding tourist crowd Gwaii Haanas is a destination to die for – happily, with a little help from knowledgeable local guides, it shouldn't come to that.

WORTH A DETOUR: Take the opportunity to see a pod of orcas swimming past the island from the relaxing vantage point of a natural hot tub.

HOTSPRINGS ISLAND

North America/Canada

Within Gwaii Haanas National Park Reserve is Hotsprings Island (also known as Gandla'kin), one of the jewels in the crown of the Queen Charlotte Islands.

Simply getting there calls for a well-planned expedition. It can be independently reached by kayak, or alternatively it's possible to book a trip as part of a select group who will be decanted into kayaks from a mother ship, close to the island. These expeditions often take in more than Hotsprings Island during the day-long outing, offering a more general chance to explore the wondrous Gwaii Haanas Reserve. For those whose wallets are bigger than their muscles, hiring a floatplane from Moresby Camp might be the answer. Whatever the means of transport, once on Hotsprings Island the first delight is exploring the fascinating shoreline and craggy interior. There are stunning scenic views out over Juan Perez Sound – a kayaker's paradise – and to the San Christoval Mountains back on the west coast of Moresby Island. After that, what could be more relaxing than dabbling in the island's dozen hot springs and seeps, followed by a plunge into one of the spring-fed hot pools carved into the volcanic rock.

JEDEDIAH ISLAND

DON'T MISS
The remains of an aboriginal fish weir.

North America/Canada

The phrase 'small but beautifully formed' could have been coined to describe British Columbia's Jedediah, located between the larger islands of Lasqueti and Texada in the Straits of Georgia, off Vancouver Island. Jedediah Island is a tranquil haven that extends to 2.4 sq km (0.9 sq mi). In the best Canadian tradition, there are no restrictions on camping, so the place becomes a favourite summer haunt for kayakers, recreational boaters and wilderness campers attracted by the pristine marine environment.

The island has five bays that offer safe harbour, with excellent camping areas around Long Bay and more isolated possibilities along the eastern shore. The coastline has bays, rocky coves, deep anchorages and sandy beaches. The unspoiled interior consists of rocky outcrops surrounded by forest containing a variety of tree species including arbutus and the ubiquitous Douglas fir, plus flat meadow areas that are ideal for pitching camp. Although a campfire ban is sometimes in operation for safety reasons, fires are generally allowed below the high-tide mark. There are a number of established hiking trails that connect the secluded bays, and visitors are asked to keep to these designed paths rather than striking off into the woods (beware – there are sometimes bears on the island!). No formal campsites exist and the only facilities provided on Jedediah Island are four pit toilets, located near the most popular anchorages. Anyone with the get-up-and-go to reach Jedediah will be aware of the 'Leave no Trace' camping ethic.

NOOTKA ISLAND

North America/Canada

YOU SHOULD KNOW
There is an access charge to the First Nations reserve at Friendly Cove.

Waterborne adventure beckons for those willing to take to their boats and explore the fabulous waters that envelop Nootka Island off the wild west coast of Vancouver Island in British Columbia. There are a number of published kayak trails that offer inspiring vistas of breathtaking coastal scenery for those who prefer to remain afloat, but that would mean ignoring the solid delights of Nootka Island itself.

The island covers an area of 534 sq km (206 sq mi). The main settlement is Yuquot (Friendly Cove), where modern-day British Columbia was born when the Royal Navy's Captain James Cook, who arrived in 1778, made the initial European contact with BC's First Nations people.

The interior is a wilderness that cries out to be explored by the experienced hiker who loves solitude and magnificent scenery. Well-established trails along the island's awesome west coast and through the interior – that may be combined for a round trip – are not for the inexperienced.

WORTH A DETOUR:
See the delights of Tahsis, a charming coastal village at the head of Tahsis Inlet, a fjord running off Nootka Sound.

HOW TO GET THERE:
Trips to the interior can be by helicopter, light aircraft, boat, horse... or just on foot.

NORTHERN ROCKIES

North America/Canada

In the top right-hand corner of British Columbia the Rocky Mountains offer amazing opportunities for lovers of wild places. Around 80 km (50 mi) to the southwest of Fort Nelson on the Alaska Highway is the Northern Rocky Mountains Provincial Park. Further along the road is Stone Mountain Provincial Park, while to the south is Kwadacha Wilderness Park. They offer a unique contiguous wilderness that encompasses much of BC's northeastern mountain landscape.

The largest is Northern Rocky Mountains Park. This expanse of valleys and ridges has a variety of water features – glaciers, lakes, large rivers, rushing streams, waterfalls and white water. The smaller Stone Mountain Park encompasses some of Canada's finest scenery. For the truly dedicated backwoods explorer, the vast Kwadacha Wilderness does just what it says on the packet. It's accessed via a 150 km (93 mi) trail from the Alaska Highway at Trutch, or an alternative route from Sikanni Chief Canyon, and offers pristine wilderness untouched by the acquisitive hand of man. This one is for experienced hikers and horse riders only, although it is possible to be flown in.

PURCELL WILDERNESS

North America/Canada

WHEN TO GO:
May–September. Hikers should note that many of the river crossings are difficult before the end of July, although a few have simple self-operated cable cars.

It's a mouthful – namely the Purcell Wilderness Conservancy Provincial Park and Protected Area – but don't be put off by that. This is a magnificent 2,027 sq km (783 sq mi) mountainous landscape where no wheeled traffic whatsoever is permitted, and nor are the sort of helicopter drops well-heeled tourists sometimes use to reach remote wilderness destinations without doing the hard approach work. The park encompasses six large catchments that drain into the Columbia River, and the original ecosystem is undamaged – remaining the only intact ecosystem in southeastern British Columbia. The park is located to the northeast of Nelson and northwest of Kimberley, not far from the US border with Washington, Idaho and Montana.

This is a truly wild place that offers determined explorers a choice of experiences to savour. Recreational opportunities include hunting, fishing, canoeing, horse riding, historic sites, climbing, wildlife observation and of course hiking. None of these is for the inexperienced, as the park contains no shelters, improved trails, public communications or supply points. Self-sufficient wilderness travellers will not be daunted, but indeed encouraged, by the opportunity to truly escape civilization. Even those who don't intend to venture into the park's rugged interior will find a day visit worthwhile, if only for splendid mountain scenery.

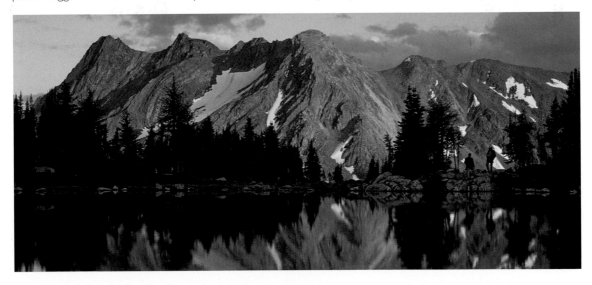

STRATHCONA PROVINCIAL PARK
North America/Canada

WORTH A DETOUR: Delta Falls in the southern section of the park – with an impressive drop of 440 m (1,440 ft) over three cascades, this is one of Canada's highest waterfalls.

Vancouver Island's largest provincial park was founded back in 1911, and now includes the UNESCO Biosphere Reserve at Clayoquot Sound, which encompasses three important watersheds in the western part of the park. Strathcona Provincial Park in the island's centre provides an unspoilt but relatively accessible tract of beautiful wild country. It can easily be reached from the surrounding communities of Gold River and Campbell River.

Trekkers will find that this rugged wilderness offers a wonderful display of assorted wild flowers in the summer months, with mixed forest covering much of the park's valley areas and foothills. The intermediate slopes are home to creeping juniper, mountain hemlock and sub-alpine fir. Strathcona's rugged mountains

remain snow-capped all year. The park is birdwatcher heaven, with unique Vancouver Island white-tailed ptarmigan to be found along with grouse, band-tailed pigeon, Steller's jay and many other species including chestnut-backed chickadee and red-breasted nuthatch. Mammals include the Roosevelt elk, Vancouver Island marmot, Vancouver Island wolf and black-tailed deer. The most popular recreational activities are hiking, canoeing, climbing, cycling, fishing and snow sports.

WORTH A DETOUR: The opportunity to view the awesome Aurora Borealis (Northern Lights) – sadly available only to those willing to make a winter expedition.

WOOD BUFFALO NATIONAL PARK
North America/Canada

Wood Buffalo National Park was established in the 1920s to protect wood bison, a subspecies of the American bison (widely called 'buffalo'). The park's population of 5,000 is now the largest herd of free-ranging bison to be found anywhere, and it encompasses a vast tract of wilderness that ranges from Caribou Mountains to the Peace-Athabasca Delta,.

In addition to the eponymous wood buffalo, the park contains much wildlife. Notable among many bird species is the critically endangered whooping crane. Animals include bears, moose, wolf, lynx, beaver and snowshoe hare. There is also a large population of garter snakes that have communal dens within the park. In addition to wildlife-watching, there are plenty of other attractions for intrepid adventurers. The possibilities for hiking, canoeing, boating, camping and fishing – with or without guides – are virtually limitless.

DON'T MISS
Fort Macleod – both the interesting NWMP (North-West Mounted Police) Museum and restored Main Street.

HEAD-SMASHED-IN BUFFALO JUMP
North America/Canada

Alberta's Head-Smashed-In Buffalo Jump tells it just as it is, or rather was. This special natural feature provides a reminder of the simple way of life once followed by the indigenous people of Canada. The location of this historic site is a point where prairie starts to give way to the foothills of the Rocky Mountains, close to the US border and not far from the town of Fort Macleod. A fascinating museum of Blackfoot culture is built naturalistically into a sandstone cliff.

This presents archaeological evidence gathered from the area and explores the mythology, ecology, lifestyle and technology of the Blackfoot peoples. The jump itself remains just as it has looked since time immemorial. This 10 m (33 ft) mini-cliff above a steep slope has been used to kill bison for at least five millennia. The buffalo were driven from a favoured grazing ground in the nearby Porcupine Hills, being channelled into narrowing lanes by many hundreds of artificial stone cairns before going off the 'jump' at full gallop. The resulting plunge broke legs and disabled these heavy beasts, allowing the hunters to finish them off at leisure and process the spoils at a nearby camp.

VALLEY OF THE TEN PEAKS
North America/Canada

Alberta's Banff National Park in the Rocky Mountains is Canada's oldest and covers an extensive 6,640 sq km (2,564 sq mi). It consists of mountainous terrain with many ice fields and glaciers. Dense pine forests that crowd the many lakes counterpoint the park's wonderful alpine landscapes.

One undoubted highlight of the park's protected wilderness is the magical Valley of the Ten Peaks, which contains ice-blue Moraine Lake.

The short but rewarding interpretive Rockpile Trail may be taken. It will take less than an hour to get to the top of the eponymous heap of rocks and back, with gentle ascent of rock-slab steps required. The effort will be rewarded by sensational vistas from viewpoints that overlook the lake and some of the famous Ten Peaks. This is some of the most spectacular scenery to be found anywhere in the Rockies.

WHEN TO GO: May–September. The Valley of Ten Peaks attracts a large number of visitors in high season (July and August).

WRITING-ON-STONE PROVINCIAL PARK

North America/Canada

WORTH A DETOUR:
The fascinating North-West Mounted Police outpost, reconstructed exactly as was after a catastrophic fire destroyed the original shortly after World War I. It's part of the protected cultural site.

YOU SHOULD KNOW
The most sensitive areas of the park have been named as a Provincial Historic Resource to protect the rock art from vandalism. Access to these areas is by official guided tour only.

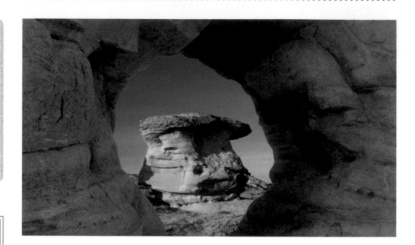

One of the most interesting places in Alberta contains both the works of nature and the impressive creations of Native Americans. The clue is in the name, for Writing-on-Stone Provincial Park contains the most concentrated collection of rock art to be found on the North American Great Plains. There are over 50 sites and literally thousands of pictographs (paintings) and petroglyphs (carvings), still held sacred by the Blackfoot people and other native tribes. The Canadian government has filed an application for UNESCO World Heritage Site status under the Blackfoot name Áísínai'Pi, meaning 'it is pictured'.

The park is a 17.8 sq km (6.9 sq mi) area of protected prairie, set against the glowering backdrop of Montana's volcanic Sweetgrass Hills to the south. It occupies part of the Milk River, where ancient grassland is broken by spectacular rocky outcrops. There are numerous coulees – low-lying areas with water in the bottom. This ideal habitat supports an impressive array of wildlife, which is high on the list of the park's sights. Animals include mule deer, pronghorn antelopes, bobcats, skunks, marmots, raccoons and northern pocket gophers. Among many bird species are prairie falcons, kestrels, cliff swallows and owls, along with pheasants and grey partridges. Reptiles include various frogs, spadefoot toads, tiger salamanders and assorted snakes. But the park's unique attraction is the native rock art, dating back into the mists of time. Much was created by nomads passing through a sacred landscape consisting of the rocky hoodoos (stone spires) that adorn the park, and tells of the everyday lives and dramas of those who created them. From the mid-17th century the tales started to include the horses, guns and metal goods introduced by European incomers, whose influx would change and ultimately destroy the indigenous way of life in less than 150 years.

YOU SHOULD KNOW
Don't hike in the winter – annual
snowfall exceeds 4.5 m (15 ft).

AGAWA CANYON

North America/Canada

There's an easy way and a hard way for those seeking to experience the natural delights of Northern Ontario's Agawa Canyon Wilderness Park. The park lies in a shallow canyon created by the erosive action of the Agawa River, between the Boreal Forest and Great Lakes-St Lawrence Forest regions. This ensures that the flora of both is represented along the well-wooded canyon, with an abundance of flowering plants in spring and summer.

The area was opened up when rail tracks were laid through the canyon in 1911, and exploited in the early 1950s when the railway company cleared a picnic area. And travelling by the Algoma Central Railway's Agawa Canyon tour train is still the easy way to visit the wilderness park, departing from the depot in downtown Sault Ste Marie. The city's grimy industrial area soon gives way to variegated woodland, rivers crossed by impressive trestle bridges and occasional panoramic vistas. It's over three hours each way, with just two hours to explore the canyon in between, choosing between five short nature trails that criss-cross the park area connecting a number of waterfalls. The experience is still very rewarding for anyone who does not have the time – or inclination – to hike in. That adds up to plenty of people, and tour trains are usually packed. But after the train has gone, those who make the effort to walk into this rugged wilderness park will more or less have the place to themselves. Even going the hard way is best essayed with a little help from the railway company. Seasoned hikers could plan their own expedition, but many prefer to opt for assistance from Algoma Central, which operates various lodges along the line. These offer the ideal starting point for a hiking trip to Agawa Canyon.

WORTH A DETOUR:
The 372-step climb to the lookout on the gorge wall, where an observation platform provides a stunning view of the canyon. There's a halfway house for those not fit enough to make the top.

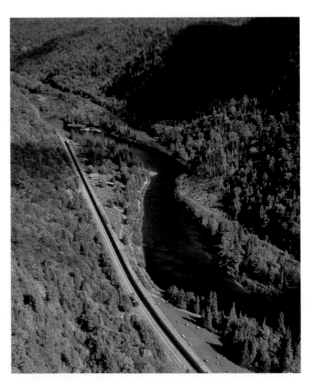

ALGONQUIN PROVINCIAL PARK
North America/Canada

WORTH A DETOUR: Organized 'wolf howlings' in late summer. Park staff encourage a wolf chorus by imitating their howls. When they get going, the wolves create a haunting melody.

Canada's greatest artist, Tom Thomson, spent every spring and summer hunting, fishing and canoeing in this park, and producing small studies of the landscape. He then returned to his studio in winter to develop these into larger oils on canvas which, almost unbelievably, were created using just four colours. Thomson's interpretations of Canada's wildernesses marked an epiphany in European settlers' attitudes to the country they had come to live in. The beauty of his work, as well as waking up a backward-looking art establishment, helped European Canadians to shake off their 'garrison mentality' and view the country around them no longer as 'Nature the Monster' but as a place of great beauty to be discovered and enjoyed.

It is possible to visit the park's museum in the morning, have a brunch of pancakes and maple syrup and be paddling a canoe on one of it's many thousand pristine lakes in the afternoon. The park is vast and covers an area about one third the size of Wales. It has over 1,600 km (995 mi) of navigable waterways and innumerable hiking trails, which can be explored on skis, snowshoes or snowmobile in winter and on foot or on the water in summer. Its vast interior is characterized by maple-covered hills, fast-running streams, craggy ridges and spruce bogs. This environment supports a vast array of wildlife. Moose, black bear, beaver and wolves live alongside over 250 reported bird species and over 40 species of (non-poisonous) amphibians and reptiles. It is a place that the phrase 'Go explore' could have been written for.

KILLARNEY PROVINCIAL PARK
North America/Canada

DON'T MISS
The view of Silver Peak from the shores of David Lake.

If there is one thing Ontario has in abundance it is well-managed provincial parks ripe for exploration on foot, snowshoe or by canoe. Killarney Provincial Park, located by the shores of Georgian Bay, itself an arm of Lake Huron, has perhaps the most spectacular scenery. Although it is small for a Canadian park at just under 500 sq km (193 sq mi), it offers a great variety of landscapes. Tectonic compression has changed the area's sandstone into brilliant white quartzite. This contrasts beautifully with the deep-blue lakes and the rich green of pine ridges. Ideally, active exploration should be punctuated with rests at the best vantage points to view the effects that sudden changes of light have on this striking palette. It was this landscape that drew the great artist AY Jackson to the area and he later successfully lobbied for the creation of the Provincial Park.

POINT PELEE NATIONAL PARK

North America/Canada

YOU SHOULD KNOW

While Point Pelee marks the most southerly point of mainland Canada, Pelee Island is its southernmost inhabited territory.

WHEN TO GO:
All year, but the shuttle service to the tip operates only from April–October.

WORTH A DETOUR:
Standing at the very tip, virtually surrounded by the waters of Lake Erie.

Point Pelee is a 20-sq km (8-sq mi) spit of land that juts out into Lake Erie, tapering gracefully to the point that marks the southernmost tip of mainland Canada. It sits on the same latitude as northern California and has a climate that allows for the greatest biodiversity in Canada. Created by hunters in 1918 as an outdoor playground, soon the motorized transport that was liberating North Americans in their pursuit of pleasure started to strangle the park. Over the years the area became crammed with summer homes and campgrounds, and traffic jams often rivalled those of rush-hour in downtown Los Angeles.

Radical action was needed to restore the area to its former glory and, in 1972, a white knight duly arrived. Legislation was passed and all land was placed under the ownership of Parks Canada, traffic was greatly restricted and a transit service was introduced to ferry visitors deep into the park. Today, the area is home to a stunning array of wildlife. It marks the take-off point for a vast number of birds heading south and the assembly point for one of the greatest migrations on Earth. Each autumn, hundreds of thousands of monarch butterflies gather on the narrow peninsula, waiting for a kind wind to assist their passage over the Great Lake and eventually on down to Mexico.

Point Pelee contains an astonishing variety of terrain for an area of its size. Long sandy beaches invite a slow amble, while boardwalks take the visitor out deep into marshland. Canoeists can wend their way through reed beds and there are numerous trails suitable for navigation all year round. Large swathes of savannah grassland are framed by lush deciduous forest in a park that has something for everyone, whether they have two wings, four wings or none.

PUKASKWA NATIONAL PARK

North America/Canada

WHEN TO GO: The National Park is open all year round, but most of the facilities at the Hattie Cove campground are open only from May–October.

Pukaskwa National Park is a place defined by its proximity to Lake Superior – the largest freshwater lake in the world. The park is virtually all wilderness, with vehicular access available only to the administration office and the Hattie Cove campground. The landscape is boreal forest, typical of the Canadian Shield, where spruce and balsam mix with that most Canadian of trees – the Jack pine. Tip Top Mountain rises to

YOU SHOULD KNOW

The shoreline is dotted with trenches. They may be 10,000 years old and were created by ancestors of the local Ojibwa people. Their function is unknown.

a height of 630 m (2,067 ft) above sea level and marks the park's highest point, and a 60 km (37 mi) trail follows the shoreline of Lake Superior. A hop-on hop-off boat-hire service operates during the summer, allowing the hiker to experience this unique marine environment more intimately. The waters of Horseshoe Bay are shallow and calm enough to allow swimming in high summer, and the shoreline is the perfect place to paddle a canoe.

DON'T MISS

Watching the waves roll in from Blackhead. Impressive in late spring.

CAPE SPEAR NATIONAL HISTORIC SITE

North America/Canada

People roll up to Cape Spear's historic lighthouse, take a quick photo and roll away again. However, the centre of the Historic Site is well worth an hour or two of anyone's time. It contains the oldest surviving lighthouse in Newfoundland – dating back to 1836 – complete with renovated lighthouse-keeper's quarters. It was also the site of much activity in World War II, when a series of tunnels and fortifications was constructed. Two gun emplacements remain as a reminder of more troubled times. Venturing away from the man-made structures on show, the Cape has much to commend it to those looking for a rugged, if sometimes very bracing, hike. The area has bird life in abundance, including shearwaters which can usually only be seen some distance out to sea. In late spring huge icebergs drift slowly down the coast like ghostly facsimiles of the rugged cape landscape. The headland is dotted with secluded coves which, in summer, provide the best land-based whale-watching in North America. Orca, minke and finback whales all come to feed on herring and capelin in the waters off the cape. Harbour seals, otters and dolphins may also be observed from these natural vantage points.

Right: Cape Spear's lighthouse

CAPE ST MARY'S ECOLOGICAL RESERVE
North America/Canada

DON'T MISS
Gannets greeting each other in French and English styles – a raised beak salute and alternating cheek beak taps.

Located at the very tip of Newfoundland's Avalon Peninsula, Cape St Mary's Ecological Reserve is about as wild a place as you could wish to find in North America. Waves crash against the rapidly eroding cliffs that mark the reserve's land boundary, while mist and fog shroud the peninsula most days. But when the wind abates and the fog clears one of the most beautiful seascapes on Earth is revealed. A lush green carpet of grass and moss covers the headlands and the land falls sharply away into the azure waters of the North Atlantic.

The reserve covers both the headland and the immediate waters around it. The main objective of the reserve was to create a low-pollution environment where birdlife could thrive. The result is a birdwatcher's paradise. Out to sea, the appropriately named Bird Rock is a limestone outcrop which has become separated from the mainland by years of erosion. Its detachment means that it is free from predators, and pearly white gannets flourish to the point that every square inch of the island is occupied by them. Kittiwakes, gannets and murres all plunge into the fish-rich waters, making the sea fizz with activity.

WHEN TO GO: The Gulf is usually ice free from May–November.
WORTH A DETOUR: Port Aux Basques – a beautiful old French fishing station right at the very tip of Newfoundland as it juts out into the Gulf.

GULF OF ST LAWRENCE
North America/Canada

In geographical science the term 'gulf' is used to describe a partly landlocked sea and although the Gulf of St Lawrence (Golfe du Saint-Laurent) seems to fit the bill, it is a misnomer. In reality the 'Gulf' is the estuary of a 'super-river' formed at the end of the last ice age.

The Gulf of St Lawrence is massive, covering an area of around 234,000 sq km (90,350 sq mi) and is of immense strategic value as it links the Great Lakes to the sea via the St Lawrence River and Seaway. It contains many of the Maritimes' most beautiful and formidable islands, including Prince Edward and Bonaventure Islands as well as the Magdalen Archipelago. Cruise ships that ply their trade in the Gulf in summer can take weeks to complete their tours, yet only scratch the surface of discovery.

The Gulf has long been of vital importance and many First Nations groups chose to live on its edge to exploit its fish-rich waters. Ever since its discovery by Europeans in 1534 it has been a vital shipping route into Canada, and the point at which the Gulf flows into the river is named the Jacques Cartier Strait, after its European discoverer. The lands around the Gulf are home to moose, caribou, bears and beavers, while its waters contain over 200 species of fish, which provide food for vast colonies of seals and pods of whales.

WORTH A DETOUR: A small detour takes you to The Spout – a giant wave-propelled geyser which squirts water at a ferocious speed through a small aperture in the rocks.

WITLESS BAY ECOLOGICAL RESERVE
North America/Canada

If you have any fear of birds and maybe have to hide behind the sofa when watching Hitchcock's *The Birds*, it is probably best to give the superbly named Witless Bay Ecological Reserve a wide berth. The reserve consists of four craggy islands – Green, Great, Gull and Pee Pee – each of which is a protected area and home to hundreds of thousands of birds. The only access to the waters of the bay is via escorted tours by locals, many of whom take time out from their regular work to show visitors this amazing landscape.

If you visit the area before the end of June, you are treated to the sight of icebergs moving across the bay like giant ice cubes, slowly melting as they drift south. The display is an awesome sight.

As you approach the islands you gradually realize that what seemed like the colour of the rocks is actually the plumage of birds. The islands are completely covered by them. Murres, puffins and kittiwakes all jostle for position on these prime pieces of avian real estate.

MAGDALEN ISLANDS
North America/Canada

HOW TO GET THERE: By ferry from Souris on Prince Edward Island or by air from Montreal and Quebec City, landing on Havre aux Maisons Island.

The Magdalen Islands (Îles de la Madeleine) form an archipelago located in the middle of the Gulf of St Lawrence, some 210 km (130 mi) from the Gaspé Peninsula. The islands, which are the visible peaks of a sub-marine ridge, run for over 60 km (37 mi) and comprise a dozen main islands along with innumerable rocky outcrops. Half of the islands are connected by long, slender sand dunes. The comparatively warm waters of the Gulf protect the island group from the harsh winters experienced on the Quebec mainland. The islands' interiors are characterized by gently contoured verdant hills, while their shorelines are marked by fragile sandstone cliffs which have been eroded into spectacular arches, tunnels and caves by the combination of powerful winds and waves. The eroded stone from the cliffs impacts greatly on the islands' littoral zones and about one third of the islands' landmass is made up of dunes and sand bars. It is easy to find solitude along its many dune-lined strands, where only the roar of the sea and the squawks of seabirds can be heard.

During the spring melt, seals can be observed hitching a ride on ice floes, while in summer the surrounding waters are ideal for windsurfing. When the wind drops, as it does every so often, the islands assume an appearance so benign that they might be from a lower latitude. But when it roars it provides a reminder that the elements govern the climate and topography of this remarkable archipelago.

MINGAN ARCHIPELAGO

North America/Canada

WHEN TO GO: From May–September is best.
WORTH A DETOUR: Watching the sun rise or set behind the magnificent monoliths that line the islands.

The Mingan Archipelago is a chain of around 30 islands and over 1,000 islets which runs for 150 km (93 mi) across Havre-Saint-Pierre on the north shore of the Gulf of Saint Lawrence. Composed of limestone bedrock with granite outcrops, this ribbon of islands has, over millions of years, been sculpted by the awesome power of sea and wind into a remarkable landscape of natural monuments. Each of these huge rock stacks has weathered uniquely, some resembling giant monsters newly emerged from the sea, while others are reminiscent of the inuksuit (stone figures) left as markers by First Nations peoples. Although the archipelago has the appearance of a fairly barren landscape, it is in fact part of a diverse marine environment. The nutrient-laden waters of the Saint-Jean and Aguanish Rivers mix with the colder

oxygen-rich waters of the Gulf to create ideal conditions. Grey, harbour and harp seals can be spotted sunning themselves on the rocks to raise their body temperature, in between fishing forays in the area's icy-cold waters. The abundance of fish and enormous shoals of plankton also attract dolphins and whales as well as Atlantic puffins, sea and eider ducks. On land, snowshoe hare, ermine and beaver flourish and the chief predators are red foxes and wolves.

RESTIGOUCHE ESTUARY

North America/Canada

WORTH A DETOUR:
Fort Listuguj, situated in the Restigouche First Nations Reservation. It's a great place to learn the legends of the area.

The Restigouche River marks the boundary between New Brunswick and Quebec and spills out into a large estuary at the western end of the Bay of Chaleur. It is fed by fast-running streams that rise in the North Appalachians and which often teem with shoals of wild salmon. The shores of this bountiful river have for centuries been the home of the Mi'kmaq people who now live on reserved land at Pointe-à-la-Croix on the Quebec bank of the estuary. .

A myriad of tributaries flow into the estuary, and it could not have been better designed for canoeing and rafting, but it is for fishing that the Restigouche is most renowned. The chance to catch and display a salmon as big as the fisherman has drawn people from around the world. For all its bounty, the estuary is a delicate ecosystem and there have been numerous incidents when fish stocks have been all but exhausted by commercial fisheries. There is also still tension surrounding the First Nation people's ancestral fishing rights.

GRAND MANAN ISLAND

North America/Canada

It may be only an hour-and-a-half ferry ride from Blacks Harbour, but Grand Manan Island has a remoteness that belies its proximity to the mainland. Home to a year-round human population of fewer than 3,000, it is also a significant stopping-off point for North American bird migration and attracts birdwatchers from around the globe. The island's name is probably a shortening of Mananook – meaning island place in the local First Nation's language. For centuries the Malecite-Passamaquoddy Indians would

risk life and limb to canoe across the often-turbulent waters to hunt, fish and collect seaweed. Norse explorers found the island over 1,000 years ago, but it was only settled by Europeans in the late 18th century. Nearly all of the settlements are dotted around the southeast coast, in comfortable little coves that provide some degree of shelter from the often ferocious wind and sea. Away from the coast Manan has a rugged interior which becomes ever more spectacular the further north and west one travels. A network of trails takes the hiker over a barren landscape of 200-million-year-old igneous rock before the land falls away into the sea via towering 120 m (394 ft) cliffs. Never crowded, the 34 km (21 mi) long island has a good system of roads which are often no more than winding country lanes.

Away from the land, the nutrient-rich waters of the Bay of Fundy attract whales and a host of seabirds, while the shallower waters closer to the shore are the perfect place to learn sea kayaking. Each season on Manan brings its own beauty. The island is covered by a carpet of wild flowers in spring, and summer and winters are tempered by the comparative warmth of the sea.

WHEN TO GO:
All year round.
The weather is best from
May–September.

WORTH A DETOUR:
The Seven Days Work cliff
formation at Whale Cove.

YOU SHOULD KNOW
The island was ceded to Britain by the Treaty of Utrecht in 1713, but the USA disputed its ownership until 1817 when they swapped it for three that are now part of Maine.

TOBEATIC WILDERNESS

North America/Canada

The Tobeatic Wilderness Area is the largest protected wild region in the Maritimes. It is an area sculpted by major glaciers of previous ice ages and its barren and semi-barren landscape is dotted with moraine and eskers. Its remoteness provides an undisturbed habitat for the rare Nova Scotia moose as well as a healthy population of black bear.

Nine major river systems have their headwaters in 'the Toby'. A network of streams, rivers and lakes makes for interesting and diverse canoeing expeditions, and solitude is almost guaranteed as the canoeist heads even a little way into this remarkable wilderness.

In autumn the colours of the mixed woodland are spectacular, but this soon gives way to a long cold winter. It is then that the wilderness assumes an eerie calm. Covered in a blanket of snow and with the lakes frozen over, the mammals of the area take their long hibernation.

WORTH A DETOUR:
The Shelburne River Canoe Route – a system of lakes connected by a river that flows from the centre of the area.

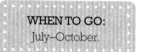

WHEN TO GO:
July–October.

SABLE ISLAND

North America/Canada

Sable Island lies like a sleeping leviathan in the North Atlantic Ocean, surrounded by barely submerged shifting sandbanks which, over the years, have swallowed more than 300 ships. The treacherousness of its waters has earned it the tag 'Graveyard of the Atlantic'. The island is long and narrow and is so battered by the elements that it is constantly changing shape. Since its discovery by Portuguese navigators, it has probably halved in size. Currently, it is around 40 km (25 mi) long and a mere 1.6 km (1 mi) wide at its broadest point. What it lacks in natural protection, the government of Canada has made up for in regulatory safeguards. Visitor numbers are strictly rationed and a code of practice must be adhered to. Indigenous wildlife includes harbour and grey seals that breed along the shoreline. However, there is one animal above all for which Sable Island is renowned: a group of more than 250 displaced horses roam wild on the island, providing a curious sight in this harsh, treeless environment. While there are several interesting and conflicting stories about how these equine exiles happened to get to the island, it is probable that they were imported in the 18th century and then abandoned.

BROOKS RANGE

North America/United States

DON'T MISS
Caribou migrations
in spring and autumn.

This impressive chain of mountains crosses Alaska from west to east, ending in Canada's Yukon, and is virtually uninhabited. The Brooks Range marks the summer position of the Arctic front, ensuring that summers are relatively mild and providing a window of opportunity for visitors. Individual expeditions are possible, but even those experienced in wilderness travel should think twice before going it alone.

The Brooks Range is the finest unspoilt mountain terrain in North America – a pristine wonderland of craggy granite, rivers and lakes teeming with wildlife. But it's that way for a reason. For the delights of the Brooks Range will never suffer the fate of so many natural wonders in the modern world – seeing a huge influx of the sort of visitors drawn to wild places whose presence ultimately devalues the very thing that attracted them in the first place. A visit to this magical place is simply too challenging for any but the most determined adventurers, able to dig deep into their wallets for the ultimate wilderness experience.

ALEXANDER ARCHIPELAGO

North America/United States

This 485 km (300 mi) long archipelago is off Alaska's southern coastline and is a chain of over one thousand islands. Once part of the mainland, these islands are the tops of submerged mountains. The Alexanders offer massive doses of everything wilderness addicts crave – steep coastlines with dramatic fjords, rugged interiors with dense evergreen and temperate rainforests. The population is thin, offering resourceful travellers with the necessary survival skills every opportunity to explore virgin terrain without seeing another human being.. There are indigenous occupants – the Tlingit, Kaigani, Haidas and Tsimshians who arrived from British Columbia in the 1800s – plus those concerned with the main commercial activities of logging, fishing and tourism.

The main islands are Admiralty, Baranof, Chichagof, Dall, Kupreanof, Prince of Wales, Revillagigedo and Wrangell. These all have scattered communities, starting points for backcountry expeditions.

DON'T MISS
With a large population
of brown bears the
Alexanders are great
for observing bruin.

NORTH CASCADES NATIONAL PARK

North America/United States

DON'T MISS
The North Cascades
Visitor Centre.

The Cascade Range begins in British Columbia and extends through Washington and Oregon into northern California. North Cascades National Park is a complex extending to around 2,800 sq km (1,080 sq mi) that consists of four linked areas – north and south park units plus Ross Lake and Lake Chelan National Recreation Areas. 93 per cent of the park has been designated as wilderness. The two recreation areas are destinations of choice for anyone keen to experience the ambiance of these rugged mountains without mounting a major backcountry expedition. Ross Lake National Recreation Area, close to the Canadian border, is the most accessible. This corridor along the Skagit River bisects the park's north and south units and encompasses three reservoirs used to generate power for Seattle. Recreational activities include hunting, fishing, kayaking, canoeing, hiking and climbing. There are trailheads connecting to an extensive network of established hiking routes, including those that continue into adjoining wilderness. The North Cascades Highway passes through the recreation area from east to west, providing access and allowing travellers to enjoy superb mountain scenery that has earned the nickname 'American Alps'. There are a number of campsites along the road. The Lake Chelan National Recreation Area is more remote, but equally impressive. It covers just 250 sq km (95 sq mi) at the north end of the lake. The Pacific Coast Trail passes through.

HOW TO GET THERE: The sanctuary is accessible by boat but most visitors fly in from Homer using one of several available air charters.

MCNEIL RIVER GAME SANCTUARY

North America/United States

The world's largest gathering of Alaska brown bears takes place annually where a series of cascades on the McNeil River provides an obstacle for migrating chum salmon. This makes them relatively easy prey for normally solitary bears, which duly congregate in large numbers to feast on Nature's bounty and fatten up for the harsh winter. A hundred or more turn up at the height of the salmon run in July to fight, play, feed and mate. A similar but smaller spectacle may been seen a little earlier at nearby Mikfik Creek, A visit to this unique sanctuary to see the bears isn't a 'gimme'. In order to offer what the name suggests, access during the bear-watching season is strictly limited, and permits should be applied for online to the Alaska Department of Fish and Game before March 1 each year. These are then are issued by ballot.

WORTH A DETOUR: Spotting large animals around Diamond Peak are black-tailed and mule deer, elk and black bear.

WILLAMETTE NATIONAL FOREST

North America/United States

After the Cascade Range duly cascades down into Oregon its western slopes are occupied by the 180 km (112 mi) length of Willamette National Forest, a protected area that offers a hugely varied landscape of mountains, canyons, rushing streams and extensively wooded slopes.

One sure-fire winner is the Diamond Peak wilderness, surrounding the shield volcano of the same name.

The Pacific Crest National Scenic Trail passes through, and some 200 km (125 mi) of established routes may be found within the wilderness, including the 16 km (10 mi) Diamond Peak Trail. A jewel-like ring of small lakes surrounds the peak's snow-capped summit.

The area features impressive stands of mixed trees such as mountain hemlock, western white pine and lodgepole. Abundant alpine flowers provide bright colour in season along the trails, on lakeshores and in meadows. Popular activities are camping, horseback riding, fishing and mountain climbing.

TRAPPER CREEK WILDERNESS

North America/United States

The Gifford Pinchot National Forest in southern Washington stretches for 115 km (70 mi) along the western slopes of the Cascade Range, covering an impressive 5,300 sq km (2,050 sq mi). One of the most interesting wilderness areas is the smallest – Trapper Creek drainage, a pristine area within the Wind River watershed, that contains one of the largest blocks of original low-growth Douglas-fir forest in the state. To that may be added a rugged landscape full of rushing streams, waterfalls as tall as 30 m (100 ft) and huckleberry fields at higher elevations.

For those capable of getting there (it requires physical effort and stamina), the outlook from the top of Observation Peak with its abandoned fire-watch post is awesome, encompassing Goat Rocks and Mounts Jefferson, Rainier, Adams and Hood.

Wildlife is varied and there is a good selection of birds – including barred and spotted owls, woodpeckers and goshawks – while commonly seen animals include Roosevelt elk, black-tailed deer and black bear. Rarer are bobcat, cougar, pine marten and grizzly bear. For those with eyes to see beyond the striking scenery, it's a dimension that adds a special something to this beautiful wilderness.

DON'T MISS
Pikes Peak; the Garden of the Gods Park.

DEATH VALLEY NATIONAL PARK

North America/United States

WHEN TO GO: May–September should be avoided. December and January are the coolest months, with average daytime temperatures of around 18°C (65°F).

Death Valley is the lowest, driest and hottest location just about anywhere, and must have seemed a fearsome place to pioneers crossing the uncharted southwestern USA during the California gold rush of 1849. Despite adverse conditions, the valley has been home to the Timbisha tribe (formerly called Panamint Shoshone) for a millennium. The 7,800-sq km (3,012-sq mi) hotspot of Death Valley is in the Great Basin, enclosed by the Sylvania and Owlshead Mountains, Panamint and Amargosa Ranges. It mostly lies in California, with small areas invading Nevada. The valley forms the greater part of the national park that bears its name, which also includes surrounding mountains, Saline Valley and most of Panamint Valley. Park headquarters is at Furnace Creek along with the world's lowest golf course and a desert resort. The visitor centre offers fascinating talks on a variety of valley-related subjects between mid-October and mid-April. To the north, Scotty's Castle is a Spanish-style mansion from the 1930s. Guided tours are available of the interior and a network of underground tunnels.

DON'T MISS

Kalmiopsis leachiana. This purple-flowered evergreen is a relic of the pre-ice age from the Ericaceae (heather) family.

KALMIOPSIS WILDERNESS

North America/United States

Tucked away at the heart of southwestern Oregon's Rogue River-Siskiyou National Forest is a hidden gem. Kalmiopsis has extraordinary geology, with an amazing variety of rock formations supporting a huge diversity of plant life of great botanical interest that has evolved to survive in harsh soil conditions caused by high concentrations of heavy metals such as magnesium, iron, chromium and nickel. The landscape of this rugged wilderness ranges from a lowly 150 m (500 ft) to a maximum elevation of 1,554 m (5,098 ft) at Pearsoll Peak. It is characterized by sharp ridges and plunging tree-clad canyons carrying rushing streams and white-water sections of the Illinois, Chetco and North Fork Rivers that attract rafters prepared to carry their craft in. Hiking trails can be challenging, as many are steep and rocky, and were not made easier by the major Biscuit Fire of 2002 that devastated much of the forest following a lightning strike. Many routes incorporate sections of old mining roads and can become confusing, so a trail map is essential. Popular day hikes lead to to Babyfoot and Vulcan Lakes. But those seeking solitude can take any other trail into the wilderness.

DON'T MISS
Kings Canyon
National Park.

CHANNEL ISLANDS NATIONAL PARK
North America/United States

Despite their proximity to the urban sprawl of Los Angeles, the Channel Islands – close to California's southern coast – are largely unspoilt. Five of them form the Channel Islands National Park, a world apart from the bustling mainland. The islands offer a stunning display of wild flowers after the winter rains and have large seabird colonies, while surrounding waters support abundant marine life including whales, seals and sea lions.

WORTH A DETOUR:
The whales – grey whales are present from December to April and a large gathering of blue whales takes place in spring and summer. For those intent on spotting the world's largest animal, this is the place to go.

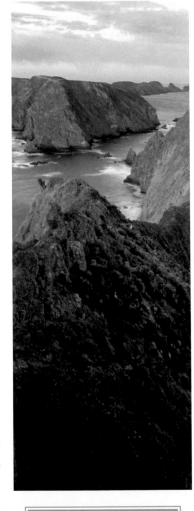

Santa Cruz is the big one at around 245 sq km (95 sq mi) and preserves a fascinating microcosm of the Californian coastal environment as once it was. There are mountains, canyons, cliffs, tide pools, pristine beaches and sea caves – including one of the world's largest, the famous Painted Cave. There are numerous reminders of former occupants – both Chumash Indians and 19th-century incomers. Nearby Santa Rosa has cliffs, beaches and central peaks and – like its neighbours – supports a considerable diversity of flora and fauna, much of it unique to the islands.

The three islets of East, Middle and West Anacapa have towering cliffs, sea caves and the Arch Rock that serves as the park's symbol. In the summer on East Anacapa rangers dive in Landing Cove with video cameras, allowing visitors to glimpse the magical undersea world of the kelp forest... without getting wet. The smallest island is Santa Barbara, a 260 ha (640 ac) triangular rock with steep cliffs that is returning to its former self as the National Park Service reverses the effects of human interference like the introduction of rabbits and cats, which did huge damage to bird populations. Wild and windswept San Miguel is the outermost island, home to tens of thousands of pinnipeds (sea lions and seals by any other name) around Point Bennett, which may be viewed in season as part of a day-long hike guided by a ranger.

YOU SHOULD KNOW
An entrance fee is payable.

OWENS PEAK WILDERNESS

North America/United States

The highest point in the southern Sierra Nevada is Owens Peak at 2,574 m (8,445 ft), which gives its name to the 300-sq km (115-sq mi) wilderness occupying the broken eastern face of the mountains beneath this saw-tooth landmark. The steep terrain has an assortment of canyons, many of them expansive, some containing springs surrounded by lush growth. This Californian wilderness is located where three ecosystems meet – those of the Mojave Desert, Great Basin and Sierra Nevada – resulting in an interesting assortment of vegetation that ranges from creosote bush scrub, cacti, classic yuccas, low-level oak and cottonwood trees to juniper-pinyon woods with pine and sagebrush at higher elevations.

Some hardened backpackers will just be passing through – the Pacific Crest Trail crosses the wilderness – but this is a great place for a day hike, and camping is permitted for those who like to explore more thoroughly. Other recreational activities include horse riding, mountain-biking, scenic viewing from the network of dirt roads and climbing.

WHEN TO GO:
Any time (in winter it's a good location for alpine skiing).

WORTH A DETOUR:
Seeing the wildlife, which includes black bear, mule deer, mountain lion, prairie falcon and golden eagle.

DON'T MISS
The ruined Five-Stamp Mill above Beveridge Canyon, surrounded by the remains of miners' cabins.

INYO MOUNTAINS WILDERNESS

North America/United States

The Inyos separate Owens Valley from Saline Valley in the Mojave Desert. The Inyo Mountains Wilderness covers 810 sq km (313 sq mi) and to the north is the Inyo National Forest, home of the world's oldest tree (Methuselah, a Great Basin bristlecone pine at a secret location that's been around for nearly 4,850 years). The park shows evidence of long-abandoned mining activity like old cabins, decaying aerial tramways and an old stamp mill. Four hiking routes are historic mining trails. These are the Burgess Mine Trail, pivotal Lonesome Miner Trail, French Spring Trail and one of the most accessible hikes, the Snowflake Mine Trail starting from the Snowflake Talc Mine and climbing the Beveridge Ridge before dropping down to the old mill site. The Beveridge Canyon Trail leads to the main mining area in an isolated location in the Mojave Desert.

YOSEMITE NATIONAL PARK

North America/United States

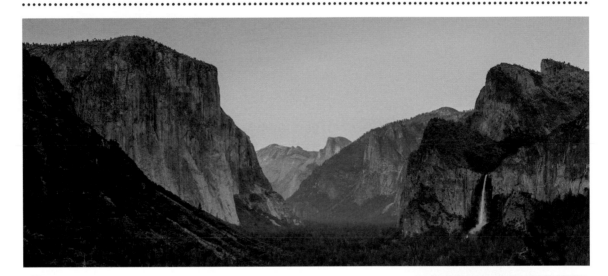

Central California's Yosemite National Park attracts three-and-a-half million visitors each year to the western slopes of the Sierra Nevada range, but it's still a wild place. The park covers 3,100 sq km (1,200 sq mi) and the vast majority of those eager tourists are interested only in Yosemite Valley, a tiny 18-sq km (7-sq mi) fraction of the whole. This is the main entry point to the park and contains a concentration of visitor facilities – but also natural wonders that make this a scenic sensation to savour. It contains the Merced River, fed and carried down the valley by a succession of eye-catching waterfalls, while high granite walls rise to stunning rock features that include the El Capitan monolith, Cathedral Rocks, Cathedral Spires, Sentinel Rock and the Three Brothers.

For those who seek wide-open empty spaces there's plenty more to enjoy. Beyond the valley lies the 95 per cent of the park's area that has been designated as wilderness. This craggy landscape contains two major rivers, numerous streams and thousands of lakes and ponds. There are mountains, glaciers, meadows and forests within a vast expanse of unspoiled alpine scenery. The total area forms one of the largest undisturbed habitat blocks in the Sierra Nevada mountains.

WHEN TO GO:
Any time (although tyre chains are often required on back roads in winter and some roads are closed).

YOU SHOULD KNOW

There's no guarantee that the awesome Yosemite Falls will actually be falling – the waterfall is fed mainly by snowmelt and often runs dry in August, remaining so until the winter snowfalls arrive.

DON'T MISS
The Grand Canyon of the Yellowstone Park, carved into the rock by the river, downstream of Yellowstone Falls.

YELLOWSTONE NATIONAL PARK

North America/United States

America's first national park – established in 1872 – is still one of the most impressive. At its heart is the high-altitude Yellowstone Lake, situated over the caldera of America's largest active supervolcano. This is responsible for the lava flows and rocks scattered by ancient eruption that can be seen all over the park, including one of the world's largest petrified forests. Volcanic activity is also responsible for the huge number of geothermal features (half the recorded number in the world) found in Yellowstone. The Old Faithful geyser is but the highlight of the park's 10,000 dramatic hot springs, geysers and boiling-mud spectacles. Yellowstone is rich in flora and fauna and has a large number of archaeological sites. A number of official suppliers offer visitor-support activities including transportation, boating, fishing, guided hiking and wildlife viewing, while a wide variety of ranger-guided activities can be booked. But for many the park's the star, and the opportunity to simply drive around, see some of the amazing hydrothermal features, spot wildlife and soak up the stunning scenery is all the stimulus needed to enjoy this extraordinary place, preserved for posterity in the 19th century by forward-thinking conservationists.

BRYCE CANYON NATIONAL PARK

North America/United States

WORTH A DETOUR Seeing stars. Bryce Canyon is one of the darkest spots in the continental USA, providing the opportunity to see a blazing night sky.

Compared to many a vast American national park, Bryce Canyon has modest vital statistics, measuring just 145 sq km (56 sq mi), and its remote location ensures that this dramatic landscape is never overburdened with visitors.

Massed ranks of slender hoodoos that can rise to a height of 60 m (200 ft) create a spectacular multicoloured jumble of red, orange and white rock seen from the canyon rim, which fluctuates between an elevation of 2,400 m (7,875 ft) and 2,700 m (8,860 ft). The 29 km (18 mi) scenic drive ends at the park's high spot, Rainbow Point, but there are eight waymarked walking trails that can be completed in less than a day, each taking from one to six hours for a round trip from trailheads. Two overnight trails (backcountry permits required) extend the total length of the park's various hiking routes to 80 km (50 mi).

Anyone who prefers to let a horse do the hard work can book riding trips between April and October. There are two official campgrounds within the park for those who wish to explore at leisure or indulge in one of the park's most popular activities, landscape photography.

Left: Yellowstone National Park

ZION NATIONAL PARK

North America/United States

Attracting over three million visitors annually, Utah's most popular national park is renowned for breathtaking canyons. People are drawn to this 600-sq km (230-sq mi) park near Springfield by extraordinary features such as the enormous Kolob Arch, typical of amazing rock formations that abound. Zion Canyon itself is 24 km (15 mi) long and up to 800 m (2,625 ft) deep, winding between precipitous walls as the north fork of the Virgin River rushes along the canyon floor. Zion National Park (so named when the original name of Mukuntuweap failed to roll off anyone's tongue) offers incredible views to those who prefer to remain firmly perched on top of four wheels and let the engine do the walking, but this is really a place to hike, climb, camp, bike or explore on horseback. It isn't a vast empty wilderness where no fellow-travellers will seen from one day to the next, but the nature of the landscape is such that there's plenty of opportunity to get away from the crowd and find deserted side canyons or rock scrambles to explore. There are numerous trails within canyons and along the rims, rated from easy through moderate to strenuous and technical, so there's something for everyone. But the ultimate Zion experience is the Narrows hike, which follows the Virgin River and involves lots of time in the water – sometimes waist-deep pools. The hike is 26 km (16 mi) long and may be done from top to bottom, with or without camping overnight, which allows time to check out tempting features like Kolob Creek and Orderville Gulch. It's possible to tackle the Narrows bottom-up, although only as far as Big Springs. A permit is needed for all but casual hikers at the lower end.

YOU SHOULD KNOW

Most roads are open to private vehicles all year, but between April and October the Zion Canyon Road is served by a free shuttle bus only.

WORTH A DETOUR:

The awesome view along Zion Canyon from Angels Landing – a prominent rock formation reached by a short but demanding trail that was cut into the rock in the 1920s.

DON'T MISS
The Painted Wall is a sheer cliff 685 m (2,250 ft) tall and shot through with light-coloured granite veins.

BLACK CANYON
North America/United States

The Black Canyon of the Gunnison National Park may be the country's third-smallest national park – but few other experiences match the scary-yet-breathtaking opportunity to perch on the edge and peer down at the jagged rockscape far below. This spectacular canyon earned its name because it is so narrow – a mere 460 m (1,500 ft) across in places – and deep – over 610 m (2,000 ft) – that it remains in almost permanent gloom. The sun illuminates the canyon only briefly, and even then falls upon dark walls of volcanic schist. The main focus of visitor interest and most of the park's facilities are to be found on the Black Canyon's South Rim. The main entrance road passes the main viewpoints. There are 12 named overlooks, plus opportunities for independent exploration. The North Rim, accessed by a gravel road, is a better option for those who prefer relative solitude. It has overlooks that equal the spectacle to be seen from the South Rim, a primitive campground and three demanding trails down to the canyon floor.

MONUMENT VALLEY
North America/United States

The movie *Stagecoach*, that saw John Wayne's breakthrough, was shot in Monument Valley. Director John Ford returned to use the valley as a location time after time, and many more film crews have followed. The Colorado Plateau has the greatest concentration of national parks and monuments in the USA, including the Grand Canyon, Canyonlands and the Petrified Forest. Monument Valley isn't among them – it lies within the Navajo Nation Reservation – but has unique scenic qualities that make this atmospheric place special in its own way. The arid floor consists of reddish siltstone and sand deposited by the ancient rivers that eroded the valley, dotted in places with low scrub vegetation. But the main attraction is the magnificent array of red sandstone spires and buttes, sculpted by wind and water over countless millennia.

CHIRICAHUA NATIONAL MONUMENT

North America/United States

YOU SHOULD KNOW

Fill up in Willcox – there are no gas stations between the town and Chiricahua National Monument.

It's billed as 'A Wonderland of Rocks' and the description is more than justified. This may not be America's largest untamed landscape – checking in at just 48 sq km (19 sq mi) – but there's still more than enough rugged terrain to allow an all-day vanishing act by those of solitary bent. Chiricahua National Monument in southern Arizona, some 190 km (120 mi) from Tucson, occupies a remote location. The Chiricahua Mountains are so-called 'sky islands', rising imperiously from a sea of surrounding grassland. The extraordinary rock formations are the main attraction, and these were grotesquely carved by water and ice over millions of years from rhyolite originally formed after the Turkey Creek Volcano erupted, a mere 27 million years ago – a sobering reminder of the human race's fleeting presence in a natural world of infinite age. This thought perhaps explains the awe experienced by those who see this enduring rockscape.

Exploring this special place may be done from the 13 km (8 mi) scenic drive on a paved road, or by using 27 km (17 mi) of hiking trails suitable for anything from short walks to day-long expeditions. There is a comprehensive trail guide available at the visitor centre. One day is the least amount of time anyone should want to spend at Chiricahua, and a select few use the 25-pitch campground to extend their stay

(no pre-booking). Quite apart from stunning scenery, there's an opportunity to visit the fascinating Faraway Ranch Historic District, home of the Erickson family of Swedish immigrants who arrived in the late 1880s and subsequently developed a thriving homestead and guest ranch. The grounds may be explored and regular house tours take place.

DON'T MISS

The one-room log cabin built by the first European settlers, Ja Hu Stafford and his wife Pauline, after they arrived here in 1880.

DON'T MISS
Yellowstone
National Park.

GRAND CANYON

North America/United States

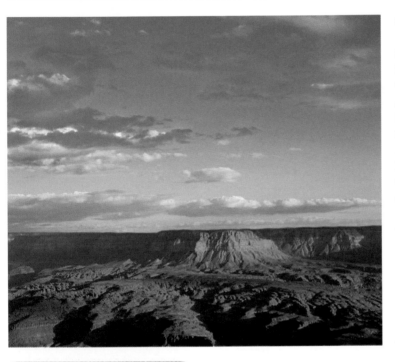

Thanks to 17 million years of relentless effort by the Colorado River, Arizona has one of the world's great natural wonders. A massive rift in the Colorado Plateau, the Grand Canyon lives up to its billing at around 440 km (275 mi) long, ranging between 29 km (18 mi) and 6.5 km (4 mi) wide while plunging to a depth of 1,800 m (5,900 ft) in places. Most of this awesome gorge lies within Grand Canyon National Park, with headquarters in Grand Canyon Village on the South Rim. This historic settlement dates from the arrival of the Santa Fe railway in 1901 and has many buildings dating from that era. Numerous museums and information centres add a dimension to the Grand Canyon experience.

For most, simply seeing this vertiginous canyon is enough, although it's worth noting that Desert View Watchtower at the eastern end of the South Rim, built on a promontory in 1932, is one of the few places from where the canyon floor and Colorado River can actually be observed. Most of the stunning views are of the opposite rim. The less-popular North Rim is considered to have the finest outlooks, yet most visitors stick to the South Rim in order to enjoy the facilities at Grand Canyon Village. It's necessary to make the choice – the drive from one rim to the other is 345 km (215 mi) and takes five hours. For those who want more than scenery, the canyon offers unique hiking opportunities, but only for those prepared to hang tough and carry a lot of water in their backpacks.

WHEN TO GO:
Not winter, when the canyon may see heavy snowfalls that can prevent access to either rim. The North Rim sees greater precipitation and the single access road can be closed for months.
Its facilities are closed from mid-October–mid-May.

LOSTWOOD NATIONAL WILDLIFE REFUGE

North America/United States

DON'T MISS
Look out for the
population
of sharp-tailed grouse.

North Dakota contains one of the most important wildfowl breeding sites in the USA, and this area bordering both Montana and Canada is protected by the Lostwood National Wildlife Refuge. It lies in the so-called prairie pothole region – meaning it has a large number of lakes, ponds and boggy patches that provide a perfect habitat for geese, ducks and other aquatic birds. This has earned it a designation as a Globally Important Bird Area, and the annual Burke County Birding Festival is held every June.

WHEN TO GO:
Any time, although summer sees the maximum population of breeding birds. Winter weather can be harsh, but cross-country skiing, snowshoeing and hiking take place despite strong winds and fearsome wind-chill.

The 110-sq km (42-sq mi) block of old prairie was first settled in the early 1900s, but proved inhospitable to incoming farmers and has been reclaimed and restored since the mid-1930s with wildlife conservation a priority. In 1975, the Lostwood Wilderness Area was established within the refuge. This 23-sq km (9-sq mi) enclave provides further protection to the bird life, encompassing vital breeding sites and preventing disruptive activity. However, hiking and photography – plus cross-country trekking on skis or snowshoes in winter – are permitted. In the wider refuge, there are numerous trails providing the opportunity to explore. Although the principal importance of the refuge lies in its 4,000 wetlands, Lostwood is within the Missouri Coteau region, which consists of prairie and hills. Nearly three quarters of the refuge is virgin prairie, making for a varied habitat that supports all sorts of creatures in addition to the large seasonal and resident bird population. There are around 250 bird species in the refuge.

DON'T MISS
The tree-sized saguaro cactus with its distinctive upstretched arms.

SONORAN DESERT

North America/United States

North America's largest and hottest place, covering 310,000 sq km (120,000 sq mi), is the Sonoran Desert. Over 2,000 plant types live and thrive in the harsh conditions, while the desert supports over 500 species of animals, birds and reptiles, plus countless insects.

This is America, so the desert must try to pay its way. It is exploited by – among others – animal grazers, so the Sonoran Desert National Monument has been established in Arizona to preserve an unspoilt tract.

To quote President Bill Clinton, after the national monument was established: 'The area encompasses a functioning desert ecosystem with an extraordinary array of biological, scientific, and historic resources. The monument's biological resources include a spectacular diversity of plant and animal species. The monument also contains many significant archaeological and historic sites, including rock-art sites, lithic quarries, and scattered artefacts.' These can still be found by those prepared to look.

BISTI BADLANDS

North America/United States

WORTH A DETOUR: The Bisti Trading Post – a cluster of abandoned buildings, including an overgrown children's playground.

The USA's badlands are arid, uneven ground that early pioneers dismissed as 'bad lands' to settle on. The Bisti Badlands in the remote northwestern corner of New Mexico is a scenic expanse of weirdly eroded rocks and colourful mounds which must have seemed a nightmare place to early 19th-century travellers as it interrupted steady progress across the prairie.

This little-visited 16-sq km (6-sq mi) patch of high desert is designated as the Bisti Wilderness Area, but the

badlands actually extend much further than official boundaries. Tracks criss-cross sandy hills at the southern edge of the rocky areas, which are risky options for low-slung cars. The wilderness itself offers a vivid mix of colours – red, orange, brown and grey – and mostly consists of small hills, shallow ravines, dry washes and unusual rock formations, some of which look more like sculptures than natural artworks. Away from the approach road, a surreal landscape envelops the bold interloper, going where there are no hiking trails and progress is made by following ravines with care – the terrain is often unstable, and loose petrified wood litters the surface, often mixed with fossils.

SIERRA BLANCA WILDERNESS

North America/United States

White Mountain Wilderness Area soars to a breathtaking (literally) height of around 3,500 m (11,500 ft) and the mountains run in a north-south direction, bordering the Mescalero Apache Reservation at the southern end. The area is heavily wooded, but grassy oak savannahs and meadows are to be found, particularly towards the crest. This is a dramatic landscape of abrupt height changes, varied vegetation, rock promontories, bold escarpments and old avalanche slides.

Any backcountry explorer is sure to spot numerous representatives of the abundant wildlife with (among others) black bears, elk, mule deer, bobcats, coyotes, badgers, foxes, porcupines, skunks and squirrels in residence, along with a thriving bird population headed by wild turkeys. The chance to get among these creatures comes courtesy of a network of lonely wilderness trails, mostly following canyon bottoms.

WORTH A DETOUR: A visit to the Mescalero Apache's Cultural Museum on Route 70 south of Ruidoso, for fascinating insight into the history and culture of this ancient race.

WHEN TO GO: Spring–autumn is best (winters can be harsh), although the park is open all year.

BADLANDS

North America/United States

South Dakota's Badlands National Park is the USA's largest mixed-grass prairie. It serves as a poignant reminder of vast tracts of similar grassland – where buffalo roamed – that once covered much of America's Middle West, stretching from Saskatchewan down to Texas. The national park covers 990 sq km (380 sq mi), within which 260 sq km (100 sq mi) has been designated as the Badlands Wilderness. The rolling prairie shares this vast wild place with dramatic expanses of rock, eroded into fantastic shapes and patterns.

For centuries these badlands were the hunting ground of the Lakota Sioux tribe, and the last armed clashes between these proud indigenous people and the US Army took place hereabouts at the end of the 19th century. This story – plus a fascinating review of the park's long history from prehistoric times, as evidenced by the wealth of fossils to be found here – is brought to life at the Ben Reifel Visitor Centre, named after the Sioux Nation's first congressman, which has numerous interesting exhibits, some interactive, and a theatre showing the fascinating park movie.

A typical half-day tour consists of a session at the visitor centre during a run around the paved Badlands Loop Road, perhaps with a side trip along the gravelled Sage Creek Road, and pauses at four scenic overlooks. It's easily extended to a full day by using one of five waymarked hiking routes that require from half an hour to three hours for a round trip.

DON'T MISS

Shenandoah
National Park.

INDIANA DUNES NATIONAL LAKESHORE

North America/United States

Although the long run of beaches along the lake is the principal recreational resource, Indiana Dunes National Lakeshore has much more than that to offer. It is a treasure house of natural delights, including areas of swamp, bog, marsh, prairie, riverbank, forest and oak savannah. The biological diversity is staggering, with around 1,100 ferns and flowering plant species to be found. The bird life is vibrant, with over 350 species recorded, including many migrants that rest before moving on. Birdwatching is therefore a popular activity, as is hiking along diverse trails that provide anything from a stroll to a day-long expedition. This wonderful expanse of sculpted soft sand may be close to civilization, but it's still easy to get away from it all. By choosing one of the less-popular locations and going during the week it is perfectly possible to imagine that this magnificent lakeshore is the wildest of places scarcely touched by human hand.

LUSK CREEK WILDERNESS

North America/United States

WORTH A DETOUR: The evocative reminders of ultimately fruitless human endeavour in Lusk Creek Wilderness: old homesteads, fruit trees and overgrown cemeteries.

Shawnee National Forest at the southern tip of Illinois is an oasis of natural wonders amid a (relative!) desert of intensively farmed land. The wildernesses – Bald Knob, Bay Creek, Burden Falls, Clear Springs, Garden of the Gods, Panther Den and Lusk Creek – all are impressive wild places, but if one has to be singled out it is the Lusk Creek Wilderness.

This wilderness extends to a mere 28 sq km (11 sq mi), but for once that old saying doesn't stack up – size definitely isn't everything, as Lusk Creek is both the second-largest wilderness in the state and a miniature masterpiece to be savoured by lovers of unspoilt wild places. This perfectly formed mini-wilderness consists of rugged terrain and winding canyons – a type of landscape not common in Illinois – where broad ridge tops overlook terraces, narrow ravines and sheer rock walls. Lusk Creek Wilderness is dotted with sinkholes and caves, there is some old-growth timber and wild flowers are abundant in spring.

Lusk Creek is one of the purest streams in Illinois, attracting fishermen, canoeists and those who simply want to stroll the banks. Horse riding, hiking and camping are other recreational activities that may be practised, but most casual visitors find that simply walking around in tranquil yet dramatic surroundings is satisfaction enough – especially when the highlight is being surprised and delighted by one of the most spectacular overlooks in the state at a precipitous hairpin turn in Lusk Creek Canyon.

BIG BEND NATIONAL PARK

North America/United States

WORTH A DETOUR: Dropping by at least one of the five visitor centres: informative exhibits illuminating the fascinating geology, natural and cultural histories of the park.

This is a truly untouched wild place, much of it appearing today just as it did to the first European pioneers centuries ago. Big Bend National Park in West Texas is three parks in one – big river, desert and mountains. It lies in Brewster County, one of the USA's least-populated areas, and this fabulous park covers 3,250 sq km (1,255 sq mi), protecting much of the Chihuahuan Desert's unique ecology and topography. Once there, it is possible to enjoy a wide variety of activities. Simplest of all is viewing awesome desert landscape from one of many scenic drives on paved roads. For more adventurous types, the park has numerous unimproved dirt roads suitable only for reliable four-wheel-drive transport, allowing exploration of the remotest places, perhaps combined with backcountry camping (permit required). In either case, it's essential to leave the vehicle from time to time to merge with the landscape. Even from paved roads a few steps lead to timeless desert solitude.

YOU SHOULD KNOW

Big Bend really is remote and it's wise to stock up with gas, water and provisions before driving in.

WORTH DETOUR: Finding incised petroglyphs and painted pictographs on rocky ledges and cliff faces. There are hundreds within BWCAW, created by the Ojibwe people.

BOUNDARY WATERS CANOE AREA

North America/United States

The Superior National Forest in Minnesota's Arrowhead Region lies between the US-Canadian border and the north shore of Lake Superior. In this 16,000-sq km (6,180-sq mi) tract of woods and water commercial activities like logging take place alongside the type of recreational activities offered by sparsely populated wild places. These include (in season where appropriate) berry picking, mountain-biking, camping, going afloat, hiking, fishing, hunting, cross-country skiing, snowshoeing, snowmobiling, driving scenic byways, off-roading, wildlife viewing and birdwatching. One of the most interesting and exciting possibilities is exploration within the Boundary Waters Canoe Area Wilderness (BWCAW), which extends along the national forest's northern limit. Renowned for pristine lakes – and the sporting fish that thrive therein – this is the USA's most-visited wilderness.

WHEN TO GO:
The show of bright autumn
foliage is world-famous.

MARK TWAIN NATIONAL FOREST

North America/United States

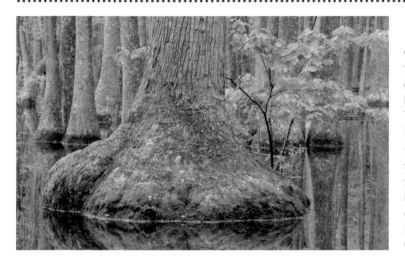

Missouri native Mark Twain is commemorated by the national forest that bears his name, which consists of around a tenth of his home state's woodland.

The Mark Twain National Forest (MTNF) covers some 6,100 sq km (2,350 sq mi) in south and central Missouri, spreading into 29 counties. The native timber had all been logged out when President Franklin D Roosevelt's Depression-era Civilian Conservation Corps – a New Deal work-creation programme – started replanting deforested areas and laid the foundations for what became MTNF, established in 1939 and mostly falling within the Ozark Highlands.

The forest is not in one block, but consists of nine separate tracts with six ranger districts and headquarters at Rolla, Missouri. It offers a variety of recreational opportunities for those who like to hunt, fish, hike, ride on horseback, camp or observe abundant wildlife, which includes over 300 species of birds, 75 types of mammal and 125 different amphibians or reptiles. Mountain-biking and driving are permitted on most forest roads, although not in wilderness areas, and there are also a number of roads where all-terrain vehicles may be used.

There are several prime locations for lovers of wild places. These include the rugged Bell Mountain Wilderness Area with 22 km (14 mi) of wilderness trails, and parts of the St Francois mountain section noted for streams, rivers, lakes, rocky bluffs, woodland trails and fine landscape views. The forest has recreation areas such as Sutton Bluff and Marble Creek with campgrounds and scenic trails. Marble Creek is the trailhead for a section of the long-distance Ozark Trail that leads to Crane Lake. Other popular forest destinations are the Council Bluff Lake Recreation Area, surrounding the forest's largest stretch of open water, and the Silver Mines Recreation Area with its abandoned mine workings.

YOU SHOULD KNOW
Greer Spring in Oregon County, Missouri, is the largest spring on forest land in the USA. It discharges 840,360,000 litres (185,000,000 gal) per day, which is 9,750 litres (2,150 gal) per second. This dramatic scenic outflow can be reached and admired after a short hike from Missouri Highway 19.

BLACK CREEK WILDERNESS

North America/United States

On the Lower Coastal Plain of southern Mississippi, Black Creek is the state's largest wilderness at 20 sq km (8 sq mi). The creek is Mississippi's only designated Wild and Scenic River and bisects the wilderness. In truth, the emphasis should be on scenic rather than wild, for this is a gentle landscape of oxbow lakes and impressive clumps of old-growth timber that include bald cypress, loblolly pine, sweet gum, red maple, sweet bay and oak.

The Black Creek National Recreation Trail runs for 65 km (40 mi) along the Black Creek drainage. To be travelled only on foot, it passes through the length of the wilderness. Nothing motorized – a prohibition that includes bicycles – may enter the wilderness, and horses are not permitted on the recreation trail. The river has plenty of wide sandbars ideal for pulling up a canoe, pitching camp or having a leisurely picnic in incomparable surroundings. Black Creek cannot be described as the USA's wildest wilderness, but it remains in pristine condition and on many days visitors will find it hard to believe that canoes have ever navigated the river or another human foot has fallen on this delightful floodplain.

> **WORTH A DETOUR:**
> Leaf River Wilderness. Although very similar to Black Creek, this is a smaller tract of floodplain, with rising ground at the western edge.

> **DON'T MISS**
> A rewarding side trip to East Creek Natural Area.

GREEN MOUNTAIN NATIONAL FOREST

North America/United States

There is something for everyone here, for Green Mountain National Forest (GMNF) covers more than 1,600 sq km 620 (sq mi) of protected land in central and southwestern Vermont. The forest is characterized by great scenic beauty and a wonderful rural atmosphere, with rugged mountain scenery and extensive forests punctuated by charming traditional villages.

There are endless opportunities for wild-place action on the extensive 1,450 km (900 mi) network of local trails. The forest has three alpine and seven Nordic ski areas for winter sports enthusiasts who come out to play during the long winters that turn the forest into a white wonderland. Hunting (in season) and fishing are also popular pastimes. So, too, is wildlife-watching and photography, with numerous bird species and mammals including black bear, moose, beaver and white-tailed deer to be spotted. Boating opportunities exist, too.

KISATCHIE HILLS WILDERNESS

North America/United States

YOU SHOULD KNOW

The four wilderness trails are all primitive and very remote and – although it is not compulsory – it is recommended that hikers or horse riders should come prepared to take risks and also leave a check-in form at their chosen trail entrance to inform the Forest Service of their presence and intentions – just to be on the safe side.

Within Louisiana's Kisatchie National Forest may be found 35 sq km (14 sq mi) of the steepest and most interesting terrain in a state not noted for rugged grandeur. Kisatchie is the only national forest in Louisiana. It is located in seven parishes – Vernon, Rapides, Grant, Natchitoches, Webster, Claiborne and Winn – in the northern and central part of the state. The forest protects a wonderful natural world of bayous beneath old-growth pine and bald cypress stands. This magical place may be explored from a comprehensive 4,800 km (3,000 mi) network of forest roads where vehicles (including all-terrain vehicles) are mostly permitted. One of the no-go motorized zones is the aforementioned Kisatchie Hills Wilderness Area, known locally as 'The Little Grand Canyon'. Relatively small but perfectly unspoilt, the only way of seeing this wilderness is to travel on foot or horseback.

There are three established trailheads that provide easy access, although it's possible to enter from any direction. This scenic area features sandstone bluffs and outcrops, flat-topped mesas and varied woodland. There is a designated trail system but no restriction stopping hardy hikers from stepping into the unknown, and camping is permitted. The four intersecting wilderness trails are for true adventurers. The Backbone Trail speaks for itself, and passes through 11 km (7 mi) of demanding terrain. The others are shorter – High Ridge Trail at 2.5 km (1.5 mi) and the Turpentine Hill Trail, of similar length. The shorter Explorer Trail provides a wonderful taste of wilderness hiking for those unwilling or unable to tackle the more demanding trails, but even there the wilderness is no place for casual strollers. Those who want to spend time in the district will find nine campgrounds in the area, all primitive and some not designed for vehicle use.

HOW TO GET THERE:

The wilderness trailheads are on Forest Road 59, the Longleaf Scenic Byway, and Forest Road 339. These may be reached from Interstate 49 using exit 119 and driving for 8 km (5 mi) down Louisiana Highway 119 to find FR 59, where the wilderness is on the right. A right turn onto FR 339 also borders the wilderness back to where it meets the forest proper.

WORTH A DETOUR:

The opportunity to drive the Longleaf Scenic Byway from end to end – it's a 27 km (17 mi) paved road connecting Louisiana Highways 119 (east end) and 117 (west end). Better still, find time to add a visit to the Longleaf Vista Day-Use Complex and tramp the interpretive trail – a short loop through the woods with informative signs describing native flora. There are great glimpses of the adjacent wilderness and short spur trails lead to a mesa offering panoramic all-round views over the forest.

CATSKILL FOREST PRESERVE

North America/United States

WORTH A DETOUR:
The view from the top of Slide Mountain, the highest peak in the Catskills – the main trail to the summit was built in 1892, the first hiking route constructed in the forest preserve at public expense.

The Catskill Forest Preserve consists of all state-owned land within Catskill Park, encompassing New York State's Catskill Mountains. The preserve amounts to an impressive 1,150 sq km (445 sq mi) that is, as the name suggests, mainly wooded. But it also includes wetlands and meadows, lakes, rivers, waterfalls and cliffs.

It is a natural playground affording all sorts of recreational opportunities, not least of which is the ability to get away from civilization and enjoy the solitude of the woods, where the only companions are birds and forest animals, the latter including bear, coyote, bobcat and mink.

The 98 major peaks within Catskill Park form a stirring skyline, and forest preserve land is classified as one of three types – wilderness, wild forest and intensive use. The last mainly consists of official campgrounds, most of which – while having vehicular access – offer only basic facilities. One exception is the huge north-south Lake campground with many pitches and swimming areas in both lakes.

Wild forest is mostly second- or third-growth woodland that has been disturbed by human activity before being allowed to regenerate. Certain vehicles are permitted on the old logging roads and those leading up to many fire towers that offer superb vantage points with panoramic views over the arboreal sea. These areas are popular with those who prefer driving, with or without accompanying woodland walks.

WHEN TO GO:
Any time (there are lots of ski
areas in or near the park for
winter sports).

WHITE MOUNTAIN NATIONAL FOREST

North America/United States

It is big, beautiful, wild and spreads into two states – New Hampshire and Maine. It's the 3,175-sq km (1,225-sq mi) White Mountain National Forest (WMNF), unsurprisingly contained within the White Mountains. This range offers the most rugged upland terrain in New England and forms part of the mighty Appalachians. It may be big enough to allow wilderness seekers ample scope, but WMNF attracts six million visitors each year. Indeed, the only national site in the USA to draw more is the Great Smoky Mountains National Park, further south on the Tennessee–North Carolina border. As for wilderness, there are five

areas within WMNF, accounting for over 460 sq km (178 sq mi) of forest lands. The Presidential Range/Dry River Wilderness is notable for cloud-shrouded mountains named after prominent US citizens who made their mark on American history, including several presidents, and attracts serious peak-baggers. The Sandwich Range Wilderness consists of rugged terrain that rewards super-fit hikers with outstanding views over mountains, lakes and forest. The Great Gulf Wilderness is a small but spectacular cirque, a natural amphitheatre formed by glacial erosion. The largest is Maine's Caribou-Speckled Mountain Wilderness, a place of craggy rockscapes characterized by open ledges, deep notches and wooded ridges. The 'speckled' description comes from vivid splashes of autumn colour created by stands of hardwood trees. Pemigewasset Wilderness encompasses a river watershed surrounded by steep mountain ridges. It is the newest – and most widely used – of the forest's wilderness areas.

YOU SHOULD KNOW

The Old Man of the Mountain, a rock formation on Cannon Mountain in Franconia Notch State Park near Lincoln looked just like the profile of a man's craggy face when viewed from a particular angle. The old boy was so distinctive that he became New Hampshire's state symbol, but he collapsed in 2003 and is no more.

CRANBERRY WILDERNESS

North America/United States

WORTH A DETOUR:
'Hell For Certain' – a particularly lovely, isolated branch stream feeding into Middle Fork Williams River; white-water running in the rushing waters of springtime or lazy river tubing in placid late summer water; the secret hollows along the Big Beechy Trail.

The last North American ice age sent its glacial fingers as far south as West Virginia. When they retreated, at their southernmost point they left behind a geological anomaly – a 3-sq km (1.2-sq mi) peat bog ecosystem. Maintained by chance microclimate, it's like a piece of Canadian taiga isolated in the dense, temperate woods and rushing mountain rivers of West Virginia's enormous Monongahela National Forest. The bog is called Cranberry Glades Botanical Area. Its spongy soil is so fragile and so full of site-specific flora, including orchids and carnivorous species like the pitcher-plant, that it can be crossed only on protective boardwalk trails.

Cranberry Glades is the jewel in the crown of the 145-sq km (56-sq mi) Cranberry Wilderness named after it – and of the additional 105-sq km (40-sq mi) 'Cranberry Backcountry' to its west, where wilderness restrictions are fewer). In the 1970s it almost became West Virginia's biggest strip coal mine and, like most of the eastern United States, it was once clear-cut by timber companies. Now, parts of Cranberry Wilderness have already had 100 years to recover. Along the Middle Fork of the Williams River, icy water tumbles across boulders in long cascades or runs through beautiful tall ferns and broad-leaf woods filled with exuberant outbursts of rhododendron. Side trails drop off the high ridges past waterfalls and into mysterious hollows. Others keep the high ground among red spruce and Appalachian hardwoods, with magnificent views across the broad mountains and deep valleys typical of the Allegheny Plateau. As a designated sanctuary for black bears, Cranberry Wilderness has become a haven for all forms of wildlife. It's a privilege to share it briefly with what the 1964 US Wilderness Act describes as 'a community of life where man himself is a visitor who does not remain'.

DON'T MISS
Crater Rim Drive;
Chain of Craters Road.

HICKORY CREEK WILDERNESS

North America/United States

Hickory Creek Wilderness is an unspoiled gem located in Pennsylvania's mighty Allegheny National Forest. It is characterized by beech and black cherry woodland, with open spaces dotted with stands of oak, maple, birch and hemlock. At ground level there's a rich variety of mosses, ferns, shrubs and wild flowers. One of the most rewarding experiences within the national forest is following the Hickory Creek Wilderness Trail. This 18 km (11 mi) loop offers a great experience for lovers of wild places, who will understand the lonely challenges faced by the first European pioneers as they explored the forest and empathize with their long-ago experiences.

The round trip makes a good overnight expedition. Occasional yellow blazes mark the way, but these are being allowed to fade naturally and obstructions like fallen trees are mostly left untouched. If this sounds daunting, just sampling the start of the trail gives a flavour of the place.

GREAT SWAMP NATIONAL WILDLIFE REFUGE

North America/United States

WORTH A DETOUR: The Raptor Trust – based in Millington, surrounded by the Great Swamp. This is the place to see a huge collection of captive raptors.

This unspoiled corner within 50 km (30 mi) of Manhattan is so special it has been declared a National Natural Landmark. Although habitat within the refuge is varied, its predominant character – as the name suggests – is wetland. This environment provides a home and refuge for a huge population of resident and migratory birds. Around 250 species have been recorded and the refuge serves as a vital stopping place on North America's eastern migration corridor. But the 'wildlife' tag applies to numerous four-footed denizens such as deer, coyote, fox, muskrat, raccoon, beaver, red and grey squirrel, plus the occasional bear. There are also turtles, snakes, amphibians, fish and innumerable insects, together enjoying a wonderful natural habitat rich in wild flowers and native vegetation.

There are roads through the Great Swamp at the western end, including Pleasant Plains Road where Refuge Headquarters and the Helen C Fenske Visitor Centre may be found, along with a nature shop.

RED RIVER GORGE

North America/United States

WHEN TO GO:
March to November,
although humidity can be
high in July and August.

More than 70 million years of weathering have formed the scenery surrounding the central section of Kentucky's Red River Gorge. The river offers excellent canoeing; the tough upper reaches suit experienced canoeists, while the quieter central section is normally safe and easy, with fine views of the rocks around the gorge. 'The Red' is also a world-renowned rock-climbing and abseiling location, with established routes in overhanging sandstone ranging from easy to very difficult.

While several of the spectacular rock arches, such as the famous Sky Bridge, are easily accessible and much visited, many more – there are around 100 – are found on quieter, more demanding trails and can be visited in peaceful solitude. Clifty Wilderness is a spacious, rugged, undeveloped part of the gorge, where a few longer trails wind through towering cliffs and narrow ravines. Traces of its earliest inhabitants, the Native Americans, and of pioneers and settlers can be seen in the area. These are treasured and protected by the Forest Service, which is diligent in its care for all aspects of this extraordinary landscape.

FALL CREEK FALLS STATE PARK

North America/United States

WORTH A DETOUR:
The Cable Trail, a difficult but
rewarding short clamber to
the base of Cane Creek Falls.

Protected within a 81-sq km (31-sq mi) State Park, Falls Creek Falls is a compendium of some of temperate-zone America's most dramatic natural formations – with the added bonus of being highly accessible. Cane Creek is fuelled by several streams even before it enters Cane Creek Gorge and drops hundreds of feet in less than a mile. Cane Creek Cascades drop 14 m (46 ft) before falling 26 m (85 ft) at Cane Creek Falls (into the same plunge pool as the 38 m (125 ft) Rockhouse Creek waterfall). Piney Falls tumble 29 m (95 ft) into a minor gorge above its confluence with Cane Creek; and even 76 m (250 ft) Coon Creek Falls seems inconspicuous right next to Fall Creek Falls itself. There are limestone sinks, cave systems, trails and swing bridges (slatted walkways, tethered at each end) high above the gorges. But there are also car parks close to the best overlooks, and facilities that owe nothing to nature.

WORTH A DETOUR:
The fabulous outlook over the Potomac-Garrett State Forest, Savage River State Forest and Crabtree Creek from a rocky outcrop near the crossways of Route 135 and Walnut Bottom Road.

BACKBONE MOUNTAIN

North America/United States

Maryland's Potomac-Garrett State Forest is a 47-sq km (18-sq mi) tract of rugged upland forest situated between the towns of Oakland and Westernport. This magical sweep of wild woodland, tumbling streams and deep valleys is a great place to start exploring Backbone Mountain, which straddles the border between Maryland and West Virginia. It is a prominent ridge of the Allegheny Mountains, part of the Appalachians and great Eastern Continental Divide, around 65 km (40 mi) long and runs on a northeast-southwest line from Maryland's Savage River Reservoir to Black Fork on the Cheat River in West Virginia. Within the State Forest on its Maryland flank may be found Crabtree Woods, a fascinating remnant of the once-vast expanse of old-growth forest that has largely been logged out. It contains mixed hardwoods such as red oak, sugar maple, basswood and cucumber trees, offering a wonderful display of contrasting colours when the foliage starts to turn in late September or October. The forest as a whole offers fishing, trails to suit casual strollers and hardened hikers alike, plus a choice of mountain-bike routes.

GEORGE WASHINGTON NATIONAL FOREST

North America/United States

WHEN TO GO: March–November, although July and August get humid. For a short time in October roads are jammed with people admiring the autumn colours.

The Appalachians, a glorious range of thickly wooded parallel ridges, deep valleys and shining rivers, sweep southwest, forming the Virginia–West Virginia border. The forests were home to Native Americans, then settlers, who cleared and farmed the fertile land. Logging and mining in the 19th century ravaged and scarred the landscape and almost wiped out the indigenous wildlife. Thanks to the vision and determination of those who recognized the threat to the nation's natural resources, the government intervened to purchase deforested mountains from 1918 onwards.

The forest is within easy reach for millions of city dwellers, who are drawn by its peace and grandeur and outdoor activities which include hunting, fishing, horse riding, camping and canoeing. Some spots can be quite crowded, but much of the more remote and undeveloped forest has been designated wilderness, and even at busy times walkers can find solitude on the hundreds of miles of hiking trails, which include part of the long-distance Appalachian Trail.

The varied terrain of the forest supports a huge variety of trees and plants and many animals and birds, including white-tailed deer and black bear, wild turkeys and bald eagles. It is splendid walking country and a climb to one of the higher ridges is rewarded with a stunning panorama of rolling, tree-clad ridges, in autumn dazzling with scarlet-and-gold foliage, receding into a softly misty distance.

CONGAREE NATIONAL PARK

North America/United States

WORTH A DETOUR: The Low Boardwalk through bald cypress and water tupelo forest; mysterious cypress 'knees', tangles of roots that grow up to 3 m (10 ft) in the air.

The astonishing old-growth bottomland hardwoods at Congaree have no equal in the USA. Over 75 species, force-fed by constantly refreshed silts washed down in regular flooding, grow to record dimensions. Their collective canopy arches high above, chased by poison ivy and grapevines. In this silent, warm, watery cathedral, darting bright colours reveal some of the 173 species of birds that fill the forest.

The area was only saved because it is a floodplain and not a true swamp. The trees thrived in the rich wetlands but stayed too green to float down-river. The best way to see it is by canoe. Cedar Creek meanders lazily through 32 km (20 mi) of oxbows, loops and bends before it joins the Congaree River. Heron, river otters, wild boar, box turtles and innumerable other wildlife in the dappled swamps turn pleasant drifting into an adventure of slightly Jurassic wonder.

DON'T MISS
The March/April wild turkey courtship dance.

CUMBERLAND ISLAND NATIONAL SEASHORE

North America/United States

The largest and southernmost of the Atlantic barrier islands protecting the coast of Georgia, Cumberland Island also includes the biggest island wilderness in the entire USA. Towards the ocean, a perfect sand beach runs up to a kilometre deep the length of the island, backed by dunes which give way to dense palmetto stands, pines and – magically – sun-dappled pastures and woods of ancient oaks festooned with Spanish

moss. On the west coast woods and meadows yield to 69 sq km (27 sq mi) of marshes, creeks and tidal mudflats, teeming with 300 species of waders, sea birds and dazzling migrants.

Once owned by the Carnegie family, part of the island remains private and closed to visitors; but palatial mansions remain, as ruins or restored luxury hotels, along with the more poignant chattel houses of 'the Settlement' where a small community of fishermen and farmers long ago sweated a living. Hotel guests get a special kind of access to the island's secrets, including wildlife-watching at dawn and dusk when other visitors have mostly gone. Rangers try to keep visitor numbers down to about 300 at any time.

DON'T MISS
The birdlife around
the Eco Pond.

FLORIDA BAY

North America/United States

Florida Bay is a vast triangle of ultra-shallow sea at the tip of the Florida Peninsula. Here, land and sea are defined by topographic and ecological integrity, and mutually dependent. Beneath Florida Bay's shimmering surface lies a marine wilderness as rich in novelty, colour and rarity as any of the Everglades' mainland natural marvels. The shallow sea only just covers gigantic meadows of seagrass. As a nursery for hundreds of marine species, and food for larger creatures like the manatee and green sea turtle, the grasses ultimately sustain the whole of Florida Bay's ecosystem. Bigger fish lurk round the mangrove islands and in the coastal estuaries and brackish waterways where mangroves form long tunnels and the channels of water run slightly deeper.

With Polaroid (non-reflective) glasses you can see deep into the water. Canoes are easy (and quiet) to manoeuvre among both mangroves and mudflats, and offer the best opportunities of seeing anything from a saltwater crocodile to some of America's rarest and most beautiful wading birds.

CALAKMUL BIOSPHERE RESERVE

North America/Mexico

WORTH A DETOUR: The view from the top of the Mayan pyramids; howler and spider monkeys – possibly teasing a crocodile.

In the language of the ancient Central American Maya culture Calakmul means city of twin pyramids. Its massive pyramids have long been reclaimed by tropical forest and jungle, but the Calakmul Biosphere Reserve is intended to protect archaeological history as much as the precarious regional ecosystem. The forest here would be familiar to a returning Mayan. Five of Mexico's six 'big cats' (jaguar, puma, ocelot, margay and jaguarondi) share the regrown wilderness with 80 other mammals, 358 bird species, reptiles, fish, butterflies, bats and amphibians. Tropical fauna make splashes of colour in the halls of green trees where monkeys swing and parrots chatter. At dusk every day, between two and five million bats wheel into the sky from Calakmul's bat cave to forage for insects. The taxonomy of such rich biodiversity even includes the family of man. It's a balancing act. Calakmul is already expanding both its core wilderness areas and the buffer zones which contain the Mayan ruins and where the *ejidos* (Mexican communities living on communal land) can benefit directly from the forest.

NEVADO DE COLIMA

North America/Mexico

HIGHLIGHTS:

Carizalillo Lake, where weekenders come to camp, kayak and picnic high on El Nevado. Swimming in the pool fed by the spring at the bottom of a canyon below the campsite clearing at 3,521 m (11,550 ft). The green water of Laguna Maria, on the trail to El Volcan, a mirror reflecting the smoking crater.

YOU SHOULD KNOW

In the Nahuatl language, Colima means God of Fire who Rules, and refers to Volcan de Fuego's eruptions.

From any angle – north to Guadalajara or southwest to Colima on Mexico's Pacific coast – the twin cone peaks of Nevado de Colima (El Nevado) and Volcan de Fuego de Colima (El Volcan) stand out from a distance. El Volcan is active, with a history of major eruptions and semi-permanent fizzing and growling. At any time it can, and does, spill showers of red-hot rocks over its flanks, and as recently as 2005 shot columns of ash 5 km (3 mi) high into the sky. It's a dangerous but fascinating force of nature, still growing in the old caldera formed by the much older and completely dormant El Nevado, a just-comfortable 9 km (5.5 mi) out of range. Between and surrounding the two lie thick forest and scrub, the 204 sq km (79 sq mi) Nevado de Colima National Park.

Snowcapped El Nevado looks down from 4,335 m (14,220 ft) on its fiery, 3,900 m (12,795 ft) neighbour. It rises out of hot, dusty (and now deforested) plains, through increasingly cooler subtropical and temperate zones of lush coniferous forest near the top. The trees are full of movement, of white-tailed deer, coyote and endemic birds like the highland guan, Aztec thrush and thick-billed parrot as well as woodpeckers, doves and hawks. Reaching El Nevado's summit is a strenuous two-day hike from the edge of the park; but in a 4x4 you can get to La Joya, a cabin at the end of the track from where a short but demanding hike brings you to some of El Nevado's loveliest terrain.

CUMBRES DE MAJALCA NATIONAL PARK

North America/Mexico

YOU SHOULD KNOW

The Mexican phrase to express being dumbstruck with amazement is *Ay Chihuahua!* (Don't ask: just practise). The boundary between the Cumbres de Majalca National Park and the backcountry is not clear. Be prepared to meet police or soldiers looking for the bandidos regularly alleged to patrol the area.

It is epic terrain. South of the US–Mexican border on the Rio Bravo, the wide-open hill country familiar from Texas becomes even wilder and more rugged. Chihuahua is Mexico's biggest state (half the size of Spain, or the whole of Britain), where the purple mountains of the Sierra Occidental descend to the southeastern plateau of the Chihuahua Desert. The state capital, also called Chihuahua, is one of just two sizeable local cities (the other is Juarez on the US border). The rest is a geological badlands of mountain bluffs and box canyons, where outstanding natural beauty has been baked and then frozen into the land itself. The harsh climate and difficult access have helped preserve its natural secrets. Cumbres de Majalca National Park is one of its best.

It is completely unexpected. The volcanic mountains of the Sierra de Majalca sub-range rise to only 2,600 m (8,530 ft), but from them spring a number of arroyos (fast-flowing streams) that cut dozens of valleys into the 1,000 m (3,280 ft) high plateau. Most of it is mantled by thick oak and pine forest; but after rain, every clearing is carpeted with green and dotted with the wild flowers of the high prairie. Everywhere, enormous boulders or chimneys (cumbres) of volcanic rock stand isolated – whittled, split and smoothed by water and wind. Like Easter Island statues, the extraordinary volcanic sculptures seem to have individual characters, but share the natural majesty of simply being immense. The dominant forest is typical of its altitude and the extreme hot and cold temperatures. It is a perfect habitat for the black bears who live here, among coyote, eagles, falcons, woodpeckers, and deer. Visitors come for the hiking, mountain-biking and rock climbing, and become smitten by the Cumbres' sheer beauty. Fortunately, the dramatic geological oddities share their grandeur with more wildlife than people.

HOW TO GET THERE:
By car from Chihuahua City – 30 km (19 mi) north on Highway 45, then left on a gravel track for the same distance.

WHEN TO GO:
Any time – but in mid-winter the high ground is likely to be under snow.

HIGHLIGHTS:
The boulders of Salsipuedas (especially if you enjoy rock climbing). The geometry eroded into the Penon de El Cuadrado rock formation. The imaginative formations known as Sleeping Beauty, Soldier's Peak and Eagle's Nest.

RIA CELESTUN BIOSPHERE RESERVE

North America/Mexico

WORTH A DETOUR: The 'petrified forest' of hundreds of sun-bleached, long-dead trees – a surreal landscape; swimming 'underground' in a freshwater sinkhole.

This is the place where the word 'ecotourism' was invented in 1983. The Ria Celestun Biosphere Reserve protects some of the best-preserved wetlands in the northwestern Yucatan Peninsula, on Mexico's Gulf coast. Enormous flocks of intensely pink flamingoes (up to 18,000 at a time) strut and flap offshore like a pink Mexican wave. There are storks, egrets, parrots, cardinals, pelicans and hummingbirds among the 320 species here. Crab and shrimp crowd the brackish water where mangroves thrive, and there are turtles, crocodiles, manatee and spider monkeys above and below.

Ria Celestun Biosphere Reserve is not especially big – 591 sq km (228 sq mi) – but it has added significance in being the source of most of the fresh groundwater in northwestern Yucatan. Every development on its increasingly crowded fringes interrupts the free exchange of fresh and saline water, and impacts immediately on the fragile balance of the ecosystem. A new bridge slightly diverted a freshwater channel, causing a reed marsh to stagnate and a large flamingo feeding area to close down. Threats like these to such a beautiful exhibition of natural dynamics can be removed only by inspiring the local economy to put ecotourism first.

WORTH A DETOUR: Take the rare opportunity to sample radically different ecosystems in a short time, and without having to carry lots of supplies. Wilderness areas are seldom as accessible or fringed by such a choice of facilities.

SIERRA GORDA BIOSPHERE RESERVE

North America/Mexico

The state of Queretaro in Mexico's central highlands is the meeting point of north and south bio-regions, and it makes Sierra Gorda Biosphere Reserve the most ecologically diverse in the country. The reserve includes deciduous and evergreen tropical forests, cloud forest and dense oak and pine; spiny shrubs and giant barrel cacti in its arid semi-desert areas; and barely penetrable jungle bursting out of its canyons and deep valleys, watered by huge sinkholes and underground river systems.

Historically difficult to access, and with a small population bound by poverty, the Biosphere Reserve was established by integrating Sierra Gorda's farms and villages into co-dependency with habitat conservation. There are roads and villages, and some industry – but local people have encouraged the wilderness areas to creep in and around them. Across almost a third of the whole state of Queretaro, their efforts have increased tourism but reduced its environmental impact. It is welcome evidence of an unusual empathy between man and Nature.

Sierra Gorda is on the monarch butterfly's flight path, and is visited by 300 kinds of migrant and native birds. It's a matter of mood which kind of forest to hike in – leafy glade, cooling waterfall or earthy-smelling oak.

SUMIDERO CANYON

North America/Mexico

Sumidero Canyon, east of Tuxtla Gutierrez in Mexico's extreme southeast, began as a seismic event on the edges of the North American, Cocos and Caribbean plates. It evolved over millions of years from a gash on the edge of the Chiapas High Plains to a majestic chasm carved a kilometre deep out of limestone and basalt by the Grijalva River. The Sumidero Canyon National Park encloses the canyon along 30 km (19 mi) of the river. The topography of its roughly 219 sq km

WORTH A DETOUR:
The giant *Crocodylus acutus*, the American crocodiles for which Sumidero is a perfect, and rare, habitat.

(84 sq mi) varies between 360–1,729 m (1,180–5,670 ft), and a road connects a series of vantage points called *miradores* from which to look down on the canyon's finest features. Hiking the area is tough and uncomfortable. It's better to head straight for the Ecological Reserve established on the river bank. It nestles in a crook of the river before the canyon proper. The lower ground encourages huge ferns and dense jungle foliage around small pools and marshy ground, the habitat of crocodiles and spider monkeys.

DON'T MISS
Hiking in the forest with a local Mayan who is an expert in traditional forest lore.

BLADEN NATURE RESERVE

Central America/Belize

Visitors are forbidden in the Bladen Nature Reserve. The only way to go there is on a pre-arranged educational research tour or as a volunteer researcher for the scientific teams permitted to do medical or environmental research. The reserve is entirely surrounded by other protected areas which provide a natural buffer zone against encroachment on its own pristine rainforest.

It's breathtakingly lovely – but rugged. The reserve descends the southeast slope of the Maya Mountains and across the Bladen Branch of the Monkey River. The limestone karst under its southern half is full of conical hills and outcrops honeycombed with sinkholes, cave systems and underground streams. Nobody has lived in the area since the Mayans and, although attempts are made at illegal activities like logging, Bladen has never been much disturbed. It is a verifiable tropical Eden, the adventure of a lifetime, and well worth the effort.

COCKSCOMB BASIN WILDLIFE SANCTUARY

Central America/Belize

DON'T MISS
Cayman Turtle Farm.

WHEN TO GO:
December–May (the dry season, and the only months Victoria Peak may be visited) – although wildlife generally is much more active from June to July (the start of the rainy season). December is best for migrant birds.

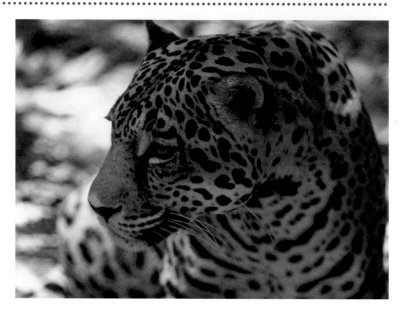

Isolated in the far south of Belize between the Maya Mountains and the coast, the Cockscomb Basin Wildlife Sanctuary is the world's only jaguar reserve. It is also one of the few reserves that accept casual visitors on the same basis as serious naturalists. This rudimentary respect stimulates visitors' curiosity and sense of adventure: it's a very effective method of sharpening vision and hearing before hiking into the great unknown.

Learning to 'read' the forest is paramount at Cockscomb. The reserve's 728 sq km (280 sq mi) of jungle are watered by dozens of streams and underground watercourses that emerge in sparkling waterfalls and clear, deep pools ringed by boulders. As in every kind of terrain, but here especially, pug marks and broken vegetation speak for the teeming wildlife – adrenalin-pumping proof of fabled big cats too canny to be easily spotted. There are several trails (graded by difficulty and physical ability) where you can feel completely absorbed into the patterns of nature the sanctuary is at pains to illustrate. The all-day hike to Outlier Mountain covers most important habitats from jungle swamp and tropical rainforest to the rugged tangle of the mountain itself; but shorter trails are intended to be as much about fun as learning something. For the really committed, the four-day hike to 1,120 m (3,675 ft) Victoria Peak needs a permit from the Belize Audubon Society and a licensed guide. The area has not yet been fully explored since it was returned to a wilderness decades ago, and you can expect to discover unknown orchids and encounter rare animals. Cockscomb Basin's willingness to treat serious conservation as potential recreation should be a blueprint for other wildlife sanctuaries of similar stature. Not many of them encourage inner-tubing down their rivers for the thrill of 'looking a crocodile in the eye at its own level'.

WORTH A DETOUR: Belize's only example of comfrey palm forest, on the banks of the Sarstoon River; the red mangrove forest – the best in Central America.

SARSTOON/TEMASH NATIONAL PARK

Central America/Belize

The Sarstoon River forms Belize's southern border with Guatemala. The Temash River opens onto the Gulf of Honduras 16 km (10 mi) up the coast in Amatique Bay. Sandwiched between the two deltas are 170 sq km (66 sq mi) of mangrove forests, sandbar and silt-filled creeks, swamps and marshes merging into some of Belize's most pristine jungle forests. It is an ancient place of innumerable shades of green shadow, splashed with flashes of primary brilliance. It is home to species not found elsewhere in Belize, like the scarlet macaw, white-faced capuchin monkey, countless butterflies and Morelet's crocodile. Seldom disturbed by human intrusion, the deeper forests are full of fresh tracks of bigger, rarer mammals like the tapir, jaguar and ocelot – legends of invisibility, but frequently glimpsed.

The crowning glory of the Temash River are the towering red mangroves reaching up on both banks to 31 m (100 ft) or more, and stretching for miles into and along the coast. Orchids and bromeliads decorate the solid 3 m (10 ft) wall of their roots. Between the rivers, the delta of shallow, brackish waters nourishes underwater grass plains where manatee feed and shoals of fish flit away their nursery years.

INDIO-MAIZ BIOLOGICAL RESERVE

Central America/Nicaragua

WORTH A DETOUR: Staying the night within the resrve. It's the only way to get a real impression of the species' diversity and behaviour – even though night-time jungle noises can be spine-chilling.

Ascending the San Juan River on Nicaragua's border with Costa Rica is one of only two ways to enter what some biologists call the gem of Central American nature reserves.

The Indio-Maiz Biological Reserve is the biggest area of contiguous rainforest outside the Amazon. Much of it is still not fully explored, but from the Caribbean side it is permitted to use the Indio River (via the San Juan) to get deep inside the 2,590-sq km (1,000-sq mi) reserve, most of which is prohibited except to scientists. The only other access point is from the west, via the Bartola River near the historic settlement of El Castillo. This route also connects to the San Juan River, but is used by many more people for frequent, shorter token visits just inside the reserve.

Visitors must have a guide, and the guide must be a Rama Indian. In a supreme irony of modern 'conservation', the Rama people are no longer allowed to live along the Indio River as they have done for centuries, but visitors can use their former homes to camp within the reserve for a few nights. That aside, their expert knowledge brings the richness of the jungle forest to vivid life. There are deer, sloths, giant anteaters, boars, pacas, pumas, howler and spider monkeys, manatees, freshwater sharks (the world's only species), turtles, crocodiles, caimans, iguanas, yellow-and-black poison dart frogs, reptiles of every hue, toucans, hummingbirds, parrots, and whole rainbows of butterflies, orchids and other tropical flowers.

BRAULIO CARRILLO NATIONAL PARK

Central America/Costa Rica

DON'T MISS
The Rainforest Aerial Tram through the canopy layers, or the zipline through the canopy itself.

It takes 30 minutes to go from Costa Rica's capital, San Jose, to Braulio Carrillo National Park, and it's like time-travelling. Although Costa Rica was slow to recognize its own environmental wealth, it responded with enthusiasm to the challenge of preserving it. More of the country is protected as wilderness or an ecological buffer zone than – proportionately – anywhere else in the world. Braulio Carrillo National Park is one of Costa Rica's biggest and best, and it's right on the capital's doorstep.

It covers the western side of the volcanic Cordillera Central, from the edge of the coffee farms and cattle ranches on the highland plateau straight up the mountains to the chilly mists of cloud forest between extinct volcanoes; and then down the Caribbean slope to La Selva's great swathes of humid lowland jungle. To cross it is a tough four- or five-day adventure with a guide (and permission). It's dangerous, too; from top to bottom 84 per cent of it is primary forest and jungle, and the wildlife includes some of the world's most lethal snakes, touch-poisonous amphibians and other colourful, murderously attractive threats. Fortunately, three Ranger stations on the park's edge provide easier access to short marked trails. The Barva Station is the start of a climb to the lake in the crater of the dormant Barva Volcano. The cloud forest here harbours local heroes like the strawberry poison arrow frog, the terrifying fer-de-lance snake, and the continent's biggest venomous snake, the bushmaster. Zurqui Station has two major trails taking in the rivers and waterfalls of different forest ecosystems full of howler and spider monkeys, deer, tapir, and the luminous, shimmering glory of quetzals, scarlet-rumpled tanagers, toucans and golden hummingbirds. The old-growth trees, butterflies and burgeoning wildlife have flourished here for thousands of years – untouched and virtually unseen until Braulio Carrillo was declared a national park. There's no easier place to sample such extraordinary diversity.

YOU SHOULD KNOW
Unfortunately bandits haunt the park, often armed. Be wary.

DON'T MISS
The wreck of the
Antilles, a French liner
that ran aground in 1971.

PENAS BLANCAS MASSIF

Central America/Nicaragua

The Penas Blancas (White Rocks) Massif in north central Nicaragua takes its name from the calcium streaking the rock face. In the recent past, the massif's generous fertility encouraged the development of coffee and other farms on its lower slopes. The realization that stripping the mountains of its rainforest damaged its vital but fragile ecosystem caused a dramatic rethink. Now the lower slopes have been returned to nature, and the Penas Blancas Massif can be appreciated for its unique contribution to the region's biodiversity.

The Massif is self-enclosed, and above 1,000 m (3,280 ft) it has never been developed, and its steep valleys and multiple peaks are a mist-filled realm of untouched cloud forest. Black oak, granadillo and walnut trees shelter giant ferns, heleconias, orchids and bromeliads. Among the colourful parakeets, warblers, hummingbirds and tanagers the resplendent quetzal is the loveliest, and restricted to its mountain habitat. Waterfalls crash jaw-dropping distances from the Massif's sheer rock walls, and the network of streams and creeks makes hiking wearily wet. There is no prolonged summer interval of hot days.

LA FLOR WILDLIFE REFUGE

Central America/Nicaragua

One of Nicaragua's most beautiful beaches lies on the Pacific coast just north of the border with Costa Rica. La Flor is the annual site of a spectacular natural drama. Between July and January, hundreds of thousands of sea turtles haul themselves out of the ocean to nest and lay their eggs here.

How turtles recognize the beach where they were born is as much a mystery as how they synchronize their mass invasions. La Flor is one of only two beaches on Nicaragua's Pacific Coast they use; and although all kinds of turtle can be seen there, it is olive ridley's turtles (known as *paslama* in Nicaragua) which appear night after night, sometimes in groups of 30,000–50,000. They have to struggle through the fine soft sand, competing for the best spaces; laboriously clear a hollow in which to lay around 100 eggs; cover it so that the eggs can develop at the right temperature; and escape back to sea before being spotted by hovering predators. La Flor exists primarily to protect the turtles, but its forests are big enough to house monkeys, iguanas and big bird colonies which treat the eggs – and hatchlings – as a larder.

WORTH A DETOUR:
Camping on La Flor around the time of a full moon. It takes at least 24 hours to see how the ocean, beach and forest interact on behalf of the turtles, their eggs, and their predators, with some degree of success for them all.

CORDILLERA DE TALAMANCA

Central America/Costa Rica

WHEN TO GO: Any time. Seasons don't really exist in the Cordillera de Talamanca – but the west slope is a little drier from December–March.

Still largely unexplored, the Cordillera de Talamanca is the southern spine of Costa Rica, the continental divide between North and South America and the watershed between the Pacific and the Caribbean. The range soars upwards to Costa Rica's highest peak, Cerro Chirripo – 3,820 m (12,530 ft) – towering over

a forbidding wilderness of plunging valleys, glacial lakes and some of the rarest terrain in the whole world: the high-altitude, neotropical ecosystem called paramo. It looks like science fiction: peat bogs and swampy grasslands peppered with enormous spiked plants and strange shrubs in profusion. The paramo is one of an astonishing number of habitats in the Cordillera, created by differences in altitude, weather patterns, soil and topography. Since every one of them is a mix of flora and fauna from north and south, Talamanca's wildlife is among the world's most abundant and diverse. The isolation of the lush forests of Talamanca's valleys harbours 600 kinds of bird, 500 species of trees and bushes, 150 kinds of orchids and around 265 amphibians and reptiles. Ocelots, tapirs, pumas and jaguars are not rare here. People are.

WHEN TO GO: November–April, for sunshine and the cooling Papagayo offshore breeze; or the beginning of the rainy season in May, for the revival of the lush green flora.

RIO BONGO ESTUARY

Central America/Costa Rica

The Pacific coast of Costa Rica's Nicoya Peninsula is an endlessly scenic series of curving white beaches punctuated by rocky headlands and mangrove-filled river estuaries. Nicoya's northern section is a mecca for surfing *cognoscenti* and intrepid backpackers. The southern section is paradise itself – and the Rio Bongo estuary is its pristine heart. Reaching it involves a 7 km (4 mi) hike north from the village of Manzanillo. It's easy to be entranced by the thick forest crowding the edge of an enormous sweep of fine sand. Be wary. The beach becomes a long spit running parallel to the river. Where it emerges into the sea it's only waist deep, but ford it at your peril. The Rio Bongo is famous for its large colony of crocodiles. The Rio Bongo beach is one of the most important nesting sites for leather-back sea turtles in the eastern Pacific – and the 1.8–2.4 m (6–8 ft) colossi are very picky about their habitat. Happily, the whole beach is protected by a private landowner who refuses to allow any kind of development that might disturb them. His sensible rules include prohibiting camping, but permitting 'night hiking' so that visitors can observe the turtles.

TORTUGUERO NATIONAL PARK

Central America/Costa Rica

The water world of Tortuguero National Park on northeast Costa Rica's Caribbean coast is an ecological adventure playground. It covers a huge region of lowland palm swamps, tropical wet rainforest and mangroves, criss-crossed with natural channels and connected lagoons as well as the freshwater creeks that feed the Tortuguero River itself. Boating on its lazy currents is the only way to get close to its many secrets and electrifying surprises – although the park includes some montane rainforest where volcanic hills climb to 100–300 m (328–985 ft). Hiking among its waterfalls and swimming in rock pools is a beautiful experience, but Tortuguero's magic is in its water margins, where freshwater and salt water mix and all four elements merge. With such a wide variety of habitats and the comparative rarity of visitors (in a whole day gliding through the network of canals and rivers, it's possible never to come across another boat), the region is alive with movement. More than half of all Costa Rica's bird and reptile species live here. Monkeys, sloths, anteaters, lizards, caimans, and crocodiles exist in the kind of profusion that makes sightings inevitable, even from a boat. Every corner is a nest, breeding ground, or habitat for something in the canopy, mangroves or dense jungle forest islands.

Four kinds of marine turtles lay eggs on Tortuguero's sandbanks, including the biggest visiting population of green sea turtles anywhere on the Caribbean coast. Visitors can join 'night walks' to see them crowd ashore.

The downside of Tortuguero's fertility and abundance is the threat from commercial interests like logging, which can only upset the ecological balance. In practice, that means the more people who come to admire its natural beauty, the more likely Tortuguero can be properly protected.

HIGHLIGHTS:
The jungle trail running from the Park Ranger HQ known as Cuatro Esquinas near Tortuguero village. Remember the wonderland underwater – with Polaroid lenses it's easy to see the seven kinds of river turtles, manatees, river otters and 50 fish species (including the menacing alligator gar) weaving through the seagrasses below the boat.

CHIRIQUI HIGHLANDS

Central America/Panama

WHEN TO GO: Any time. Temperatures vary enormously according to altitude rather than season, and the park is a network of microclimates.

The province of Chiriqui forms Panama's border with Costa Rica on the Pacific slope of the continental divide. Its coastal lowlands are a mix of dense jungles and lively surfing resorts, backed by miles of orderly farmland where the volcanic soil guarantees astonishing fertility. The region is famous for its coffee farms stretching high up into the Chiriqui Highlands, quilting the slopes of Panama's highest peak and only volcano, the dormant 3,478 m (11,410 ft) Baru Volcano. As the farms thin out, montane rainforest takes over, dotted with small villages perched on rocky crags in a landscape of waterfalls and tall trees. It's suspiciously European,

and no surprise to discover that most of the villages were built by engineers who came to work on the Panama Canal. Higher still lies a wilderness of primary cloud forest, a cool, misty world filled with the clamour of birds of the brightest colours and fanciest names. Between the mountain villages of Boquete and Cerro Punto, the Quetzal Trail follows a high ridge around the Baru Volcano. Besides the legendary sacred bird of the Aztecs, the oak, cedar and laurel trees and the ferns and mosses harbour the spectacled foliage-gleaner, the prong-billed barbet, the buffy tufted-cheek and a jeweller's display of hummingbirds.

WHEN TO GO: Any time, but the turtles come to nest between April and October.

ISLA BASTIMENTOS

Central America/Panama

Of the 68 Bocas del Toro islands spread across 100 km (62 mi) of the Gulf of Chiriqui on Panama's Caribbean coast, only Isla Bastimentos anchors a National Marine Park. Only the central section belongs within the park, providing a land bridge between three enormous and mutually dependent marine tracts which are the highlight of any visit.

The indigenous villages and tourist developments on the island see eco-conservation as serving their own interests: Bastimentos is an advanced model of how to combine leisure with ecotourism. There's plenty to explore.

The 16.6 sq km (6.4 sq mi) of interior land corridor is primary rainforest with a full complement of monkeys, sloths, turtles, frogs, lizards, caimans, armadillos, colourful birds, ferns, hardwood trees, bromeliads and orchids. To the south the forest floods to become Panama's largest red and white mangrove swamp, opening onto the shallows of Almirante Lagoon – a sub-marine meadow of waving seagrass.

RIO DULCE

Central America/Guatemala

YOU SHOULD KNOW

When pirates roved the Spanish Main, Lake Izabal was a popular pirate haven. The little town of El Estor got its name from English pirates who used to sail up the Rio Dulce to replenish supplies at 'The Store' – El Estor. The Castillo, the fort of San Felipe de Lara upstream of the present-day road bridge, was built by the Spanish to repel the Englishmen's regular visits.

The eastern corner of Guatemala between Belize and Honduras is a self-contained watery wonderland called Rio Dulce. The Dulce River itself is short – 42 km (26 mi) – but it is the central feature of a much bigger region of small rivers and jungle islands, of protected swamps, mangroves, and primary tropical rainforest. The river is the outlet for Lake Izabal, Guatemala's biggest, which is fed in turn by the rivers running off the Sierra de las Minas into the Polochic Valley. The glorious logic of this topography and the climate is the ripeness and fertility of all the different kinds of wilderness the region supports. The feeling remains strong despite a thriving tourist industry based on several small towns and villages on its banks, and the major road bridge that crosses it. The human presence actually makes access to Rio Dulce's secrets easier: without it, the jungle would be forbidding and, frankly, scary. But even with its civilization, the giant-size vegetation feels all-consuming.

The Garifuna town of Livingston, on Amatique Bay at the mouth of the Rio Dulce, is the only large community at one with its environment – so it's the place to find a guide as well as to have fun. Since Livingston is accessible only by boat, Rio Dulce's fabulous natural riches are on the doorstep. There are hundreds of connecting channels overhung by trees trailing flowers and filled by chattering monkeys, long-beaked waterbirds and screaming parrots. There are 'hot' waterfalls created by underwater geysers, huge 'meadows' of packed lily pads in bloom, a 10 km (6 mi) white limestone gorge with 120 m (400 ft) high walls festooned with trailing greenery and orchids, and acres of reed beds. A motorized dugout (cayuco) opens up the most remote, toucan-friendly creeks and provides a water taxi to some of the amazing jungle trails.

HOW TO GET THERE:
By bus to the town of Mariscos on the south shore of Lake Izabal; or by boat to Livingston

WHEN TO GO:
Any time. The rainy season expands the wetland jungle delta where the Polochic River enters the lake, and the wildlife explodes all along the Rio Dulce.

HIGHLIGHTS:
Turning off the outboard and paddling your own cayuco among the untouched and seldom-visited pristine jungles and crystal-clear freshwater rivers like Rio Obscuro and Rio Zarquito on the southwest bank of Lake Izabal. Return via the Biotopo de Chacon Machacas – the manatee sanctuary in the seagrass lagoons of the Golfete, a 5 km (3 mi) wide section of the Rio Dulce edged by a lattice of mangrove channels.

SIERRA DE LAS MINAS

Central America/Guatemala

WORTH A DETOUR: Tasting the utter purity of the water – the dense forests of the biosphere's northern section filter it repeatedly.

Undisturbed since the Olmecs and Maya mined jade and obsidian, the Sierra de las Minas has been protected by the deterrent factor of its geography. Its shallow soil and steep slopes discouraged farming, and its topography caused local microclimates of opposite and irregular extremes. Scientists love its integrity: six ecosystems and three ecoregions operating in symbiotic harmony, but with different results from anywhere else with a similar range. This is because the Sierra is 3.2 km (2 mi) high, 48 km (30 mi) wide and runs east–west for about 160 km (100 mi) through Guatemala's northeast highlands. Its shape causes 'weather-shadows'.

The astonishing variety and quantity of the wildlife can only be appreciated by taking in the Sierra's entire altitudinal range. Between San Agustin Acasaguastlan and Chelasco on the Biosphere Reserve's northern edge there is a 32 km (20 mi) wilderness trail which more than justifies the strenuous effort required. From the bird-filled cloud forests of mossy hardwoods and bamboo stands the trail winds down through evergreen forest so perfect that the Sierra is referred to as 'one of the world's most important tropical gene banks for conifer endoplasm' (it means seed banks are a good thing). The descent proves repeatedly that there's more wildlife and more varied fauna even than in the legendary Peten area to the north. It's an extra hike to visit the Motagua Valley – but Motagua has the added attraction of being chaparral country.

WHEN TO GO: Any time. The first rains of May bring out the dazzling wild flowers and green the highlands. The Highlands' climate is rainy from May–October.

WESTERN HIGHLANDS

Central America/Guatemala

Central America's highest peak, 4,220 m (13,845 ft) Tajamulco, explodes with the colour of wild flowers in spring. But at any time the Western Highlands region is the most spectacularly beautiful in all Guatemala. Getting the most from visiting means revising the usual definitions of nature in the wild. The Sierra Madre's three active volcanoes spit regular fire and fumes, yet their flanks are still terraced for crops wherever possible. In the rain-drenched highlands, forests at every elevation grow giants of their species, with dense under-brush to match. Only the summits are treeless altiplano, a mist-wreathed, chilly grassland broken by worn boulders. Yet both landscapes are productive in the hands of the indigenous farmers and shepherds. The Western Highlands and its people have evolved together and belong to each other. It is their symbiosis that makes the region so bewitching.

DON'T MISS
The Gorge Trail, which follows a ridge of humid rainforest between two cascading mountain rivers.

PICO BONITO

Central America/Honduras

The resort beaches lining the Caribbean at La Ceiba are dominated by the looming bulk of Pico Bonito. The highest – 2,436 m (8,000 ft) – peak in the Nombre de Dios range, Pico Bonito rears up from sea level immediately behind the resort. Its jagged silhouette stretches away into the blue yonder, an invitation to an adventure that starts just a few minutes' drive away. The lure is the diversity of wildlife habitats in close proximity; the coastal jungle rises through strata of tropical wet, broadleaf and lowland dry forest, diversifying into cloud forest at around 1,200 m (4,000 ft) – a rare combination guaranteeing the best chance of seeing the widest variety of endemic species. These strata are subdivided by another influence – the mountain's unusually steep valley formations. Tumbling rivers and rushing streams create dozens of cascades and waterfalls on every level. Each harbours its own population of birds, butterflies and bigger animals, from monkeys to river otters. Their abundance is dependent on the harsh topography, which makes Pico Bonito very hard to access.

RIO PLATANO BIOSPHERE RESERVE

Central America/Honduras

WORTH A DETOUR: Spend as much time as possible in a pipante (dugout) or on a raft on the Rio Platano. It's the best vantage point to see every kind of wildlife.

The 'Banana' River used to be the source of 'red gold' – the mahogany that furnished Europe. It is the major river of the Mosquito Coast and is still home to the remnants of three of Honduras' indigenous peoples: the Miskito, Pech and Garifuna. The Biosphere Reserve was created as much to provide a sanctuary for these cultures as to protect the fabulously complete coastal ecosystems in which, historically, they thrived. It is a humid, haunting wilderness of steaming mangroves, islets of jungle, coastal lagoons and creeks draped in moss-shrouded rainforest.

The best surprises are to be found with the guidance of one of the villagers. Each guide is part of the region's living continuity, familiar with its wildlife and weather. Near the Rio Platano's headwaters at Warsaka, and at Lancetillal nearby, there are 1,500-year-old petroglyphs incorporated into major ruins whose occupants used the rainforest as larder and pharmacy just as its current residents do. Descending the river by cayuco (motorized dugout) provides a glimpse of the subtle complexities controlling every kind of life in these isolated wetlands and shows how Miskito culture is integrated into the ecochain.

YOU SHOULD KNOW
The Mosquito Coast gets its name from the Meskito people, not because it's a mosquito-infested swamp. Although, in fact, it is.

CERRO VERDE

Central America/El Salvador

Cerro Verde is the centrepiece of three volcanoes set close together on the border between the departments of Sonsonate and Santa Ana. Together they are a powerful reminder of El Salvador's always precarious position along the Pacific Ring of Fire, and although Cerro Verde is extinct and Izalco 'quiescent', the third, Santa Ana, still spurts out sulphurous fumes around its boiling crater lake. All three can be climbed, but Cerro Verde offers a grandstand view of both its neighbours, and Izalco, El Salvador's iconic volcano cone (it used to be on the country's banknotes), is in any case most dramatic seen from a distance. Santa Ana's craters are much more interesting. It has four, descending in size from the rim to what was recently a sulphurous lagoon, and is now a reawakened, boiling and bubbling cauldron. There's a wonderful trail from Cerro Verde all the way to the 2,365 m (7,760 ft) rim of Santa Ana, with progressively more staggering views as it rises through the forest and into the volcanic debris. On Cerro Verde itself, the supernutrients in the volcanic soil have created a cone wreathed in layers of dense secondary forest that have replaced the coffee farms for which it is still famous at its lower levels. Left to itself, the mountain is ablaze with wild flowers packing the lush vegetation below the towering trees. At about 2,000 m (6,560 ft), the tropical conditions draw the clouds into a misty veil of tepid drizzle, and Cerro Verde's rim and crater are covered in beautiful cloud forest. The Una Ventana a la Naturaleza Trail (a window on nature) leads you into the crater itself where, untouched for 300 years, the trees are giants.

YOU SHOULD KNOW

Izalco is the youngest volcano in El Salvador. For 200 years it was in a state of continuous eruption, and its flaring lava streams were visible well out into the Pacific Ocean. Sailors relied on it as 'the lighthouse of the Pacific'. Eventually a hotel was built on Cerro Verde so visitors could enjoy the sight in comfort. A few weeks before the hotel opened in 1967, Izalco's eruptions stopped completely and permanently. Since 2005, when it sprang back into life, Santa Ana (aka Ilamatepec) has been the subject of an 'active' warning.

WHEN TO GO:

Any time. The rainy season from May–November brings out the best of the flowers and greenery.

EL IMPOSIBLE NATIONAL PARK

Central America/El Salvador

YOU SHOULD KNOW

The main entrance to El Imposible is on the park's southeast edge at San Benito, beyond the tiny village of San Miguelito. It's important to get a visitor's permit in advance either in San Salvador or by calling the park so they can arrange a guide who will collect the permit money on arrival. Guides are usually volunteers who work for a tip in US dollars.

Don't be put off by the name. A century ago, coffee was farmed on the steepest mountains. At one point high up, the trail was too narrow for two mules to squeeze past each other: it was 'impossible'. Now the plantations have been returned to secondary forest, in a bid to buffer a precious remnant of El Salvador's once huge primary forests and to form El Imposible National Park on the western edge of the Apaneca-Ilmatepec range. Protection came just in time for many species of bird, mammal, reptile, insect and even amphibians which survive only here. More crucially, by reversing the inroads made by farming and logging, El Imposible has been saved as the source of seven rivers which water a huge part of El Salvador. That's why visitor numbers are controlled and travellers must seek a permit from the government agency, Salvanatura – but the payoff is that the conservation process has restored the mountains to their pristine beauty.

There are only around 36 sq km (14 sq mi) of primary dry forest, but they range in altitude from 274–1,311 m (900–4,300 ft). The mountains and steep gullies are an outstanding sanctuary for over 500 bird species and 1,000 species of trees and plants. One 8 km (5 mi) circuit called Cerro El Leon begins in the florescent humidity of a deep gorge and leads through dense forest of constantly changing fauna and flora to astonishing panoramic views near the summit of Montana de los Aguilares, and returns by way of the Ixcanal and Guayapa river valleys. It's the best trail for birdwatching and for butterflies. Less strenuous is the short – 2.2 km (1.4 mi) – trail from the Mixtepe Visitor Centre at the park entrance to Mirador El Mulo. It's a perfect introduction to the forest, and leads to a lookout point with dramatic views of the Guayapa valley.

HOW TO GET THERE:
By car, or by bus from Cara Sucia or the Ahuachapio River bridge.

WHEN TO GO:
October–February, when it's dry. The rainy season makes the steep hills too muddy and difficult.

HIGHLIGHTS:
The lovely Los Enganches trail to the beautiful forest swimming hole at the junction of the Guayapa and Venado Rivers. It continues upriver to Piedra Sellada (the Stamped Rock), a stone carved with Maya script, and one of several archaeological sites buried in the wilderness. The Hasta La Luna trek follows no trail but leads into El Imposible's heart, and to a stunning series of cascades where you can cool off.

LOS COBANOS

Central America/El Salvador

WORTH A DETOUR:
Taking a boat ride into deep water above the seaward fringes of the reef, where dolphins, sea turtles, rays and the larger game fish come to feed and cavort.

Punta Remedios is a pimple of a headland jutting into the Pacific Ocean from the flattened curve of El Salvador's western coastline. It's a hotspot of marine biodiversity, and has recently come under eco-sensitive scrutiny as El Salvador's first Natural Marine Protected Area, known as Los Cobanos. It includes nearly 40 km (25 mi) of coastline from Playa Barra Salada to just short of the port of Acajutla, all the mangrove forests to their inland limit, and exactly 36 times as much ocean as landmass, with the coral reef at the area's heart.

The wildlife comes in quantity as well as quality. At low tide a thousand rock pools teem with small fish and shellfish, and it's easy to pick a path through the shallow water around mangroves. It's not just a children's paradise. Wading birds pace the flats while ocean predators patrol the skies above the reef looking for the nursery shoals. Big game fish come in raiding packs, a target for fishermen and sometimes each other. Migrating 15 m (50 ft) humpback whales pass close to the shore. In the crystal water, scuba divers and snorkellers get the best view of the reef flora and fauna, and of the giant snapper, barracuda, mahi-mahi, wahoo, yellow-fin tuna, rooster fish and turtles that abound. Los Cobanos has got the lot, and pelicans too.

WHEN TO GO:
November–March/April.
The summit area above Los Planes is closed at other times for the cloud forest fauna breeding season.

MONTECRISTO–EL TRIFINIO NATIONAL PARK

Central America/El Salvador

The preservation of the Cerro Montecristo cloud forest is a triumph of political optimism in a region once plagued by sectarian confrontation. The mountain is 'shared' by El Salvador, Guatemala and Honduras. Its 2,418 m (7,935 ft) summit marks the exact spot where the three countries meet, and is proudly known as El Trifinio. Here, visitors are monarchs of all they survey – explorers in a wild and beautiful world that repays the hardships of getting there with a superabundance of plant and animal species born of the region's isolation and blend of exotic microclimates. Montecristo has cloud forest on a gargantuan scale, and the biodiversity to match. Wreathed in mist, oak and laurel trees grow to 30 m (100 ft) with a vault-like canopy shading giant 8 m (26 ft) tree ferns among the mosses, lichens, trailing bromeliads and psychedelic orchids near the forest floor. Even at intermediate altitudes where cypress stands and pine–oak forest dominate (and sometimes alternate – the microclimates produce strange anomalies!) normal expectations are confounded by the richness and rarity of the wildlife.

SIERRA DEL ROSARIO

The Caribbean/Cuba

WORTH A DETOUR:
The Orchidarium at Soroa which displays hundreds of species of orchid, many endemic.

As part of a determined reforestation programme, many areas of Cuba are national parks. The Sierra del Rosario is a lovely swathe of rolling, wooded mountains, tobacco plants and orchards which used to be an important coffee-growing area, and small-scale coffee production continues. The village of Las Terrazas, originally built for forestry and conservation workers but now also home to artisans and farmers, has a museum, cinema and research institute. A hotel complex offers horse riding, mountain-biking, fishing and boating as well as delightful long and short guided walks into the lushly verdant evergreen and semi-deciduous forest. Many of the hundreds of species of plant and wildlife found here are unique to Cuba. South of Las Terrazas is Soroa. Originally a coffee plantation, the hotel here organizes activities and hikes.

SIERRA MAESTRA

DON'T MISS
Santo Domingo, in its deep, verdant valley.

The Caribbean/Cuba

The biggest mountain range in Cuba, the Sierra Maestra rises steeply from the southeast coast. Pico Turquino, at over 1,970 m (6,465 ft), is the country's highest mountain, and the ascent is a long, challenging hike best undertaken as a two- or three-day guided trek. Refuges are spaced out along the whole route and guides will organize overnight stops. The walk combines green valleys, open uplands affording panoramas of unfolding mountain ranges and the brilliant-blue Caribbean, and cool forests rich in flora and fauna (pygmy owls and hummingbirds are often spotted).

The Comandancia de La Plata, Castro's revolutionary base, is a shorter hike and can be completed in a day. After the steep road from Santo Domingo to Alto del Naranjo, this trail runs west along sheer ridges to where, in a deep gully, hidden under a canopy of trees, Fidel and Raul built their settlement. Here, visitors can inspect a scatter of huts (including dormitories and stores), Castro's operational headquarters and Che Guevara's hospital. A little museum displays photographs and memorabilia, such as Fidel's fountain pen and the radio equipment used by Che for his Radio Rebelde broadcasts to the nation.

CULEBRA NATIONAL WILDLIFE REFUGE

The Caribbean/Puerto Rico

DON'T MISS
Mirador Laime viewpoint is the best spot to take photographs.

HOW TO GET THERE:
Flights from San Juan and Fajardo airports; regular ferry service from Fajardo.

WHEN TO GO:
November–July.

Culebra was declared a National Wildlife Refuge in 1909 but was, effectively, a firing range for the US Navy until 1975. Now administered by the US Fish and Wildlife Service, the refuge includes the deeply indented coastline, palm-fringed beaches, parts of the rocky, forested interior and all the satellite islets; all this, and its exceptional wildlife, attracts visitors to this small island with its easy-going brand of ecotourism. Limited development means wonderfully clean seawater, and Culebra's fringe and barrier reefs are some of the most vibrant in the Caribbean. They provide excellent feeding for seabirds and large fish and some very fine snorkelling – anything from angelfish to barracuda may be encountered in the brilliant, glassy waters.

Large coastal mangrove swamps are roosting sites for the endangered brown pelican and nurseries for fish and crustaceans, while the isolated beaches (most are accessible only by tracks) and untouched forest (the Mount Resaca area can be explored by trail) are perfect habitats for a multitude of nesting birds. Terns are particularly numerous on Culebra – a large colony of sooty terns colonizes the Flamenco Peninsula, while roseate, sandwich, bridled and royal terns are widespread. Other birds frequently seen include boobies, tropicbirds and ospreys.

The northern beaches and tiny Isla Culebrita are also nesting sites for endangered sea turtles. Loggerhead, hawksbill, green and leatherback turtles all bury their eggs in the soft sand; the sites are closed during the

summer hatching season. Culebra is only about 11 km (7 mi) long and there is little traffic on the few roads; mountain bikes are a good transport option. By day, the empty beaches of Cayo Luis Pena and Isla Culebrita can be reached by water taxi, although a kayak is a pleasing and ecologically sound way to visit these little desert islands.

EL YUNQUE

The Caribbean/Puerto Rico

WHEN TO GO:
April to June are quiet months in the forest; in the hot summers, islanders flock there to cool down; winter (high season) can be hectic.

DON'T MISS:
A night in the rainforest. Camping is permitted off-trail, but it is very basic. Several hotels around the forest perimeter provide an enticing combination of comfort with the unforgettable music of the creatures of dusk and darkness.

Sometimes the rich Taino, European and African heritage of Puerto Rico seems overshadowed by modern American life, but the island probably owes the survival of its rainforests and rich biodiversity to US colonial rule. Logging and rapid urban expansion resulted in serious deforestation and soil erosion, but in the 1920s extensive areas of conservation forest were set aside and now thousands of tropical plant, bird and animal species flourish in a variety of natural habitats. Much of eastern Puerto Rico is covered by the forests, hills, streams and waterfalls of El Yunque (previously known as the Caribbean National Forest), the only tropical rainforest under US administration. Now a UNESCO Biosphere Reserve, it is carefully managed and has hiking trails and visitor and research centres. A range of forest types grows here, including most of Puerto Rico's ancient virgin forest – many of the reddish-barked Palo Colorado trees, with their trailing vines, are around 1,000 years old. Sierra palms, ferns and mosses thrive in wetter conditions and, on peaks and ridges, heavy rain and constant winds bend and stunt the cloud, or dwarf, forest. This sumptuously diverse landscape supports a wealth of wildlife. Although the endangered Puerto Rican parrot (which nests in the Palo Colorado trees) is rarely seen, more than 50 bird species, many unique, inhabit the reserve. Resident reptiles include the Puerto Rican boa. Some of the shorter, paved trails to popular destinations (waterfalls, viewing towers and peaks) can get busy, but longer wilderness trails in the undeveloped south of the forest are often deserted. Serious walkers may leave the crowds behind and relish the cool, pristine beauty of this mountainous subtropical rainforest.

JARAGUA NATIONAL PARK

The Caribbean/Dominican Republic

The largest protected area in the Caribbean, Jaragua National Park lies in the southwest of the Dominican Republic's Barahona Peninsula. The dry, thorny forest hosts a preponderance of cacti alongside endemic shrubs such as the medicinal canelilla, and guanito palms. The land is dotted with caves and many are decorated with petroglyphs and pictographs dating back to 2590 BC; they provide shelter for 11 species of bat. More than 50 endemic species live here: 36 in Hispaniola, 26 in Jaragua itself, 4 on Beata Island and 3 on Alto Velo Island. Among these are two iguanas and, at 16 mm (0.6 in), the world's tiniest reptile, the Jaragua Sphaero – a dwarf gecko. The park is also home to 130 species of birds – some 60 per cent of the country's total – over half of which are seabirds. The country's largest population of pink flamingoes lives at Oviedo lagoon, and vast colonies of white-crowned pigeons and the largest known colony of the plain pigeon, a West Indian endangered species, can be found here. On the islands the sooty tern has formed its largest Caribbean colony.

WHEN TO GO:
December–February or
July–August.

DON'T MISS
On a hill close to the lake
is the Las Caritas Indian
Cave where you'll find
Taino engravings of faces.

LAKE ENRIQUILLO

The Caribbean/Dominican Republic

The largest lake in the entire Caribbean, Lake Enriquillo is unique. Situated some 44 m (144 ft) below sea level in the southwestern area of the island, it has a fascinating ecosystem due to its hypersalinity. Not only twice as salty as the sea, it is also sulphurous. Lake Enriquillo was declared a national park in 1995, although in 1974 Cabritos Island – one of three islands in the lake – became a national park in its own right. The lake is named after Enriquillo, the Taino Indian chief who resisted the Spanish colonizers while hiding in this area; his statue can be seen at a museum in Santo Domingo.

The difficult conditions provide a habitat for a large number of birds and reptiles, including the American crocodile. The largest population in the world may be found here; each day they swim to the mouths of freshwater streams and spend their nights and lay their eggs on Cabritos Island – a flat, arid 9.6 km (6 mi) long island where cacti grow in profusion. Two species of iguana – Ricord's and rhinoceros – abound.

DON'T MISS
You might see whales
in Samana in February.

ARMANDO BERMUDEZ NATIONAL PARK

The Caribbean/Dominican Republic

The scenery of the Armando Bermudez National Park is glorious; the forested slopes, including most of the surviving virgin rainforest, encompass the largest areas of the country's originally forested landscape. Rivers allow a lush subtropical mixture of West Indian cedar, orchids, palms, bamboo and tree ferns to thrive; at higher elevations, the trees are mainly Caribbean pines. This is twitcher paradise where Hispaniolan parrots, palmchats – the national bird – Hispaniolan trogons, loggerhead flycatchers and several endangered species such as the La Selle thrush can all be seen. Mammals – wild boar and the endangered Hispaniolan solenodons, a creature like a large shrew – are far less visible.

Campsites and trails bring climbers and hikers, but for others the goal is the summit of Pico Duarte. You must take a guide and a mule and camp en route. After travelling through aromatic pine forests with meadows affording fabulous views, the tough push to the ancient, barren summit is worthwhile.

EASTERN NATIONAL PARK

The Caribbean/Dominican Republic

Formed from limestone, the wooded southeastern peninsula of the Dominican Republic has shoreline cliffs, white sandy beaches, rocky spurs and mangroves and is riddled with tunnels and caves where pre-Columbian pictographs may be seen. The easiest cave to visit is Cueva del Puente, but it's a tough hike nevertheless. Whether approaching from land or sea, take water with you. Around 112 species of birds are to be found here, including the ashy-faced owl and the Hispaniolan lizard cuckoo, both of which are endemic.

The coastal ecosystem provides habitats for hundreds of species of plants, birds, fish and marine mammals,

such as the rhinoceros iguana, bottlenose dolphins, manatees, and several different species of sea turtle.

Catalina Island has a wealth of glorious white sandy beaches with crystal-clear waters, so the snorkelling and diving is renowned. Saona Island has two small communities and excellent anchorage. There are no hotels, so visit for the day or anchor your boat offshore and stay longer.

WHEN TO GO: December–February and July–August.

COCKPIT COUNTRY

The Caribbean/Jamaica

One of the joys of flying from Montego Bay are the views of an extraordinary and beautiful region of Jamaica. From this bird's-eye viewpoint, it looks like a vast inverted egg box: all verdant mounds and hollows, unscarred by roads or settlements. This is Jamaica's unique Cockpit Country. In 1665 the British army took Jamaica from its Spanish colonists, many of whom released their slaves and fled to Cuba. In western Jamaica, the slaves, or Maroons, hid in this wilderness. After many years of guerrilla warfare, they forced the British to cede land, autonomy and freedom to them in the treaty of 1738, and their descendants live there still.

HIGHLIGHTS:
Wait-a-Bit, the visitor centre at the entrance to Cockpit Country, and the Peace Cave where Cudjoe, the Maroon's Ashanti leader, and the British signed the peace treaty.

Formed 12 million years ago, the limestone plateau has subsequently been eroded, producing a large area of regularly spaced, rounded conical hills and flat-bottomed pits, or sinks, probably caused by collapsing cave systems. During storms, soil is brought down from the hills into the valleys, some of which are cultivated and only accessible by trails from surrounding villages. Much of the area remains impenetrable virgin forest.

The region is extremely important for wildlife. More than three-quarters of Jamaica's birds are found here, including both the black- and yellow-billed parrot. The island's largest predator, the Jamaican boa, makes its home here, too, as do the endemic blue swallowtail and Jamaican giant swallowtail butterflies and many kinds of bat that roost in the 300 or so caves. At least 101 unique species of plant can be found, some growing on a single hill. These include ferns, bromeliads and six varieties of orchid. You'll need to take a local guide when hiking here – it's easy to get lost and dangerous to go off–trail, as you can fall through thin layers of limestone into a sinkhole.

YOU SHOULD KNOW
In the 17th century the British chose the name Cockpit Country because the area reminded them of the cock-fighting pits that were prevalent across Jamaica at that time. Cock-fighting is now illegal, although it still takes place occasionally.

CENTRAL RAINFOREST RESERVE

The Caribbean/St Lucia

WHEN TO GO: The dry season is December–June, but don't forget there can be frequent sharp showers in the rainforest.

St Lucia is one of the Caribbean's Windward Islands and best known for its tourism. Most visitors either visit on cruise ships or remain in their all-inclusive holiday resorts. In recent years, however, the Forestry Department has actively promoted the beauty of the mountainous interior. Clad in tropical rainforest, it contains many rivers that tumble down to the sea.

The Central Rainforest Reserve encompasses 77 sq km (30 sq mi) of the central mountain range. Mount Gimie, the highest peak in the region, rises to 958 m (3145 ft) and is a steep, tough hike of about seven hours. Many shorter hikes are available, however, such as the Enbas Saut Falls trail, which starts 9.6 km (6 mi) east of Soufrière on the island's southwestern coast.

An hour-long trip at the base of Mount Gimie takes you, via many wooden steps, to two waterfalls and

natural pools at the head of the Troumassee River. Most hikes require a forestry guide, but this trail can be followed without one. There are splendid mahogany and mahoe trees to be seen and some huge ferns. The trail includes both true rainforest and cloud forest and it's good for spotting birds. The St Lucia black finch, the blue-hooded euphonia, the mountain whistler and even the St Lucian parrot, endemic to the island, may be sighted here.

DON'T MISS
Château Dubuc
lighthouse.

CARAVELLE PENINSULA

The Caribbean/Martinique

Martinique's Caravelle Peninsula is a nature reserve that juts out into the Atlantic on the northeastern side of the island and is an excellent place in which to hike. It's arid and beautiful, with varied landscapes and offering stunning views of the rocky coastline.

Start your trip at the 17th-century Château Dubuc, a ruined plantation with wonderful vistas across Treasury Bay. From here hike one of the two paths that lead through the reserve, or go off-piste. The longer

trail is 12 km (7.5 mi) and takes some three-and-a-half hours to traverse. It gives the hiker an opportunity to see the different ecosystems of the Caravelle, as well as many types of flora and fauna – some 80 species of sea and land birds, including rare and endangered species, frequent the area.

MORNE TROIS PITONS NATIONAL PARK

The Caribbean/Dominica

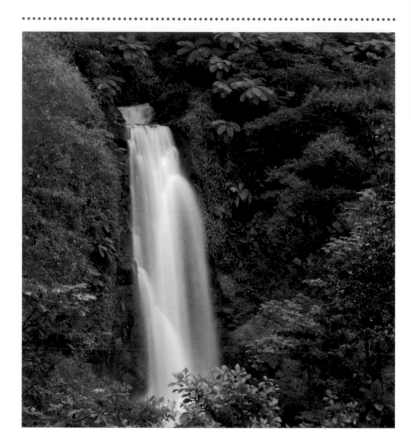

WORTH A DETOUR:
The aerial tramway near Titou Gorge gives a unique view up to the rainforest canopy and down through clouds of birds and butterflies to the forest floor, where agoutis (rather like long-legged guinea pigs) may be spotted rummaging.

Rugged little Dominica lacks beaches and has avoided mass tourism, but its waters are perfect for diving and whale-watching, and its mountainous, forested interior rewarding for birdwatchers and walkers. Much of this 'nature island' is protected and the Morne Trois Pitons National Park is also a UNESCO World Heritage Site because of its rare combination of volcanoes, fumaroles and hot springs with pristine rainforest and a remarkable biodiversity.

Some very popular short walks, such as the Trafalgar Falls and Emerald Pool Trails, pass through luxuriant rainforest where huge, ancient trees with buttressed trunks are festooned in creepers and bright with flowers, to reach cool lakes, plunge pools and waterfalls. Longer trails lead to high, secluded lakes and volcanic peaks – the easiest to climb is the Morne Anglais, in the south of the park. From high ridges where trees are dwarfed by wind and rain, there are views over remote waterfalls and valleys to the circling sea. The most demanding and exciting hike is to the Boiling Lake and the Valley of Desolation. A three-hour guided climb through rainforest brings the walker to a ridge above the lake, whose water is heated by geothermal activity. It is unwise to linger long here, for the ever-present dense clouds of steam and vapour over the lake are sulphurous. The invisible water can be heard churning as it simmers at just below boiling point. The floor of the Valley of Desolation steams, hisses and belches with numerous scalding geysers, bubbling mud pots, hot springs and steam vents in a blighted expanse of sulphur-stained rocks.

TAYRONA NATIONAL PARK

South America/Colombia

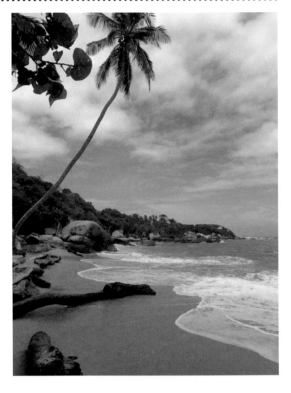

Colombia has made huge strides in recent times to clean up its image as a dangerous, crime-infested country where powerful drug barons operated largely unchecked by the forces of law. Now it has become once again a relatively safe and desirable tourism destination. Nowhere is the transformation more dramatically apparent than in the Tayrona National Park in the remote far north of the country. What was until relatively recently a no-go zone for visitors, where Marxist guerrillas battled with right-wing paramilitary groups for control of the cocaine business, has now reverted to a secluded paradise containing some of the Caribbean's most stunning unspoilt beaches and most pristine tropical forest. Tayrona was designated a national park in 1964. Its 150 sq km (58 sq mi) are remarkable for their biological diversity. The park is flanked on its southern edge by the foothills of the world's highest coastal range, the Sierra Nevada de Santa Marta, which includes the country's tallest peak, at 5,775 m (18,950 ft). Tayrona is one of the few places on the planet where you can stand on a tropical beach and see snow-capped mountains. It is home to more than 200 species of bird, including the extraordinary royal flycatcher, and mammals such as howler monkeys, collared peccaries and the elusive jaguar (a nocturnal hunter which you are most unlikely to see). Tayrona is situated 35 km (22 mi) east of the old coastal city of Santa Marta. There are no roads inside the park so you have to walk or hire a horse for the 45-minute trek through the jungle to the coast at Arrecifes, where a sequence of glorious beaches unfolds to the west.

YOU SHOULD KNOW

A key part of Tayrona's appeal is its lack of development so you should come well prepared with your own supplies of essentials such as sun screen and mosquito repellent.

WORTH A DETOUR:

If you can tear yourself away from the beach, it's worth making the two-hour trek through the rainforest to the ruins of a pre-Columbian native village at Pueblito.

CANAIMA NATIONAL PARK

South America/Venezuela

DON'T MISS

The darkly brooding cliffs of Cañón del Diablo (Devil's Canyon) at the base of Angel Falls.

The name of this vast park, encompassing some 30,000 sq km (11,600 sq mi) of remote jungle may not be a familiar one but Canaima contains the mighty Salto Ángel or Angel Falls. Angel is the world's highest waterfall; at 980 m (3,215 ft) it is 16 times the height of Niagara Falls. The phenomenon is caused by the Churún River plunging dramatically off the edge of the Auyantepui plateau into the dense rainforest below. So high is the drop that before the water hits the pool at the base, much of it has turned to mist.

You can view the waterfall by flying over it in a small plane but it is far better to take your time with a three-day overland trip. The sense of anticipation as you trek the final leg is palpable; you hear the dull roar of the huge cascade long before it comes into view. And spending a night in a simple camp at the base of the falls means that you see them in the magical light of sunrise.

WORTH A DETOUR: With any luck your guide will point out the heliamphora, a carnivorous plant that grows only on the summit and traps insects in its seductive red flowers.

RORAIMA

South America/Venezuela

Until the last 100 years the large plateau forming the summit of Roraima was largely cut off from the impact of humans. The distinctive 'table-top' profiles of such sandstone mountains are the result of geological processes two billion years ago, making them among the most ancient formations on the planet. Roraima's impenetrable flanks have produced a unique ecosystem on the plateau: endemic species of plants, insects and small creatures found nowhere else on Earth.

Roraima's biological diversity makes the six-day trek up onto the 2,800 m (9,200 ft) plateau a thoroughly rewarding one for anyone possessing reasonable levels of fitness. The payoff is a genuinely other-worldly experience of a kind that is increasingly rare. The mysterious atmosphere on the barren surface of the summit with its strange rock formations, glinting quartz crystals and bizarre plant life is only enhanced by the frequent mists that cover it.

IWOKRAMA RAINFOREST

South America/Guyana

Travelling some 160 km (100 mi) south of Georgetown, Guyana, brings you to Iwokrama, an area of unsullied tropical rainforest which owes its remarkable survival to a pioneering 1996 initiative of the Guyanese government. The Makushi Indian people, whose traditional homeland this is, have been given support and training to develop new and non-destructive ways of earning their living, such as low-impact harvesting of timber and opportunities to work in ecotourism.

The Iwokrama reserve boasts a range of habitats in addition to rainforest, including lakes, river systems,

savannah and, at its heart, a 1,000 m (3,280 ft) mountain range from which the area takes its name. Your base is the international field station beside the Essequibo River where you live alongside scientists conducting ongoing conservation and research into Iwokrama's extraordinary profusion of flora and fauna. Nearly 500 species of bird, 130 different mammals and over 400 types of fish (including South America's biggest) are found here.

WHEN TO GO:
September–March.

DON'T MISS
The quinoa plant,
sacred to the Incas.

CHIMBORAZO

South America/Ecuador

Snow-capped peak Chimborazo is Ecuador's highest mountain and sits at the southern end of what the 19th-century German explorer Alexander von Humboldt dubbed the 'Avenue of the Volcanoes' in the Andes. Although it is technically not a difficult climb, basic mountaineering experience of snow and ice conditions is required for the ascent of Chimborazo; this normally takes three days with an organized expedition. Because there is a real risk of avalanches during the warm daylight hours, the final eight-hour summit climb is undertaken at night. If you are not in this league, however, it is still possible to appreciate the magnificent landscape with day-treks; for example, by climbing close to the snowline between the two refuges, an ascent of 200 m (655 ft). The highlands surrounding the mountain are protected as a forest reserve; hiking here will familiarize you with the unusual native vegetation and also give you the chance to see llamas and alpacas roaming freely.

YASUNÍ NATIONAL PARK

South America/Ecuador

HOW TO GET THERE:
The oil town of Coca, eight–ten hours by bus from the capital, Quito, is the main jumping-off point for Yasuní. To reach the park from here involves a 90-minute drive followed by a two-hour river trip.

WHEN TO GO:
Any time of year (but note that May–July are the wettest months).

WORTH A DETOUR:
Spot the formidable harpy eagle, one of the world's largest birds of prey.

The extensive area of Ecuador east of the Andes range is known, appropriately enough, as the Oriente. And in the far east of this region, brushing up against the border with Peru, lies Yasuní National Park. Covering nearly 10,000 sq km (3,860 sq mi), Yasuní is the largest mainland national park in the country and one of Ecuador's last true wildernesses.

Most of the park consists of upland tropical forest, but there is a liberal sprinkling of lakes, rivers and other distinctive wetland environments, too, such as seasonally flooded forest and igapó, lowlands that are more or less permanently under water.

What makes Yasuní so special, for biologists and nature lovers alike, is the fact that for reasons that are still not clear this area was spared the ravages of the last ice age; as a consequence it has retained a degree of biodiversity found in few other places on Earth. Yasuní is home to more than 500 species of bird and nearly two-thirds of the mammals found in Ecuador, including three of the continent's 'Big Five' – the tapir, jaguar and giant otter. A recent botanical study discovered 473 different tree species in a single hectare (2.5 acres) – thought to be a world record. The fecundity of this remarkable place has been recognized by UNESCO, which in 1989 declared it an international Biosphere Reserve.

It comes as no surprise that such a well-preserved natural environment should be a long way from civilization. It is not an easy place to get to and you certainly should not visit the park without a guide (it is a jungle out there, after all). Most people savour the delights of Yasuní on organized tours which are plentiful and relatively cheap.

YOU SHOULD KNOW
Lucrative oil deposits in Yasuní mean an uneasy co-existence prevails at present between the ecology lobby and the oil industry.

GALÁPAGOS ISLANDS

South America/Ecuador

So many stories and myths surround the Galápagos Islands, in the remote South Pacific 1,000 km (620 mi) west of the Ecuador mainland, that it is sometimes hard to believe that they exist at all, rather than inhabiting a parallel universe beloved of natural history film makers. Charles Darwin first brought the Galápagos to the world's attention when he visited the archipelago in 1835 and used his observations of the islands' wildlife to formulate his revolutionary theory of evolution. What made such an impression on Darwin was the extraordinarily rich ecosystem which had developed in an isolated location. This ecosystem may be rich but it is also incredibly fragile and struggling nowadays to deal with the pressures of the modern world, not least those resulting from mass tourism. The Galápagos Islands are high on the destination list of most serious nature lovers but be warned that visiting them does not come cheap; indeed the authorities now deliberately hike the prices in an effort to restrict the human flow. Although you can plot your own itinerary once there, you will definitely see more of the remarkable wildlife on an organized boat tour; a typical tour offers onboard accommodation as you cruise among the islands, and numerous onshore excursions. There are opportunities aplenty for observing the astonishing number of species that are unique to the Galápagos, including penguins, frigate birds, blue-footed boobies, the ubiquitous sea lions, marine iguanas (the world's only seagoing lizards) and, most famously of all, the majestic giant tortoises. Nowhere else on earth can you get up as close and personal to wild creatures which seem so unfazed by your presence.

WORTH A DETOUR:
If your visit coincides with the mating season, you should see the bizarre courting ritual of the male frigate bird which inflates a flap of scarlet skin on his chest to the size of a balloon.

YOU SHOULD KNOW
UNESCO now has the Galápagos Islands on its Danger List.

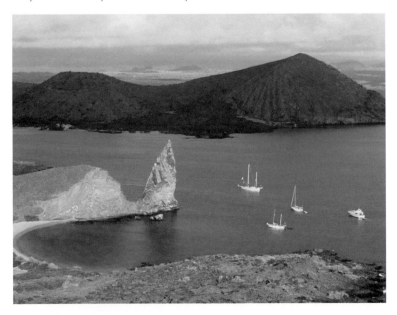

MACHALILLA NATIONAL PARK

South America/Ecuador

WORTH A DETOUR: The coral reefs in the Machalilla seas are some of the most impressive along the entire coast and are excellent for snorkelling and diving.

On Ecuador's central Pacific coast Machalilla National Park was created in 1979 to preserve its most beautiful stretch of coastline and one of the few remaining expanses of tropical dry forest on the continent. Tranquil, isolated beaches are backed by coastal scrub and densely forested hills, while inland the terrain rises and the dry forest gives way to the lush vegetation of a cloud forest. There are few maps or waymarkers, so you will be dependent on the expertise of local guides. Ceibo trees tower above you on the various hiking trails through the virgin forest as your guide points out exotic orchids and numerous endemic plant species, such as the ivory palm. You will certainly hear if not see howler monkeys and, if you are lucky, spot anteaters and two rare species of deer, as well as over 350 types of bird. Agua Blanca is a small village in the park with noted archaeological remains from pre-Columbian times. A nearby sulphur pool offers an enticing and refreshing dip, in spite of its pungent odour. For a change of habitat, you can take a boat trip from Puerto López to Isla de la Plata, one of several offshore islands, which provides important breeding grounds for frigate birds and boobies.

WORTH A DETOUR: The cylindrical burial towers that dominate the landscape in the plains west of Titicaca and are reminders of an ancient pre-Inca culture.

ALTIPLANO

South America/Peru

Altiplano means 'high plain' in Spanish and the term is now used to denote a vast plateau in the central Andes. The wide, empty grasslands of the Altiplano occur at altitudes of 3,500 m (11,480 ft) or more so it is essential to acclimatize yourself properly before visiting. After Tibet, the Andean Altiplano is the biggest area of high plateau on Earth. The rarefied air at this altitude is exceptionally clear, affording wonderful views of seemingly limitless horizons beneath stunning cobalt skies. Lake Titicaca is the world's highest navigable lake. A boat trip to explore some of the 70 or so islands is an unmissable experience, giving the visitor a chance to witness the fishing communities of the local Quechua Indians as they struggle to retain their distinctive culture against the onslaught of modern commerce and tourism. These communities are also to be found on Titicaca's remarkable floating islands. Resembling enormous rafts, these islands are built from the buoyant totora reeds which grow in abundance around the lake.

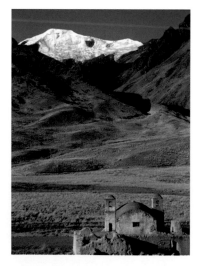

WORTH A DETOUR:
The Belén valley west of Chachapoyas, with its river lazily meandering through a fabulously green valley floor and ringed by misty hills.

CHACHAPOYAS

South America/Peru

If you harbour Indiana Jones-style fantasies of coming across mysterious archaeological remains as you hack your way through dense jungle, then a trip to the Chachapoyas region in Peru's Northern Highlands is a must. The virgin cloud forests surrounding the little market town of Chachapoyas are littered with archaeological sites testifying to an enigmatic ancient culture which at one time rivalled the Incas. The Chachapoyas were a fierce warrior people who liked to show off their trophies of conquest and also practised human sacrifice. The only way to reach most of the ruins is on foot or horseback. Many of the remains have been reclaimed by the jungle and are hard to spot so, even if you decide to strike out on your own, you would be well advised to hire a local guide. The most spectacular ancient site (and a relatively accessible one) is the mighty stone citadel of Kuélap, perched breathtakingly on a mountain-top surrounded by thick forest. Location and vistas rival Machu Picchu, without the crowds.

Only disclosed to the outside world a few years ago, the Gocta Falls deep in the jungle north of Chachapoyas are one of the world's tallest waterfalls, at 771 m (2,530 ft). It's a tough five-hour trek but worth it.

LOMAS DE LACHAY NATIONAL RESERVE

South America/Peru

DON'T MISS
The odd-looking, rabbit-like vizcacha.

A little over 100 km (62 mi) north of Lima, the bleakness of the Sechura desert which fringes the coast all the way to the border with Ecuador is unexpectedly punctured by the Lomas de Lachay, a spur running down from the Andes. The rolling mists that blow in off the sea in the winter months produce condensation in the hills which triggers an explosion of growth and life. No fewer than 74 plant species have been recorded in this relatively confined area, one-third of which are now on the critically endangered list. Among the 55 types of bird found here are several species of the delicate hummingbird. Mammals include the zorro (red fox), Andean skunk, and grey deer which have been successfully re-introduced in recent years. An area of 51 sq km (20 sq mi) is protected as a Reserva Nacional. There may be few other facilities in the reserve but it does offer good waymarked trails and some camping areas. Among the profusion of flora and fauna there are also strange rock formations, the result of forces eroding the local granite; some have been given fanciful names, such as Cerro la Virgen, said to resemble a praying Virgin Mary. Although these hills are now uninhabited, rock paintings provide evidence that they were once the home of ancient tribes.

MANU RIVER

South America/Peru

DON'T MISS
The giant catahua tree,
used by local tribes to
make dugout canoes.

HOW TO GET THERE:
Make this the adventure it
deserves to be and travel
overland from Cuzco. It's a
24-hour boneshaking drive
to Atalaya where you board
a boat for the day's river
journey to the park entrance.

Peru takes its responsibility to protect its wilderness areas rather seriously. The entire watershed of the Manu River is contained within the Manu National Park, the country's largest. As with most of the Amazon jungle the river provides the only means of getting around. Manu National Park is half the size of Switzerland but a mere one-fifth is open to visitors (the rest is accessible only to indigenous tribes and authorized scientists), but Manu is right up there as one of the most biodiverse spots on the planet; not for nothing did UNESCO declare it a Biosphere Reserve in 1977.

The park's boundaries encompass altitudes ranging from 365 m (1,200 ft) to 4,000 m (13,120 ft), and the resulting variety of environments, from lowland jungle to mountain cloud forests, is home to a staggering array of vegetation and wildlife. The numbers are almost unbelievable – there are 13 types of monkey and 1,200 butterfly species alone – but it does mean that, with the help of an experienced guide, you should be richly rewarded with sightings.

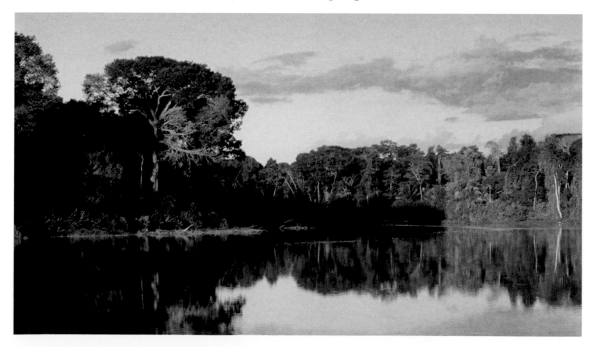

BENI BIOSPHERE RESERVE

South America/Bolivia

WORTH A DETOUR:

If you are visiting at the end of July the three-day village fiesta at nearby San Ignacio de Moxos is one of the most colourful and exciting in the country.

The enormous Amazon Basin in the northeast of Bolivia still contains great swathes of pristine tropical forest. One of the best is the Beni Biosphere Reserve which lies in the Llanos de Moxos region west of Trinidad. The reserve protects 1,350 sq km (520 sq mi) of mixed savannah and rainforest and, as its label suggests, is rich in flora and fauna. Around 500 bird species have been recorded here and 100 different types of mammal, including big favourites like the anteater, peccary, jaguar, river otter and spider monkey (although as usual you can count yourself fortunate if you see any of the stars as most are shy and elusive, often hunting or foraging at night). A large adjacent area of forest has been set aside for the exclusive use of the local Chimane people.

The only visitor facilities in the reserve are at El Porvenir on its southern edge, close to the main road between La Paz and Trinidad. This is savannah and the forest proper is some way away but various tours are offered from the visitor centre, a former ranch which offers basic accommodation. You can either take day-long guided hikes out into the jungle or tours on horseback around the more open areas. Viewing towers give you a different perspective on the wildlife. A popular excursion (although that is a relative term in this remote spot) is the river trip by canoe to the Laguna Normandia, a lake filled with rare black caimans. These impressive amphibians may look entirely at home in this lovely setting but in fact they are the descendants of creatures rescued from a failed leather business in the city.

LAGUNA COLORADA

South America/Bolivia

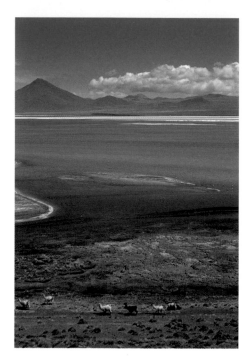

High up on the puna grasslands of Bolivia's southern Altiplano sits a very unusual lake. The name, Laguna Colorada or 'Coloured Lake', provides a clue. Forget the palette of blues, greys and browns you would normally associate with a lake; this one has a striking reddish hue, caused by the algae that flourish in these mineral-rich waters. If you walk around the shores of the lake you can see evidence of the minerals themselves in deposits of white sodium and magnesium.

Although the lake covers an area of 60 sq km (23 sq mi), its average depth is a mere 0.8 m (2.6 ft), making it a haven for waders and other waterfowl. Many different species of duck and geese flourish in these brackish waters but the undoubted stars of the Laguna Colorada show, and what most people come here to see, are the flamingoes. All three of the continent's native species are to be seen here, including the world's largest population of the smaller James flamingo. The stupendous array of colours in this harsh, other-worldly landscape – the lake's waters, the greens of the puna scrub, the delicate pinks of the flamingoes, the snow-capped peaks on the horizon, and all beneath a brilliant blue sky – takes your breath away; literally so, since the altitude is well over 4,000 m (13,120 ft).

The Laguna Colorada is in the north of the large Eduardo Avaroa Wildlife Reserve, which extends over 100 km (62 mi) down to the borders with Chile and Argentina. Herds of wild llama and vicuña roam the wide open plains and the reserve contains unusual features, including other coloured lakes, a volcano (which can be climbed) and geothermal areas with hot springs and bubbling mud pools.

HOW TO GET THERE:

This is a sparsely populated area with few facilities so you should not consider visiting it other than on an organized tour. Three- or four-day tours by 4×4 can be arranged in the nearby towns of Uyuni and Tupiza.

WHEN TO GO:

July–October (but remember that the high altitude means that it can be bitterly cold, with temperatures at night falling well below freezing).

WORTH A DETOUR:

If you can brave the cold, the night skies of the Altiplano are some of the best you will ever see.

WHEN TO GO:
July–October for the best climate, although an autumn visit (March and April) gives you a greater chance of seeing the reflective surfaces.

SALAR DE UYUNI

South America/Bolivia

Uyuni is the world's largest salt pan, covering more than 12,000 sq km (4,630 sq mi). The Altiplano (high plain) here has no outlet to the sea so mineral-rich waters off the mountains once collected at the lowest point; high salinity levels left salt deposits which formed a giant saltwater lake. A permanent cover of water has long since evaporated but beneath the thick surface crust of salt the ground remains largely saturated. There is an industry devoted to salt extraction and processing. It is a tough way to earn a living and many locals have realized that a more lucrative avenue is to sell curios and artefacts made from the white stuff to the growing tourist market.

Most people visiting the Salar take an organized 4x4 tour which generally involves one night on the salt flats in basic accommodation. Longer tours also take in the Eduardo Avaroa Wildlife Reserve to the south. If you are fortunate enough to see the salt flat just after rainfall, you can enjoy the reflections of the sky and clouds in the surface water – an astonishing optical effect where the horizon seems to disappear altogether.

CHACO FOREST

South America/Paraguay

DON'T MISS
The rhea, the giant flightless bird that is South America's equivalent of the ostrich and emu

What the small, land-locked nation of Paraguay lacks in the way of facilities for travellers is more than compensated by the integrity and lack of degradation of much of its natural landscapes. The Chaco is one of the continent's great remaining wildernesses and its second-largest ecosystem after the Amazon.

With both tropical and subtropical climates, the Chaco encompasses a range of environments; wide plains and seasonally flooded savannahs characterize the lowlands, which provide major feeding grounds for waterbirds. The huge dry forest of El Gran Chaco is a harsh, unforgiving landscape of prickly scrub and stunted trees where searing temperatures and fiercely hot winds hold sway. But, unpromising as it sounds, it is also one of the best places to seek out the continent's larger mammals. Both great cats – the puma and the jaguar – live in the Gran Chaco, as well as peccaries, tapirs, anteaters, giant armadillos and the guanaco, a member of the camelid family.

APARADOS DA SERRA NATIONAL PARK

South America/Brazil

In the far south of Brazil the dominant landscape feature is an extensive highland plateau, its rock formations the result of layer upon layer of sediment deposited from the nearby Atlantic Ocean. Volcanic and other subterranean activity some 150 million years ago covered the tableland with a thick crust of basalt rock. The forces of wind and water subsequently carved out great cracks in the basalt at the plateau's edges, creating a series of magnificent canyons for the modern visitor to wonder at. The most impressive of these is Itaimbezinho, which forms the centrepiece of the Aparados da Serra National Park. The canyon is nearly 6 km (3.75 mi) long, 720 m (2,360 ft) deep and between 600 m (1,970 ft) and 2 km (1.25 mi) wide. It is a sublime spectacle at any time, but its grandeur is enhanced still further by the regular fogs that roll in off the Atlantic.

The canyon's most striking feature is its sheer rock escarpments, mostly covered with plants. The park lies in a temperate zone, with well-defined seasons, but the special topography of the Itaimbezinho canyon means that it hosts two distinct habitats: the canyon floor is subtropical, while the slopes and higher levels, which see relatively little rainfall, display a thick cover of cloud forest. The surrounding tableland is dotted with stands of umbrella-shaped araucaria pine.

Guided trails, including one that runs around the canyon rim and a more challenging one that descends to its floor, take you into the heart of the park. Aparados da Serra is home to an abundance of bird and animal life. The maned wolf, puma, ocelot and tapir can be found.

HOW TO GET THERE:
The park lies 66 km (41 mi) northeast of São Francisco de Paula. It is a difficult place to get to unless you take a guided tour or have your own transport (4x4 advisable).

WHEN TO GO:
Winter (May–August) is the best time to visit; it may be cold but the visibility is clearest and there is less chance of sea fogs spoiling the views. Spring (October and November) can also be chilly but offers a dazzling display of wild flowers.

WORTH A DETOUR:
See the canyons containing two spectacular waterfalls.

YOU SHOULD KNOW
Visitor numbers to the park are limited to 1,000 per day so if you are not on an organized tour you are advised to book your visit in advance.

ANAVILHANAS ARCHIPELAGO

South America/Brazil

HOW TO GET THERE:
Anavilhanas is an eight-hour boat ride from Manaus. It's a little quicker by bus but much less atmospheric.

WHEN TO GO:
Any time of year. This region gets a lot of rain; if you really want to avoid the wet stuff, June–October tends to be the driest period.

The Rio Negro or Black River in western Brazil is one of the major tributaries of the Amazon. Rising in the mountains on the Venezuelan border it joins with the Rio Solimões at Manaus to form the Amazon proper. A day's boat journey upstream from Manaus brings you to the small jungle town of Novo Aírão, gateway to the world's largest group of freshwater islands – the Anavilhanas Archipelago. Over time geological barriers downstream caused the river to flow in narrower channels and the resulting water pressure backed up to create a huge lake-like area up to 20 km (12.5 mi) wide, which is studded by more than 400 densely forested islands – the consequences of sedimentary deposits. Much of the forest here is seasonally flooded, known in Portuguese as *igapó*; during the wet season, many of the islands in the archipelago are completely submerged.

Boat tours introduce you to the Anavilhanas Archipelago, which has its own ecosystem and an abundance of plant and animal life. Macaws and parrots are a common sight, as are toucans and howler monkeys. Among the river creatures you are likely to see are delightful Amazonian dolphins. The dry season exposes some superb beaches on a number of the islands, their fine white sands making a vivid contrast with the unmistakeable black waters of the river. It may not be the seaside but you can still enjoy chilling on these beaches, especially as the Negro's acidic waters mean there are far fewer mosquitoes around than normally in the jungle.

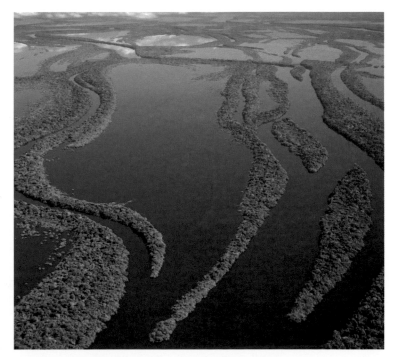

BOIPEBA ISLAND

South America/Brazil

DON'T MISS

The amazing array of sea life in the natural pools that form off the beaches at low tide.

Boipeba is one of the three main islands of the Tinharé Archipelago. Its larger neighbour, the Ilha de Tinharé, is a famous holiday destination, and the two are separated by the vividly named Rio de Inferno (Hell River). The change of atmosphere crossing this narrow and, in spite of its name, relatively placid channel is quite remarkable; the crowds and the buzz that surround the beaches of Morro de São Paulo on Tinharé

vanish completely when you step onto its unassuming neighbour. There are no roads and no cars, just the odd tractor and jeep, so travel is on foot or by boat. Besides the palm-fringed beaches the landscape is one of sand dunes, salt marshes, extensive mangrove swamps and, in the interior, dense Atlantic rainforest. The waters around the island are crystal clear most of the year and are superb for snorkelling and diving, especially the coral reefs off the Ponta de Castelhauos at the southern tip of the island. If you are feeling more energetic, surfing, canoeing and horse riding are also available.

CAATINGA WILDERNESS

South America/Brazil

DON'T MISS

If you visit in the wet season you will see the landscape transformed by wild flowers and lush growth.

This vast and sparsely populated region gets its name from the thorny scrub which is its dominant vegetation. Only the hardiest of plants survive in the harsh, semi-desert conditions of these uplands. One of the toughest of all, the cactus, is a common feature of the landscape. Other kinds of tree have adapted to the intense heat and drought-like conditions by remaining leafless for long periods. An integral part of the *sertão*, the Brazilian bush or outback, the Caatinga is a bleak and lonely place where scattered communities eke out a living from subsistence farming. The towns of Campina Grande and Caruaru are the main gateways for exploring the region if you are heading inland from the coast. The São Francisco River is also an important artery and a vital green lung through what is the largest area of dry forest on the whole continent. With a mere one per cent of it enjoying any form of protection, however, the Caatinga is very much at the mercy of commercial pressures and human activity. The large ranches with their herds of grazing cattle and *vaqueiros* cowboys may look picturesque enough but the introduction of new and intensive agricultural practices is accelerating a process of desertification throughout the region. This is particularly bad news for the bird life, which is surprisingly rich given the unpromising habitat.

DON'T MISS
The vertical walls of
dark-red rock at sunset.

CHAPADA DOS GUIMARÃES
South America/Brazil

The Mato Grosso in western Brazil is a region of flat uplands which extend to the horizon in every direction. At its centre is the Chapada dos Guimarães, a sandstone plateau that rises over 350 m (1,150 ft) from the surrounding plains. The national park that covers much of the plateau – 300 sq km (116 sq mi) of it – holds an array of spectacular natural sights you won't want to miss. Although the Chapada is an increasingly popular attraction, it still retains a distinct aura of remoteness and mystery. It can claim, however, to be at the heart of things in one very specific sense, lying as it does at the geodesic centre of the South American continent (it is equidistant between the Pacific and Atlantic oceans). There are a number of hiking trails around the national park, some of which can only be undertaken with a guide. Natural features include waterfalls, canyons, caves and bizarre rock formations. The Véu de Noiva (Bridal Veil) waterfall drops 86 m (282 ft) down a sheer cliff, while the Cidade de Pedra (City of Stone) is a mesmerizing collection of sandstone shapes around the canyon edges. A flash of blue seen here belongs most probably to macaws which build their nests on the cliff faces. At several sites ancient rock paintings have been preserved.

ITATIAIA NATIONAL PARK
South America/Brazil

WORTH A DETOUR: Lago Azul (blue lake) with its beautiful setting and clear waters that are ideal for bathing.

Established in 1937, Itatiaia was Brazil's first national park and is still a place where you can escape the crowds and get back to nature with relative ease. The unusual name comes from an indigenous word referring to 'rocks with sharp edges'. The park covers an area of 120 sq km (46 sq mi) on the slopes of the Mantiqueira mountain range; the variation in altitude it encompasses makes for a startling diversity of landscapes, from dense Atlantic forest in the foothills (a type of forest that is now critically endangered in Brazil) through treeless, grassy slopes at higher levels and on up to the mountains themselves. Within the park's borders are two major peaks: Agulhas Negras at 2,787 m (9,145 ft) and Prateleira at 2,540 m (8,335 ft), both of which are popular climbs for those with mountaineering experience.

Because the area escaped use for coffee cultivation or other agricultural purposes its ecology has remained remarkably intact and unchanged. On the various walking trails through the park you will see giant tree ferns, bromeliads, orchids and other characteristic features of subtropical forest. Itatiaia is graced with numerous waterfalls and natural springs which feed the Paraíba River (an important source for Rio's water supply).

LENÇÓIS MARANHENSES NATIONAL PARK

South America/Brazil

WORTH A DETOUR: The beaches at Lençóis Maranhenses are exceptional by any standards and you will almost certainly have them to yourself.

Brazil is a huge country but it's a fair bet you won't see anything else quite like the Parque Nacional dos Lençóis Maranhenses. Only a few hundred kilometres from the Amazon delta you do not expect to find a desert, but that is what you get: an area of over 1,500 sq km (580 sq mi) composed in the main of giant white sand dunes. Their dramatic shapes have been formed over thousands of years from sand deposited by rivers at their mouths, which has then been swept back inland by winds and ocean currents. The dunes now stretch up to 50 km (31 mi) inland and extend 43 km (27 mi) along the coastline.

The play of sunlight and shadow on the dunes is a captivating sight. But this is an equatorial climate, with little of the aridity of the Sahara or Arabian deserts. When it rains in the first half of the year it does so with a vengeance and the flat areas between the dunes fill with water, creating hundreds of freshwater lagoons. Some, like Lagoa Bonita and Lagoa da Gaivota, are enormous and provide wonderful swimming opportunities in their crystal-clear waters. Other activities to enjoy in the park include boat trips on the Preguiças river and around the mangrove swamps and riding the dunes in a jeep (authorized drivers only!).

WORTH A DETOUR: If you're lucky your guide will help you spot the golden-backed uacari, one of South America's most charming but least-known monkeys.

RIO NEGRO FOREST RESERVE

South America/Brazil

There aren't many places on the planet that can still lay claim to being uncharted territory but the upper reaches of the Rio Negro in the far northwest of the Amazon basin come as close as any. The Negro has its source in the Colombian uplands 2,230 km (1,390 mi) away. Close to the source, and hard up against the border with Colombia, lies the Rio Negro Forest Reserve, a protected area covering 38,000 sq km (14,670 sq mi) of virgin tropical forest. Bounded on one side by the Rio Negro and on the other by its tributary the Uaupés, the reserve contains swathes of *igapó*, seasonally flooded forest, as well as rainforest and scrubland.

The only way to explore the reserve is by hiring a local guide to take you on day-treks or camping trips. In terms of wildlife the Rio Negro Forest Reserve is the Amazon at its extravagant best; over half of all the species recorded in the Amazon basin can be found here. Multicoloured toucans and parrots, pink dolphins frolicking in the river and capuchin monkeys swinging through the canopy should provide ample compensation for any failure to spot more elusive creatures.

YOU SHOULD KNOW

North of Serra do Cipó are the towns of Diamantina and Serro, two examples of the *cidades históricas* (historic cities), founded as mining camps in the early 18th century.

SERRA DO CIPÓ NATIONAL PARK

South America/Brazil

The Espinhaço Mountains bisect the state of Minas Gerais from north to south, dividing the central Brazilian Highlands from the coastal plain to the east. At the southern end of the range lies the Parque Nacional Serra do Cipó, established to protect a typical cerrado landscape of high-altitude grasslands and open savannah of a kind that is increasingly threatened with degradation from human settlement and commercial exploitation. Covering an area of 338 sq km (130 sq mi), the park is criss-crossed by a series of watercourses forming part of the São Francisco basin. Formidable canyons and gorges have been created where the valleys have cut through the mountains; the Cānion dos Confins and the gorge of the Rio do Peixe are two of the best. The park is also blessed with an abundance of waterfalls. Serra do Cipó is renowned for its biodiversity and boasts a high proportion of endemic species. The conditions in this harsh scrubland hardly seem propitious for growth but a variety of unusual plants manage to prosper in the sparse and sandy soil, helped by the proximity of fresh water. Among more than 50 species of mammal found here are anteaters, deer, armadillos, monkeys, ocelots and otters. This is also classic habitat for the capybara; you should have no difficulty spotting the world's largest rodent.

Besides trekking, Serra do Cipó offers opportunities for horse riding and for kayaking on the Cipó River. As you explore the area keep an eye out for traces in the foothills of the old stone road built by slaves for the prospectors who came looking for gold and precious stones in centuries past.

DON'T MISS

The clear waters in the pool beneath the Great Waterfall make a marvellous bathing spot.

ATACAMA DESERT

South America/Chile

YOU SHOULD KNOW

The atmospheric conditions in the Atacama Desert make it a famous location for star-gazing and there are a number of observatories in the area.

If the name Atacama has a familiar ring about it this is probably because in a school geography lesson you will have learned about it as the driest place on Earth. In parts of the Atacama, rainfall has never been recorded. The world's highest desert occupies the entire far north of Chile, extending 1,000 km (620 mi) south from the Peruvian border. It is a huge region but its most spectacular sights are to be found in a relatively compact area at the desert's heart, clustered around the town of San Pedro de Atacama. Here you can experience the best of the Atacama in microcosm: a dazzling altiplano (high plains) landscape of salt flats, sand dunes, lagoons and hot springs, set against a backdrop of snow-capped volcanoes.

Immediately south of San Pedro the rough white crust of Chile's largest salt flat stretches away The monotone visual palette is dramatically punctured by large flocks of flamingo and other waders attracted to the shallow lakes scattered around the salt pan. On its northern edge the aptly named Valle de la Luna is a world of strange rock formations, the result of millions of years of erosion. The valley is at its most striking at either end of the day when the sun's rays bathe the encircling peaks in hues of pink, gold and purple.

In the other direction El Tatio is the world's highest geothermal field, at 4,320 m (14,170 ft). Early morning is the best time to see the geysers at full strength; the sight of steaming fumaroles against the brilliant azure of the altiplano sky is one of many memorable images the Atacama has to offer.

WHEN TO GO:
Any time of year (but remember you are at considerable altitude so nights can get very chilly).

WORTH A DETOUR:
A relaxing soak in one of the thermal pools at El Tatio.

YOU SHOULD KNOW

Most of the tours involve kayaking and have a minimum age restriction (usually 12).

BERNARDO O'HIGGINS NATIONAL PARK

South America/Chile

Bernardo O'Higgins was the unlikely sounding name of Chile's first head of state after the country had shaken off the Spanish colonial yoke and gained its independence in 1818. A fully paid-up member of the Chilean liberation struggle, O'Higgins was the illegitimate son of an Irishman who is now remembered as one of the nation's founding fathers. His name crops up frequently, but certainly nowhere more substantially than in Chile's largest national park. Straddling the 50° latitude in the deep south of Patagonia, the Bernardo O'Higgins National Park covers a staggering 35,000 sq km (13,510 sq mi). The park has been much less touched by human hands than its more famous neighbour, the Torres del Paine, largely because it is only accessible by boat. The granite pillars of Torres del Paine may be justly famous among the trekking community but Bernardo O'Higgins is the place to come if you want to hike away from the crowds. Including much of the Southern Patagonian Ice Field within its boundaries, this is a truly elemental world of glaciers, waterfalls, lakes, craggy peaks and untouched fjords. Huge swathes of native forest are interrupted by pampas and the occasional isolated *estancia*. This is the realm of the condor but also of the guanaco, a smaller relative of the llama. It takes several hours to reach the park by boat up the Última Esperanza sound. The name translates as 'Last Hope' but you should certainly not despair as the views on the way are astonishing, as is your eventual arrival at the base of the Serrano glacier, beautiful Mount Balmaceda rising up behind. The only way to do the park full justice, though, is to take one of the longer escorted tours which involves kayaking and camping.

HOW TO GET THERE:
Most visits to the park start from Puerto Natales, 50 km (31 mi) to the south. The nearest airport is at Punta Arenas.

WORTH A DETOUR:
If the weather and season are right, the chance to kayak among floating icebergs on a meltwater lake.

TORRES DEL PAINE

South America/Chile

DON'T MISS
Being at the Las Torres viewpoint at dawn to watch the peaks suffused by the first rays of the sun.

Mention the words Torres del Paine to a serious walker and the chances are you will be met with an expression of awed reverie. This national park in the far south of Chile has long been a legendary destination among the trekking community, and the eponymous 'Towers' – a cluster of 2,600 m (8,530 ft) granite pillars that make up the Paine Massif at the heart of the park – have become the defining image of Patagonia in many people's minds. There are enough different aspects of elemental nature here to satisfy the most seasoned of travellers: rugged mountain terrain, thundering rivers in deep-sided valleys, wide-open steppes and dense green forests. And being so far south you find a magical extra ingredient in the mix: huge glaciers and lakes with floating chunks of shimmering blue ice the size of a house.

The breathtaking scenery in this national park fully deserves its reputation but it does mean that it is a popular place and can get very busy with hikers in the summer months. Most walkers come to tackle the 'W', one of the world's classic treks, so called because of the route's shape on the map. The 'W' takes four to five days to complete and there are good campsites and mountain shelters throughout the park. The route includes a number of fantastic viewpoints (miradores) and the Valle Francés, a steep-sided valley with spectacular mountain views on both sides. If you have the time and the stamina, the Circuit Trail (seven to ten days) takes you round the back of the peaks and gets you away from the crowds.

WORTH A DETOUR: Spot Chile's national flower, the copihue, grows in these forests. The distinctive shape of its red flowers gives it its common name of Chilean bellflower.

VALDIVIAN COASTAL RANGE

South America/Chile

The Valdivian Coastal Range forms part of the Cordillera de la Costa, the western range of the Andes mountains which hugs much of Chile's Pacific coast. Also known as the Cordillera de Mahuidanchi, the range lies towards the southern end of the whole chain. Its ecological significance lies in the fact that it is a rare surviving example of temperate rainforest, a habitat which has been particularly vulnerable throughout the world to intensive logging and other commercial interests. Broadleaf evergreens are the dominant tree type; they flourish in the moist and humid climate created by the prevailing westerly winds blowing off the ocean. The elegant canelo tree is a particularly common sight in the Valdivian forest with its shiny whitish-green leaves. Its durability and adaptation to harsh conditions have given it the nickname of 'winter's bark'. Although a less-visited part of the country, the Valdivian hills and forests have much to offer the lover of nature. A good place to sample the area's delights is in the Parque Oncol, a 754 hectare (1,860 acre) reserve centred around Cerro Oncol, at 714 m (2,340 ft) the region's highest point. Numerous walking trails and viewing platforms give excellent views of the ocean as well as the area's many volcanoes further inland.

Right: Torres del Paine

PUMALÍN PARK

South America/Chile

Parque Pumalín (Pumalín Park) is the creation of one man, the American clothing magnate and entrepreneur Doug Tompkins. Tompkins is one of a new breed of environmental philanthropists dedicated to supporting innovative projects in conservation and sustainable living. He purchased his first parcel of land in the area 20 years ago and has added to it steadily since, so that today the park covers an area of nearly 3,000 sq km (1,160 sq mi) in northern Patagonia, running south from outside Hornopirén to just north of Chaitén. This has always been one of Chile's wildest and most rugged regions and Doug Tompkins wants to keep it that way, while at the same time giving visitors an experience of the natural world that is both enriching and humbling.

Pumalín preserves a pristine landscape of temperate forest and pasture criss-crossed by sparkling upland rivers. A jagged coastline with deep inlets carved out by the ocean adds to the drama. By local standards the visitor facilities in the park are exemplary and could serve as a model for the country's national parks. As well as a network of well-marked hiking trails there are sensitively sited lodges and campsites.

There are two points of access to the park. Most people visit from the south where there is a visitors' centre and other facilities at the small cove of Caleta Gonzalo, 60 km (37 mi) north of Chaitén. It is the northern end, however, accessed by boat from Hornopirén, that is wilder and more spectacular and offers hot springs.

DON'T MISS
The giant alerce tree, a member of the cypress family. It can grow to over 60 m (200 ft), making it the largest tree species on the continent.

YOU SHOULD KNOW

You must have a permit to trek or climb in the Aconcagua Park during the summer. This can be obtained only in Mendoza.

ACONCAGUA

South America/Argentina

The Andes mountain chain runs the entire length of the continent but it is Argentina that can claim the loftiest peak of all within its borders. At 6,960 m (22,835 ft) Mount Aconcagua is the highest summit in both the western and southern hemispheres. It is also one of the most accessible of the world's great peaks, attracting hundreds of climbers every year to its three routes to the top. Provided you are fit and have some experience of climbing at altitude there is no reason why you shouldn't undertake an organized ascent with professional guides, although you will need to allow a good two weeks.

If you hadn't planned on such hardcore activity you can still enjoy many of the splendours of the Alta Montaña on a tour of the Andes highlands west of Mendoza. Beyond the city the road soon starts to climb, leaving behind fertile slopes covered in vineyards (this is Argentina's premier wine-growing area). The hills become increasingly barren and denuded of vegetation as the ascent continues. Pastures and grassland give way to mountain streams, sudden deep valleys and rocks of strikingly varied hues. Just beyond the winter ski resort of Los Penitentes and at an altitude of 2,700 m (8,860 ft) you encounter one of the region's great sights, the Puente del Inca. This natural stone bridge over the Rio de las Cuevas owes its coppery-gold colour to minerals in the water. A short way on is the entrance to the Aconcagua Provincial Park. If you have not signed up for the full climbing experience you can still enjoy hugely rewarding day and overnight treks to base camps.

HOW TO GET THERE:
Buses from Mendoza ply this route regularly as it is the main road over the Andes to the Chilean capital, Santiago.

WHEN TO GO:
For an area notorious for its unpredictable weather your best bet is to visit during the summer months, from December–March.

WORTH A DETOUR:
If the skies are clear there is a magnificent view of the summit of Mount Aconcagua from the Laguna de Horcones, a small lake close to the park entrance.

CABO DOS BAHIAS

South America/Argentina

HOW TO GET THERE:
The reserve is about 30 km (19 mi) south of Camarones by the RP1, a slow, gravel road.

WHEN TO GO:
October–March for penguins, although the reserve is a fascinating place all year round.

WORTH A DETOUR:
Meeting the penguins. Although the nesting area is fenced off, they potter about and are naturally curious. Visitors who sit and wait will be rewarded, although penguins do nip if anyone gets too close.

Patagonia's coastal highway runs almost all the way to Tierra del Fuego. The landscape is often hypnotically vast and empty, although in places the road is within sight and sound of the ocean. Here, an extraordinary abundance of wildlife – whales and dolphins, seals and sea lions, penguins and seabirds – nest, breed and feed. The Valdes Peninsula in the north is a prime whale-watching location, while the popular Punto Tombo Reserve is home to South America's largest nesting colony of penguins. Cabo dos Bahias, south of Camarones, is an isolated wilderness of scrub and rugged shore, where land and sea creatures thrive in a peaceful, protected reserve.

Large numbers of Patagonian foxes and the usually timid guanacos (wild llamas) and ostrich-like, flightless rheas, wander fearlessly inland. Seals and big, aggressive sea lions colonize the rocky foreshore, and killer whales (orcas), which are actually large dolphins, patrol the waters for sustenance. Numerous resident seabirds include cormorants, skuas and petrels. In spring and summer, beach and hinterland become an enormous nursery where some 25,000 pairs of Magellanic penguins raise their young.

These strikingly marked birds – elegant black-and-white stripes divide dark backs from white fronts – have discordant calls and are also known as jackass penguins. Males come ashore and dig burrows where females lay eggs in October; parents share feeding duties until the chicks learn to swim in February. In March, the young start their migration north, followed by the adults. Watching thousands of penguins seemingly 'planted' in holes and surrounded by grazing guanacos is fascinating – and rather surreal.

WORTH A DETOUR:
The opportunity to try your hand (and feet) at a spot of ice trekking on the glacier – equipment and full instruction provided, but not available to children under 12.

LOS GLACIARES
South America/Argentina

The Los Glaciares National Park is formed from the eastern slopes of the Andes in southern Patagonia. Extending for 170 km (106 mi) along the national frontier with Chile, the 6,000-sq km (2,320-sq mi) park encompasses a range of habitats as its terrain spreads down from the mountains: to the east lies Patagonian steppe, giving way, as the ground rises, to huge montane beech forests. What most people come to this national park for (and the reason why it is a UNESCO World Heritage Site) is hinted at in its name: *glaciares* is Spanish for glaciers and there are 47 of them in the park, occupying close to half its total surface area. This extraordinary fact becomes more credible when you consider the mind-boggling dimensions of the larger glaciers like Upsala and Viedma; the latter is the biggest in the country at nearly 1,000 sq km (385 sq mi). Together they make up the Southern Patagonian Ice Field, the largest ice mass on the planet after Antarctica and Greenland.

The most celebrated and visited of the park's glaciers is the Glaciar Perito Moreno in its southern section. Although there are fabulous views of the glacier from the well-sited walkways on the Península de Magellanes, the best way to appreciate the splendours of this frozen world is to take a boat tour on Lago Argentino. As well as visiting several smaller glaciers, the boat weaves its way between giant icebergs floating on the lake as it draws close (but not too close!) to Perito Moreno's 60 m (197 ft) high ice wall. If you are very lucky you may experience the phenomenon known as 'calving' in which huge chunks of ice succumb to water pressure and break away from the face of the wall.

IBERA WETLANDS

South America/Argentina

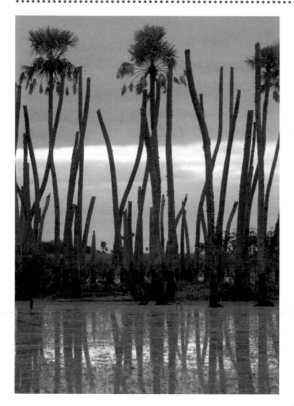

WORTH A DETOUR:
Spotting the capybara, the world's largest rodent. Luckily, unlike many of the other South American mammals, the capybara is far from reclusive and can often be seen grazing in large family groups at the water's edge.

The Esteros del Iberá or Ibera Wetlands are one of Argentina's most important wildlife havens. Situated in the subtropical northeast of the country in the Entre Ríos or Mesopotamia region – so called because it is bounded by the two great rivers of the Paraná and the Uruguay – the Esteros del Iberá were once part of the main course of the Río Paraná. Sluggish currents have combined with silting and sedimentation over time to form the present patchwork of lakes, water channels, swamps, densely wooded marshes and savannah. Floating islands, known as *embalsados*, are a special feature of the waterways, a consequence of aquatic plants and other vegetation accumulating on the water's surface.

This is no ordinary wetland; covering a total area of 13,700 sq km (5,290 sq mi), the Esteros del Iberá is the second-largest wetland in the world after the Pantanal in Brazil. In recent years it has been afforded a measure of protection as a nature reserve but environmentalists, worried about continuing threats to its delicate ecosystem, carry on campaigning for tougher controls and greater regulation. There are no paved roads in the reserve so most visitors don't take their vehicle in.

Even though you are largely leaving behind the sounds of human activity it is surprising to discover just how noisy the natural world can be, especially when you are talking about howler monkeys and more than 350 bird species. Waders feature prominently of course, among them the splendid Jabiru stork and the ruddy tiger heron. There can be few more magical experiences than being poled through the marshes in a noiseless flat-bottomed boat as the air around you is filled with the rich and raucous polyphony of the natural world.

YOU SHOULD KNOW
In the language of the pre-Columbian people who once inhabited the area Iberá means 'glittering water'. When the sun is setting, or beneath a full moon, it is easy to see why.

CALCHAQUÍ VALLEYS

South America/Argentina

DON'T MISS

If you are visiting in the autumn (March–May) you will see lines of red peppers drying in the sun on many of the hillsides.

The Andean northwest of Argentina is a dry, semi-desert world of striking rockscapes and sparse vegetation that is far removed from the lush pampas to the south. Even so, such an unpromising landscape can yield surprising pockets of fertility, such as the Valles Calchaquíes region. The dramatic contrasts between green valleys, surrounding sun-parched uplands and an ever-present backdrop of snow-capped mountains help to explain the particular appeal of this remote area, lying south and west of the provincial capital Salta. The main artery through the region is the Calchaquí River and most of the valleys link to it. Tumbling mountain torrents have carved a number of remarkable canyons out of the sandstone plateau.

In this thinly populated landscape the few scattered settlements are oases of shade and tranquillity, offering traditional adobe houses, cobblestones, pretty squares and artisan workshops. Cachi is a typical example and boasts an unbeatable setting beneath the towering profile of Mount Nevado del Cachi – 6,380 m (20,930 ft). An area of 650 sq km (250 sq mi) at the heart of the Valles was designated a national park as recently as 1996; the Los Cardones park takes its name from the ubiquitous cardón or candelabra cactus, one of the few plants to flourish in these parts. With no other trees growing here, the wood of this giant cactus, which can grow to over 5 m (16 ft), is widely used by local communities as a construction material and for furniture. Its unmistakable profile will certainly be one of your abiding images of a visit to the Valles.

DON'T MISS
An early morning walk in the forest – the best time to see the birdlife.

MISIONES FOREST

South America/Argentina

The province of Misiones lies in the far northeast of Argentina, in a strip of land that extends like a crooked finger between Paraguay and Brazil. The climate and topography are subtropical, and Misiones has some of the largest and least spoilt areas of surviving Atlantic rainforest. Your best bet is to head up to the Brazilian border and avail yourself of the services and infrastructure that have been established around the Iguazú Falls. The magnificent falls are one of the planet's top natural wonders and what of course everyone comes here to see. But set as they are within a sizeable national park it is surprisingly simple to head off on a nature trail into the depths of the forest.

The dense canopy and the luxuriant undergrowth support a staggering array of plants and wildlife. If you are patient and tread softly, you should be rewarded with plenty of sightings, especially of multicoloured butterflies and gorgeous tropical birds like toucans and parrots.

VALLEY OF THE MOON

South America/Argentina

WHEN TO GO:
April–September. Afternoon tours offer the added bonus of a wonderful sunset.

Ischigualasto Provincial Park lies high in the semi-arid Sierra de Valle Fertil amid the lower ranges of the Andes in northwestern Argentina. This name derives from the Diaguita for 'land without life'. The park is an extensive area – around 600 sq km, (230 sq mi) – of barren, eerie emptiness scattered with twisted rock formations. Millions of years ago its dramatic red-sandstone canyons contained rivers whose swirling waters eroded the rocks, which were further sculpted by millennia of weather into strangely shaped red and ash-grey monoliths. This lifeless landscape is known as the Valley of the Moon.

The valley is a palaeontological treasure trove, where fossil-bearing rocks form a unique, undisturbed sequence of deposits, with perfectly preserved fossils representing the entire Triassic period. Among the important dinosaur fossils are the remains of the carnivorous *Herrerasaurus* and of the small predator *Eoraptor lunensis*, the 'dawn raptor', one of the earliest dinosaurs ever discovered. Fossils of other vertebrates and of ferns, horsetails and giant tree trunks have given palaeontologists a chance to study the evolution of dinosaurs and mammals and to build up a picture of their environment. The lunar landscape was, around 200 million years ago, a floodplain with meandering rivers and dense vegetation.

Right: Valley of the Moon

AFRICA

FARAFRA OASIS AND THE WHITE DESERT

Northern Africa/Egypt

DON'T MISS
At sunrise, the weird chalk shapes in the White Desert glow pink and orange.

WHEN TO GO:
November–March. Nights in the desert can be extremely cold in winter and the area gets very crowded during Egyptian holidays.

YOU SHOULD KNOW
Although the old name Land of the Cow probably referred to Farafra's association with the cow-headed goddess Hathor, cattle in the oasis still look strikingly like those depicted on tomb and temple walls in Luxor.

A huge fertile depression in the Libyan Desert, the Farafra Oasis is the most isolated and least populated of Egypt's oases. No archaeological evidence of occupation in pharaonic times has been found, although it is known that during the reign of Rameses II it was called Ta-iht, the Land of the Cow. It is bordered to the west by the impenetrable Great Sand Sea where, it is said, the army of the Persian king Cambyses disappeared en route to Siwa. Repeated searches have revealed no trace of the lost men. All that remains of an important Roman settlement is a tumbled fort, although a ruined Roman cemetery lies outside the town and evidence of Roman and Byzantine travellers is scattered around springs and pools all over the oasis, particularly at Ain Hadra, an important watering place on the ancient caravan route. Now sleepy Farafra is home to Bedouin who live in traditional mud-brick houses, often painted blue to ward off the evil eye. At nearby Bir Sitta, a sulphurous spring offers a soak after a day in the desert.

The extraordinary White Desert begins about 32 km (20 mi) north of the town; the vast, flat, milky wasteland is broken by hundreds of jagged, blindingly white chalk rocks, shaped by millennia of desert winds into pinnacles, twisted spires, misshapen mushrooms and a bewildering menagerie of mutant creatures. West of the road stand the inselbergs – steep, symmetrical rock cones with flattened tops, strangely similar to those seen on Mars. These give some welcome shade for walkers and campers. This surreal landscape is much visited by tour groups, but away from the most popular clusters of photogenic chalk formations, its mystery is compelling.

VALLEY OF THE WHALES
Northern Africa/Egypt

WORTH A DETOUR:
The visitor centre and information booths may seem incongruous, but they are sympathetically built and the information is invaluable.

Southwest of the Faium Oasis, the Wadi al-Rayan is a protected area of lakes and waterfalls popular with birds and animals and with weekend Cairenes escaping the city's heat. A long unpaved track leads from the wadi out into the desert to a level, pale expanse broken by occasional rocky outcrops. This is the Valley of the Whales which, in 2005, became Egypt's first Natural World Heritage Site. More than 40 million years ago, when oceans covered much of the Sahara, this arid spot was very like the Florida Everglades – a swampy coastal region whose waters teemed with fish and marine life and whose banks swarmed with reptiles, animals and birds. A remarkable variety of well-preserved fossils, including mangrove roots, sharks and turtles, give palaeontologists a vivid picture of life before the waters ebbed, but it is the fossilized skeletons of whales that give the valley its name and importance. This extinct subspecies of whale, the archaeoceti, was carnivorous, streamlined, 18 m (59 ft) long, and land-based. Many of these fossils have not only flippers but also hind legs, feet and toes, and represent a major stage in evolution: the emergence of the whale as an ocean-dwelling mammal. This incomparable open-air museum is now carefully managed by UNESCO. Marked walking tracks lead around the exhibits, where fossilized whale skeletons lie stretched out on the sand, ringed by stones and low ropes. The site's remoteness and scale are impressive and slightly disorientating.

YOU SHOULD KNOW
None of the fossils should be touched and there are very heavy penalties for removing anything.

GREEN MOUNTAINS

Northern Africa/Libya

HOW TO GET THERE:
Several good roads lead from the main coastal road up into the hills.

WHEN TO GO:
April–November.

WORTH A DETOUR:
Outside Slonta, a little hill town, stands a tiny temple dedicated to a pre-Greek deity. The naively carved human faces and animals are unlike anything else in Libya. Nothing is known of the cult.

YOU SHOULD KNOW

The Green Mountain Sustainable Development Area was initiated in 2007. This ecotourism initiative aims to protect classical sites and the rugged landscape – which has been described as 'one of the last ten paradises of the Mediterranean' – from haphazard tourist development.

Most of Libya's vast, barren landscape does not receive sufficient rainfall for settled agriculture. Desert lakes are salt and the network of wadis, apart from brief periods after rain, is dry. The Green Mountains (Jebel al-Akhdar) of northern Cyrenaica, where streams and waterfalls flow almost year round, are the exception. The mountains, with their cover of pine, wild olives, cypress and juniper trees, are gloriously verdant. In the south, the desert stretches to the Chad border; to the north, the range drops precipitously to a coastal plain which curves from Benghazi to Derna. Cyrenaica was a province of ancient Greece, and several important cities lay on the coast. Then, the lovely Green Mountains were a precious granary; now, this area is little known.

It is possible to explore the Green Mountains from Al-Bayda and Shahat and visit some of Libya's finest classical sites. These include Ptolemaia, Apollonia and magnificent Cyrene, the most complete of the Greek cities. Inland sites like the Temple of Aesculapius at Al-Bayda are less visited. In Qasr Libya a museum displays the remarkable mosaics found in two small Byzantine churches. Laid in AD 539, most depict paradisiacal scenes of flowers and wildlife, although one shows the Pharos Lighthouse at Alexandria.

Wadi al-Kuf was the scene of fierce battles in 1927 when, until they were bombed, Libyan resistance fighters halted the advance of the Italian forces. The caves where the guerrillas sheltered can be seen in the steep, rocky walls of the valley.

The fertile rounded hills of the Green Mountains still produce cereals, potatoes and fruit. This is one of the few areas in Libya with a pleasant summer climate, and cliffs, canyons, springs, woodland and deep, shady valleys make for marvellous, relatively cool walking in beautiful, unspoilt countryside.

WORTH A DETOUR:
Photogenic Tarmesia, whose deserted stone houses blend into the crags where they perch.

JEBEL NAFUSA

Northern Africa/Libya

Towns and villages – many deserted and derelict – cling to the rocky hillsides of the Jebel Nafusa range. In the 7th century the Berbers retreated here and built underground houses, *dammous*, to protect them from the advancing Arabs and the weather. The most impressive of these are dwellings built into the sides of wide, deep pits, reached by tunnels. From a distance, they are invisible. Huge, fortress-like granaries, *qasrs*, some of which are still in use, protected their treasure – the crops. Although now living in modern homes, most of Libya's Berbers still farm the Jebel Nafusa. Nalut, near the Algerian border, has an old town built on a rocky bluff, and Gharyan, at the eastern end of the range, has some well-preserved underground homes. In the middle, Yefren, built among woods high above the coastal plain, is a lovely old town. A large Jewish community once lived here and a fascinating, ancient synagogue survives. Steep slopes, deep ravines and high, sunny pastures with breathtaking views north and south make for exhilarating walking.

UBARI DUNES AND LAKES

Northern Africa/Libya

YOU SHOULD KNOW
To avoid offending the locals, cover up when bathing.

WHEN TO GO:
October–April. Winter night temperatures in the desert can drop below zero.

Much of the desert which covers Libya is a flat, gravel wasteland. To experience the thrill and romance of the Sahara dunes, visitors must head for one of the sand seas. The most accessible is the Ubari Sand Sea, a boundless expanse of reddish sand waves – crescent and ridge dunes which, with their compacted bases, are relatively stable. Early and late, they glow with rosy sunlight and their shadowy valleys make perfect campsites. As the temperature drops and the campfire crackles, the

brilliance of the stars in an inky sky and the total silence are awe inspiring. Although 4x4s are a quick and easy option, they do break up the surface of the dunes and a trip into the sand sea by camel is infinitely more satisfactory.

A first sight of the Ubari lakes from the heights of the dunes is unforgettable, for they lie in the tawny sands like gleaming slivers of lapis lazuli set in the deep green of palms and reeds. There are several north of Tekerkiba, and three – Umm al-Maa, Mavo and Gebraoun – are sizeable. A fourth large lake has almost dried up, as have several of the smaller ones. They are remnants of a wetter past and are now very salt, so that bathing in them – Gebraoun is the easiest to get into – is a float rather than a swim.

BOUHEDMA NATIONAL PARK

Northern Africa/Tunisia

YOU SHOULD KNOW
This is one of the few remaining places in the world where the sand or dune cat has been sighted.

HOW TO GET THERE:
By road from Gabès.

WHEN TO GO:
During the winter months – the summer is far too hot.

WORTH A DETOUR:
The remnants of ancient civilizations that occupied this area. There are Neolithic places of worship, Berber tombs, a prehistoric site and old mines to be seen.

Probably Tunisia's most important national park, Bouhedma was created in 1980 and is now a UNESCO Biosphere Reserve. The 165-sq km (64-sq mi) park is dominated by a type of gumtree and scrub, the last traces of the savannah that once spread along the northern edges of the Sahara desert.

Lying beneath the Bouhedma Escarpment, but including the rocky slopes, the park is unique in North Africa and looks and feels more like parts of Kenya or Tanzania. This is the place to visit if mammals are of particular interest to you. Dorcas gazelles, scimitar-horned oryx, golden jackals, Cape hares and Ruppell's foxes can be seen, as well as gundis – rodents that live on the rocky foothills of the escarpment.

Bouhedma has needed some protection as grazing livestock, land clearance and poaching had begun to degrade the landscape. As part of this effort several animals, such as addax and dama gazelles, have been successfully re-introduced.

There are also about 300 plant species and many birds. These include

ostriches and several species of raptor, such as golden eagles, Lanner falcons and Pharaoh eagle owls. The highest peak, which reaches 840 m (2,756 ft), is home to juniper, olive and Pistacia – a genus of trees in the cashew family.

Both permanent and seasonal watercourses can be found here, the most important of which is the source of Ain Cherchera. Be alert as you walk, however: there are scorpions all across Tunisia.

A small ecomuseum and forest station is situated at the entrance to the park, the former offering excellent guidance on its flora and fauna.

ICHKEUL NATIONAL PARK

Northern Africa/Tunisia

Comprising a large lake and wetland area by the side of Ichkeul Mountain, Ichkeul National Park is the only natural area in North Africa to be recognized as a World Heritage Site. Easily reached from the capital, Tunis, this is a wonderful place to visit.

Connected to a large lagoon which is itself connected to the ocean, the 85-sq km (33-sq mi) shallow and brackish Lake Ichkeul is an essential refuge for more than 200 species of trans-Saharan migratory birds that gather here each spring and autumn. During the winter season between 200,000 and 300,000 birds can be seen on the lake and its surrounding marshlands. Herons, white storks, spoonbills, flamingoes, ducks, geese, waders and endangered white-headed ducks rest up while, overhead, buzzards, kites, ospreys, falcons and harriers hunt for the perfect meal.

The lake itself is full of life, including otters, frogs, toads, snakes, turtles, crabs and fish such as eels, sole, sea bass and anchovies. Plenty of pondweed provides both food and shelter for many species.

On Mount Ichkeul, jackal, genet, wild cat, porcupine, wild boar and mongoose thrive – there is even a large boa population. During winter, when the area receives the most rainfall, the mountainside is carpeted with flowers and, just at the entrance, a small herd of water buffalo can be seen, often with white egrets on their backs, eating the insects bothering their hosts.

During summer the lake becomes more saline as the rains depart and salt-loving plants begin to colonize the edges. The locals have been known to use lake water for drinking and irrigation and, despite its being illegal, cattle, sheep and goats graze in the park, too. Hunting, fishing and quarrying also continues, albeit clandestinely.

HOW TO GET THERE:
Arrange a taxi from Menzel Bourguiba or Bizerte, or choose a tour when in Tunis.

WHEN TO GO:
Winter or spring.

WORTH A DETOUR:
The small ecomuseum just inside the entrance to the park. Your guide will be able to explain all the exhibits if you don't speak French or Arabic.

YOU SHOULD KNOW
Between 1996 and 2006, Lake Ichkeul was on the World Heritage Sites endangered list. However, the Tunisian government stepped in and measures were taken to rehabilitate the lake. It had become too salty, causing a reduction in the numbers of birds relying upon it. In 2006, the park was removed from the endangered list.

KHROUMIRIE MOUNTAINS

Northern Africa/Tunisia

WHEN TO GO: It is possible to go at any time of year, but be aware of possible winter snow. Even at the height of summer the Khroumirie Mountains remain reasonably cool.

The Khroumirie Mountains are situated in the eastern reaches of the Atlas Mountains. The average height of these peaks is 800 m (2,625 ft) and their 550 km (340 mi) of footpaths and trails provide a wonderful hiking experience. At 1,014 m (3,327 ft), the highest peak is Jebel Biri.

This region enjoys a Mediterranean climate, and the town of Ain Draham, deep in the Khroumirie Mountains and developed by the French as a hunting resort, has a European look with its steeply sloped red roofs. It is an excellent base for a visit, surrounded as it is by many paths and tracks leading through this lovely forested region. Trees include mimosa, eucalyptus, pine, juniper and – the dominant species – cork oak. These last are large evergreens with gnarled and twisted branches that live for about 150 years, growing a thick layer of rough bark that can be harvested without damage to the tree about 12 times during their lifespan. The cork layer regenerates, making the trees a renewable resource.

This woodland shelters mammals such as deer, wild boar, jackals, foxes and mongoose, as well as birds such as partridges, green woodpeckers and cuckoos. Tortoises may be seen trudging about on sunny slopes and rocky verges. Hiking through this shady cork forest, with its springs and waterfalls and valleys, is an absolute joy. The region receives more rainfall than most in North Africa, and some snow falls during winter. Much of the wildlife suffered from over hunting by the local population, so steps were taken to protect it.

DON'T MISS
Merzouga and its surrounding area.

ERG CHEBBI

Northern Africa/Morocco

The Erg Chebbi dunes near the village of Merzouga are the most impressive of the two ergs in southeast Morocco. The landscape is flat, desolate, stony desert, but suddenly, and seemingly out of nowhere, these vast Saharan sand dunes rise up to 150 m (490 ft) high, blown there by the wind. They cover an area 22 km (14 mi) long and 5 km (3 mi) wide and are an astonishing sight.

It is possible to take a camel ride to the top of the dunes, or hire a quad bike, but the very best way to experience them is on foot. Go to watch the sunset: an awe-inspiring visual feast of red, pink, orange, yellow and purple – and if luck is on your side, you might even see a green flash.

A walk into the dunes in the dark is also exciting, lit only by the moon and a myriad of sparkling stars in the sky above. Infinitely more stars are visible when there is no ambient light, and the realization of the immensity of the universe is humbling.

DON'T MISS
The ancient walled city
of Fez el Bali is unlike
anywhere else in the world.

JBEL TAZZEKA NATIONAL PARK

Northern Africa/Morocco

Located in the Middle Atlas Mountains some 97 km (60 mi) east of Fez is the old garrison town of Taza, which is the perfect base from which to explore Jbel Tazzeka. This 1,980 m (6,496 ft) peak rises in the centre of the surrounding national park, which is famed for its scenic beauty. There are many routes to take, short or long, but on reaching the summit of Jbel Tazzeka the reward is majestic views of the surrounding forested mountains and snowy peaks in the distance. The park is a great area for hiking through forests of cedar, cork oak and even olive trees; splashing through clear springs; marvelling at waterfalls and lakes; and exploring canyons and caves. The undergrowth is largely tall ferns and bracken, interspersed with pink cistus – a good habitat for large frogs, brilliantly colourful lizards and birds such as rollers, shrikes, short-toed treecreepers and hoopoes. During spring and summer gorgeous butterflies abound. Don't be surprised to meet goat herders or farmers ploughing small plots with oxen or donkeys. Crops are surrounded by yellow-and-white daisies and blood-red poppies, which add to the pleasure of walking here.

THE DADES AND TODRA GORGES

Northern Africa/Morocco

WORTH A DETOUR: El Kelaa M'Gouna, an oasis in the Dades valley that is the centre of Moroccan rose cultivation. It is a great hiking area and every May a traditional Rose Festival is held.

The Dades and Todra Gorges rank high on the list of memorable sights in Morocco. The pair lie fairly close to each other in the Atlas Mountains, 110 km (70 mi) northeast of Ouarzazate.
In early spring the almond blossom is enchanting, softening the spectacularly vivid red and rocky landscape.

Historically, the Berbers fortified this fertile area with hundreds of kasbahs: great, castellated buildings made of red mud, straw and lime, their turrets and walls decorated with carvings. Some are inhabited but many stand empty, gradually being reclaimed by the earth.

The entrance to the Dades is by paved track, although it is far more interesting to hike than to attempt to drive. There are fantastic rock formations and a walk through the gorge, with its sheer rock walls, is unforgettable. Both gorges are a big draw for rock climbers, with many different routes to attempt.

The Todra Gorge is the more dramatic of the two. It is 600 m (656 yd) long and cuts through the mountains, the 300 m (985 ft) walls guarding a passage at some points a mere 10 m (33 ft) in width. A few families live and farm nearby and can often be seen with sheep, goats or camels.

PICO DE FOGO

Western Africa/Cape Verde

DON'T MISS
The Bandeira de São Felipe, Fogo's liveliest festival that takes place in April.

Some 483 km (300 mi) from the coast of Senegal, West Africa, lies the Republic of Cape Verde. An archipelago of ten islands and eight islets, its capital, Praia, is on the largest island, Santiago. Fogo is Cape Verde's fourth largest island and the only one with an active volcano: Pico de Fogo.

Two eruptions shook the island during the last century. In 1951 lava poured down the southern flanks of the volcano and created two new cones. The 1995 eruption was incredibly dramatic. After days of small

earthquakes, flaming lava shot 400 m (1,310 ft) into the sky, raining down into the crater. An ash cloud 5 km (3 mi) high covered Fogo and it was seven weeks before the lava stopped flowing altogether.

At 2,892 m (9,488 ft) and dominating every view, Pico de Fogo looms high, and a hike or two around and into the caldera is hard work and exhilarating, providing extraordinary views not only of the volcano itself but also of Santiago. Volcanoes are famously fertile and Pico de Fogo is no exception. The crater is known as Cha das Caldeiras and within it the vast floor is relatively flat, although strewn with lumps of lava. Two small villages exist here, cultivating vegetables and fruit, including grapes that are turned into locally renowned wine.

WORTH A DETOUR: The bird-count tours, on foot and by boat. Visitors may help the professionals spot water birds.

THE LANGUE DE BARBARIE NATIONAL PARK

Western Africa/Senegal

Saint-Louis, situated on a narrow island some 25 km (15 mi) from the mouth of the Senegal River is a charmingly dilapidated city in three parts. The historic centre is on the island itself, while Sor, with its tidal marshlands, is on the eastern mainland, separated from the island by the river. To the west the river is separated from the Atlantic by a narrow sand spit, the Langue de Barbarie.

At 30 km (19 mi) long, the sand spit itself has little vegetation – mostly casuarina trees that have been encouraged to grow to help prevent erosion – and can best be explored by pirogue. These small, flat-bottomed boats are used by local fishermen and can be easily handled in shallow water. The trip alone is interesting as the pirogue gently moves through the many sandbanks and small islands. This is an area of great importance to migratory birds, as well as being a haven for marine turtles, many of which nest here.

KIANG WEST NATIONAL PARK

Western Africa/The Gambia

Established in 1987, Kiang West National Park is probably the most important and least visited wildlife park in The Gambia. Located on the south bank of the Gambia River, it is only 145 km (90 mi) from the capital, Banjul. The journey, however, is hard as the road is in poor repair. The river forms the park's northern boundary.

Kiang West is uninhabited, flat and low. Three bolongs, or creeks, run through the interior, which mainly consists of savannah and deciduous woodland, with mangroves and tidal flats. There are many trees: red acacia, kapok, and several species native to the Sahelian biogeographic area that divides the Sahara desert from the southern savannahs. Most of The Gambia's mammals are found here, including antelopes, warthogs, spotted hyenas, leopards, servals and caracals. This is habitat for marsh mongoose, pythons, cobras and Nile crocodiles. West African manatees and humpback dolphins can sometimes be spotted in the Jarin creek.

The Gambia is famous for its birds and this area is home to half the country's species – more than 300 have been recorded. During the dry season many raptors are found such as eagles – including the bateleur, Kiang West's logo – hawks, harriers, falcons and the ubiquitous vultures. Other birds include hornbills, with their recognizably awkward flight, weavers, parrots, kingfishers, sandgrouse and chats. It is not essential to take a guide, but guides are knowledgeable and quick to point out birds that you might otherwise miss. Make for Tubabkollon Point. Here you are close to the river, and antelopes and warthogs can be spotted from the nearby escarpment. A waterhole within walking distance can be observed from a viewing shelter. Here you'll see many animals, including monkeys, coming to drink as the dry season tightens its grip.

HOW TO GET THERE:
4×4 on the southern Trans-Gambia highway to Dumbuto, the main base of Kiang West. You can also take tours that go partly by road and the remainder of the way by river boat.

WHEN TO GO:
During the dry season, from November–April.

HIGHLIGHTS:
The Nganingkoi Bolon tidal creek where you will see many wading birds, and possibly marsh mongoose hunting for crabs. The view from the top of Mount Muhavura.

YOU SHOULD KNOW
Kiang West National Park warrants more than a quick look, and it is easy to stay nearby. You can organize this independently or through a tour company.

PENDJARI BIOSPHERE RESERVE

Western Africa/Benin

YOU SHOULD KNOW
The dirt roads within are better maintained and easier to drive than the roads accessing the park. A map is available at all the park entrances and you are requested to drive slowly and carefully to minimize disturbance to the wildlife. The best time to see animals is in the early morning or late afternoon, near the river or lakes. Take binoculars, sunscreen and plenty of water.

Situated in the northwest of Benin, Pendjari National Park, some 12,000 sq km (4,635 sq mi) in size, is part of the largest complex of Protected Areas in West Africa, crossing the borders of Benin, Niger and Burkino Faso.

During the 1950s Benin, then part of French West Africa, listed Pendjari as a Protected Area and it became a hunting ground for French colonials. Today, Pendjari still retains three areas for hunters and their professional guides, under the ownership, control and supervision of the local people. A percentage of the fees received for hunting permits is used to improve the lives of those living near the park boundaries; the remainder helps preserve and improve the Biosphere Reserve, which it became in 1986. Much emphasis is placed on the growth of ecotourism and research, and this is a fantastic area through which to hike, go mountain-biking, take canoe trips, join organized safaris or drive independently.

With a backdrop of the Atakora range and its rocky cliffs, Pendjari park is lush in part, thanks to the eponymous broad river winding through it, bordered by thick, canopied forest.

Renowned for its populations of large mammals, the savannah and grassland is home to cheetahs, lions, leopards, hyena, African wild dogs and jackals. Other large mammals include elephants, buffalo and hippos. Pendjari contains several types of antelope and monkeys, but most of all, there are birds.

Within its boundaries over 300 species of bird can be found. Birds of prey include kestrels, kites, harriers and eagles such as the booted eagle and the African fish eagle. Smaller species include chats, babblers, waxbills, whydah, white-throated francolin and many more. Purple glossy starlings flash past, their iridescent plumage almost shockingly vivid, disappearing into the shelter of baobabs, palms and other African tree and shrub species.

HOW TO GET THERE:
It is an eight-hour drive from Cotonou, Benin's economic and administrative capital, but only a five- or six-hour drive from Burkina Faso and Niger respectively.

WHEN TO GO:
October–mid-February. Pendjari is open year round, but the trip is more difficult during the rainy season.

HIGHLIGHTS:
The local tribal villages and the Tata Sombas of the Betamaribe. Benin has several ancient and treasured cultures.
The many spectacular species of birds and butterflies.

DON'T MISS
The pygmy hippopotamus
and the white-necked
picathartes which nests in
colonies on cliffs in the forest.

GOLA FOREST

Western Africa/Sierra Leone

Bordered by the Atlantic Ocean, Guinea and Liberia, Sierra Leone is severely underdeveloped. Its inhabitants still suffer from the after effects of a disastrous civil war, only resolved in 2000. Gola Forest is the largest area of lowland rainforest in Sierra Leone. It is divided into four distinct areas. Gola North is rugged, fairly high and drained by the Mogbai River, while Gola East and West, separated by the Mano River, are low-lying and swampy. Tiwai Island is a game sanctuary. The closed canopy forest, which contains 200 species of tree, supports most of West Africa's wildlife. Around 50 species of mammal live in Gola, including 10 primates. Several species are vulnerable or endangered, including chimpanzees, elephants and pygmy hippopotami. Other species have only recently been found, such as the leopard, zebra duiker and bongo. There are about 330 different birds. Nine are threatened, 6 are vulnerable and one, the rufous fishing owl, is endangered. The 770 species of flowering plants in the forest help the very high diversity of butterflies to flourish; over 600 species have been found there, 3 of which are new discoveries.

COMOE NATIONAL PARK

Western Africa/Côte d'Ivoire

WORTH A DETOUR: Big-game fishing is available on the Comoe River if hiking doesn't appeal.

Located in northeastern Côte d'Ivoire, south of the country's border with Burkino Faso, is Comoe National Park. West Africa's largest game park was inscribed on the UNESCO World Heritage Site list in

1983, but added to the endangered sites list in 2003. The political turmoil that has overtaken the country during recent years has made 65 per cent of the park 'beyond the control of the staff'. The Comoe River, which flows south from the northeastern section of the park, is the reason Comoe contains such remarkable plant diversity, including shrub savannahs and dense rainforest normally found much further south. It is best visited when its floodplains seasonally become tall grasslands, tempting many species to leave the forest in search of food.

The park contains a great many birds and mammals. Among these are 17 types of carnivore, including African wild dogs and leopards. Chimpanzees, baboons, colobus monkeys and the endangered Diana monkey can be found here, as can duikers and bushbucks. African elephants, buffaloes, warthogs and hippos are also present, but in fairly small numbers.

WHEN TO GO:
The dry season is
December–February.

TAI NATIONAL PARK

Western Africa/Côte d'Ivoire

Declared a Forest and Wildlife Refuge in 1926, Tai National Park became a UNESCO World Heritage Site in 1982, 46 years later. Situated between the Cavally and Sassandra rivers in the southwest of Côte d'Ivoire, this is the largest area of primary tropical rainforest in the whole of West Africa.

Vast trees soar to heights of 46 m (150 ft), their massive trunks using supporting roots for extra strength. The dense canopy excludes sunlight, making for good hiking as it keeps the undergrowth down. Tai has two recognizable types of forest: the north and southeast supports trees such as palms and ebony on poor, thin soil, while in the southwest the trees are all tropical, rain-loving species, 150 of which are endemic. There are 47 species of large mammal living in this forest, five of which are endangered. It is not particularly easy to see large mammals – many are elusive – but there are African elephants, leopards, golden cats, various species of duiker, pygmy hippos, Cape buffaloes and colobus monkeys. The chimpanzees of Tai National Park have become famous thanks to years of study carried out by Swiss researchers. The apes live in groups of 70–80, and during the dry season visitors can hear them cracking nuts open with stones.

CRYSTAL MOUNTAINS NATIONAL PARK

Western Africa/Gabon

DON'T MISS:
A visit to Albert
Schweitzer's hospital
at Lambaréné.

Gabon lies on the equator and contains three well-defined areas: mountains, savannah and the coastal plain. The economy – boosted by oil revenues – is relatively well distributed and the government has made conservation a high priority. Some 10 per cent of the country is protected in 13 national parks.

The Crystal Mountains National Park is a section of a wide, rocky escarpment situated in the northwest of the country between Equatorial Guinea and the Ogooué River. Mount Iboundji, in the north of the mountain range, reaches just 1,575 m (5,167 ft) and is the highest peak in Gabon.

Stunningly beautiful, the park is the epitome of a tropical African jungle – teeming with life and famed as a biodiversity hotspot. The flora is exceptional. Trees include hardwoods such as ebony and mahogany as well as okoumé and ozigo, all of which produce valuable timber, and there is an extraordinary array of flowers, including endemic orchids and begonias. At higher elevations, clouds envelop the forest, producing a mystical landscape of tangled undergrowth, trees shrouded in lianas, and climbing vines.

This equatorial rainforest provides habitat for a wide variety of wildlife. Elephants, leopards, antelopes, jackals and zebras roam the savannah; crocodiles and hippos haunt the river; lowland gorillas and many other primates swing through branches in chattering groups. Pythons and vipers hunt for small prey at ground level, while toucans and parrots screech in the canopy above.

Left: Tai National Park

LOANGO NATIONAL PARK

Western Africa/Gabon

HOW TO GET THERE:
It is easiest to book a trip to Loango in advance. The lodge and its satellite camps will arrange transport by plane or road, and boat, from Libreville.

HIGHLIGHTS:
Elephants and forest buffaloes walking on the beach at sunset or the whale-watching season from July to September.

In 2002 Gabon's president Omar Bongo Ondimba created 13 national parks. The existing Petit Loango and Iguéla Reserves were joined to form Loango National Park. Its habitat includes forest, savannah and lagoons as well as swamps and untamed coastline, and it quickly became a popular spot for ex-pats living in Libreville. Situated between the Nkomi and Ndogo lagoons, south of the capital, and based on the concept 'tourism pays for conservation', it became the focus of small-scale, low-impact, high-end tourism.

The coastline boasts the continent's largest number and variety of whale and dolphin species, including humpback and killer whales, with the exception of South Africa. The ocean also contains many large fish, and Loango is renowned for its record-sized Atlantic tarpon. Fishing in these waters is an exciting experience.

Four types of sea turtle breed on this coastline, including the olive ridley and the leatherback, both of which are endangered. From November–February, visitors may join the data-collection team, going out at night in search of nests or hatchlings. Three species of crocodile may also be seen on such a night-time trek.

Fabulous wildlife abounds in Loango throughout the year and, although the animals are shy, there is a good chance of a sighting from a 4x4, on foot, from a hide or from a boat. Trips around Iguéla lagoon are very rewarding, and birdwatching expeditions can be arranged. Expect to see Pel's and vermiculated fishing owls, Forbes's plover, and African river martins among others.

The savannah and forest is home to many mammals, large and small, and although Loango is not like the big game parks in East Africa, on a safari there is a good chance of observing several species such as zebras, herds of buffalo, lowland gorillas and chimpanzees in unusual settings.

DON'T MISS

The area just after a sharp shower. The mist caused by evaporating rainfall shrouds the vegetation in cloak of tiny water particles.

KAKUM CONSERVATION AREA

Western Africa/Ghana

The Kakum Conservation Area supports a rich diversity of wildlife, including the white-bearded colobus monkey, bush pigs, porcupines and the timid forest elephant. Many species of birds and butterflies also flourish in this lavish land of plenty. The conservation area has a number of hiking trails that take ramblers deep into the forest to a land of fast-flowing tropical rivers and spectacular rapids. It is the 65 m (213 ft) tall giant hardwood trees, however, that are the main attraction in Kakum.

Administrators in Kakum have come up with an ingenious way of giving their trees greater economic value by leaving them in situ than they would have if they were cut down for timber. Visitors can now climb high into the canopy by way of a 500 m (547 yd) long tree-top walkway to experience the environment of the high-tree dwellers. If vertigo can be avoided, it is a great way to view a world that is seen only by canopy dwellers and wildlife cameramen.

BANC D'ARGUIN NATIONAL PARK

Western Africa/Mauritania

WORTH A DETOUR: Birdwatching – especially from the island of Niroumi, where the colonies of bar-tailed godwit, ringed plover and dunlin represent over half of the total Atlantic population.

Mauritania is a vast country in West Africa on the western fringes of the Sahara Desert. Its main resource, other than some low-level mining, comes from its Atlantic coastline in the form of fishing. But even here the right to fish very often belongs to others. This makes the National Park of Banc d'Arguin all the more vital for the protection of the ecology of the area.

The park covers the largely desert coastal region of the country between the capital Nouakchott and Nouadhibou. Away from its arid core, Banc d'Arguin contains an astonishing variety of habitats. The area of most significance to the biodiversity of the region is a large expanse of mudflats, particularly those adjacent to the island of Tidra – the largest of 15 significant islands off the coast. Millions of birds head south to escape the European winter and breed in the park, making the mudflats of Banc d'Arguin the largest bird conservation area on Earth. The fish-rich waters are also a magnet for dolphins and sea turtles. The most remarkable part of the park is its mangrove swamp. It has the most diverse flora in the park, and offers up clues about the area's very different geological past and about our ever-changing planet.

YOU SHOULD KNOW

Travel to and within Mauritania is difficult. Take official advice on safety and security before travelling.

BANDIAGARA ESCARPMENT

Western Africa/Mali

When journeying through the flat, unexciting and scorched landscape of Mali, the traveller could be forgiven for recalling the words of Samuel Johnson, who said that there are places 'worth seeing, but not worth going to see'. Such thoughts are quickly dismissed as the road begins a steady incline and one of Africa's greatest natural wonders rises mirage-like out of the desolate landscape. The gigantic Bandiagara Escarpment – a 150 km (94 mi) long towering sandstone cliff of rich ochre colour – runs from Ouo in the west to the Honbori mountains in the southeast and, as well as being a geological phenomenon, is a place of no little human intrigue.

The cliff face itself varies in height from 100 m (328 ft) to 500 m (1,640 ft) and is broken by deep ravines and scree-lined passages. The higher levels of the escarpment have a rich and diverse flora which has all but disappeared at lower levels. Archaeological research has revealed that high up in the cliffs a system of caves and tunnels was created over 2,000 years ago. The caves then lay empty for over a thousand years until the Tellem pygmies arrived and built houses in the crevices. The remains of these elevated structures can still be seen. Today, the cliffs act as protection for a string of over 300 villages belonging to the local Dogon people. It is hard to leave the area without the feeling that you've visited a place out of time. The flat-topped and cone-roofed clusters of Dogon buildings blend in to seem part of nature and the people themselves have an animist system of beliefs and rituals that is far removed from anything else on Earth.

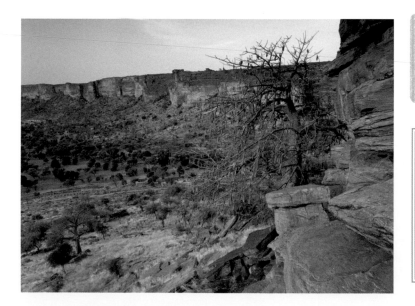

WHEN TO GO:
October–February, when the weather is relatively cool and dry.

YOU SHOULD KNOW

The Dogons believe they originated from Sirius B, a white dwarf star that circles Sirius. It is not visible to the naked eye and their belief pre-dates the detection of the star by Western astrologers in 1915.

AFRICA

DON'T MISS
The distant view of the
Air Mountains that appear
to bubble up out of the desert.

AIR AND TENERE NATURAL RESERVES
Western Africa/Niger

Located in northern Niger towards the border with Algeria, the Air and Tenere Natural Reserves together form the largest protected area in Africa – roughly the size of Scotland. The combined reserve was created in 1988 and includes the western portion of the Tenere Desert and the eastern peaks of the Air Mountains.

Unfortunately, years of civil strife have seen wildlife numbers plummet. The addax antelope, ostrich, and dama gazelle have all but disappeared from the region, while the once numerous Barbary sheep and Dorcas gazelle are now seldom seen. Still, the Tenere Desert contains one of the world's largest sand seas and some of the highest barchan dunes in the Sahara.

The Air Mountains are positively verdant by comparison. Comprising several massifs above a craggy plateau, they support a wide variety of grasses, shrubs and small trees. The mountains are also a good landmark for migrating birds.

MOUNT CAMEROON

DON'T MISS
A guided
walking safari.

Western Africa/Cameroon

Dubbed 'the roof of West Africa', Mount Cameroon at 4,095 m (13,435 ft) above sea level is not only the region's highest peak but an active volcano. It is part of a basalt ridge that rises from the Gulf of Guinea. It is also as wet as it gets. The region surrounding the mountain receives some of the heaviest rainfall on Earth at an incredible average of 10 m (33 ft) per year. This, coupled with the tropical heat of the lower slopes of the mountain, creates a hothouse environment for a diverse and spectacular range of plant life. Some of the insect-attracting plants that thrive there have heads as big as bicycle wheels. Despite its elevation, the mountain is more of a hike than a climb, but the vertical journey takes the traveller through four distinct habitats. At sea level the area features dense mangrove forest, which soon gives way to lush evergreen forest.

ZAKOUMA NATIONAL PARK

Central Africa/Chad

WHEN TO GO:
The wet season, from June–September, is less oppressively hot.

The *raison d'etre* of a game reserve is to bring people close to the wild animals they would normally have little access to. This is a happy marriage, as the visitors bring much-needed revenue, which in turn goes towards preserving the animals' habitat. Safety and security in exchange for the disturbance created by a few motor vehicles is no bad deal. For the staff and wildlife at Zakouma National Park this would be a great luxury. Its close proximity to the war in Darfur has had a catastrophic impact on the area, and poaching has become endemic. Some wildlife has been killed for food, but one animal has suffered more than most. In a land where per capita income is less than $200 a year, the elephant has been targeted by organized criminal gangs for its tusks, which can fetch $100,000 a pair when sold in China or Thailand. In 1970 the elephant population in Chad stood at over 300,000; today it is below 10,000.

Travel through the park is possible only by journeying with the park rangers who, by necessity, must be as heavily armed as the poachers. But Zakouma is a beautiful place. It is a land of wide open plains broken only by a few clumps of trees, where lions take shelter before heading into the cover of the long parched grass to stalk their prey. This is a magical place, where heat haze distorts distance, and clouds of dust rise out of the sun-baked earth, disturbed by the hooves of gazelles. But it is the mighty African elephant that most symbolizes the park. As sensitive as it is strong, its plight is shaming.

WHEN TO GO:
The heat is less searing from December–February.

TIBESTI MOUNTAINS

Central Africa/Chad

The Sahara extends across North Africa from its Atlantic coastline in the west to the Nile Delta in the east. At 9 million sq km (3.5 million sq mi), and growing steadily still, it is the largest arid region on Earth. The Tibesti Mountains appear like a mirage from the desert. Composed of black basalt from a now-dormant volcanic chain, they have over the years been sandblasted into a stunning lunar-like landscape. Travel through the range is beset with problems. Sand gets into everything and the area is subject to the largest diurnal temperature range on Earth.

Emi Koussi, at 3,415 m (11,204 ft) is the highest and most challenging peak of the area. But, without doubt, the most stunning spectacle the area has to offer is a 5 km (3 mi) wide 750 m (2,460 ft) deep salt-filled crater, Trou au Natron. The contrast between the black mountains and the blinding white of the crater as the sun beats off both provides one of the world's most extraordinary sights.

BALE MOUNTAINS

Eastern Africa/Ethiopia

This lush landscape of forested mountains and pristine streams offers superb scenic satisfaction, but also introduces visitors to local culture in a manner that provides a blueprint for sustainable ecotourism. The people are friendly and guides may be found to lead visitors into the forest, either on foot or mounted on horseback. Bold trekkers will be rewarded with a wealth of tree and plant life, with distinctly different flora as the elevation increases, right up to heather-covered moors at the highest levels. The hillsides are aflame with torch lilies between June and November, while the bright-yellow flowers of Hypericum lanceolatum are everywhere. Honey production is a significant activity and there are far worse tipples than the punchy mead that much of it mysteriously becomes.

The Adaba-Dodola forests harbour a wealth of birdlife, from Abyssinian catbirds to yellow-fronted parrots. These will be more visible than the forest animals – although the likes of Menelik's bushbuck, assorted monkeys, baboons, spotted hyenas, porcupines, warthogs, mongoose, jackals and Ethiopian wolves are there. The chances of getting lucky – and enjoying a good all-round experience – are much increased for visitors who book one of the organized mountain expeditions that use primitive but established camps.

HIGHLIGHTS:
A day trip from Dodola town to the Lensho River.
The spectacular Shebelle Waterfalls.

YOU SHOULD KNOW
There is a real threat of terrorist activity in Ethiopia, and not even Addis Ababa is deemed entirely safe for visitors.

OMO VALLEY

Eastern Africa/Ethiopia

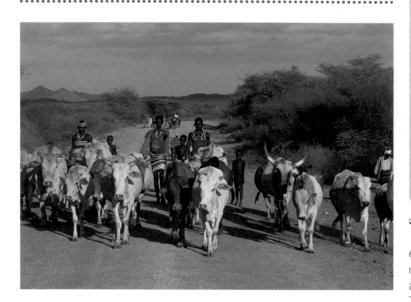

HOW TO GET THERE:
With difficulty. The area is remote, roads are unpaved and only a few specialist tour companies inside or outside the country organize trips to the area, although there is a guest lodge along the river that has a private airstrip for charter flights from Addis Ababa.

WHEN TO GO:
Avoid the rainy season (April and May) when the river floods, Nile-style.

The important Omo River falls entirely within southern Ethiopia, rising in the Shewan Highlands and rushing down to Lake Turkana in the Great Rift Valley. Ethiopia's most remote wilderness surrounds the Omo Valley. The valley's natural beauty may be stunning and justify a visit in its own right, but the opportunity to visit colourful local villages adds a fascinating extra dimension. This UNESCO World Heritage Site is a cultural melting pot where the earliest-known fossil remains of *Homo sapiens* were discovered.

The river flows through two national parks – Omo and Mago – but these have few if any facilities and are defined more by lines on maps than much evidence on the ground. With just one significant road providing access – from Konso via Woito to Bako or Omorate – this really is a splendid opportunity for adventurous types to organize the expedition of a lifetime. But however ambitious the journey, there simply won't be time to see and do everything. Photography, birdwatching, wildlife-viewing, fishing, nature hiking and exploring in a 4x4 are just some of the tempting possibilities, but the real joy of this place is people-watching.

There are at least 20 different African tribes within the area – all interesting, all with their own customs, all living a traditional way of life that may be seen today but will inevitably be swept away by 'progress' within a few more generations. Peoples of the lower Omo Valley include the Dizi, Dorze, Hamar, Me'en, Mursi, Nyangatom and Suri. The villages contain mud-and-thatch houses – often of beehive form – and this is the place to see the extraordinary sight of women with mouths stretched to accommodate huge round clay plates. The effort of getting to the Omo Valley may be considerable, but the reward will be a storehouse of memories to treasure.

GODA MOUNTAINS

Eastern Africa/Djibouti

HOW TO GET THERE:
A hired 4×4 vehicle is the transport of choice, with or without the services of a local guide.

WHEN TO GO:
A visit to Tadjoura, on the gulf of the Tadjoura Sea and overlooked by the Goda Mountains. Once a slave-trading centre, Djibouti's oldest town is now a busy port notable for white-washed houses and splendid nearby beaches.

Located to the northwest of the Gulf of Tadjoura in North Africa's smallest country, the Goda Mountains rise to a height of 1,750 m (5,741 ft) and are Djibouti's largest 'green' enclave – a vegetated oasis amid the country's stony desert landscapes and an area where mist often rises above the lush green slopes and it actually rains sometimes. Small mountain villages like Bankoualé, Dittilou and Randa seem a world apart from the scorching plains at the foot of the mountains and offer the blessed relief of a cooler climate.

It is possible to enjoy a day's hike in the mountains or find accommodation there at a few locally run campsites or in simple huts reserved for tourists in unspoilt areas, either of which can provide a base to explore before it's too late. Much of the forest has been cleared over the past 200 years and only one-tenth of its original area remains. Drought, fires, deforestation and overgrazing by ubiquitous livestock are, sadly, continuing the process.

The Day Forest National Park, accessed from the National 9 road, aims to protect much of what is left and contains most of Djibouti's biodiversity. One of three national parks in Djibouti, it is small but has a unique ambiance. It harbours rare plants and birds, some – like the Djibouti francolin – endemic. Birdwatching attracts visitors, while animals such as warthog, monkeys and antelope may also be seen. The forest is located where the plateau of the Goda Mountains is bordered by the Goh and Hamboka cliffs. The Day Massif contains juniper trees and an impressively dense pine forest. However, the attempt to preserve the junipers seems to be a losing battle, as there are now almost too few to ensure survival, let alone mass regeneration.

LAKE ASSAL

Eastern Africa/Djibouti

WHEN TO GO:
Avoid high summer, when the heat can be unbearable.

Anyone who's ever wanted to walk on water must head for Lake Assal, a crater lake 120 km (75 mi) to the west of Djibouti City. This amazing body of water is fed by salt springs that make it more saline than the Dead Sea. Lake Assal is an impressive 157 m (515 ft) below sea level – making it the lowest point in Africa. Remoteness and the fierce climate combine to ensure that this eerie landscape remains largely untouched. The lake is in the Danakil Desert and extends to an area of 54 sq km (21 sq mi). It is surrounded by brooding volcanoes (happily dormant) whose dark presence contrasts dramatically with the lake's brilliant aquamarine colour. A visit to Lake Assal is not for those who like gentle scenery and a temperate climate.

YOU SHOULD KNOW

It is possible to go into the water at Lake Assal to frolic (drowning is an impossibility, sitting up almost feasible) – but it's advisable to wear shoes as the bottom is littered with sharp salt crystals.

It is in an inhospitable area seared by desert winds that is one of the hottest places in Africa, with temperatures capable of reaching nearly 60°C (140°F) and light so bright that a good pair of polarizing sunglasses is an essential travelling companion. But for lovers of wild places and dramatic landscapes its austere charms will be deeply satisfying.

The banks are covered in large salt crystals, and saltpans surround the lake. The local Afar people still produce salt to trade into Ethiopia, as they have for centuries, and may be seen coming and going with their camels. The visitor is likely to be offered an unusual souvenir – a large bag of Lake Assal refined salt, costing only a few francs.

MERU NATIONAL PARK

Eastern Africa/Kenya

International fame came to Meru National Park when Joy Adamson's book *Born Free* chronicled the reintroduction of the lioness Elsa to the Kenyan wilderness back in the late 1950s. This was an important step forward for the conservation movement yet, despite such a positive association, many tourists overlook Meru. This may be a legacy of mismanagement in the 1970s and 1980s, when poaching was endemic and visitors wisely stayed away. Today, that situation has been remedied after an intensive rehabilitation programme conducted by the Kenya Wildlife Service, supported by the International Fund for Animal Welfare. So Meru is once again a haven for wildlife and a stimulating destination but, happily for those who appreciate wilderness exploration, it remains one of Kenya's lesser-known parks.

WORTH A DETOUR:
The Meru home of George and Joy Adamson of *Born Free* fame. Elsa herself is buried in the park and some of Joy Adamson's ashes were scattered over the grave of her beloved lioness after the pioneering conservationist was murdered in 1980.

The 870-sq km (335-sq mi) park consists of riverine palm forests, with wooded grasslands in the west and thorny bush land to the north. The area experiences high rainfall that encourages the growth of tall grass and nourishes extensive swampland, which means that animals are sometimes difficult to spot. But with or without the help of a guide it is possible to see many species, including lion, leopard, cheetah, giraffe (not so hard to detect!), zebra, elephant and hippopotamus, black rhino and rare antelopes. In addition, the bird population is thriving and more than 300 species have been recorded within park boundaries.

WATAMU MARINE NATIONAL RESERVE

Eastern Africa/Kenya

WORTH A DETOUR: Gede ruins – the remains of a 12th-century Swahili village, mysteriously abandoned around 1400 and now an atmospheric place overgrown with baobabs and tamarinds.

The jewel in the crown of Kenya's 50-plus national parks, reserves and sanctuaries must surely be the tiny but glittering Watamu Marine National Reserve. Its glory lies in its extraordinary marine environment. This consists of the Mida Creek mangrove forest with its teeming bird-like intertidal rocks, sandy beaches, mudflats, coral cliffs, fringing reefs and a glorious coral garden. The latter lies less than 300 m (328 yd) from shore in the azure Indian Ocean, crying out to be explored by glass-bottomed boat. Diving and snorkelling are even better options for those who want to become part of this unique underwater world,

As well as corals – there are around 150 species here, hard and soft, including sponges, brain and fan corals – over 500 types of fish inhabit the waters. The larger denizens include whale shark, barracuda, manta rays and giant octopus, while there are countless brightly coloured reef fish. Another major attraction is the green turtle population, actively encouraged in this haven by a serious conservation programme that involves the active co-operation of local fishermen. Also to be seen is the occasional dugong – the fabled sea cow said to be the inspiration behind mermaid legends.

DON'T MISS
It's possible to see chimps acclimatized to human presence in nearby Gombe Stream National Park.

MAHALE MOUNTAINS

Eastern Africa/Tanzania

The Mahale Mountains National Park represents the heart of Africa unspoilt, a place with no roads, covering 1,600 sq km (620 sq mi) of lakeshore and spectacular upland terrain, with beaches and azure water easily mistaken for those of an Indian Ocean paradise island. The added dimension is mysterious, jungle-clad mountains that tower above the lake.
The park is home to around 800 chimpanzees, one of the largest cohesive populations left in Africa. There's every chance of a sighting – about 60 of them belong to the M Group, which has become used to humans as a result of a research programme dating back to the 1960s.
Some visitors may get no further than the waterside – swimming, snorkelling or fishing in the pristine waters of the world's least-polluted freshwater lake. Others will be seduced by camping safaris to the interior, where forested slopes are home to an amazing array of colourful birds and easily observed red colobus, red-tailed, and blue monkeys. Most will want to do a bit of both, to wring every last drop of rewarding experience from the trip of a lifetime.

RUAHA NATIONAL PARK

Eastern Africa/Tanzania

Ruaha is a vast wilderness of semi-arid bush country that is home to a teeming population of animals and birds. Africa's most iconic animals are here in numbers. The park has 10,000 elephants, the greatest number in any East African park. There are giraffe, zebras galore, many large lion prides, leopard, cheetah, hippo and crocodile, along with numerous great kudu – characterized by the males' magnificent corkscrew horns. Among other species to be seen are lesser kudu, striped and spotted hyena, packs of rare African wild dogs, roan antelope, impala and waterbuck. The bird population is impressive too, boasting some 450 different species.

DON'T MISS

The nearby Stone Age ruins at Isimila, 15 km (9 mi) west of Iringa, dating back 60,000 years.

SERENGETI

Eastern Africa/Tanzania

WORTH A DETOUR: Fascinating rock paintings executed by the indigenous Maasai people – ask in the village of Kolo for a guide to the cave site.

Tanzania's largest, oldest and most popular national park is a world-famous UNESCO World Heritage Site – with good reason. For Serengeti is home to one of the most awesome events in the animal world, when six million hooves pound the plains during an annual migration that sends a million wildebeest, 300,000 Thomson's gazelle and 200,000 zebra in search of fresh grazing to support a population explosion of 8,000 calves every day, before the 1,000 km (620 mi) return journey sorts out the weak from the strong. The 40 km (25 mi) columns of animals are a moving spectacle as they brave crocodile-infested river crossings to fulfil their annual destiny, but Serengeti has much more to offer. This land of parched savannah, wooded hills, termite mounds and orange dust has different faces, becoming transformed in the rainy season to a green expanse spangled with flowers. The variety of wildlife is extraordinary and this is one of the best places in Africa to watch game doing its own thing in the wild. Apart from the great migration, a highlight of any visit is the sight of one of the great predators pursuing a kill. The park has lion, leopard, cheetah, buffalo, giraffe, elephant, rhino, eland, topi, impala, jackal, hyena and many more, right down to the insect-eating aardwolf. There are also at least 500 bird species.

The park is so vast that even a full complement of visitors can quickly vanish into the blue yonder, allowing everyone so minded to enjoy undisturbed solitude in this wonderful wilderness.

THE KITULO PLATEAU

Eastern Africa/Tanzania

WORTH A DETOUR: Matema Beach – a fabulous spot on the shore of Lake Nyasa, a half-day hike from the park. It has two affordable church-run hostels.

The glittering jewel in the crown of Tanzania's Southern Highlands is the Kitulo Plateau. Locals call it Bustani ya Mungu – the Garden of God – and anyone lucky enough to reach this enchanting place will instantly understand why it has earned that name. For this is where one of the world's most impressive floral displays may be seen during the rainy season. Around 350 types of vascular plant erupt into a botanical spectacle of extraordinary diversity from November onwards, dazzling visitors with sheer variety and scale. Prominent alongside 45 different ground orchids are plants such as aloes, asters, geraniums, giant lobelias, lilies and brilliant red-hot pokers, together creating a riot of competing colour.

The plateau levels out at 2,600 m (8,530 ft) and is protected by Kitulo National Park, which extends to an area of around 415 sq km (160 sq mi). This is an important watershed for the Great Ruaha River, with well-watered volcanic soils supporting the country's most important montane grassland. In addition to this rolling grassland, the area has rounded hills, rivers, waterfalls, crater lakes and forest. Visitors should aim to find the Numbi Valley, a picturesque spot where small streams emerge from grassy hillsides as if by magic. There are good hiking trails on the plateau, giving access to flowers and a vibrant bird population. The latter is so beguiling that it attracts birdwatchers who see Kitulo's flowers and brilliant butterflies as a great backdrop to the main attraction – rare birds such as Denham's bustard, blue swallow, and Cisticola njombe.

DON'T MISS
A guided night walk in the forest.

KIBALE FOREST

Eastern Africa/Uganda

It's a primary primate destination – a beautiful 775-sq km (300-sq mi) tract of preserved Ugandan tropical rainforest that supports no fewer than 13 primate species, from chimpanzees to several types of Central African monkey, such as L'Hoest's, Ugandan red colobus and Ugandan mangabey. A network of shaded trails offers almost unlimited hiking possibilities within the forest, also giving opportunities to visitors with a specialist interest. Birdwatchers are drawn by over 300 species, including African grey parrots, noisy hornbills, African pitas, green-breasted pitas and the endemic Prirogrine's ground thrush. Lepidopterists are attracted by shimmering displays of butterflies while botanists (including university researchers) come for the varied flora. In addition to seeing numerous agile primates, animal watchers may be delighted by occasional encounters with buffalo, leopard, bush pig, otter or assorted antelopes. The park's forest elephants (smaller and hairier than plains counterparts) commute to and fro from Kibale to the adjacent Queen Elizabeth National Park, the two protected areas together providing one of the country's most important ecotourism areas. In fact, the latter is Uganda's most-visited game reserve.

KIDEPO VALLEY

Eastern Africa/Uganda

WORTH A DETOUR:
A visit to the local Karamajong community, which welcomes visitors interested in their timeless way of life. Cultural entertainers will put on a splendid show of traditional dancing for a small fee.

The Kidepo Valley National Park in the Karamoja region is tucked away in Uganda's northeastern corner, where it meets Sudan. It's the country's most remote national park, boasting rugged landscapes unsurpassed in any other. Kidepo is the ultimate destination for true lovers of unspoilt wild places, for this pristine 1,500-sq km (580-sq mi) wilderness of semi-arid valleys is little visited by tourists. Indeed, the word best used to describe those who do make the pilgrimage is 'adventurers'.

Many determined travellers who make the effort needed to visit Kidepo Valley are birdwatchers – often as part of organized ornithological expeditions – attracted by the huge variety of feathered species (around 475) to be found in the varied habitat of semi-desert scrub, open thorn scrub, grassy savannas, assorted woodland and granite outcrops. Among 'specials' not found in any other Ugandan park are some of East Africa's rarest birds, including the Karamoja apalis and black-breasted barbet. But the range is eye watering, from ostrich down to a huge variety of colourful songbirds, with an awesome selection of birds of prey. The animal population suffered during Uganda's catastrophic Idi Amin years, but has recovered. Over 80 mammal species live in Kidepo, including nearly 30 found in no other park. Along with rarities like the bat-eared fox and caracal, visitors can expect to spot the likes of giraffe, elephant, buffalo, lion, leopard, cheetah, reedbuck, waterbuck, kongoni, orobis, kudu, klipspringer, dik dik, zebra, warthog, jackal and mongoose, plus a healthy reptile population.

LAKE MBURO

Eastern Africa/Uganda

DON'T MISS
The Haunted Forest
at Okaukuezo.

For a small national park by African standards, with an area of just 260 sq km (100 sq mi), Lake Mburo offers a very special experience. There are actually five lakes within the park – home to hippos, crocodiles and numerous water birds. The lakes are fringed with swamps that give sanctuary to papyrus specialists like the Sitatunga antelope and the rare Papyrus gonolek, a striking red, black and yellow bird.

This gives a clue to Lake Mburo National Park's key attractions – animal watching and birdwatching. This part of Uganda is covered in acacia woodland, with rich biodiversity supporting its own distinctive fauna. Those intent on seeing a wide variety of game will not be disappointed. There are nearly 70 species of animal to be found within the park, including Uganda's most visible population of giant eland plus impala, topi, the rare

roan antelope, zebra and buffalo, with predators like leopard, jackal and hyena waiting to pounce on all but the fittest. Birders have 360 recorded species to pursue, including half a dozen forest rarities and 60 different water birds. The park has strategically placed hides overlooking salt licks where animals may constantly be observed coming and going, while boat trips on Lake Mburo provide an unmissable perspective on the park's flora on fauna, including those wily crocs, hippos and birds such as pelican, fish eagle and the rare shoebill stork.

WORTH A DETOUR:
Mungilo Waterfall, just
outside the park boundary.

SEMULIKI VALLEY

Eastern Africa/Uganda

This remote section of the Semuliki Forest in western Uganda is an extension of the Congo's vast Ituri Forest. It provides a wonderful chance to escape Uganda's regular tourist circuit and experience the only real jungle in East Africa.

The very best way of enjoying Semuliki Valley is to camp within the park and spend time exploring on foot. A hike along the winding Semuliki River will seem like paradise for birdwatchers, while everyone can enjoy the bright butterflies and perhaps glimpse animals such as pygmy hippo, crocodile, forest elephant, buffalo, leopard and assorted primates (including chimps). For anglers, the river offers great sport fishing. There are campsites within the park (tents supplied or bring your own).

One unmissable highlight is Semuliki's hot springs, located in a section of mineral-rich swamp land that attracts a fascinating variety of wildlife and is served by a network of trails. The highlights are a jet of super-heated water and pool of boiling water that bubbles up from the depths. The park's party trick is to take some food and boil it on site – eggs a speciality.

Right: Semuliki Valley

AKAGERA NATIONAL PARK

Eastern Africa/Rwanda

WORTH A DETOUR: The opportunity to camp alongside one of Akagera's lakes, where pods of hippos splutter and grunt, large crocodiles sunbathe, and assorted wildlife comes to drink.

The most remote source of the Nile is northeast Rwanda's Akagera River, meandering through a landscape of lakes and swamps on the Tanzanian border. In 1936 a 2,500-sq km (965-sq mi) area to the west of the river was reserved to form Akagera National Park.

All the classic African animals were well represented, including hippo, crocodile, lion, leopard, elephant, giraffe, zebra and many types of antelope, along with a stunning bird population numbering around 500 species. But the preservation of this fabulous place was inevitably set back by the tragic events of the 1990s, when over a million Rwandans died as a result of ethnically motivated genocide. Refugees returning after the civil war flooded the savannah and this severe human pressure drove much of the wildlife back into the park's more remote areas.

However, this remains big game country with every chance of spotting the big ones – giraffe, elephant, buffalo and zebra herds, plus occasional lions and leopards on the prowl. A dozen species of antelope still inhabit the park, including impala and the statuesque Cape eland.

WHEN TO GO: Prime dry season months for forest hiking are December and January or June–August.

NYUNGWE FOREST

Eastern Africa/Rwanda

Southwestern Rwanda's Nyungwe National Park contains the largest tract of montane forest left in East or Central Africa. Nyungwe Forest with its high canopy is a wonderland of 250 types of tree including ebonies and mahoganies, towering tree ferns, tangled vegetation and orchids galore. Notable among the flora is the spectacular giant lobelia.

Nyungwe is home to 275 bird species, countless butterflies, 80 different mammals including 13 primate species, plus assorted amphibians and reptiles. Birders will spot feathered gems, with 24 specials endemic to this part of the Rift Valley high on the list. These include giant hornbills, great blue turacos and red-breasted sparrowhawks. Looking for primates is hugely satisfying, with chimpanzees a popular quarry.

WHEN TO GO: Any time (it was famously said of the Virungas by Dian Fossey that 'they're so high up that you shiver more than you sweat').

VOLCANOES NATIONAL PARK

Eastern Africa/Rwanda

In the far northwest of Rwanda, towering to an impressive 4,500 m (14,760 ft), the Virunga Mountains are home to the oh-so-rare mountain gorilla. The flanks of this rugged range are protected by Volcanoes National Park – Africa's first national park, gazetted in 1925 to protect those priceless primates.

The gorillas were saved from extinction after American primatologist Dian Fossey brought their plight to international attention. She founded the Karisoke Research Centre in the 1960s and devoted her life to studying these amazing animals. She was murdered at her home in 1985 – probably by poachers – and is buried in the park among a gorilla population that owes its continued existence to her efforts. Seeing these magnificent but gentle creatures up close in their natural habitat is a deeply moving experience, and a fitting memorial to Fossey, whose story was told in the film *Gorillas in the Mist*.

NANKHUMBA PENINSULA

Southern Africa/Malawi

Malawi is landlocked, but it certainly isn't short of water – the country is dominated by and shares a name with Africa's third-largest lake, which is surrounded by exceptional landscapes characterized by high mountains, plateaux, rocky outcrops and sensational vistas.

One of the most attractive sections of Lake Malawi's long shoreline is Nankhumba Peninsula at the picturesque southern end. It's a serious tourist destination, capitalizing on the lake's undoubted charms. Lake Malawi National Park encompasses the peninsula's northern tip and is a UNESCO World Heritage Site, the citation referring to its importance in the study of evolution as a result of the incredibly varied endemic fish population. The park is also home to important Neolithic sites, but the fish are the main attraction, providing an extraordinary display of kaleidoscopic colour and seeming entirely devoid of fear, feeding from the hand and swirling boldly around snorkellers. But the lake is (much!) bigger than the park's relatively unobtrusive tourist facilities and the peninsula as a whole remains an achingly beautiful place.

WORTH A DETOUR: Chembe village on Cape Maclear – a fishing community at the end of a dirt road from Monkey Bay with basic facilities, offering an ideal opportunity to see how the locals live.

NYIKA NATIONAL PARK

Southern Africa/Malawi

Malawi's largest national park covers an area of 3,200 sq km (1,235 sq mi) and this unique wild place does just what the name suggests. The translation of Nyika is 'source of the water' and the national park is indeed one of the country's most important catchments. It extends across a great plateau in northern Malawi and is a vast granite dome hosting an environment like no other in Africa, consisting of rolling grassy hills interspersed with wooded valleys, surrounded by steep escarpments.

The grasslands are richly endowed with wild flowers, including over 200 types of orchid, and the montane vegetation attracts large numbers of antelopes – which in turn serve as a generous larder for one of Central Africa's most concentrated leopard populations. The occasional lion or elephant may be seen, along with zebra and smaller animals like bush pig or warthog. Over 400 species of bird have been recorded in Nyika National Park. Notable among these are the endemic red-winged francolin, wattled crane and rare Denham's bustard.

The park attracts specialist visitors like birdwatchers and landscape photographers, but also makes a superb destination for those who simply want to get away from civilization and enjoy this atmospheric wilderness, which is often shrouded in cloud during the rainy season. There are all sorts of attractions to be found, such as a Neolithic shelter, waterfalls, trout pools and the pretty Lake Kaulime. The area may be explored from park headquarters at Chelina Camp, in the centre of the Nyika Plateau, where the log-cabin lodge provides good accommodation that makes a perfect base. Safaris may be undertaken on foot, mountain-bike or horseback, and 4x4 excursions are the easiest way to see as much as possible of this striking country if time is limited.

HOW TO GET THERE:
Access is by one dirt road branching off the highway to Katumbi border post, some 60 km (37 mi) north of the town of Rumphi. It continues across the plateau (where it delineates the border with Zambia) before reaching Chisenga border post.

WHEN TO GO:
In the rainy season (November–April) to see Nyika's fabulous display of wild flowers.

WORTH A DETOUR:
A side trip to Vwaza Marsh Game Reserve – just 50 km (31 mi) south of Nyiki. This remote reserve is not much visited, but its mopane and miombo woodland provides an exceptional opportunity to view a great variety of animals and rich birdlife.

YOU SHOULD KNOW
A small 80-sq km (31-sq mi) section of the Nyika Plateau (also called Nyika National Park) falls inside Zambia, but there is no road access so all visitors from that side of the border have to travel via Malawi to see Zambia's own small but perfectly formed wild gem.

DON'T MISS
Emperor's View – one
of the very finest viewpoints.

ZOMBA PLATEAU

Southern Africa/Malawi

In the south of Malawi is a great massif that rises to 1,800 m (5,900 ft). It supports vast tracts of cypress, cedar and pine woodland, interspersed with a riot of mixed vegetation. Although there are plenty of animals and birds galore, Zomba is not the place to attract dedicated wildlife-watchers – the animals are shy and, although leopards, bushbuck or baboons may occasionally be glimpsed, the cover is so dense that such events are a rarity. However, one type of impressive sighting is guaranteed – brilliantly coloured giant butterflies are everywhere – and more visible birds include the ubiquitous white-necked raven and green louries with their vivid red underwings.

But the main attraction here is stunning scenery. Colonizing Brits in pith helmets once described the sweeping panoramas to be seen from Zomba Plateau as 'The finest views in the British Empire' and it's breathtakingly apparent why they came to that bold conclusion. Far-reaching vistas overlook Lake Chilwa to the north, Shire River to the west and Mount Mulanje to the southeast.

Most of the plateau is managed by Malawi's Department of Forestry, which is doing a fairly sensitive job that respects the original ecosystem. This means that a good network of dirt roads exists, which is ideal for 4x4 sightseeing excursions around this wonderland of tumbling streams, waterfalls and lakes. Other popular recreational activities are trout fishing in season, hiking and horseback riding. For those tempted to spend more than a day enjoying this unique landscape, there is a luxury hotel on the edge of the plateau, along with a large campsite with facilities.

CHIMANIMANI MOUNTAINS
Southern Africa/Mozambique

WORTH A DETOUR: The spectacular waterfall of the Muvumodzi River within the reserve (also known as the Martin Falls), plunging dramatically into a deep, rocky bowl.

This rugged range – part of a chain stretching from Cape Town to the high mountains of East Africa – straddles the frontier between Mozambique and Zimbabwe, mostly falling within the Chimanimani Transfrontier Conservation Area. Tourism may be a major contributor to the area's future but for now it is still a truly wild place – with lushly forested slopes that provide the opportunity to explore on foot and highlands that remain a wilderness – that progress seems to have passed by.

The biodiversity of the Chimanimani Mountains is legendary, but to enjoy their solitude it is first necessary to leave the cultivated areas around villages behind. Local guides are easily found, and essential for everything

but the most cursory day hike. For anything longer, it is sensible to hire porters who will act both as guides and carry camping equipment. With their help, it is possible to reach the plateau with its sensational rock formations and far-reaching views, where curious animals such as klipspringers are likely to take a close look at the intruders to their lofty domain. Elephants are quite common lower down, where the forest birdlife is abundant.

DON'T MISS
Groups of traditional fishermen netting fish from the shore.

MAPUTO SPECIAL RESERVE
Southern Africa/Mozambique

Around 80 km (50 mi) south of Mozambique's capital of Maputo is a world apart from the bustling city with its teeming streets, cultural diversity and fascinating museums. Although sharing its name, the Maputo Special Reserve on Santa Maria Peninsula in the country's southern part is an area of outstanding natural beauty forming part of the Lubombo Transfrontier Conservation Area – a grouping of national parks from South Africa, Swaziland and Mozambique itself.

In the aftermath of prolonged civil war Mozambique is some way behind its neighbours in catering for the well-heeled local and international visitors who will eventually transform the national economy. But there's a downside to go with the fact that the reserve therefore remains wild and unspoilt by over-exploitation for tourism. That downside is that a 1975 stocking of the reserve from South Africa's Umfolozi Game Reserve introduced a huge population of elephant and rhino that perished in the war. Just 200 elephants and no rhinos survived the conflict. However, numbers are now recovering well with a splendid selection of wildlife – such as elephant herds, hippos, leopards, lions, antelope, zebra, armadillos and red squirrels.

QUIRIMBAS ARCHIPELAGO
Southern Africa/Mozambique

Northern Mozambique's Quirimbas Archipelago is a mesmerizing chain of 31 islands in the Indian Ocean that contains some of the world's richest coral reefs, supporting a fabulous array of marine life that equals snorkelling and scuba-diving heaven. Still, the archipelago's seductive attractions are a relatively well-kept secret and these enchanting tropical islands have never been seriously exploited for tourism and remain a conservation jewel all but untouched by intrusive development.

The islands stretch from the coastal town of Pemba up to Cape Delgado and the Tanzanian border, a distance of around 320 km (200 mi). Some are linked to the mainland by coral reefs, sandbars and mangroves. The fortunate few who stray from the beaten track to pay one or more of them a visit are richly rewarded. It won't always be so, for Mozambique's proactive Ministry of Tourism is busy planning a serious campaign to make the most effective economic use of the country's abundant natural wonders, with the buzzword being 'ecotourism'.

It doesn't come much more eco that the Quirimbas. These fine islands – some tiny, some uninhabited, some with lodges built of local materials that hardly seem to intrude on the beauty that surrounds them – are formed of rugged coral punctuated by golden beaches where it is truly possible to feel isolated. Key islands include Ibo, Quisiva and Matemo, which harbour former Portuguese outposts that supplanted pre-colonial settlements – a striking example being Stone Town on Ibo, a monument to Swahili culture over the centuries.

WORTH A DETOUR:
The Bazaruto Archipelago, to the south, where you can see the fabled dugong, or sea cow.

KASANKA NATIONAL PARK

Southern Africa/Zambia

This is not a national park in the conventional sense, for Kasanka in Zambia's Central Province is operated by a non-profit-making charitable trust that aims to secure the park's biodiversity and make it self-sustaining with the help of carefully managed tourism. The park has assorted habitats – lakes, rivers, swamps, dambos (shallow drainage channels), riverine forest, grassland – and is handsomely endowed with the miombo woodlands characteristic of the area.

Despite being relatively small at 450 sq km (175 sq mi), Kasanka is a well-preserved wilderness that serves as a haven for many endangered species – including Sitatunga antelope and blue monkeys from the animal kingdom, plus Ross's lourie and wattled crane from the wonderful world of birds, which here numbers over 400 recorded species. This figure underlines the fact that Kasanka has a rich diversity of flora and fauna. There are no vast herds of animals but it's possible to spot a variety of interesting creatures. In addition to the rarities, visitors can look for hartebeest, antelope, bush pig, warthog, duiker, baboon, leopard, waterbuck, reedbuck, hippo, crocodile, otter, elephant, jackal, civet, mongoose and more.

There are three affordable campsites with basic facilities in the park. It is wise to check in advance rather than simply turning up, as conditions may preclude camping, or all three sites may be fully booked. It is also possible to stay at one of Kasanka's two lodges, an option which many combine with a trip to nearby Shebill Island Camp in the vast Bangweulu Wetlands. Local lodges offer the choice of budget self-catering chalets or a more expensive full-board package.

YOU SHOULD KNOW

Petty crime is a problem in Zambia, with bag-snatching, mugging and thefts from parked cars not uncommon.

WHEN TO GO:

November and December when Kasanka sees a spectacular congregation of several million fruit bats. The least favoured months are January–May.

LOWER ZAMBEZI NATIONAL PARK
Southern Africa/Zambia

YOU SHOULD KNOW

Fishing (for tiger fish, bream and vundu catfish) is popular. The canny locals have discovered that pungent cheap soap is a top bait.

Still relatively undeveloped, Zambia's newest national park is an unspoilt wilderness that extends to an impressive 4,000 sq km (1,545 sq mi). It lies some 450 km (280 mi) downriver from Victoria Falls, where the mighty Zambezi River crosses the fertile floodplains of the Lower Zambezi Valley. Across the river is Zimbabwe's Mana Pools Reserve, and the two parks combine to create a huge wildlife sanctuary. There is a steep escarpment along the northern boundary of the park, confining most animals to the plain. The river's edge is characterized by lush vegetation, the floodplain is fringed with winterthorn trees and mopane forest, while broadleaf woodland cloaks the surrounding hills.

There may not be as many different animal species in Lower Zambezi National Park as can be found in some other parks, but they are present in vast quantities and this place offers keen wildlife-watchers a unique experience. This involves taking to the water and observing the likes of abundant hippos, large elephant herds, crocodile, impala, buffalo, zebra, kudu, puku antelope and baboons, all seeming relatively unfussed by waterborne intruders, thus allowing canoeists to get very close. The birdlife is exceptional with a huge variety of species to be spotted, including fish eagles, trumpeter hornbill, Meyer's parrot, Lilian's lovebird, crested guinea fowl, black eagle and vast flocks of quelea.

Day safaris are offered by park lodges – guided or unguided – that allow adventurous visitors to drift downstream at a leisurely pace all day, before being spared the need to paddle back by the arrival of the lodge's motorboat as dusk approaches with the welcome offer of a return tow.

WORTH A DETOUR:
If there's one place where the cost of booking a bushcamp or safari lodge is justified by the return, this is it – the park has some of the very best in Africa.

SESRIEM CANYON AND SOSSUSVLEI

Southern Africa/Namibia

WORTH A DETOUR:
The rock formations
and caves within the
Sesriem Canyon – a vivid
geological record written in
sedimentary rock, and the
habitat of eagle owls.

The dunes of the Namib Desert are 30 million years old. Whipped by fierce winds into sharp, undulating ridges like colossal red-and-black waves in a granulated ocean, they cover 32,500 sq km (12,550 sq mi), stretching 300 km (186 mi) north up Namibia's coast from Luderitz, and as much as 140 km (87 mi) inland. Nowhere in that vast region are their changing colours and moods more spectacular than in the alien magnificence of Sossusvlei. These are the tallest dunes in the world, over 300 m (1,000 ft). Just to gaze on them is humbling. Between the hours of dawn and dusk they might be coloured blood red, lilac, palest gold, deep yellow or intense orange like rust; and shadowed by a patchwork of soft blue and green, deepening to ultramarine and black.

Incredibly, the bone-dry Sossusvlei dunes mark the estuary of the Tsauchab River, swamped in mid-flow by the encroaching desert. The river evaporates into white clay pans like Dead Vlei and Nara Vlei on the edge of Sossusvlei. Sometimes enough water reaches the pans to provide a mirror reflecting some of Africa's most spectacular views, and to bring the desert alive with flowers and birds. But visitors may not stay here: camping is a 63 km (39 mi) drive 'upriver' at Sesriem. A trail from the campsites leads to the 40 m (131 ft) deep and 1 km (0.6 mi) long Sesriem Canyon, carved over a million years by the Tsauchab River. Even from a few metres' distance, the canyon is invisible among the camelthorn trees and scrub. In many places its walls almost meet overhead, and the pools of water it retains are a magnet for birds and animals.

YOU SHOULD KNOW
Visitors clever enough to book a campsite at Sesriem during high season may enter Sossusvlei an hour before sunrise, which means getting a very privileged view of the dunes and their denizens.

SKELETON COAST
Southern Africa/Namibia

WHEN TO GO:
Any time. From May–September a strong wind blows the fog further inland, bringing moisture and reviving plant and animal life.

The Bushmen called it 'The Land God Made in Anger'. To the Portuguese it was 'The Gates of Hell'. The Skeleton Coast used to mean the whole of Namibia's Atlantic coastline. Now it refers to the 20,000 sq km (7,720 sq mi) National Park that protects the northern one third of Namibia's coast, from the Ugab River to the Angolan border. It is an untouched world shrouded in chilling mists and prolonged fog. The cold Benguela Current sweeps north, pushing Antarctic air into the arid African heat. Although it never freezes, the Skeleton Coast is spitefully inhospitable – but it is a sanctuary to fur seals and marine and wading birds for which the nutrient-rich sea is a perpetually full larder. Inland, huge crescent, hummock and transverse dune systems lie between canyons of rust-coloured rock; and in this rainless transition zone, desert scrub is watered by the mist. It's the transition that brings so much wildlife to the area. Rare desert elephants live here, with oryx, springbok, giraffe, ostrich, hyena, black rhino and even lion. Most find refuge in the depths of the canyons and dry river beds where the temperature is higher – pursuers and pursued using the foggy world for hunting cover.

YOU SHOULD KNOW

The Skeleton Coast is literally a geological jewel. Some of its beaches, especially near Mowe Bay, consist of gemstones polished by wave action.

Between the Hoanib and Kunene Rivers the Skeleton Coast may only be visited as part of a 'fly-in safari' that must be organized by a government-licensed concessionary. This northern section is where the coast's hostile reputation is confirmed. The shore is littered with long-ago shipwrecks, surreal sculptures of mechanical bones wedged in the sands. Somehow they are simultaneously pathetic and magnificent: failures in a contest with the raw power of unforgiving nature. Yet for some of Africa's most threatened creatures, the harsh struggle to stay alive here is their shield. The dynamism of that wilderness struggle is what brings visitors.

SPITZKOPPE

Southern Africa/Namibia

YOU SHOULD KNOW

Spitzkoppe is famous among photographers for its fabulous colours and shapes. In Namibia, the massif is considered so beautiful and unusual that images of it inspire a kind of reverence.

WORTH A DETOUR:

The various sites of Bushmen rock paintings. The most complex – and complete – are at 'Bushman's Paradise', where you use a chain handhold to clamber up a smooth slope to see them, on the underside of a long rocky overhang.

On the flat, arid scrub desert of Namibia's coastal plain between Usakos and Swakopmund, Spitzkoppe rears on the horizon as the jagged silhouette of a sleeping dinosaur. Sometimes called the 'Matterhorn of Namibia', the granite massif is the eroded remnant of a volcano that collapsed 100 million years ago. Its twin peaks reach 1,800 m and 1,584 m (5,905 ft and 5,197 ft), but their effect is made much more dramatic by rising, sheer, over 700 m (2,300 ft) above the plain. Wind and rain have sculpted the rocks into weird and wonderful formations, carving out gullies and caves which harbour unusual flora like the yellow butter tree and the poison tree, which oozes a white sap used by Bushmen to poison their hunting arrows. Several sheltered rock faces carry ancient paintings by this indigenous San people.

Spitzkoppe is a magnet for experienced climbers, who over the years have established a system of permanent lines for hikers to pull themselves over rocky obstacles along the various trails. This opens up the mountain for less athletic visitors. There are so many trails to so many beautiful, hidden corners, and they cater to every level of fitness. They lead to spectacular views across the plains to the Pondok Mountains (the

name comes from the Afrikaans for 'looks like an African hut'), or to vistas along the spine of the Klein Spitzkoppe 10 km (6 mi) to the west. Climbing is much harder than it may look. Even for experts the rock can be too hot to touch, and the round, weathered surfaces defy any sane grip – but outside the summer there are climbing tours to the summit which require spending three nights on the mountain. The less committed will be content with the lower campsites sited in isolated privacy among boulders.

SIBEBE ROCK

Southern Africa/Swaziland

WHEN TO GO:
June–November, when the
western highlands are drier
but cooler.

Swaziland is landlocked by Mozambique to the east and South Africa everywhere else. It's a topographical jigsaw, with highlands predominant in the west, and hot, dry lowlands to the east, both crammed into an area no bigger than Wales in the UK or New Jersey in the USA. In a single day visitors can easily drive from the cool mountains, forests and waterfalls of the highveld, through hilly central grasslands, to the open savannah of acacia and broadleaf and the baking bushveld of stunted thickets, knobthorn and dry riverine forests. Many drive straight through to South Africa, cheating themselves of some of Africa's loveliest landscapes, and missing world-class geological oddities for which Swaziland is famous.

Outside Mbabane, Swaziland's capital at the northern end of the Ezulwini Valley, a gravel road follows the Mbuluzi River as it winds down the incomparable Pine Valley. The villages and rondavel homesteads seem to grow naturally out of this pastoral beauty: it's made for hiking or horse riding. Then quite suddenly, as river and road loop round a protruding bluff of smooth rock, the trees and shrubs fall away to reveal the bald rock crown of a truly massive granite dome pushing into the blue sky. This is Sibebe, second only to Australia's Uluru as the world's largest single rock. Close-to, it's impossible to guess its real size.

The colossal granite monolith is only visible from far away, sheer on all sides, and unbroken anywhere except by gullies formed by erosion. It's even more spectacular from its own summit. It feels like being on top of the world, with views (on a clear day) as far east as the great 'big five' game reserves of Hlane and Mkhaya, and to the south, the twin peaks called Sheba's Breasts, the legendary site of King Solomon's Mines. Informally, Swazis call Sibebe Rock 'the tumescence of Swaziland' – and they might not be joking.

YOU SHOULD KNOW

Swaziland is sometimes called Africa's last truly traditional kingdom. 'Kingship', personified in the Swazi royal family, is also a mystical notion that informs everyone's daily life and provides the glue securing traditional culture to modern customs. The whole country stops for two major annual rituals – the Incwala, or sacred ceremony of Kingship, and the Umhlanga Reed Dance, in which unmarried girls collect reeds (umhlanga) to make a symbolic windbreak demonstrating their protective loyalty to the Queen Mother, known universally as Indlovukazi, or 'She-Elephant'.

KGALAGADI TRANSFRONTIER PARK

Southern Africa/Namibia

HIGHLIGHTS:
The Gemsbok Wilderness Trail, Mabuasehube Wilderness Trail, or the Nossob 4×4 Eco Trail, each of which is expertly planned to take in the highlights of different areas and habitats.

Formerly known as Kalahari Gemsbok National Park, Kgalagadi is a joint enterprise by Botswana and South Africa on their Namibian border. With only five park entrances from the three countries, visitors may have to jump through a few bureaucratic hoops to fulfil border as well as park controls. Frankly, it's worth every effort to gain access to one of Africa's and the world's great open wilderness areas.

In size alone Kgalagadi represents the rare phenomenon of an entire ecosystem with minimal human interference. The park covers 36,000 sq km (13,900 sq mi) of semi-desert savannah, red dune systems, acacia scrub and woodland, and endless sparse tracts of Kalahari couch grass covered in camelthorn bushes. They are landscapes that belong naturally to huge herds of antelope, and visitors will find migrating oryx, blue wildebeest, grey duiker, red hartebeest, steenbok, impala, gemsbok and the occasional rare eland.

Where they go, the predators follow. No campfire is complete without an evening serenade of the grunts, screams, snarls and coughing roars belonging to some of Africa's most famous carnivores, but a much better time to see them is around midday when leopard, cheetah, spotted hyena and the giant, black-maned Kalahari lion can often be found resting in the shade of camelthorn or acacia trees. Mammals of all sizes concentrate in or near the dry courses of the Auob and Nossob Rivers, including meerkat, pangolin (aka the scaly anteater), honey badger and bat-eared fox. The Nossob is also a byword for spotting an unusual variety of raptors, like the bateleur, snake eagle, lappet-faced vulture, pygmy falcon, kestrel, kite and pale chanting goshawk.

With 200 other migratory and resident species, the birds participate in Kgalagadi's magnificent annual cycle of regeneration. The visitor's privilege is to be able to follow its wildlife cast of millions, playing out the game of life in all its glorious, gory detail. Amazing.

YOU SHOULD KNOW
Visitors must plan their day to reach their destination before sundown. Driving or any kind of travelling at night is forbidden.

TSODILO HILLS

Southern Africa/Botswana

WORTH A DETOUR:
The Tsodilo Hills paintings aren't the only demonstrations of ancient ideas: in one of the rock grottos on 'the female' (from which the gods ruled the world) the stones have been crudely fashioned into a 2 m (7 ft) high, and 6 m (20 ft) long, python's head.

From a distance the desert horizon is a flat line broken by a series of quartzite cliffs rising sheer from the savannah to 410 m (1,345 ft). This is the highest peak in Botswana, and one of four in a line of descending height called the Tsodilo Hills. Standing alone in the western corner of the Kalahari Desert, in Ngamiland near the edge of the Okavango swamps, the hills have a history to match their geological oddity. Alternately baked and scoured by freezing winds, they are the repository of the world's biggest collection of indigenous rock paintings, the summary of 100,000 years of known religious worship and sacred ritual. Throughout that time the Tsodilo Hills have been physical representations of the San Bushmen's spiritual culture. According to height, they are 'the male', 'the female' and 'the child' (with the nameless fourth knoll ascribed to 'the male's first, discarded wife') in the San creation myth, and the resting place of ancestral spirits. Even now, a San guide taking visitors to what is known collectively as the 'Rock that Whispers' will first ask 'permission' from the hill deities to do so. The 4,500 rock paintings (and thousands of other artefacts) are spread between 400 sites across 10 sq km (3.8 sq mi) of the hills. Most of them, including the best, are on the northern side of 'the female' and, significantly, they are different in style and content from any other known rock art. The feeling of being in a place of mystery and magic can be overwhelming: visitors may come for the archaeology or the cultural aesthetics, but they leave with a profound sense of human indomitability. By investing their enduring faith in these barren, inhospitable and isolated hills, the San Bushmen have created an ark of beauty out of burning hot rock.

YOU SHOULD KNOW

Some visitors feel the atmosphere so keenly they cannot bear to stay in the area. Many report feeling an 'unlooked-for empathy' with the San belief that hunting or causing death of any kind in the vicinity will bring misfortune.

SEHLABATHEBE NATIONAL PARK

Southern Africa/Lesotho

YOU SHOULD KNOW

With a pre-arranged permit, camping is allowed throughout the park.

WHEN TO GO:

Any time. Summer rain means frequent thick mists; but it is cold in winter and light snow is common.

If the 'Kingdom of the Sky' has a garden, it is Sehlabathebe National Park, an impossibly remote, sub-alpine paradise protected by its average altitude of 2,450 m (8,038 ft) and its position on Lesotho's eastern border with South Africa, on the lip of the Drakensberg Escarpment.

A tectonic quirk raised the Sehlabathebe area higher than its surroundings, pushing a very rare outcrop of Clarens formation (cream-coloured) sandstone clear of the Drakensberg basalt which forms southern Africa's highest mountains immediately to the north.

Whittled by the Tsoelikane and other tributaries of the nascent Orange River to the west, the sandstone contributes sensational landscapes like near-vertical cliff faces, river gorges, weird rock formations riddled with caves, waterfalls, magnificent promontories looking over plateaux studded with small lakes – and the sandy sediments which fill its valleys and provide the mineral sustenance for some of the planet's loveliest open grasslands. There are marshes and meadows at every altitude, completing the conditions for an unusual range of biodiversity. Game is restricted to rhebuck, eland, baboons, oribi antelope, mongoose, otters, wild cats and jackals, but the birdlife is magnificent, especially in the highest tarns. With all this, and vast skies and distant views, Sehlabathebe makes gods of hikers and riders. There are no fences.

Sehlabathebe is a designated wilderness that shares a boundary with South Africa's uKhahlamba Drakensberg Park, and a position at the southern end of the 300 km (186 mi) Maloti-Drakensberg Transfrontier Project which rings north and east Lesotho. Although visitors bask in the park's remote perfection, the beautiful surrounding backcountry adds to the quality of the experience by reintroducing the human element. The wilderness survives only if the Basotho people can benefit from it.

TSEHLANYANE NATIONAL PARK

Southern Africa/Lesotho

Small by international standards, Tsehlanyane is the jewel in a much larger environmental scheme, and of growing importance to its ultimate success. The park covers 56 sq km (21.5 sq mi) of the highest and most rugged terrain in the Lesotho Highlands. Set deep in the Front Range of the Maloti Mountains, Tsehlanyane's plunging valleys have an altitude range of 1,940–3,112 m (6,365–10,210 ft) and are predominantly sub-alpine. Their beauty is not exclusive – the whole Maloti range is breathtaking – but it is of rare quality. Tsehlanyane includes one of Lesotho's very few remaining old-growth indigenous forests, and preserving it is proving crucial to the Maloti Mountains' role as a source of pure, fresh water, and to a high level of endemism.

The much larger scheme is the development of the Maloti-Drakensberg Transfrontier Project. Tsehlanyane and its environs represent a massive extension of a biological corridor that now runs for hundreds of miles around northern Lesotho along the Drakensberg range that forms its border with South Africa. It is a fragile ecosystem, challenged by human encroachment of every kind – but it's proving to be a model of sustainable development, benefiting the Basotho people as much as the wildlife. Already visitors to Tsehlanyane can see previously non-existent herds of migrating eland, troops of baboons, grey rhebuck and 20 other frequently sighted medium-sized mammals. Even leopards have returned. Yet Tsehlanyane is not a wholly pristine wilderness. There are still villages dotted about. The Maloti Mountains are full of archaeological sites charting Basotho culture over several millennia. Tsehlanyane's forests include che-che woodland and stands of berg bamboo among local flora and fauna that have direct cultural significance for the Basotho.

WORTH A DETOUR:
Riding. It's the ideal travel mode for the steep hillside trails. Tsehlanyane is full of streams, cascades and rock pools for a super-bracing dip, and a really stunning 39 km (24 mi) trail connects the park with Bokong Nature Reserve, perched on a cliff overlooking the Lepagoa Valley and home of the Lepagoa Falls.

TIMBAVATI GAME RESERVE

Southern Africa/South Africa

WORTH A DETOUR:
See the 'white lions' of Timbavati. Lion prides in the region carry the recessive gene which can result in an ultra pale-furred lion. Nobody can guarantee seeing one but doing so is the experience of a lifetime.

South Africa's Kruger National Park is an enormous wilderness showcasing Africa's most spectacular wildlife. Timbavati borders the Kruger's central section, one of a number of private concessions along the Kruger's length which benefit from having no fences to hinder game moving freely between them. Timbavati's 680 sq km (262 sq mi) of low bushveld is the meeting place of the mopane woodlands and the Timbavati floodplain. The combination of savannah grasslands and dense shelter makes the region one of southern Africa's best for viewing all kinds of game. Besides the 'big five' of lion, leopard, buffalo, elephant and rhino, visitors are almost certain to see impala, kudu, giraffe, baboons, zebra, monkeys, cheetah, hippos and crocodiles.

Early morning and late afternoon safaris are adventures into the real world of dangerous predators – and even from a vehicle it's not unusual to have to back off quickly if an elephant or buffalo feels threatened. Of course, getting as close as possible to some of Earth's greatest living creatures is the whole point.

Timbavati is organized so that it's never crowded, although it can feel like it during the dry season when three or four 4x4s are tracking game to the same waterhole. It takes expert knowledge to get the best from going on safari, which means staying at one of Timbavati's private lodges. Some are bushcamps, others are five-star luxury eco-resorts camouflaged in the vegetation next to waterholes for easy viewing. Each has a speciality, like night tours or river trips by dug-out canoe among crocodiles and Africa's most dangerous mammal, the hippo. Some are better placed to see the 500 bird species that regularly visit the Kruger and its environs.

DON'T MISS
Most of the camps
have special activities
for children, if needed.

MADIKWE

Southern Africa/South Africa

YOU SHOULD KNOW

The region of Madikwe is
immortalized in the works
of Herman Charles Bosman
(1905–1951), the South African
writer and poet. His most
famous story is called *The
Mafeking Road*, after the track
which runs straight through
the reserve.

Madikwe includes 750 sq km (290 sq mi) of acacia-studded grasslands and bushveld plains that disappear in a blue haze on the horizon, broken only by outcrops of burnished rock and the occasional solitary hill. It is a transition zone between the desperately arid Kalahari thornveld and the dense forests watered by a permanent river and seasonal wetlands in the foothills of the majestic Dwarsberg Mountains. Madikwe is how travellers imagine the African wilderness, with columns of elephant and buffalo shimmering under a heat haze, and the inky blackness of the night canopy. It supports a phenomenal number and variety of game: the biggest elephant herd outside the Kruger, and of buffalo anywhere; white and black rhinos; cheetah, giraffe, hyena, zebra, kudu, springbok and dozens of other species; and a mixture of desert, plains and wetland species among its 300 birds.

Madikwe's success as a reserve has been bolstered by Operation Phoenix, the world's biggest translocation programme. With the enthusiastic support of its residents, in little more than 20 years Madikwe has seen re-introduced species like wild dog and black rhino flourish and spread as former farm and ranching land was returned to a wilderness. Local enthusiasm has been crucial, and one of its cornerstones has been the local desire to create South Africa's 'best' reserve.

|AI-|AIS/RICHTERSVELD TRANSFRONTIER PARK

Southern Africa/South Africa

WHEN TO GO:
April–October. Depending on good rains, springtime (July to October) brings out the full floral splendour of |Ai-|Ais/Richtersveld.

Nobody does camouflage better than Nature. The unification of Namibia's |Ai-|Ais reserve and South Africa's Richtersveld appears to be the twinning of two equally inhospitable mountainous deserts that face each other across a loop of the mighty Orange River. A closer inspection reveals that the two halves of the Transfrontier Park complete each other to form a single botanical hotspot called the Succulent Karoo biome. The apparently barren landscape of interminable rocky hills scarred by rugged kloofs (gullies), dry river beds and valleys filled with immense boulders is a fragile ecosystem adapted to over 1,700 plant species, most of them rare, and over a 100 of which are endemic. As the eye adjusts to the spectacular topography, it begins to take in the enormous variety of life forms it supports. Many are bizarre, like the halfmens boom (half-person tree), a 3 m (10 ft) cactus with a crown of leaves like dreadlocks. Wild animals are also numerous, although elusive in Richtersveld's vastness. Even so, hikers will come across klipspringer, springbok and steenbok, baboon, mountain zebra and leopard. The unfamiliar flora attracts 150 specialist bird species, and in the Orange River and some of the larger pools elsewhere, the region has its own endemic fish, like the yellowfish, the Orange River mudfish and the sharptooth catfish.

On the Namibian side are two of southern Africa's most amazing natural wonders. One is the hot springs at |Ai-|Ais itself. The other is the second-largest natural canyon in the world. Hiking 90 km (56 mi) of the 166 km (103 mi) Fish River Canyon is one of the great African adventures. There's no marked trail. Hikers take five days to pick their way down the bluffs of the canyon and follow the intermittently flowing Fish River through a chasm with sheer walls 550 m (1,800 ft) high to a world of magnificent, alien beauty.

ROYAL NATAL NATIONAL PARK

Southern Africa/South Africa

WORTH A DETOUR:
Swimming in the rock bowls at the top of Gudu Falls, then using chain ladders to climb the cliff chimney called 'The Crack' for the reward of seeing the vast panorama of the rugged Drakensberg; return by clambering down the near-vertical 'Mudslide'.

Royal Natal National Park was created long before anyone realized the importance of bio-corridors in conserving flora and wildlife. Now it forms part of the mighty uKhahlamba Drakensberg Park, itself subsumed into the Maloti-Drakensberg Transfrontier Project that rings the border between Lesotho and KwaZulu-Natal. As interest shifts towards the grander plan, it's easy to overlook the jewel in the Drakensberg crown: the original nature reserve, Royal Natal. It is dominated by the Drakensberg Amphitheatre, a wall of rock 5 km (3 mi) long standing 500 m (1,640 ft) straight up from the surrounding plain. Two 3,000 m (9,840 ft) peaks, the Sentinel and Eastern Buttress, guard each end and several large domes rise from the summit plateau. A French missionary christened the highest of these Mont-aux-Sources because seven rivers begin here, including the Orange River. It is a spectacular landscape at any level and from every angle. Experienced hikers get the best of it on the two-day 45 km (28 mi) Mont-aux-Sources Trail, although it's possible to drive to the top as well. One of the most scenic trails leads visitors boulder-hopping along the Tugela Gorge, through thick forest with stands of yellowwood trees, over flower-studded grassland and up a chain ladder through a rock tunnel to a cliff with an eye-popping view of Tugela Falls, one of the world's highest waterfalls, dropping 948 m (3,110 ft) in five distinct leaps.

IMFOLOZI WILDERNESS

Southern Africa/South Africa

HIGHLIGHTS:

The guided walking trails – Emoyeni Mpila, Enkulu and Masinda Ncane – led by local community members who take visitors close to startlingly 'wild' animals.

Both iMfolozi and its neighbour Hluhluwe had been game reserves for a century when they were officially amalgamated as the 960-sq km (370-sq mi) Hluhluwe-iMfolozi Game Reserve in 1989. Game conservation had not always been completely unselfish: iMfolozi (formerly Umfolozi) was once the private hunting precinct of King Shaka Zulu, and both sections have been threatened by hunting warriors as well as poachers.

Hluhluwe in the north is more mountainous, broken by canyons, fast rivers and tropical forests filled with the colours of exotic birds. Its hills and dense shrubbery are the ideal habitat for black rhino, which thrive here. To the south, iMfolozi flattens into a wilderness of acacia-dotted savannah and undulating, thicket-cloaked hills squeezed between two branches of the iMfolozi River.

iMfolozi Wilderness is (relatively) crammed with Africa's biggest and best. The reserve is famous as a sanctuary for both black and white rhino, and visitors can expect game drives and guided trail safaris to

the hides overlooking wilderness pans and waterholes to which all wildlife must come. Elephant, lion, cheetah, leopard, hyena, buffalo, warthog, wildebeest, baboon and jackal pass in a pageant of African splendour. At any time on the savannah they may be joined by zebra, giraffe, waterbuck, nyala, kudu, bushbuck and great herds of impala.

The grasslands themselves harbour wild dog, meerkat and dozens of smaller species, and everywhere colourful tropical birds fill the air or patrol the mudflats round the waterholes and river banks. At iMfolozi it really is possible to believe in the notion of an ark of creation.

DON'T MISS
Birds! The African finfoot,
pinkthroated longclaw, crab
plover and many more.

KOSI BAY

Southern Africa/South Africa

WORTH A DETOUR: Tembe
Elephant Reserve on Kosi's
doorstep (home to the 'big
five' and a lot more).

In the northeastern corner of Maputaland, on the border with Mozambique, Kosi Bay sustains an African microculture that has survived there for over 700 years. Kosi Bay is inhabited exclusively by Maputaland's three oldest existing communities of kwaDapha, eMalangeni and Nkovukeni peoples, members of the Tembe tribal group indigenous to the area. They live in symbiotic harmony with the 12 km (7.5 mi) long system of Kosi Bay's four lakes, which they maintain as the fundamental element of their very existence.

It is a fragile ecosystem. The chain of lakes is connected by a series of channels that lead to the most pristine estuary in South Africa – a sandbar-choked lagoon with just one narrow exit into the Indian Ocean. High tides constantly refresh the system, and the differing salinity of each lake supports a colossal variety of plant life on its banks, including rare forests of raffia palm, five mangrove species, figs, orchids and papyrus. The lakes themselves are strung with a web of fish kraals, sited to make the most of every twist in the watercourse and every flood and eddy in the water itself. The fish are so plentiful that Kosi Bay is known as 'the aquarium', and its crystal-clear waters are great for snorkelling and scuba-diving. However, even fishing can be a risky business. Zambesi sharks come up the channels, and hippos and crocodiles live among its marshes, reed beds and overhanging swamp forests. Lots of them. The forests are also home to bushbuck, duiker and several kinds of monkey.

TSITSIKAMMA NATIONAL PARK

Southern Africa/South Africa

Most South Africans think of Tsitsikamma as an eco-playground and adventure centre for extreme sports, with Tsitsikamma National Park as its heart. The park includes a marine section extending 5 km (3 mi) into the Indian Ocean, and an 80 km (50 mi) coastline. Tsitsikamma Forest sits on a 200 m (656 ft) high, thickly forested plateau rising sheer from the waves, bounded by the Bloukrans River to the west and the Eerste River to the east. Its owes its conservation to the development of trails and facilities for mountain-biking, group hiking, bungee-jumping (Bloukrans Bridge over the Storms River gorge is the highest bungee jump in the world), quad bikes, scuba diving, canopy ziplining and trail-driving – yet wildlife flourishes and Tsitsikamma's beauty remains legendary. Visitors love its setting between the ocean and the Tsitsikamma Mountains, assuming both belong to the National Park. They look, but they seldom see.

The Tsitsikamma Mountains are a true wilderness with no formal trails or activities. Their solitude is enhanced by their location within the Formosa Nature Reserve, which itself lies between the remotest part of Tsitsikamma National Park and the Bavvianskloof Wilderness Area inland towards the Great Karoo. The only crowds are of birds which fill the rich afromontane forests, ravines, river banks and towering ferns and shrubs of the wet fynbos. Near the pools below mountain cascades there may be bushpig or blue duiker, leopard or elephant; or, more likely, butterflies, amphibians and smaller mammals.

DON'T MISS

The mountains' highest peak, 1,675 m (5,495 ft) Formosa, for glorious views over Nature's Valley and the coastal forest.

EASTERN CAPE – THE WILD COAST
Southern Africa/South Africa

WORTH A DETOUR:
The coastal hike from Coffee Shack past Baby Hole and Hlungwane Waterfall to the spectacular 'Hole in the Wall' – a pierced rock formation in which crashing waves set up a rhythmic slapping.

Not so long ago South Africa's apartheid culture banished 'unwanted blacks' west and north of the Kei River, creating the semi-autonomous Transkei, an unloved territory deprived of economic opportunity and subsidy. For decades Transkei was ignored as a deeply rural backwater, while the rest of South Africa's beautiful Cape coast was heavily developed in the name of local and international tourism. Known as 'The Garden Route', it's still beautiful – but Transkei's pristine coastal dunes, beaches and bays are both beautiful and empty. Rolling hills and grasslands reach back from the rock cliffs and dune systems. Aloe groves fill deep ravines. For roughly 250 km (155 mi) from the Great Kei to the Mtanvuna River, the Wild Coast is a gift of nature, unpolluted by light or noise, and accessible only to those willing to hike or ride a horse to get there.

The only communities are the long-established thatched rondavels of fishermen, and the occasional backpacker lodge or small hotel, managed and owned by local people. When democracy turned South Africa on its head, the Xhosa communities of the Wild Coast quickly realized the value of preserving their natural asset intact. Nowhere else in the world is there such an idyllic coastline with a benign, all-year climate, and still virtually undeveloped. The Wild Coast does include several small nature reserves like the tiny Silaka Reserve which protects an enclave of towering forest and lush grasslands; but most are like the Hluleka Reserve south of Port St Johns, useful signposts to areas of unspoilt natural beauty and tranquillity. It's an addictive combination and visitors will discover that the more they entrust themselves to local knowledge about the Wild Coast, the more they will be enriched by its isolated charm.

CIRQUE MAFATE, RÉUNION

Réunion

Conan Doyle would recognize it as his Lost World, accessible only by helicopter or long, hard trek. Summit peaks of bald rock lance the tropical sky, almost strangled by a cloak of thick forest and green jungle that plunges down to absurd, handkerchief-sized clearings between the mountains. Separated by huge crags, ravines and waterfalls, the isolated clearings are connected only by difficult trails that wind through tumbled boulders overrun by rainforest vines and giant ferns. The Cirque Mafate is the Indian Ocean volcanic island of Réunion's 'island within an island', one of a 'three-leaf clover' of adjacent calderas (cirques)

in the north of Réunion (the only active volcano is in the south), each differing radically from the others and from the rest of Réunion. Cirque Cilaos is the most developed. Cirque Salazie is the most exuberantly florescent, and famous for the perfect straw to make straw hats. Mafate is the most remote, protected by inaccessibility. It has always been so: it was untouched until it became the refuge for a few maroons centuries ago. Eventually some stayed, founding the eight ilets ('islets', or villages) on the only flat ground they could clear between the almost sheer mountain walls. To hike between the islets, succinctly placed in staggering landscapes of rock and sky and falling water, is to enter enchantment. There is a tamarind forest where the trees grow to 20 m (66 ft), bent by wind and covered in trailing bearded capuchin. Grass-covered ledges skirt precipices, and swaying bridges cross fearsome gorges.

DON'T MISS
The Creole culture that persists in Cirque Mafate. It includes a relaxed version of French café culture.

YOU SHOULD KNOW
The hiking is world-class, with or without a guide.

WORTH A DETOUR
The unique plants and wildlife at the very top of Mount Maharira in the south of the park, found only there.

RANOMAFANA NATIONAL PARK

Madagascar

When Madagascar split from the African continent it became a living laboratory of evolution and diversity. Isolation prevented almost all forms of species exchange, so that 90 per cent of its flora and fauna is now endemic and exclusive. Yet four-fifths of all Madagascar's landmass has been stripped and ransacked for short-term commercial gain. Ranomafana National Park protects the best of what's left.

The National Park owes its existence to the golden lemur. Its discovery in 1986 prompted research which revealed 30 species of lemur monkeys, and 60 more in the extended lemur family. Some are really bizarre. The indri has panda markings and somersaults from tree to tree, wailing like a humpback whale. The aye-aye is the stuff of nightmares, with bat's ears, teeth that never stop growing, and a Scrooge-like long skinny finger that enables it to perform the role of a woodpecker where no woodpeckers exist.

Ranomafana's montane rainforest is watered by dozens of streams feeding the Namorona River, which nourishes more orchid species than in the whole of Africa and flora and fauna like nowhere else on Earth.

TSINGY DE BEMARAHA

Madagascar

Tsingys are plateaux of karst limestone undercut by groundwater into cavern systems and tunnel fissures, and simultaneously eroded from the top. Collapsed caverns form canyons up to 120 m (395 ft) deep with rock walls cracked into a series of razor-sharp pinnacles. The whole region is a biofortress protected by its impenetrable geography. It's full of unknown, unnamed flora and fauna, besides a legion of known species endemic not just to the reserve, but often to specific altitudes on specific pinnacles. The forest crams into the spaces at the foot of each tsingy, often creating its own microclimate, and three or four distinct habitats chart its height and exposure to the extreme heat and humidity. These are magic mini-worlds – but travellers willing to risk their real dangers (just to stumble is to be lacerated) will find lemurs, amphibians, butterflies and birds. in landscapes that exist nowhere else.

WHEN TO GO: April–November (closed December–March, the rainy season).

EUROPE

HORNSTRANDIR

Northern Europe/Iceland

WORTH A DETOUR:
The cliff of Hornbjarg, 534 m (1,752 ft) at its highest. From there, one of the loveliest hikes follows tumbling streams and cascades down into Hornvik cove.

Hornstrandir, at the tip of the most northerly 'prong' of Iceland's West Fjords, has a coastline out of all proportion to its actual size. The variety – of chilling precipices of black rock, grassy slopes tumbling down to sandy coves, wave-smashed pinnacles and beaches formed from crushed shells – lends itself to constantly evolving marine landscapes. Hornstrandir's majestic cliff formations are backed by vivid-green grasslands.

Everywhere, vistas across lakes and streams to faraway promontories and snow-touched peaks are also reminders of the austerity that living creatures here must endure. It takes a full summer for the ice of the previous winter to melt – so every blade of grass and every field mouse survives on the edge, and visitors need to be hypersensitive to scuffing mosses that may have taken years to root properly.

WORTH A DETOUR: Exploring the geology of the fissures along Thingvellir's western rim, and along the meanders of the Oxara River.

THINGVELLIR

Northern Europe/Iceland

Thingvellir means 'plains of parliament', and it is where Iceland instituted the world's first legislative assembly, the Althing, in the year 980. Geologically, Thingvellir is just astounding. It is a major rift valley set out like a textbook illustration of plate tectonics. It is where the North American and Eurasian plates drift apart – visibly. A small Natural History Exhibition with an overview of the whole valley explains the significance of the shield volcanoes, glaciers, lava fields and the 114 m (374 ft) deep Lake Thingvallavatn spread below; and visitors can walk down one of the largest faults, Almannagja, to the Oxararfoss waterfalls. Most of the lake's water flows out through Flosagja and its tributary fissures to the east. The greatest adventure at Thingvellir is to go 'fissure diving' in Silfra. It's the crack in the Earth's crust between the plates, and divers swim 'from Europe to America' between the two faces of rock, wafted effortlessly along on the gentle current. Silfra is 40 m (130 ft) deep in open water, and 60 m (197 ft) deep in its side caves. Below the surface, the clear water turns a surreal bright blue. Non-divers may prefer to discuss Viking politics while basking in the hot springs.

DON'T MISS
On Heimeay, hike up Eldfell past steaming fissures to the brilliantly coloured mineral deposits at the top.

SURTSEY
Northern Europe/Iceland

Iceland grows about one inch wider each year as Europe and North America continue to pull apart. Tension between the two tectonic plates creates a weak fault line in the Earth's crust which cracks under pressure of the welling core magma. Over tens of millions of years the process threw up the submerged mountain chain called the mid-Atlantic Ridge, and pushed Iceland above sea level. Surtsey, newest of the 45 rocky outcrops of the Vestmannaeyjar (Westmann Islands) off Iceland's south coast, is a rare surface demonstration of our planet's dynamic fundamental geology. In June 1963, fishermen saw the sea boil as fiery lava broke the surface, vented from a volcano that rose 130 m (426 ft) from the sea floor in a day, and continued to challenge ice with fire for nearly four more years. By then Surtsey had grown to 2.8 sq km (1.1 sq mi) of still-smoking lava, but although it was already being nibbled by wave and wind, it was untouched by human intervention. In fact, since its birth, only scientists have been permitted to set foot on it, to take advantage of the unrivalled opportunity to chart both its raw geology and its gradual colonization by coastal flora and fauna. It is an utterly pristine work of nature, in all its forms.

Visitors may be forbidden on Surtsey but the other Westmann Islands were formed by the identical process, and Heimeay suffered its own volcanic eruption in 1973. Side by side, visitors can compare the newly created terrain of crusty lava with the beautiful, austere, sub-arctic landscapes into which it might mature. It's already happening on Surtsey. By boat (and the smaller the better), it's quite easy to study the colonizing vegetation and tentative animal life – and to enjoy it at least by analogy on Heimeay, so close by.

YOU SHOULD KNOW
Surtsey was named for Sutur, the Norse giant of fire. Its original eruption blasted columns of ash 9,150 m (30,000 ft) into the sky to the accompaniment of non-stop lightning storms. Travellers are asked to applaud this demonstration of Icelandic mythology and not reveal that volcanic ash clouds create electrical charges by friction, just like clouds of vapour.

THORSMORK NATIONAL PARK

Northern Europe/Iceland

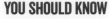

DON'T MISS

The Laugavegurinn or 'Hot Spring Trail' to Thorsmork from the north.

YOU SHOULD KNOW

In March 2010, after 200 dormant years and without any warning at all, two brand-new volcanic fissures several hundred metres long opened on the Fimmvorduhals Pass. Authorities evacuated the entire area. Scientists fear it could trigger a future catastrophic eruption of Katla, the colossus buried under the Myrdalsjokull ice cap overlooking the pass – but instability is the chief characteristic of Iceland's vulcanology. Visitors should be aware of the risks and be prepared for the worst.

Thorsmork is Iceland's sacred, hidden valley. For at least a thousand years it has been dedicated to Thor, the Norse god of thunder and lightning. Thorsmork means 'Thor's Woods', and in a country that plundered all but one per cent of its trees for firewood, Thorsmork's forested beauty confirms its continuing status. It is approached across 30 km (19 mi) of lichen-covered gravel cut by the myriad shallow channels of the Markarfljot River, braided with its tributary glacial streams. They converge where the mountains rise up on either side into the glaciers of Tindfjallajokull and Eyjafjallajokull. As the river turns north through the hills, it reveals an outlet finger of the Gigjokull spur glacier pushing down a side-gully into a steel-blue lagoon, and magnificent box canyons like Stakkholtsgja gorge, where the towering rock walls narrow to the feathery waterfall at its far end. Another turn in the river and suddenly Thorsmork opens out, an oasis of green vegetation in the rain shadow of the huge glacial and volcanic complexes of Eyjafjallajokull and Myrdalsjokull – both ice caps over major volcanoes. Birds fill the air, attracted by the lichens, mosses, alpine flowers, grassland and birch trees that soften the dynamic geology of volcanic glaciers, moraine and lakes.

Thorsmork is an outstanding destination for hiking and, especially, horse riding. Icelandic horses deal with fording rivers better than any vehicle, besides doing minimal damage. The most popular trek is from the lush valley up across the rocky fastness of Fimmvorduhals Pass between the glaciers, to the glorious 60 m (197 ft) waterfall of Skogarfoss near the coast. The descent passes 20 major cascades before the main falls' sheer drop over the escarpment – where a double rainbow forms in the spray every time the sun shines.

LYSEFJORD
Northern Europe/Norway

WHEN TO GO:
Any time – but there are
many more boats, buses and
facilities June–September.

HIGHLIGHTS:
Sailing as close as possible
to 400 m (1,312 ft) high
Hengjanefossen, plunging
down the cliff face. The
waterfall looks good from
the north rim, too, but the
major shoreline attraction is
Preikestolen (Pulpit Rock),
a 600-sq m (6,460-sq ft) flat
mountain ledge towering
604 m (1,981 ft) above
Lysefjord. Drivers will
appreciate Lysevegen,
a spectacular road with
27 hairpin bends rising
900 m (2,950 ft) out
of Lysebotn.

The two southernmost of Norway's major fjords meet near the 'oil city' of Stavanger. Lysefjord heads eastwards off Hogsfjord, through a cleft in the rock like the Pillars of Hercules in the Bosphorus. It looks even more like a creation of the gods as it suddenly opens up a dramatic vista along most of its 40 km (25 mi) length, revealing walls of rock facing each other over just 2 km (1.5 mi) of water, and rising to peaks over 1,000 m (3,280 ft) high. The effect of the sheer slabs of light-coloured granite (Lyse means 'light') is magnified by the water's other-worldly shade of deep green where it plunges to its maximum depth of 422 m (1,384 ft). Lysefjord was carved by brutal glacial action into the kind of austere landscape that inspired Norse sagas. Its sides are so steep that nobody can live there. That means one of Norway's most characteristic natural wonders remains pristine wilderness, easy to access, and highly popular as a destination. There are two ways to see Lysefjord – from the top or by boat.

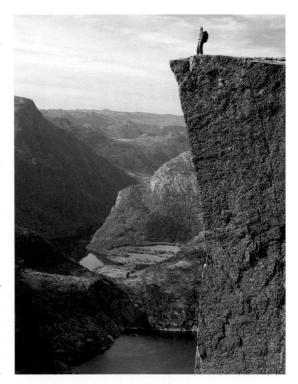

Boating is glamorous and comfortable. From Lysebotn, the ancient (and only) community at the fjord's innermost end, Lysefjord stretches straight ahead in an overwhelming geometric perspective of sky, rock and water. Almost the same view from the Kjerag Boulder – a giant sphere of rock wedged in a crevice over a sheer, 1,000 m (3,280 ft) drop into the water – feels like looking across the roof of the world, and visitors feel this sense of majesty wherever they look across the fjord to faraway mountain ranges. Fortunately, it's easy to combine a boat trip with a hike to Lysefjord's rim in the same day.

UTLADALEN CANYON

Northern Europe/Norway

DON'T MISS
Exploring the web of trails that criss-crosses the Utla River in search of ever more spectacular mountain panoramas.

Sognefjord, north of Bergen, is Norway's longest fjord. It course follows a series of sharp peaks and abrupt rock buttresses, separated by many short, hanging valleys. A glacier scoured out the huge, steep-sided canyon of Utladalen – and the silts it left behind are the reason that Utladalen is so very much more pastoral than the wild, jagged peaks around it.

Utladalen is the gentler face of Jotunheimen's dramatic landscapes. Its pine forests are old, and a sheltering cloak to remote hill farms. The rugged terrain is softened by grassy spurs and slopes of scree or shale, and dozens of streams and waterfalls. The occasional farms lend an air of domesticity in tune with, but quite different, from the harsh extremities of the alpine Hurrungane mountain region which soars up alongside.

The contrast is what attracts both ramblers and the many hikers for whom Utladalen is part of a highway. It has only one obvious attraction – Norway's highest free-falling waterfall, 275 m (902 ft) Vettisfossen – but the valley holds more unregulated major waterfalls than anywhere else. Outstandingly beautiful, geologically fascinating and spiritually fulfilling, Utladalen is a manifestation of the compelling chain that binds human enterprise to nature at its most robust.

YOU SHOULD KNOW
Jotunheimen is the 'Home of the Giants' of Norwegian folk lore.

KULLABERG NATURE RESERVE

Northern Europe/Sweden

Kullaberg occupies the very tip of the Kullen peninsula and packs an extraordinary variety of terrain into its 35 sq km (13.5 sq mi). Cliffs of ancient archean rock rear above the sea, and below there are beech forests, meadows filled with wild flowers, steep gullies and promontories that drop off the central ridge where climbers come to practise. The cliffs themselves are mined by the sea into secret swimming holes, tide pools and prehistoric caves that were inhabited 10,000 years ago. Many of the best are accessible only from the water, but visitors can rent kayaks locally to reach them and some of the 800 climbing routes with intriguing names like Napoleon's Hat or The Kulla Man's Door. The lighthouse at Kullaberg's tip stands only 70 m (230 ft) above the sea, but is visible for 50 km (31 mi); in one form or another it has signalled the murderous dangers of the peninsula for a millennium.

WORTH A DETOUR:
Pick your way from the cliff-top down to the sea through a Nimis, a ramshackle extravaganza of driftwood towers and tunnels. The structure was created by Lars Vilks, who in 1996 declared the land around it to be an 'independent republic' called Ladonia.

SAREK NATIONAL PARK

Northern Europe/Sweden

WORTH A DETOUR:
Laddepakte, Skarjatjakka and Skierfe are easily accessible mountain peaks, Look out for the bizarrely exuberant herbaceous flora of Rapadalen, and dense stands of mountain birch and osier that encourage the presence of bear, arctic fox, lynx, wolverine and the large elk of the region.

The World Heritage Site of Laponia is known more prosaically as Sweden's northernmost province of Norrbotten, and it is the ancestral home of the nomadic Sami reindeer herders. It is a harsh, remote world, far above the Arctic Circle, of glacial lakes and valley wetlands, alpine massifs, ravines, rivers and spectacular mountain peaks rising above glittering ice fields and glaciers. Most of it is a trackless wilderness, protected by a series of national parks that border Norway to the west, and stretch almost to Finland in the east.

Each park has a signature terrain, but their common heart is Sarek, where Sweden's greatest concentration of high peaks sits in icy majesty. Of some 250 distinct mountains, 87 are over 1,800 m (5,900 ft) and eight soar over 2,000 m (6,560 ft), packed into a rough circle spanning 50 km (31 mi). Although the park contains nearly 100 glaciers, it suffers a lot of rain which can turn streams into torrents without warning. In fact, crossing rivers is a major hazard in Sarek, where two bridges over key trail junctions are the only facilities available to help hikers. The bridge over the Smaila River at the park's centre is all-important. From the outside it takes two to three days to reach — from Rinim through the Pastavagge; from Kisuris through the Ruotesvagge; or, from Aktse along Rapadalen.

Rapadalen is Sarek's main artery. Fed by the waters of 30 glaciers, the Rapapaato River flows like threads, braided and spread across the broad valley floor, settling in ponds and small lakes. The water is coloured a bright ice-green against the emerald shrubs on its soggy banks, and fingers of mist shroud nearby mountain tops and hover inside canyons. It's one of Europe's most beautiful places, and worth every effort to see.

YOU SHOULD KNOW
Sarek National Park is not for the inexperienced. Professional polar explorers come here to train.

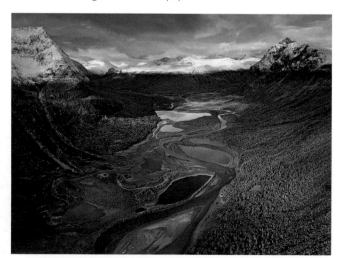

STOCKHOLM ARCHIPELAGO

Northern Europe/Sweden

WHEN TO GO:
Any time, but note that
winter ferry services are
greatly curtailed.

Swedes call it the 'garden of skerries' (rocky islets) or Skargarden. The archipelago of more than 24,000 islands radiates from Sweden's capital city, Stockholm, in an arc 70 km (44 mi) deep and 150 km (93 mi) from north to south. Size and vegetation diminish with distance, so that the smallest outcrops of bare black rock are closest to the lashing storms of

open water. In a continuous geological process, the whole land mass has been rising infinitesimally, exposing new skerries and enlarging the existing islands; and uniquely among the world's major archipelagoes, the islands are extremely close together – many only 100 m (328 ft) apart. Since they are typically formed from the mixture of volcanic ash, sand and clay called greywracke, a bedrock created billions of years ago, Skargarden is simultaneously very old and very young.

DON'T MISS
Saimaa seals,
exclusive to Lake Saimaa.

LAKE SAIMAA

Northern Europe/Finland

The Saimaa lake district of southeast Finland is a watery maze of thousands of lakes, 14,000 islands and skerries, green forests, reed beds and narrow strings of grassland dividing one watercourse from another. Created by uniform glacial upheaval, most of the lakes run roughly parallel to each other, and water flows slowly hrough the vast system of connecting channels above and below ground. The twisted, elongated shapes of the lakes and the islands together offer 15,000 km (9,320 mi) of pristine shoreline. You can sail or hike, or both, for days without seeing another person. Even the little summer houses visible

on many small islands, or among the forests crowding the shore, are too discreet to disturb the tranquil beauty that characterizes the majority of the region. Visitors can stay in some of them, although facilities are suitably spartan. Part of Lake Saimaa's ethos is demonstrating rugged individualism, and that includes cooking on an open fire fish caught locally, as well as hurling yourself into freezing water for fun.

LEMMENJOKI NATIONAL PARK

Northern Europe/Finland

YOU SHOULD KNOW

Visitors may still encounter the occasional gold prospector. However, be advised that they are characteristically solitary.

Nothing else in Europe matches the size of Lemmenjoki National Park, at the 'top of Europe'. It's an uninhabited, roadless wilderness of forests, rivers, low fells and huge mires in the arctic north.

The fragile ecosystem that Lemmenjoki protects has a cultural as well as ecological importance. The park combines natural features which enable the nomadic Lapp people to survive from one year to the next. Along the Repojoki River, the Sallivaara Reindeer Round-up site of fences and cabins is a reminder of the herders' harsh way of life – but Lapps know that Lemmenjoki can also be a garden of opportunity. The slopes of the 70 km (43 mi) long Lemmenjoki River valley and the banks of both Kietsimajoki and Vaskojoki are thick with typically Lappish, short and wide, old-growth pine trees called *aihki*, which are favoured by succulent moose. Above the river valleys pine gives way to birch and the habitat of the rock ptarmigan on the bald hilltops and fells. Where the valleys are broad, aapa bogs and deep mires crammed with rarities of arctic flora buzz with a sub-stratum of birds and insect life; and although the spruce forests reach their northern limit in Lemmenjoki's south, the park is permanent home to brown bears, wolverines and golden eagles. Lemmenjoki has unequivocal grandeur, as though its big sky, vast forests and great rivers shake their combined fist at the brutal harshness of the elements; but it also demonstrates how richly varied and fulfilling life – in all its forms – can be on the margins.

OULANKA NATIONAL PARK

Northern Europe/Finland

Oulanka National Park sits in the cross-hair of the Arctic Circle and Finland's border with Russia, roughly equidistant from Kuusamo and Salla. It's a Finnish 'National Landscape' which celebrates a uniquely Finnish version of the northern boreal forest zone that encircles the world. The hilly uplands to the lowest river valleys, range from only 150 m (492 ft) to 380 m (1,246 ft), but they are carved by two major rivers and their tributaries into a series of canyons and gorges famous for their white-water rapids, waterfalls, and long, shallow cascades. In the valley bottoms, rich silts deposited by river meanders and oxbows encourage lush meadows full of sub-arctic wild flowers, boreal moths, and butterflies like the copper violet. Big temperature variations between the fells and meadows support even greater species versatility; and the region's calcium-rich bedrock gives a further twist to the selection of rare flora, especially close to Oulanka's chalk springs and ponds. The herb-scented forests higher up shelter mosses where visitors will find plants like the dark-red helleborine, dwarf milkwort, and the calypso orchid (Oulanka Park's symbol). Hiking here is heaven on the senses.

Oulanka's dramas are played out on and by the rivers. The Oulanka River enters the park as rip-roaring rapids plunging down the Oulanka Canyon, and descends a series of stunning ravines to meet the Kitkajoki just before the Russian frontier. Hiking down the Oulanka takes visitors through a selection of the park's finest scenery, across hanging bridges where streams come hurtling in from the side, past Rupakivi Rock and the deafening roar of the Klutakongas waterfalls and rapids, to eventual tranquillity in the water margins of its eastern edge. Not surprisingly, Oulanka's charms make it one of Finland's favourite destinations, for hiking, water-rafting, rapid-running and even swimming, as well as botanizing for idle pleasure.

DON'T MISS

The breathtaking scenery along the lower course of the Kitkajoki River, from Juuma to the Russian border.

DON'T MISS
In June, you can see
Denmark's largest
orchid, the Lady's Slipper,
in the Bjergeskoven forest.

ROLD SKOV

Northern Europe/Denmark

One of Denmarks's largest forests, Rold Skov, covers about 80 sq km (31 sq mi) in the Himmerland region between Aalborg and Randers on the Jutland peninsula. The forest is an agglomerate of state- and many privately-owned small forests, brought together by common interest not in preservation for its own sake, but in the development of an ecologically integrated plan for a reserve which necessarily spreads in and around villages, farmsteads and small towns.

For visitors it helps that Rold Skov is a patchwork of discrete sections. In one, prominence is given to restoring great plantations of North American spruce and fir species, adding to existing forests of dense, old fir which flourish in the moraine soil of sand and gravel. In the Rebild Hills and Bjergeskov sections, there are growths of natural, old beech forest, where the gnarled and twisted trees have survived long-ago pruning and damage from game. Two sections, Troldeskoven and Urskoven, are set aside to revert eventually to virgin forest. With no human intervention trees will fall, creating their own glades and new flora to fill them. Almost equally important as the forest ecology itself are the cultural artefacts and associations scattered throughout Rold Skov. The Northern Well is 600–700 years old, and the Bjergeskoven section alone holds Bronze Age burial mounds, the Stenstuen dolmen, and ancient, parallel sunken roads. Evidence of various methods of charcoal-burning is everywhere.

SKAGEN, GRENEN AND THE RAABJERG MILE

Northern Europe/Denmark

WHEN TO GO: Any time. Skagen is always a birdwatcher's paradise, but May is spectacular for raptors and many other migrants.

If the Jutland peninsula were a silhouette portrait, Skagen would be the cowlick on top of its Pompadour hairstyle. It is the meeting point of the Baltic and the North Sea, a place of colliding white water and achingly beautiful blue and gold luminescence. Empires have been won and lost on Skagen's whimsical meteorological vagaries.

The eccentric resort town of Skagen anchors local geography with its system of stabilized dunes, and the opposing forces of the Skagerrak and Kattegat have gradually moved their principal battleground to Grenen, the curling tongue of sand on Skagen's northern edge which consequently grows by 8 m (26 ft) each year and shifts its shape from day to day. Visitors can ride a blue-and-red tractor-train called the Sandormen (Sandworm) from the dunes to the water's edge, and stand with a foot in each sea.

MOLS BJERGE NATIONAL PARK

Northern Europe/Denmark

DON'T MISS
The old beech woods
of Troldeskoven
(Troll Forest).

In a country as flat as Denmark, rolling hills and coastal cliffs have special significance. Mols Bjerge National Park takes its name from the 137 m (450 ft) hilltop of Mols itself – the best-known natural feature of a much bigger 180-sq km (69-sq mi) reserve that includes heath, pastureland, forests, bogs, meadows and a whole range of coastal and marine features. It sits on the twin headlands of southern Djursland, east of Arhus, and extends north as far as Ronde in the west, across to Hyllested on the Kattegat coast. It includes the open water of Begtrup Bay and much of Ebeltoft Bay, two stretches along the Kattegat, and the island of Hjelm.

Mols Bjerge is a representative catalogue of Denmark's finest landscapes, all of it discreetly signed with trails that make those highlights accessible to hikers and ramblers of every level of experience, and as special as possible for children and the wheelchair-bound. The trail from the Forest and Nature Agency Visitor Centre at Ovre Strandkaer, next to Mols, is typical. It runs through pine and broadleaf woods and across gentle open hills full of grazing longhorn cattle to a spot with far-flung views over Ebeltoft Bay. Ebeltoft is an historic 13th-century market town of huge charm and has an ancient harbour flanked by sandy coves. To its south the fascinating salt marsh of Ahl Plantage is crammed with wild flowers, herbs and grasses adapted to its brackish moisture, right next to what was once the mighty Bjornkaer and Egedal forest of oak which fuelled the 17th-century salt-extraction process, and is now recovering its grandeur. A lovely 6 km (4 mi) nature path north to Gravlev passes rich meadows and mixed broadleaf woods.

LLECHWEDD SLATE CAVERNS

Northern Europe/Wales

DON'T MISS
Lobsgows, a meal of blended mashed potato, corned beef and beetroot.

Paradoxically, once some industrial enterprises have served their purpose and been abandoned the result can be great natural drama. Around Blaenau Ffestiniog in North Wales, quarries still produce slate, and spoil tips continue to grow. Llechwedd Slate Caverns is the place to learn about the Welsh slate industry and the hardy miners who made it possible, when demand for this quality roofing material arose in the 19th century. At the surface is a re-created Victorian Village with pubs, shops, a lock-up, bank and smithy, plus a collection of narrow-gauge wagons once used to haul slate. Below ground it's possible to ride the Miners' Underground Tramway through a network of tunnels and vast chambers enlivened by tableaux, and explore the Deep Mine on foot, where dramatic *son et lumière* presentations re-create Victorian mining conditions. The abiding memory of Llechwedd Slate Caverns will surely be the truly awesome grandeur of those magnificent underground cathedrals of commerce, hewn from the living rock with the help of no more than basic tools, gunpowder and muscle power. Although those tough miners are no more than a memory, their work remains as a dramatic spectacle that Mother Nature herself might envy.

NICHOLASTON BURROWS

Northern Europe/Wales

WHEN TO GO:
From late spring to early autumn if lazy beach time is a priority. Avoid July–August if solitude is a desirable part of the package.

The Gower Peninsula in southwest Wales has plenty of splendid marine scenery along its southern coastline. Even in high summer it does not get crowded, because getting there requires a hike through extensive Nicholaston Woods (home to protected ash trees and rare plants such as purple bromwell, butcher's broom and bloody cranesbill). The western part of Oxwich Bay (where there's car parking) can get busy in summer, but even then the eastern end next to Nicholaston Burrows never gets too busy, and those with a keen interest in nature may care to explore the Oxwich Burrows reserve, a wonderful expanse of salt- and freshwater marshes.

In the other direction lies Three Cliffs Bay with its impressive jutting rock formations. When the tide is out beachcombing often produces dividends, especially for lovers of seafood such as cockles and scallops. It's easy to spend a couple of active days exploring the Burrows and environs.

BRECON BEACONS

Northern Europe/Wales

Good enough for the tough-as-nails SAS to use as a training ground, these stern hills to the south of Brecon are neither over-populated nor the easiest of terrain – particularly in winter, when the local mountain rescue team is frequently called into action. That said, at other times of year the Brecon Beacons offer rewarding outdoor opportunities, although they are notorious for sudden weather changes. The range consists of peaks forming a horseshoe around the head of Taf Fechan River, including Pen y Fan, Corn Du, Cribyn and Fan y Big. They're connected by an extended ridge with long parallel spurs.

These are the core of the Brecon Beacons National Park, but there are other sections, giving an overall area of 1,350 sq km (520 sq mi). The Black Mountain is to the west and then comes the sandstone massif of Fforest Fawr. To the east of the beacons lie the Black Mountains on the English border. The park contains some of the most spectacular upland formations in southern Britain and the landscape is mainly high moorland, with forestry plantations and pastureland in the many valleys.

Sightseeing from the comfort of a car is satisfying, with so much rugged scenery to appreciate, but the national park is made for those who enjoy outdoor activities. These include a gamut of leisure possibilities, including hang-gliding, parascending, caving, rock climbing, watersports, canoeing, fishing, horse riding, cycling, mountain-biking, walking and camping. The park's rich past and natural heritage offer another dimension, with numerous archaeological and historical sites to be found. Around 170,000 visitors come each year, which is far too few to deny the secretive SAS their lonely, undisturbed route marches in the park's remote wilderness areas.

HOW TO GET THERE:
Working clockwise from the west, the main towns surrounding the Brecon Beacons National Park are Llandeilo, Llandovery, Brecon, Hay-on-Wye, Abergavenny, Pontypool, Blaenavon, Brynmawr, Merthyr Tydfil, Glyn Neath and Ystradgynlais. Several good roads cross the park from north to south and the A40 runs from east to west.

WHEN TO GO:
Spring, summer or autumn.

WORTH A DETOUR:
Waterfalls. There are dozens in the national park, mainly towards the southern edge, the tallest of which is Sgwd Henrhyd with a drop of 27 m (90 ft), on National Trust land near Coelbren.

YOU SHOULD KNOW
In 2005 the first hiking route to cover the entire length of the Brecon Beacons National Park was inaugurated. The Beacons Way runs from the village of Bethlehem in Carmarthenshire to the foot of Ysgyryd Fawr near Abergavenny, the most easterly of the Black Mountains. The long-distance Taff Trail from Brecon to Cardiff also passes through the national park.

Left: Brecon Beacons

CLWYDIAN RANGE

Northern Europe/Wales

One of only eight protected landscapes in Wales, the wild and wonderful Clwydian Range is a 35 km (22 mi) chain of heather-clad hills stretching from Prestatyn Hillside in the north to the Nany y Garth pass in the south, from the Vale of Clwyd in the west towards the Dee Estuary in the east. Denbigh and Ruthin are in the vale and Mold is on the Dee side.

This is one of the most precious tracts of countryside in North Wales, rising from fertile farmland through coppice woodland and small hedged fields on the lower slopes to open heather moorland punctuated with limestone outcrops and wooded escarpments on the tops. Deep valleys slash the flanks, notably those carrying the Rivers Alyn and Wheeler. Where the limestone breaks through, there are grasslands rich with orchids and other wild flowers.

The Clwydian Range is best viewed from the Vale of Clwyd, but most folk will want to do more than look. These hills offer the opportunity for every sort of recreational activity, from thrill-seeking challenges like paragliding, abseiling or rock climbing through horse riding, cycling and walking to fishing. Although long popular as a 'green lung' for visitors from Merseyside and Cheshire, these delightful hills have enough roaming room to ensure that anybody who wants to get away from it all need never feel crowded, especially if avoiding summer weekends.

WORTH A DETOUR
Gweryd Lakes, towards the south of the range. In enviable surroundings, it offers coarse and trout fishing and is an excellent base for sallying forth into the hills.

DON'T MISS
The open-air Minack
Theatre, perched on
a cliffside.

PORTHCURNO

Northern Europe/England

The Cornish coastline is world famous, and Porthcurno is an ideal place to appreciate its visual grandeur. This little village is almost at the tip of England – an honour reserved for nearby Land's End – but with its triangular beach and flanking cliffs Porthcurno delivers all the rugged splendour anyone could want. The steeply shelving beach has coarse sand and faces to the southeast. It is tucked neatly into the western end of Porthcurno Bay, a sweep of awesome cliffs punctuated by tantalizing coves culminating in rectangular Logan's Rock. The coastline around Porthcurno is designated as an Area of Outstanding Natural Beauty. The granite cliffs are up to 70 m (230 ft) tall and can be appreciated by exploring the many footpaths, one of which is the long-distance South West Coast Path. Green Bay is a small sandy cove immediately adjacent to Porthcurno Beach that can be reached at low tide. Further towards Logan Rock is Pedn Vounder, another small beach accessed by a steep path from the cliff top. Near the top is a white granite pyramid that serves as a navigational aid. It replaced the building that housed the terminal of an undersea telegraph cable to France, laid in 1880. In the other direction is Porth Chapel Beach, which is named for a ruined medieval chapel.

Lifeguards are on duty at Porthcurno between Whitsun and mid-September (there can be dangerous rip-tides off the beach) and a dog ban is in force on the beach from Easter to the end of September. Cornwall cheerfully overdoses on holidaymakers in high season and Porthcurno is a justifiably popular destination, but at other times of year it is possible to find total solitude amid some of the Cornwall's most dramatic coastal scenery.

HOW TO GET THERE:
Porthcurno is after St Levan down a dead-end valley road, off the B3315 some 14 km (9 mi) southwest of Penzance and just 5 km (3 mi) from Land's End. There is a large car park above the beach, which is then reached by a wide footpath.

WHEN TO GO:
Forget any thoughts of privacy in the summer months, but midweek forays out of season are very quiet.

EXMOOR

Northern Europe/England

YOU SHOULD KNOW
A huge cat is said to stalk Exmoor. Is it real? Well, the area is definitely big enough to provide sanctuary for it.

The Exmoor National Park is very special and sure to appeal to anyone who loves wild and lonely places. But there's much more than moor to be seen in this 700-sq km (270-sq mi) area of outstanding natural beauty that includes the Vale of Porlock and Brendon Hills. It spans the borders of Devon and Somerset, with nearly three-quarters located in the latter county. Exmoor has over 200 scheduled ancient monuments and countless historic sights ranging from prehistoric hill forts and mine workings to pretty medieval villages with wonderful old churches. Red deer roam free, as do Exmoor ponies, while sheep graze everywhere and the thriving bird population is represented by species as different as the peregrine falcon and Dartford warbler.

But the landscape is the star and that, too, is hugely varied. The rugged northern boundary is a Heritage Coast 55 km (34 mi) long, a stretch of dramatic coastal scenery that includes Britain's highest cliff – the grimly named Great Hangman near Combe Martin, soaring to an impressive 318 m (1,040 ft) with a sheer face of 250 m (820 ft). The shoreline is often wooded and exploring the coast reveals a wonderland of cliffs, caves and huge waterfalls. There are few settlements on the water – only Lynton-Lynmouth (connected by a cliff railway) and Porlock Weir – so mostly this awesome coast is accessible only to the most determined adventurers.

The park mostly consists of heather-covered moorland, lightly peppered with hamlets and small villages.

This hilly former royal hunting ground also has extensive areas of broadleaf and conifer woodlands. There are numerous rivers, notably the River Exe and its tributaries flowing south and several that flow out into the Bristol Channel in the north, and it would be easy to spend a month or more exploring.

WORTH A DETOUR:
A stroll across the famous Tarr Steps, an ancient clapper bridge across the River Barle between Withypool and Dulverton.

PRAWLE POINT

Northern Europe/England

DON'T MISS
In summer basking sharks and grey seals can be spotted in the water.

Devon's southern extremity is Prawle Point, a jutting coastal headland. It is to the east of Plymouth in the area known as the South Hams, across the Kingsbridge Estuary from the popular waterside town of Salcombe in the direction of Start Point. The land is mostly owned by the National Trust and the point itself is a ten-minute (uphill) walk from the NT car park. The building on the cliff above the point is a watch station manned by National Coastwatch Institution volunteers (visitors are welcome to pop in for a chat and see the display housed there). The volunteers are not alone in observing passing traffic out to sea, as this superb vantage point is a magnet for ship spotters (really!).

Actually, this is not a place to go with the intention of doing particular stuff, because the real joy is being there, surrounded by magnificent coastal scenery in a remote and unspoilt place. That said, ornithologists might beg to differ. The Devon Bird Watching & Preservation Society has a small reserve that features a modest superstar – the sparrow-sized cirl bunting, found only in South Devon. Birdlife is abundant, with major migrations in spring and autumn and a large cast of regulars, including assorted sea birds, ravens and raptors like buzzard, red kite and hobby.

Apart from being a birdwatcher's paradise, Prawle Point will appeal to those who simply want to appreciate the rugged grandeur of this beautiful coastline. The South West Coast Path passes through and it's possible to scramble down to little coves with shingle beaches and explore rocky shelves that run unevenly out to sea from the base of the cliffs. Just to the west is Macely Cove, with its enticing strip of sand enclosed by towering granite walls.

YOU SHOULD KNOW

Just after leaving East Prawle, the tall post in a field was erected to play the role of a ship's mast, allowing coastguard crews to practise the use of rocket apparatus – once a crucial aid in shore-to-ship rescues. It was often deployed locally, for many a ship has run aground on Prawle Point over the years. The strange-looking bunker on the left just before the climb to the point is a leftover from a WW2 radar station.

PENDLE HILL

Northern Europe/England

WORTH A DETOUR: The British in India Museum in nearby Colne's Hendon Mill, dedicated to telling the story of the British Raj.

The old mill towns of Burnley, Nelson, Clithero and Colne in northeastern Lancashire are grouped around isolated Pendle Hill, rising to a moorland crest 557 m (1,827 ft) above sea level. The moist climate that underpinned the area's cotton-producing industry is enshrined in the local saying 'when you can see Pendle Hill it's about to rain, when you can't, it's already started'.

There's a Bronze Age burial site on the summit but Halloween is the time for a completely different historical hike – large numbers gather to climb the supposedly haunted hill each year in memory of the

infamous Pendle witch trials of 1612 that accused a dozen locals of murdering ten people by witchcraft. One 'witch' died in prison, one was acquitted and ten were found guilty and hanged.

Pendle Hill is one of those places too wild to be tamed, and has therefore remained much as nature intended. Away from regular paths to the summit it offers compete peace and solitude, while those who like to be organized can follow cycling or walking tours.

DON'T MISS
The magnificent view of Ennerdale Water from the top of Anglers Crag.

SETTLE-CARLISLE RAILWAY

Northern Europe/England

This was the last great main rail line to be constructed in England, completed in 1876 by the Midland Railway Company. Those skilled 19th-century railway engineers built 14 tunnels and 17 major viaducts to create a route through the magnificent Yorkshire Dales, on through the lush, gently rolling hills of the Eden Valley with its charming villages and traditional market towns to Carlisle, gateway to Scotland.

The so-called 'Lancashire Dales Rail' service runs on many Sundays between the beginning of May and mid-October, offering a through trip from Blackpool via Preston and Blackburn on to Settle and Carlisle. For those drawn by the romance of bygone travel, charter trains with vintage carriages – pulled by classic steam locomotives – regularly do the Settle to Carlisle run (usually as part of a longer journey).

HOW TO GET THERE:
Access may be (officially) obtained only by
using the National Trust ferry from Orford town
quay on a 'first come, first served' basis.

ORFORD NESS
Northern Europe/England

Nearly but not quite as far to the east as it's possible to get in the British Isles lies Orford Ness – the largest shingle spit in Europe. The Ness is 15 km (9 mi) long – an atmospheric strip of marsh and mudflat, lagoons and tidal river, shingle and sand, grassland and scrub, flowers and shells. This should be a lonely outpost untouched by the hand of man, but instead it has a lighthouse dating from 1792 and an extraordinary collection of abandoned buildings. The legacy of the Ness's history as a closed site for weapons testing and other research purposes may be read from a bizarre assortment of structures dating from two hot World Wars and one Cold War. Early radar experiments took place in the 1930s and the distinctive 'pagodas' were used for testing nuclear triggers after World War II. The combination of lonely wild place, wide open spaces and big skies with a 'mystique of secrecy' generated by the former military establishment makes for weird contrasts and a fascinating visit.

NORTH NORFOLK COAST
Northern Europe/England

This Area of Outstanding Natural Beauty is a land of extensive marshes and mudflats, creeks and tidal pools, beaches and sand dunes. This is where low tide can see the sea retreating beyond sight from the shoreline, only to rush back when the tide turns, filling the gutters with extraordinary rapidity and threatening to cut off the unwary from dry land with no more warning than the ominous rumble of waves driven by a following wind.
Wonderful walks may be enjoyed in the Holkham National Nature Reserve. It stretches from Burnham Norton to Blakeney and has every feature that makes this unique coastline so special – foreshore, reclaimed marshland, salt marsh, pinewoods, scrub and dunes. A good spot to start from is Holkham Bay.

WHEN TO GO: Winter, to see the migrating wildfowl, notably protected Brent geese.

NORTH YORK MOORS

Northern Europe/England

WORTH A DETOUR: A trip on North Yorkshire Moors Railway. This slice of yesteryear offers steam locomotives, wood-panelled carriages, old-fashioned conductor service and around 30 km (19 mi) of preserved track.

Seductive as wild and lonely places may be, there's much more to the North York Moors National Park than that. As well as the wonderful heather moors, there are ancient woodlands, rivers and a wonderful stretch of Heritage Coast that includes the fascinating old port of Whitby, plus beaches and dramatic cliffs. In addition, there are picturesque sandstone villages, castles, medieval abbeys and churches to be found by those fascinated by built history.

The park's various attractions include an important archaeological site and an informative visitor centre. Superb views are on offer from the network of roads on the moorland plateau without climbing or hiking a single step. It's a place that everyone can enjoy at their own pace, in their own way.

NORTH PENNINES

Northern Europe/England

DON'T MISS
The twin highlights of Cauldron Snout and High Force on the upper River Tees.

The special character of the North Pennines – stretching down from Carlisle to Darlington – is recognized by salutations galore. This low-rise range has been designated as an Area of Outstanding Natural Beauty and at 2,000 sq km (772 sq mi) is the second-largest AONB in England, outranked only by the Cotswolds. As a result of unique geological heritage, unusual flora (including rare alpine plants not found elsewhere in the British Isles) and threatened fauna such as red squirrel the North Pennines have also achieved UNESCO European and Global Geopark status.

Quite apart from official recognition, everyone who appreciates wide open spaces and the ability to escape into the great outdoors will be instantly captivated by huge expanses of open heather moor, blanket bog, hay meadows bright with wild flowers in season, enticing dales, rushing rivers, waterfalls and wonderful woodland.

Traditional stone-built villages house welcoming traditional communities, and the North Pennines has a fascinating industrial past, with evidence of extensive lead mining and quarrying in earlier centuries still to be found, providing an added dimension to this striking landscape that spans three counties – Cumbria, Durham and Northumberland.

YOU SHOULD KNOW
Writer George Orwell moved to Jura in 1946, to escape the pressures of London life.

ISLE OF JURA
Northern Europe/Scotland

Once the exclusive fiefdom of the powerful Campbell clan, the Isle of Jura in the Inner Hebrides is now split into different estates. There are lots more red deer than people on Jura, and deer stalking is a principal contributor to the island's economy. The other is tourism. With an area of around 370 sq km (143 sq mi) and some 200 inhabitants, this starkly beautiful island remains a classic unspoilt Scottish wilderness that draws visitors who love wild and lonely places. Most people live in the pretty village of Craighouse on the east coast, which has a post-office shop, hotel, tearoom, village hall and church. A narrow road (pretentiously titled the A846) follows the eastern and southern coasts. Jura House in the south has a sheltered Walled Garden, open to the public, featuring many exotic species from the Antipodes. Respecting the awesome power of Atlantic gales, the rugged and unsheltered west coast is uninhabited, but has a number of raised beaches (rocky marine shelves above sea level). The island's western side is dominated by three conical peaks known as the Paps of Jura. Between the northern tip of Jura and neighbouring Scarba is the Gulf of Corryvreckan, complete with notorious whirlpool. Jura has many historical sites, including Iron Age forts and prehistoric standing stones, but the landscape is the main attraction. The island has assorted habitats – lough, woodland, bog, heather, grassland, mountains, cliffs, bays and beaches.

WORTH A DETOUR:
A taste of Isle of Jura Single Malt. The distillery has been operating since 1810 at Craighouse, and produces a smooth, light whisky up to 21 years old – plus one named Superstition for the island's mystical heritage.

GALLOWAY FOREST PARK

Northern Europe/Scotland

HOW TO GET THERE:
Enter the park from any of the surrounding villages – Newton Stewart, New Galloway, Gatehouse of Fleet, Dalmellington or Castle Douglas.

WHEN TO GO:
Any time (even if a winter visit goes no further than Kirroughtree Visitor Centre to introduce the kids to Santa and pick up a sustainably grown Scottish Christmas tree).

WORTH A DETOUR:
A visit to Bruce's Stone, high on the northern shore of Loch Trool, which can be reached by car (see above). This memorial commemorates Robert the Bruce's first victory over the English, when he was a fugitive hiding in the Galloway Hills.

Welcome to the Scottish Borders – one of Britain's most pleasing tracts of unspoilt countryside. Once there, the 775 sq km (300 sq mi) of Galloway Forest Park provides a wonderful opportunity to experience the natural beauty of the Borders at first hand. As the name suggests, this is a woodland park. It is operated by the Forestry Commission, an organization that majors on commercial conifer plantations, and this is indeed the predominant characteristic of Galloway Forest Park. But this is a mixed landscape of forest and moor, lochs and rivers, seashore and mountains – a combination that attracts over a quarter of a million fresh-air enthusiasts who visit every year. Their motivation is understandable. The park is in Dumfries and Galloway and encompasses much of the Galloway Hills, part of Scotland's Southern Uplands. This is a wild and uninhabited area, allowing enormous scope for independent exploration in the sure and certain knowledge that – despite all those visitors – total solitude is never far away. There is more than enough lonely backcountry to get lost in (hopefully not literally) and there are 27 waymarked trails, covering every type of landscape within the park and catering for every level of ability. Wild camping is a popular summer option, and other recreational opportunities include fishing in stunning surroundings for trout and salmon (in season), canoeing, mountain-biking, horse riding and wildlife-watching (top sightings are red deer, pine marten, otter and red squirrel, golden eagles, black grouse and nightjar).

There are three first-class visitor centres to help point newcomers in their desired direction: Kirroughtree (reached from Newton Stewart or New Galloway), Glentrool (reached from Newton Stewart) and Clatteringshaws (reached from New Galloway). The last is on the Galloway Red Kite Trail and has a superb interactive wildlife exhibition.

YOU SHOULD KNOW
The lake was originally called Winandermere, but the Victorian railway company thought that was too long, called their new station at Birthwaite 'Windermere'… and the name stuck for both town and lake.

Left: Galloway Forest Park

KNOYDART PENINSULA

Northern Europe/Scotland

Travellers tempted to visit Scotland's last great protected wilderness will even enjoy the bit that is sometimes frustrating when it comes to such adventures – getting there. Because, for all but seafarers or those rich enough to hire a helicopter, a visit to the remote Knoydart Peninsula will start with a drive up Rathad nan Eilan – the Road to the Isles. This starts at Fort William and goes through breathtaking coastal scenery as it passes through Glenfinnan and Arisaig en route to the port of Mallaig. A good alternative is making the same journey by train, using the spectacular West Highland Line.

The peninsula is sandwiched between Lochs Nevis and Hourn. This National Scenic Area, known locally as the 'rough bounds', attracts sailors, hill walkers and mountaineers – the last including those intent on Munro-bagging, with two of these must-climb mountains on offer. The pretty whitewashed village of Inverie crouches below conifer woodland on the north side of Loch Nevis, beneath the intimidating bulk of Sgurr Coire Choinnichean. The peninsula's one metalled road goes nowhere, making Inverie the largest mainland settlement in Britain not connected to the national road network. Inverie is the ideal base from which to explore Knoydart's dramatic landscape. There are guided ranger walks on Wednesdays that allow day visitors to experience this extraordinary place without staying over, timed to end before the last return ferry to Mallaig.

DON'T MISS

The remotest pub in Britain, the Old Forge at Inverie. It has six moorings, offers good food, has a roaring fire and opens all day 364 days a year.

There are a number of excellent B&Bs in and around the village of Inverie, and also some self-catering cottages. It's advisable to book early if summer accommodation is required – or take a tent – for some visitors return year after year to recharge their batteries in this tranquil haven far from the hustle and bustle of modern life.

WHEN TO GO:
Spring–autumn, unless
extreme winter sports are
the objective.

RANNOCH MOOR

Northern Europe/Scotland

Rannoch Moor can seem like the last place on Earth when the weather closes in, as cloud swirls down from the hills and relentless rain starts falling. This large triangular expanse of boggy Highland moorland stands on its inverted apex to the west of Loch Rannoch and extends to around 130 sq km (50 sq mi). The moor is a level plateau surrounded by mountains and consists of innumerable lochs and lochans, streams and peat bogs, heather and scrub.

The moor is crossed by one road and a railway, but still remains one of Scotland's loneliest enclaves, described thus by Robert Louis Stevenson in his novel *Kidnapped*: 'A wearier-looking desert a man never saw'. He must have seen it on a bad day, for when the sun comes out this dour other-worldly place takes on a sparkle all its own. Weary hikers plodding across the moor on the West Highland Way are re-energized. Others are tempted to park their cars and roam through this extraordinary landscape, while some let the train take the initial strain before doing the same. Achallader is at the moor's southern apex, Rannoch Station is at the northeastern corner, while the northwest is delineated by the mouth of Glen Coe.

LOCH CORUISK

Northern Europe/Scotland

WHEN TO GO:
April–October for the boat
trip from Elgol.

'Speed, bonnie boat, like a bird on the wing… Over the sea to Skye'. The lyrics of the famous Skye Boat Song are in fact not traditional – for it is a Victorian invention written after one Annie MacLeod heard and remembered the melody of her oarsmen's Gaelic rowing song in a boat on Loch Coruisk.

People are still going over the sea to enjoy the stunning natural beauty of Skye. One of the highlights of any trip to the island must be a visit to that self-same Loch Coruisk, a freshwater lake that takes its name from the Gaelic Coire Uisg (Cauldron of Waters). This must surely be one of the most wild and dramatic visions in all the Scottish Highlands. The northern end of the loch is surrounded by the jagged fangs of the Black Cullin range and it is hidden by those inhospitable basalt mountains. A small rill from the southern end discharges into Loch Scavaig, a sea loch.

This is handy for those who lack the time, energy or fitness to reach this isolated natural wonder on foot, for boat trips from various starting points on and off the island deposit people at the iron steps on Scavaig that give access to the short but rocky walk to Scotland's most magnificent freshwater loch.

SANDWOOD BAY

Northern Europe/Scotland

WHEN TO GO:
Any time – the beach is delightful in summer, but truly magisterial in winter when angry Atlantic waves lash the beach and flying spray clouds the cold air, beneath a dark and steely sky.

Sandwood Bay, facing the restless Atlantic Ocean close to the northwestern tip of Scotland, is a 2 km (1 mi) stretch of wide pinkish sand backed by impressive sand dunes and a small loch, which curves between craggy cliffs. An imposing sea stack guards the southern end. Even in high summer it is likely that only a few determined souls will share this special strand, for a real effort is required to get there.

As the descent to the beach begins, roofless Sandwood Cottage is on the right – providing a good spot to camp for those who think one day in this special place isn't enough.

They're not wrong. Simply sitting on the beach soaking up the stark beauty of this lonely beach is a great beginning, but after that comes the urge to explore – the sand, the dunes, Sandwood Loch, adjoining cliffs. Some imbued with pioneering spirit even set out to follow the shore up to Cape Wrath, a name that says everything about this Atlantic coastline.

WORTH A DETOUR:
The Torr Scenic Route. There are some steep descents down narrow lanes but the reward is splendid coastal scenery and distant views (on a clear day!) to the Mull of Kintyre.

GLENS OF ANTRIM

Northern Europe/Northern Ireland

The Glens of Antrim are nine stunning valleys, together offering a concentrated cocktail of awe-inspiring scenery within an area of some 50 sq km (19 sq mi), which includes glacial valleys and tundra plateau, boglands, rivers and waterfalls, vertical cliffs and sandy beaches.

Each glen has its own character, each merits leisurely exploration. Glenarm – the glen of the army – has a village of the same name. Glencloy is the glen of the hedges. Fertile Glenariff is the so-called Queen of the Glens. Glenballyemon is geographically the middle glen of nine. Rugged Glenaan is the site of legendary Ossian's grave. Glencorp is the glen of the slaughtered, named for a long-forgotten event in Ireland's violent past. Glendun, spanned by a viaduct carrying the main Cushendall-Ballycastle road, is the glen of the brown river. Glenshesk is the sedgey glen and Glentaisie is named for the princess of nearby Rathin Island.

WHEN TO GO:
Try to see the annual Doolin
Festival, held over the
weekend following the last
Friday in February.

THE BURREN

Northern Europe/Republic of Ireland

If there's a more bizarre landscape in all Ireland, it remains a secret – for surely nothing can wrest that quirky crown from The Burren. This karst limestone region – one of Europe's largest – extends to around 300 sq km (115 sq mi) bounded by the Atlantic to the west and Galway Bay to the north. The name comes from the Irish Boireann, meaning 'Great Rock', and it's certainly that. These rolling hills are made up of limestone pavements criss-crossed with a distinctive pattern (karren) of cracks (grikes) and isolated rocks (clints).

The Burren seems like a barren wilderness at a first distant glance, but closer inspection reveals rich vegetation growing in the narrow cracks. This habitat is so unusual that Mediterranean, arctic and alpine plants live side by side, with one alpine – the blue spring gentian – serving as The Burren's tourist-board symbol. This wild and empty place will not appeal to people who like their natural wonders to be big and bold, yet more discerning explorers will be captivated by green lanes where it's possible to walk for long distances amidst this unique landscape without seeing a soul. Along the way will be innumerable signs of The Burren's rich heritage – dozens of megalithic tombs, standing stones, Celtic crosses and traces of villages abandoned during the Great Famine.

The Burren's muscular coastline is magnificent – coming to a dramatic high point at the Cliffs of Moher towards the southwestern boundary. These are as big and bold as they come, towering up to 214 m (702 ft) above the Atlantic. There are spectacular coastal views from the top.

YOU SHOULD KNOW

During Oliver Cromwell's brutal mid-17th-century campaign in Ireland his lieutenant general of horse, one Edmund Ludlow, uttered a phrase that has never been forgotten and is enshrined in local history. During the course of operations to suppress resistance in The Burren, he sourly commented 'It is a country where there is not enough water to drown a man, wood enough to hang him nor earth enough to bury him.'

MOURNE MOUNTAINS

Northern Europe/Northern Ireland

The very words have a romantic ring, and the Mourne Mountains in County Down do not disappoint. This compact range due south of Belfast overlooks Carlingford Lough close to the Irish Republic. The mountains are contained within a rough triangle just 24 km (15 mi) long by 13 km (8 mi) wide with apex-points formed by Newcastle, Warrenpoint and Kilkeel.

With rugged mountains, grazing pastures, heather moorland, forests, drumlins, lakes, rivers, coastal plains and wonderful sandy beaches, walking is a major activity. Climbers, too, can find pitches to test every level of competence. Seven signed cycle trails offer varying degrees of difficulty and length, while dedicated mountain-bikers have their own marked course. Fishing and horse riding are also popular options. For those who prefer not to wander on spec, there are wonderful reserves to enjoy (Castlewellan, Tollymore and Kilbroney Forest Parks, Donard Forest, Silent Valley, Cranfield Beach and Murlough Bay).

WORTH A DETOUR:
Tollymore Forest Park, which offers excellent views of the sea and surrounding Mourne Mountains.

DON'T MISS
The Aringa Mining Experience includes an underground mine tour.

LOUGH ALLEN

Northern Europe/Republic of Ireland

This beautiful lake atop the River Shannon is shared between Counties Leitrim and Roscommon. This is a traditional tract of rural Ireland that is sparsely populated, with the lough separating the hilly northwest from a relatively flat southeast. It is a land of extraordinary pastoral beauty, with soaring mountains and plunging valleys, rolling pastures and woodland, lakes and rivers – plus a short stretch of Atlantic coastline. The lake itself is a wonderful stretch of water, fed by numerous small streams that descend the slopes of adjacent mountains, which are steep but not precipitous.

This is wild country – a place of bogs, heather and rocks with some relatively recent woodland planting. The lake is a noted angling hotspot, and eco-friendly watersports such as windsurfing and kayaking are popular. The limit of the Shannon navigation is at the north shore of the lake, with access from the extensive Shannon waterway system via scenic Lough Allen Canal at the southern end.

DON'T MISS
The wonderful coastal vista to be seen from the top of Healy Pass.

BEARA PENINSULA

Northern Europe/Republic of Ireland

The Wild West of Ireland isn't what it used to be, with tourist pressures and prosperity brought by Celtic Tiger years inevitably changing this once-remote area. One place that retains its traditional character is the Beara Peninsula in the far southwest of the country.

Marooned between the Kenmare River to the north and Bantry Bay to the south, the Beara Peninsula was once the stronghold of the O'Sullivan clan and it's easy to understand why it was one of the last strongholds to resist the conquering English in Elizabeth I's reign. Today, the established tourist trail is the Ring of Beara, a 195 km (120 mi) circumnavigation of the untamed peninsula. The ring begins in Kenmare and ends at Glengarriff, passing through Adrigole, Castletown Bere and Allihies along the way. Top attractions include ruined Dunboy Castle, Puxley Mansion, a copper-mining museum and Derreen Gardens. There are countless opportunities to explore the rugged shoreline and/or vanish into one of two mountain ranges that run down the centre, the Caha and Slieve Kish, bisected only by two roads along their entire length.

MARQUENTERRE DUNES

Northern Europe/France

WHEN TO GO: Any time. The northern bird migration takes place in April and May, the return journey from August–October.

Le Marquenterre is an impressive expanse of dunes fronting La Manche (the English Channel) that have been stabilized by pinewood plantations. The place is home to an assortment of interesting wildlife, including a colony of seals.

Le Marquenterre provides refuge for an enormous number of migrating birds stopping off to rest and refuel during the long two-way journey from Scandinavia to Africa. This strange land of dunes, pine forests and tamarisk, with salty meres and ponds rich with water plants, provides an ideal habitat.

It offers three waymarked walks – a short one taking around 90 minutes and two longer ones needing perhaps three hours. The beauty of these is that they were designed to pass numerous points ideal for observing birds. There are many hides along the way, some of which may be manned by knowledgeable guides.

HAUT ALLIER

Northern Europe/France

DON'T MISS

The magnificent Basilica of St Julien in Brioude, constructed between the 11th and 14th centuries.

The Auvergne has been described as 'France's best-kept secret' and, if it is a place that even most French open-air enthusiasts have yet to discover, the unspoilt Haut Allier is even less well known. Located in the western half of the Haute-Loire department in southern Auvergne (although the principal river is actually the Allier, a Loire tributary), this is the driest and sunniest part of the Auvergne, which constantly provides a reminder that the south of France is not far away.

The Haut Allier – unexploited for mass tourism – is emblematic of authentic rural France at its best.

The landscape is stunning and includes large tracts of wild country. The River Allier rises in the Cevennes Mountains and features extraordinary riverscapes with awesome rock formations. The river runs through and is surrounded by stunning gorges – usually having no road access – that are often densely wooded. This is France's last great wild river and the area is renowned among those in the know as white-water rafting and canoeing heaven. Primitive camping, backpacking, rambling, day-hiking and mountain-biking are also popular, using an extensive network of paths through this natural playground. Anglers come for the trout and salmon (there is an extensive fry-stocking programme designed to maintain the salmon run).

The Haut Allier (high valley of the upper Allier) is a place where it's possible to get up close and personal with Mother Nature – either at a leisurely pace or as part of an action-packed adventure, which could be anything from rock climbing through bungee-jumping to dog-sledding in winter.

ILES D'OUESSANT

Northern Europe/France

YOU SHOULD KNOW

As befits the place that marks the southern entrance to the English Channel (the Isles of Scilly being the northern entrance), Ushant has the world's most powerful lighthouse. Kreac'h is one of three on an island that has seen countless shipwrecks over the centuries, the other lighthouses being Nidvic and Le Jumet. A popular tourist purchase along the Finistère coast is a poster illustrating the most famous wreck sites.

In the wild Atlantic Ocean, close to Cape Finistère, lies the one place in Brittany that has a different name in English. Ushant is a corruption of Ouessant, one of only two inhabited islands (the other is Molène, to the southeast) in the rocky Iles d'Ouessant – rocky granite outposts separated from the mainland by treacherous seas. A visit to Ushant involves taking the car ferry – capacity just two cars, so don't bother taking yours as the island's main road extends to just 6 km (4 mi) long and the whole island is only 8 km (5 mi) long and half as wide. Ushant has one significant settlement. Lampaul has all the necessary facilities, including four hotels, and there is also a campsite for do-it-yourself visitors. Although it is a popular destination, Ushant never gets overrun and this windswept place remains a wild and unspoilt destination even in high summer. The island is surrounded by towering cliffs that plunge into the sea, with nary a guard rail in sight, and intrepid observers can find innumerable spectacular vantage points from which to study this dramatic coastline in all its moods. The interior is a virtually treeless plateau covered in heather and springy turf, with occasional stunted trees and low scrub crouching in hollows. There is gorse and a kaleidoscope of wild flowers in season.

There are few established paths so walkers go where they please, while bicycles may be hired from the ferry terminal by those who prefer pedal-power. Ornithologists love the Iles d'Ouessant, for this craggy archipelago is a welcome stopping-off point for numerous migratory birds such as the wheatear and ring ouzel, with around 350 species recorded. Beyond that, the obvious wildlife seems confined to the large rabbit population and lizards sunning themselves on dry-stone walls.

HOW TO GET THERE:

Ferries run to Ushant from Brest (two-and-a-half hours) and Le Conquet (one-and-a-half hours or 45 minutes using the fast ferry). There is a summer plane service from Brest operated by Fisist'air.

WHEN TO GO:

Any time – in February the island can be warmer than the French Riviera. April–October.

WORTH A DETOUR:

The Ecomusée d'Ouessant in Lampaul. Located in two restored houses, it provides fascinating insight into the islanders' self-sufficient way of life in the 19th century (closed on Tuesdays).

LA COUBRE FOREST

Northern Europe/France

YOU SHOULD KNOW

Be aware that certain paths and areas within the forest may be restricted on Thursdays, the day reserved for hunting. Guided walks are offered every day in season (barring Sundays and public holidays), starting at 10.00 from La Bouverie on the Côte Sauvage (take signposted road 44 from the D25).

The Avert Peninsula at the mouth of the Gironde Estuary borders the coast, and its tip offers the opportunity to go down to the woods – and shore – without feeling in the least bit crowded. With around 500 sq km (193 sq mi) to explore, La Coubre Forest is a real get-away-from-it-all destination.

As with so many things in the modern world, La Coubre Forest is not quite so original as it appears, having been planted in the 19th century to stabilize an area of sand dunes. Also, this is a commercial woodland and there are tracts of clear felling awaiting replanting – although compared to the vastness of the whole, these hardly intrude.

It's possible to drive through the forest and see some worthwhile sights – including Bonne Anse Bay, La Coubre lighthouse, La Bouverie forest lodge and Pointe Espagnol, where a path from the car park leads to a particularly fine beach with far-reaching views that was-named for a Spanish vessel wrecked in 1823. For those who like being beside the seaside in a natural environment entirely unspoilt by tourist trappings, La Coubre's sandy Côte Sauvage is a terrific find.

That should be part of any itinerary, but in truth La Coubre deserves to be explored at leisure, on foot or two wheels. The considerable expanse of this light-and-airy pine forest is criss-crossed with established trails. Serious hikers will be tempted by the long-distance path from Royan to Ronce-les-Bains and the island of Oléron, although walkers can roam the forest unchecked. For cyclists who prefer established routes to pedalling at will, there is a cycle track from Saint-Palais-sur-Mer to Ronce-les-Bains, a 60 km (37 mi) round trip that takes in both coast and woodland. There are also marked mountain-bike routes in the forest.

HOW TO GET THERE:
The D25 road between Ronce-les-Bains and La Palmyre passes through the middle of the forest, a drive of some 20 km (12 mi).

WHEN TO GO:
At any time, although July and August do see plenty of visitors, so those who like solitude might prefer the off season.

WORTH A DETOUR:
The splendid outlook from the base of the Tour de Gardour, a metal communications tower just off the D25. Follow the arrow sign from the road and park, then take the short footpath and enjoy a breathtaking panorama that takes in the forest, Atlantic Ocean and Gironde Estuary.

MILLEVACHES REGIONAL NATURE PARK

Northern Europe/France

YOU SHOULD KNOW

Don't make the assumption that the park is named after the brown Limousin cattle that may be seen everywhere. It is perhaps named for distinctive rock formations that look like cows (vaches) – or possibly as a combination of the Celtic melo (high) and Latin vacua (empty). Take your pick – it has thousands of Limousin cattle, lots of rock formations that look like cows (with a little imagination) and it's definitely both high and mostly empty of human habitation.

Unwilling to do anything by halves, when the authorities created Millevaches Regional Nature Park in 2004 they ensured it fell within all three of Limousin's departments – Corrèze, Creuse and Haute-Vienne. Equivalent to the UK's Areas of Outstanding Natural Beauty, regional nature parks aim to preserve the best of the nation's fine countryside – an asset that France happily still possesses in abundance. Millevaches makes the point in spades.

This marvellous tract of wild landscape is located in the foothills of the awesome Massif Central. It covers an area of 3,150 sq km (1,216 sq mi), thinly populated by around 40,000 people who mainly live in the villages and small towns around the edge of the park that are characterized by wonderful vernacular stone buildings. An extensive granite plateau offers heather moorland and peat bogs, open grasslands and wildflower meadows, deciduous, coniferous and mixed forests, bubbling springs, rushing rivers and lakes. In fact, it is more of a gentle dome than a plateau, ranging in height from 600 m (1,968 ft) to 1,000 m (3,280 ft). The River Varre rises here, flowing north to feed the Loire, and the Vézère originates nearby and south into the Dordogne River.

The higher areas are heavily forested with little agricultural activity. Otherwise, a pleasing patchwork of woods and meadows is punctuated by the occasional field of sunflowers or maize. As is to be expected, Limousin cattle are everywhere.

This is an area that provides real satisfaction to those who like exploring unspoilt places where they can be alone amid the vastness of nature. But for those who like a little conventional tourist fun, large reservoirs are nearby. These have beaches, campsites and picnic areas, while sailing and boating should appeal to the nautically minded.

HOW TO GET THERE:
The park is criss-crossed by a network of lanes and minor roads. Good starting points for a journey of exploration are the N141–D941 Saint-Léonard-de-Noblat to Aubusson road in the north or the A89 Tulle–Ussel road in the south.

WHEN TO GO:
Any time (but note that summer mornings can be very misty and winter days can be very chilly).

WORTH A DETOUR:
Millevaches Regional Nature Park at a glance. This unique experience is available at purpose-built Mont Bessou viewing tower at the southeastern edge of the plateau at its high point. Set in an area of woodland just north of Meymac, the tower affords stunning vistas across the park and to the distant Cantal Mountains in the south.

MASSIF DU SANCY

Northern Europe/France

WHEN TO GO:
The climate is severe and the main visitor season for non-winter-sporters is from mid-June–mid-September, when the autumn foliage is already turning.

This ancient stratovolcano in the Auvergne's Puy-de-Dôme department has been inactive for over ten millennia, so it's reasonable to suppose that no eruption is imminent. The Massif du Sancy was created around 250,000 years ago when molten rock exploded through the Earth's crust to spawn a basalt giant. Today, the massif rises majestically from the middle of a plateau and at a soaraway 1,186 m (3,890 ft) takes the crown as the highest mountain in the centre of France – outgunned nationally only by those big guys in the Alps and Pyrenees. Over time it has eroded to a chaotic jumble of steep valleys and spiky needles.

The Massif du Sancy is an imposing sight from afar, a steep-sided monolith crouching along the skyline wearing a white cap of snow long after the surrounding countryside has thawed. Both northern and southern slopes are popular skiing locations, with a number of cable cars and lifts to make the going up easy (although biting winds call for warm clothing, even in summer). Determined mountaineers who prefer doing it the hard way will not be disappointed – some of the routes up the massif's rugged flanks are extremely testing. Despite winter-sports infrastructure, this remains an empty expanse of jumbled rock surrounded by rolling backcountry with fir woods, pastures, rushing streams and waterfalls that echo the mountain's lonely grandeur. The nature of the place may be judged from the evocative names of features such as Hell's Valley and the Devil's Teeth.

CHAÎNE DES PUYS

Northern Europe/France

YOU SHOULD KNOW

When the 6 km (4 mi) road up the Puy de Dôme is too busy in summer motorists are required to park at the foot of the mountain and take a shuttle bus to the summit.

A puy is a volcanic mountain with a rounded outline. And one of the best places for seeing lots of these shapely domes is the Massif Central's Chaîne des Puys. This run of 8 lava domes, 48 cinder cones and 15 maars (volcanic explosion craters) stretches for just 40 km (25 mi) and reaches the high point at the Puy de Dôme towards the middle. This is the highest point in the Auvergne, attracting half a million visitors annually.

There's a regular bus to the summit from Clemont-Ferrand station in summer and there's parking at the lofty visitor centre, but for many the objective is not so much the destination – impressive though that may be – but getting there unaided. This involves ascending an old Roman road, *Le sentier des muletiers*, or taking the northern path via the Nid de la Poule crater. Cyclists can emulate some famous stage finishes on the Tour de France by using the road during limited periods when it is closed to motor traffic. To be fair, some people aren't that interested in the going up – for numerous paragliders coming down is the high.

If that sounds a bit touristy, the rest of the Chaîne des Puys maintains its unyielding rocky character without any compromise with the modern world. Rocky tops rise above tree-clad flanks, maars have become lonely lakes and occasional isolated farmsteads may be found in the valleys below. Those drawn to wild places can have free rein and it's possible to tramp through this unspoilt mountain landscape for hours without seeing anyone. The Auvergne is an area of great natural beauty where the timeless traditions of rural France are kept alive beneath the watchful gaze of extinct volcanoes, and nowhere is this truer than around the Chaîne des Puys.

WHEN TO GO:

Winter: Chaîne des Puys from the top of Puy de Dôme when there's snow on the ground can only be described as breathtaking.

WORTH A DETOUR:

It is thought that the summit of the Puy de Dôme has served as a gathering place since prehistoric times. Be sure to inspect the ruined Gallo-Roman temple built there and dedicated to Mercury.

PLATEAU DU VERCORS

Northern Europe/France

The Vercors is a series of plateaux and mountains in the Isère and Drôme departments, surrounded by vertical limestone cliffs and divided by deep canyons. This remote and lonely place was the scene of fierce fighting during World War II, as the French Maquis de Vercors group gallantly rose to tie up German forces that would otherwise have been available to counter the D-Day landings in June 1944.

Today's visitor can easily understand why this place was ideal for resisting the German conquerors during the war. Today, the Vercors massif is a picturesque Regional Nature Park. But those daunting cliffs and broken terrain remain the same, explaining why it took 10,000 German soldiers delivered by glider and parachute to defeat 4,000 guerrilla fighters operating in territory perfect for ambush. The Vercors has distinct sectors. These are the heavily forested Coulmes area in the northwest, the northern

HIGHLIGHTS:
The village of Pont-en-Royans with its houses overhanging the River Bourne.
Saint-Nazaire-en-Royans beneath a 19th-century aqueduct that still operates.

plateau nicknamed 'The Four Mountains' for obvious reasons, small western plateaux with their high summer pastures and deep gorges, plus the high plateaux that are the wildest and most remote part of the park. Such contrasting areas give the Plateau du Vercors enormous visual variety, but all of it is impressive. The massif is popular with get-away-from-it-all hikers and there are many signed and well-maintained trails. Many caverns can be explored without special equipment (or undue risk), while paragliding and white-water canoeing are other possibilities. Happily for the action-averse, sightseeing from the relative safety of a car offers breathtaking vistas from some of the most vertiginous roads in France.

DON'T MISS
Fourme d'Ambert, a
delicious local blue-
veined cheese.

LIVRADOIS–FOREZ REGIONAL NATURE PARK

Northern Europe/France

They're not big as mountains go, but the Forez Mountains on the borders of Auvergne's Puy-de-Dôme and Haute-Loire departments have pine forests that seem a timeless haven of arboreal tranquillity. Across the Dore river valley is the Livradois, a wooded area of undulating plateau with granite outcrops. Together with gentle hills and slopes around Billom in the west, rolling forested valleys in the southwest and the fringes of the Auvergne's volcanic mountains in the southeast, these contrasting landscapes make up the Livradois-Forez Regional Nature Park, which – in addition to dramatic scenery – is as good a place as any in the land to experience the timeless rhythms of traditional French rural life.

The park has Chateldon and the famous French cutlery capital of Thiers in the north, Ambert and Usson in the middle and Brioude, Lavaudieu and La Chaise-Dieu towards the southern end. But this vast area that stretches from the plains of Limagne to the peaks of the Forez Mountains is essentially a rural backwater dotted with small villages and isolated hamlets. The contrasting terrain gives visitors with limited time available some regional food for thought – there's so much to see that it's hard to choose.

CHARTREUSE MOUNTAINS

Northern Europe/France

WORTH A DETOUR: Le Fort du St Eynard, a well-restored 19th-century fortress just south of Le Sappey-en-Chartreuse, perched on a cliff top overlooking Grenoble.

Eastern France's Chartreuse Mountains stretch down from the Lac du Bourget towards Grenoble. This limestone range is riddled with underground passages and caves, including the famous Dent de Crolles system that extends to an impressive 60 km (37 mi) in length. Above ground, the mountainous terrain makes a great backdrop for a few centres that cater for skiers, although the undeveloped Chartreuse Mountains serve mainly as a magnet for climbers and summer hikers.

The tallest peak is Chamechaude at 2,082 m (6,831 ft), with other notable summits including Grand Som and Mont Granier. The internal valleys have small rural communities supported by pastoral farming and sustainable forestry. These little settlements have distinctive vernacular architecture. Square houses sit beneath steeply pitched tile roofs, while shingle-roofed barns with massive cornerstones are built of reddish stone. Wooded slopes rise to dramatic cliffs, above which the hiker will find a magical world of high plateaux.

CÉVENNES NATIONAL PARK

Northern Europe/France

WORTH A DETOUR: Aven Armand. This amazing limestone cavern is a fairyland of stalagmites, including the world's largest known example at 30 m (100 ft) tall.

Created in 1970, the spectacular Cévennes National Park attracts over 800,000 visitors every year, but it's still possible to escape into the vastness of the Cévennes Mountains and enjoy awe-inspiring natural beauty. Elevations within the park vary from 380 m (1,250 ft) to 1,700 m (5,600 ft) and the climate varies from the continental north to the maritime south. Coupled with differing soil types this ensures an extraordinary

variety of flora, with over 2,250 species. Notable among them are huge plantations of chestnut trees and the carnivorous sundew plant, while both alpine and subtropical species may also be found. Animal and bird life is equally diverse, with nearly 2,500 different creatures recorded. Animals such as deer, wild boar, mouflon (wild sheep with large curved horns), beaver and otter roam free, while more visible birds include vultures, woodpeckers and grouse.

There is a network of established trails that extends to 1,800 km (1,120 mi), many designed to be sufficiently user-friendly to encourage visits by families with children. Cévennes also has more Grande Routes (GR long-distance walking paths) than any other French national park.

WHEN TO GO: Summertime, when the going is (relatively) easy and the weather is (usually) in clement mood.

CIRQUES DE GAVARNIE AND D'ESTAUBÉ

Northern Europe/France

The Pyrenees have rugged mountainscapes aplenty, but two adjoining features that should not be missed are the Cirque de Gavarnie and the Cirque d'Estaubé. In this context a cirque (circus) is a valley-head formed like an amphitheatre, open on the downhill side to form a flatter area corresponding to a stage with the valley falling away behind. The upper part of the bowl is a steeper

section that might represent the sloping seating area. The Cirque de Gavarnie is a famous example of the feature. It is around 800 m (2,625 ft) across at the low point and 3,000 m (9,840 ft) wide at the top. It has an impressive natural gap in the surrounding steep cliffs called Le Brèche de Roland. The area also boasts France's highest waterfall, the Grand Cascade de Gavarnie, a tiered fall down a rugged cliff face with a drop of 422 m (1,385 ft). This awesome natural bowl ranks as a scenic masterpiece.

DON'T MISS
A jar (or two) of the
local honey to take home.

DOURBIE VALLEY

Northern Europe/France

The stunning grandeur of the three Tarn gorges takes the breath away, and of these natural masterpieces the Dourbie Valley is the most picturesque. Its wild slopes are wooded or covered with sparse vegetation at higher levels where the bare rock breaks through, and the stunning array of wild flowers has to be seen to be believed. The smallish but perfectly formed River Dourbie winds down this green valley from its source near Le Vigan in the Cévennes Mountains to join the Tarn at Millau.

The upper valley narrows into two spectacular granite and schist gorges that are 300 m (985 ft) deep. In the Cévennes foothills the river flows through the lush 'Garden of Aveyron', a peaceful green oasis where the charming villages of Nant and Saint-Jean-du-Bruel are located. The Dourbie then begins its home run to the Tarn, snaking between the Causse Noir and Causse du Larzac down an austere yet grandiose valley.

Favoured leisure activities in the Dourbie Valley are rock climbing, white-water canoeing or rafting, birdwatching, horse riding, cycling, strolling beside this lovely river, enjoying some of the best trout fishing in France or hiking up to the limestone plateaux above to find solitude beneath a big sky populated with lazily circling vultures. For some, the scenery ensures that simple sightseeing is enough. In addition to its scenic qualities, the Dourbie Valley has quaint stone-built villages like La Roque-Sainte-Marguerite with its 11th-century church and mill, located near the river below Montpellier-le-Vieux, an impressive labyrinth of rock that simply must be explored. It appears almost man made but was carved by water. The village also has impressive Montcalm Castle. Other medieval villages like Saint-Véran and Cantobre cling to the cliffside with stunning views down the valley.

HOW TO GET THERE:
The Dourbie Valley is accessible from the A75 at Millau, with the D991 actually going up the valley to La Roque-St-Marguerite, Sain-Véran, Saint-Sauveur and Nant.

WHEN TO GO:
Any time (the winter valley looks great beneath a covering of snow, with not so much as a solitary tourist to be seen).

ORLU NATURE RESERVE

Northern Europe/France

WORTH A DETOUR: Andorra, as one of over ten million annual visitors to this beguiling mountain principality who take advantage of its duty-free status and enjoy the scenery, usually in that order.

The Ariege Department to the south of Toulouse is little known outside France. The land rises to the high Pyrenees and is steeped in history, as the ruins of numerous romantic Cathar castles atop their rocky outcrops testify. One little gem tucked away in the dramatic mountain landscape of southeastern Ariege is Orlu Nature Reserve. This 40-sq km (15-sq mi) chunk of mountain terrain rises from 930 m (3,050 ft) to 2,765 m (9,070 ft) and is sufficiently demanding to ensure that – despite its relatively small size amidst the general grandeur of the surrounding Pyrenees – the determined explorer must still put in a real effort to appreciate everything this special wild place has to offer.

The expedition can start with a quick visit to the museum at the bottom of the reserve, to discover the rationale behind its status as a national hunting reserve. Rangers ensure that the wildlife is protected, scientists study it and intrepid members of the public watch it. Orlu requires the donning of stout shoes and walking. There is an easy hike in the Gaudu Valley and a more demanding three-hour climb to a sanctuary in the middle of the reserve where it's possible to stay overnight.

DON'T MISS
The Forêt d'Aitone
National Park, just to
the west of Evisa.

GORGES DE SPELUNCA

Northern Europe/France

Set between the mountain villages of Ota and Evisa, the Gorges de Spelunca, a 2 km (1.2 mi) long canyon, cuts between the two, its steep, red granite walls plunging down to the eponymous river below. The gorge is one of Corsica's famous natural sites and it is possible to walk or hike there all year round. Although there are excellent views of much of the gorge from the road, it is more rewarding to make for the mountains, where there is shade and the air is fresh and clean.

Although the gorge is accessible from both villages, most people start from the cemetery just outside Evisa. The descent, at first quite gentle, becomes steeper lower down. The trail leads through shady woods, passing wind-scoured rock pinnacles and bare rock faces to the bottom of the valley and the elegant old Genoese stone bridge, Pont de Zaglia – one of two here. The track through the gorge was once an important communications link, enabling heavily laden mules to be sent from Porto into the mountain villages. Today, the path has been restored using original stones, but it can often feel more like jumping than walking. Children will also enjoy the gorge, although it will be too strenuous for very little ones. Curiously shaped tiers of boulders, sometimes with one balanced, apparently precariously, on top of another, lead to mini-waterfalls and several natural bathing pools.

Keep an eye open for the Corsican salamander – this is a great place to see one.

WEST FRISIAN ISLANDS

Northern Europe/Netherlands

WORTH A DETOUR:
The ten-day Oerol Festival on the island of Terschelling. It takes place in mid-June and the whole island becomes a stage for the arts, with theatre, music and visual arts put on in the unlikeliest of places - barns, boathouses, meadows, dunes - as well as utilizing the two purpose-built main stages.

Germany and the Netherlands share the North Sea's Frisian Islands, with Holland having the best of the deal – it has 14 West Frisians (five inhabited) as opposed to Germany's 12 East Frisians (seven inhabited). In truth, most of the uninhabited Frisians are little more than shifting sandbars that barely stay above water at high tide and even the populated ones are sparsely settled. They are barrier islands, sheltering the shallow Waddenzee from the North Sea proper.

Starting in the west, the largest and best-populated island is Texel. A third of Texel is a nature reserve. The landscape of sand dunes has a network of cycle paths that encourage two-wheeled exploration. Next along is Vlieland, with one major settlement at Oost-Vlieland. Again, dunes are the predominant feature, leavened by meadows and woods. Historic Terschelling is notable for (surprisingly) cranberries. Inhabitants have long used bounty brought by the sea to build eccentric houses and barns, and a barrel of cranberries was washed ashore in 1840. The canny islanders planted them, they thrived and today bakeries and restaurants vie to offer the best cranberry delicacies. Ameland has just four small villages and consists mostly of dunes, but nonetheless has extraordinary biodiversity. Tiny Schiermonnikoog – heavily fortified by the Germans in World War II – hosts the Netherlands' first nature reserve. Small and flat, it nonetheless attracts huge numbers of summer visitors, including many day-trippers.

Island-hopping ferries offer tickets that allow visitors to go at their own pace and check out inhabited islands in turn. This is ideal for hikers and – this is two-wheel-savvy Holland – the many touring cyclists.

LOWER ODER VALLEY

Northern Europe/Germany

The Oder is a name which resonates in postwar European history. The river has formed a significant frontier for hundreds of years and currently marks the border between Germany and Poland. Flowing into the Baltic Sea by Szczecin in Poland, the Oder possesses one of the few delta regions in Europe that have remained largely undisturbed by human interference. A cross-border reserve has been created in its lower reaches to protect and preserve this exceptional environment. The greater part, 105 sq km (40 sq mi), is on the German side where it is known as the Lower Oder Valley National Park. The park covers a 60 km (37 mi) stretch of the River Oder with idyllic riverbank scenery, water meadows, marshes, mixed riparian forests and dry grassland on the surrounding hillsides.

The biodiversity of this relatively compact area is outstanding in Europe. The floodplain is a breeding ground for over 120 kinds of birds, including several endangered species such as the black stork and the sea eagle. Conservation methods have become more radical in recent years and large parts of the park are now completely off-limits to human activity. Even so, the Lower Oder Valley remains a mecca for serious birdwatchers who are able to get close to the wildlife on foot, on bicycle or by canoe along the riverbank. The visitor centre in the village of Criewen has lots of useful information and is a good starting-point for tours of the park. A recommended day walk is the 14 km (9 mi) circuit of the polder at Schwedt; walking on the raised dyke gives you a good vantage-point for spotting birdlife. Serious cyclists can also do a round trip up and down the two riverbanks (passport needed for the Polish section).

HOW TO GET THERE:
Local buses operate from the nearest railway stations at Angermünde and Schwedt. The park is 40 km (25 mi) east of the Berlin-Szczecin motorway.

WHEN TO GO:
Any time of year. The winter months are the best time for birdwatching.

WORTH A DETOUR:
Visit in October when the park becomes a staging post for a mass population of cranes on their migration to warmer southern climes.

YOU SHOULD KNOW
This region witnessed some of the fiercest fighting of World War II as the Germans tried desperately to stem the Soviet advance in early 1945. Many towns still bear the scars.

DON'T MISS
Seals on the sandbanks
close to the shore,
sunning themselves.

AMRUM ISLAND

Northern Europe/Germany

Amrum is the smallest of the North Frisian group of islands which
lie in the North Sea off the west coast of Germany. It is also the least commercialized and offers a very
different experience from its lively and sophisticated neighbour Sylt. Amrum is a place to come to unwind
and allow your biological clock to slow down to a gentler and simpler rhythm of life. At little more than
20 km (12 mi) long and never wider than a couple of kilometres (just over a mile), the island can be cycled
in a few hours and even walked around inside a day. Considering its size Amrum contains a remarkable
variety of habitats, including pine forests, heathland and marshes. Its crowning glory, though, and what draws
people back to the island year after year, is the Kniepsand, a huge expanse of fine white sand extending for
12 km (7.5 mi) down the entire western side of the island. If you grow tired of the fantastic beaches, the
large patchwork of dunes behind await exploration. These cover almost half the area of the island, with some
rising to as much as 32 m (105 ft) above sea level.
A single road runs down the spine of the island, linking its five villages.

JASMUND NATIONAL PARK

Northern Europe/Germany

Rügen is a popular holiday island just off Germany's Baltic coast, From
the area at the end of the Jasmund Peninsula – the Stubbenkammer –
there are outstanding views of the chalk cliffs stretching south.
These are the highest sea cliffs in Germany and demonstrate vividly
the effects of coastal erosion. The highest of all is the Königsstuhl (king's
seat) which plunges 118 m (387 ft) into the emerald-green sea. It is
a popular viewpoint, although for a view of the cliff itself you need to
head a few hundred metres further along the coast to the Victoriasicht
viewpoint. A cliff-top walk takes in
the entire coastline between the
Königsstuhl and Sassnitz, including
the craggy Wissower Klinken cliffs.
In addition a small park, Jasmund also
has fine examples of marsh, wetland
and mixed broadleaf woodland.

DON'T MISS
A ride on the
Rasender Roland
narrow-gauge steam train.

HARZ NATIONAL PARK

Northern Europe/Germany

WHEN TO GO:
April–October (but there is also excellent cross-country skiing in the winter months).

In 2006 the Nationalpark Harz was created out of the amalgamation of two former parks on either side of the old border of West and East Germany. The new park protects 158 sq km (61 sq mi) of mountainous granite terrain, much of it covered in dense forests, but there are also areas of high moorland and hidden valleys where birdsong and the babbling of crystal-clear streams are the only sounds you will hear. At the heart of the national park stands the Brocken, at 1,142 m (3,747 ft) the highest point in the Harz range. You can trek to the top or else take the delightful narrow-gauge steam railway. The Brocken itself is steeped in legend and the mists that often shroud the summit serve only to enhance the air of mystery. It is the legendary site of the great witches' gathering on the pagan festival of Walpurgisnacht; lively celebrations in the local towns and villages take place on the night in question (April 30), when lots of locals dress up as – you've guessed – witches and devils.

SPREEWALD

Northern Europe/Germany

WORTH A DETOUR:
With no hills and a well-developed network of trails running alongside the streams and canals this is a great cycling area for family outings.

Journey little more than an hour from the centre of Berlin and you could be on a different planet. The Spreewald in the southeast of the state of Brandenburg is one of Germany's most surprising landscapes. This extensive network of rivers, streams and canals was formed when mineral deposits during the Ice Age created natural barriers that forced the River Spree to divert its course and split into a multitude of channels. The resulting marshes and wetlands, with their numerous small lakes and sandy islands, constitute an important ecosystem rare in central Europe; it was duly recognized as such when in 1990 UNESCO declared the region a biosphere reserve.

The Spreewald has over 400 km (250 mi) of idyllic green waterways, many of which are navigable. You can explore them yourself in a canoe or kayak, or else take a trip in a characteristic flat-bottomed boat and enjoy the local knowledge and anecdotes dispensed by your ferryman as he propels you gently along with his pole. These punts are an integral part of a traditional way of life here; in the summer months the post is still delivered by boat to the outlying villages! The wetlands are a haven for waterbirds.

The Spreewald is the historic home of Germany's only indigenous minority, the Sorbs. At festivals and on special days you can still see them in their traditional costumes.

Left: Spreewald

KELLERWALD-EDERSEE NATIONAL PARK

Northern Europe/Germany

YOU SHOULD KNOW

The Kellerwald is one of the last remaining Central European habitats of the wild cat and the eagle owl.

HOW TO GET THERE:
Kellerwald-Edersee is 30 minutes' drive southwest of Kassel. The nearest rail stations are Bad Wildungen and Frankenberg.

WORTH A DETOUR:
Look out for the pretty Cheddar pink flower, also known as firewitch, which grows in the cracks of rock faces around the Edersee.

Once upon a time much of central Europe was covered in beech forests but the inevitable pressures of human settlement and exploitation have led to their steady decline, with the result that today they are found only in isolated pockets. The largest such pocket is in the north of the state of Hesse in the so-called 'green heart' of Germany. Such is its importance as a habitat that in 2004 the Kellerwald-Edersee National Park was established to preserve it for future generations. The broad swathe of ancient, gnarled beech trees which make up the Kellerwald – many several hundred years old – owes its survival to having been a hunting ground for the local nobility in centuries past, which protected it from logging and other forms of exploitation. The majestic red deer is still a common sight in the park but thankfully is no longer hunted

The beech may be the dominant tree here but it does allow other deciduous species to make an occasional appearance, such as large-leaved limes, ancient oaks and the ash and mountain elms found in the damp gullies which proliferate throughout the park. Numerous nature trails take you along crystal-clear streams, past rock and boulder fields (relics of the last ice age) and over meadows covered in wild flowers.

The northern boundary of the park is marked by the Edersee, an artificial lake formed by a dam which offers all kinds of water-based activities. A 70 km (43 mi) walking trail takes you right around the lake, while the Kellerwaldsteig is twice as long and links up with the adjacent nature park to the south.

SAXON SWITZERLAND

Northern Europe/Germany

Many parts of Europe have had the 'Swiss' epithet applied to them by virtue of their putative resemblance to that country's alpine scenery, although few live up to the grandeur of the real thing. One that does is the region known as Sächsische Schweiz, or Saxon Switzerland, which occupies the land between Dresden and the border with the Czech Republic. It may not boast the snow-covered peaks of its namesake, but Saxon Switzerland possesses drama of a different kind. Soaring sandstone cliffs, canyon-like gorges and flat-topped mountains combine to create a landscape like no other in Germany.

The area, which is also known as the Elbsandsteingebirge (Elbe Sandstone Mountains), owes its existence to the mighty River Elbe which has here carved a tortuous path through the Lusatian Mountains. It is well known for the extraordinary sandstone and basalt rock formations which crop up everywhere, the result of erosion by wind and water. Tall columns with weird shapes and names like Barbarine and the Pillars of Hercules are popular among rock climbers, but you do not have to go to such lengths yourself to get a buzz from this landscape. It is a paradise for children who love venturing into the myriad gullies and clefts and scrambling up the gentler rock faces.

Climb to the top of a sandstone plateau like the Pfaffenstein or the Lilienstein and you are rewarded with magnificent panoramic views of the Elbe Valley and the surrounding countryside. The ruins of a medieval fortress are an additional attraction on top of the Bastei rocks which tower 305 m (1,000 ft) above the open fields and rolling hills. An alternative and less strenuous way of appreciating the scenery is on one of the lovely old paddle steamers which ply the Elbe between Dresden and Schmilka.

HOW TO GET THERE:
Saxon Switzerland is an easy drive from Dresden, 50 km (31 mi) to the northwest. Bad Schandau, a good base for walks and excursions, is 50 minutes by train from Dresden.

WORTH A DETOUR:
Königstein Castle on its rocky perch. Its outer wall is a staggering 1.7 km (1 mi) in circumference.

SWABIAN-FRANCONIAN FOREST NATURE PARK

Northern Europe/Germany

YOU SHOULD KNOW

In a pioneering venture, the nature park currently offers GPS satellite navigation to its walkers and cyclists.

HOW TO GET THERE:
The park headquarters and visitor centre is at Murrhardt, 45 km (28 mi) northeast of Stuttgart.

WHEN TO GO:
April–October.

WORTH A DETOUR
The archaeological park near Welzheim, which includes a full-scale reconstruction of a twin-towered gateway to a Roman fort.

Germany can boast a huge variety of scenery within its borders. While the wooded hills of northeast Baden-Württemberg may not be among the star offerings, they do come as close as any other to presenting what for many is the archetypal German landscape – a mosaic of forests, valleys, fields, gentle uplands, water meadows and pastures where sheep and cattle graze.

Much of this area is now contained within the Naturpark Schwäbisch-Fränkischer Wald. Covering 900 sq km (347 sq mi), the Swabian-Franconian Nature Park gets its name from the fact that it straddles the historical frontier between the medieval duchies of Swabia and Franconia. The border itself ran along the ridge above the valley of the Murr River which more or less cuts the park in two on an east-west course to join the Neckar near Marbach.

The park provides a good example of a reasonably harmonious co-existence between man and Nature which has lasted hundreds of years. It is lovely country for walking and cycling excursions and there are any number of marked trails leading you to hidden valleys, viewpoints and peaceful lakes in the woods where a refreshing dip can be very

welcome on a hot summer's day. On your wanderings through the spruce and beech forests look out for signs of the Limes (pronounced 'lee-mays') – the frontier which for 250 years marked the northern limit of the Roman Empire in central Europe. Unlike Hadrian's Wall, the Limes was a timber-and-earthwork fortification and you can still find good traces of the ditch and earth rampart in many places; the foundations of some of the stone watch-towers are also still visible. A walking trail with information panels enables you to follow the course of the Limes right across the park.

HAINICH NATIONAL PARK

Northern Europe/Germany

DON'T MISS
Germany's greatest medieval castle, the Wartburg.

Hainich Forest is the largest unbroken expanse of mixed deciduous woodland in Germany. It's a delightfully green and peaceful place to visit, with plenty of walking opportunities. One of the more unusual is a high-level walkway near the park's visitor centre at Thiemsburg which takes you through the tree-tops to an observation tower in the heart of the forest, 44 m (144 ft) above the ground. Children will appreciate the different perspective on the forest, as they will the 'Wild Cat Children's Forest', a playground fashioned out of fallen trees and natural materials. Hainich National Park is in the northwestern corner of the Thüringerwald, an area of thickly wooded hills and picturesque valleys which was once a favoured haunt of artists of the German Romantic movement. The unhurried lifestyle and relative lack of commercialism which once attracted them still prevail.

WUTACH GORGE

Northern Europe/Germany

WORTH A DETOUR:
Even wilder and more remote, the Lotenbach Glen is definitely worth tackling.

The name 'Grand Canyon of the Black Forest', as it is sometimes billed in the tourist brochures, may be overdoing it a tad, but the Wutach Gorge is an undeniably impressive sight. The River Wutach rises on the Feldberg, the highest point of the Black Forest, and flows east and south before joining the Rhine near Waldshut. At one time the Wutach was a tributary of the Danube but geologists don't know what caused the river to change its course by 90 degrees in favour of the Rhine.

Outside the town of Bonndorf the Wutach River has punched its way through the Black Forest rocks to create a spectacular ravine with jagged, near-vertical cliffs which soar skywards and keep the valley in shadow for large parts of the day. The damp, shady conditions have generated a microclimate where unusual plants grow. Well over 1,000 types of wild flower have been recorded in this astonishingly fertile environment, which in turn attracts rare birds such as the grey egret and a glorious variety of butterflies and insects. The best way to appreciate this remarkable landscape is to hike the length of the gorge. The trail runs beside the river between the Schattenmühle and the Wutachmühle.

FICHTELGEBIRGE

Northern Europe/Germany

DON'T MISS
The chairlift ride to the summit of Ochsenkopf (Ox Head) Mountain, second highest in the Fichtelgebirge range.

The name of these mountains tells it as it always was and happily still is today – for Fichtelgebirge translates as 'Spruce Mountains'. The Fichtelgebirge stretch from the Red Main River Valley to the Czech border and form part of the distinct upland region known as the Thuringian-Franconian Highlands. In truth, these are more like rolling wooded hills than mountains, serving as a reminder that Germany has enough territory to ensure that several large areas of peaceful forest can be allowed to remain relatively undeveloped.

There are numerous towns and pretty villages within the Fichtelgebirge, but this does not detract from the area's natural charms and its unspoilt rural character attracts tourists all year round. For many, simply driving around and seeing the sights is enough, for this is a place of extraordinary granite rock formations and huge tracts of attractive woodland interspersed with moorland, meadows, wetlands and rivers. But Germany wouldn't be Germany without large numbers of enthusiastic visitors bent on embracing open-air activities. These include camping, hiking and mountain-biking in the warmer months, quickly switching to alpine skiing, snowboarding, cross-country skiing and sledding when the snow comes. More pampered incomers head for traditional spas like Fichtelberg, Bad Berneck or Bad Alexandersbad that have morphed into thoroughly modern health resorts offering thermal baths with all the luxury trimmings.

DON'T MISS
The wild flower displays in the high meadows and pastures.

LA PIERREUSE NATURE RESERVE

Northern Europe/Switzerland

La Pierreuse is the largest nature reserve in Romandie, the historical name for the French-speaking part of Switzerland which makes up the west of the country. It packs a good deal into its 34 sq km (13 sq mi). These foothills to the east of Lake Geneva constitute a prime example of a sub-alpine landscape, with cliffs, meadows, moorland and forests. The reserve is situated south of the town of Château d'Oex on the left bank of the River Sarine. Its core is a broad valley basin which is surrounded by mountains. Ibex and chamois are at home here on the screes and rocky slopes, while black grouse live on the moors and birds of prey include falcons and golden eagles. The variety of scenery in a relatively confined area, together with the surprise factor of the scattered rocks, makes La Pierreuse an excellent place for day walks. One of the best begins at the mountain station of the Videmanette cable car and runs through the reserve, crossing over four hills before finishing in L'Etivaz. It is a tough but rewarding six-hour hike with a difference in elevation of 1,000 m (3,280 ft); an easier variation is to walk down from the same starting point to the valley floor at Château d'Oex.

YOU SHOULD KNOW

Thanks to the local rock's high quartz component the area has long been famous for its hand-blown glass making. You can visit workshops in Zwiesel and Frauenau to see the ancient craft still being practised.

BAVARIAN FOREST
Northern Europe/Germany

Along with the Bohemian Forest across the border in the Czech Republic, the Bavarian Forest (Bayerischer Wald) forms the largest continuous area of woodland in Europe. It covers most of the land between the north bank of the Danube and the Czech border, an area of some 6,000 sq km (2,317 sq mi) on a southeast axis extending from Regensburg to Passau. For a country as heavily populated and highly developed as Germany the Bavarian Forest is a surprisingly wild and unspoilt region and it is certainly a place to come if you want to fill your lungs with fresh air. These uplands, which in parts rise to nearly 1,500 m (4,920 ft), are covered almost entirely in dense forest – largely spruce, but beech, oak and pine also feature. Here you can see ancient trees that have grown to gigantic proportions, some as high as 50 m (164 ft) and with girths of 2 m (6.5 ft) and more. Their enormous scale certainly enhances the sense of this being a primeval wilderness. Although mostly wooded, the Bavarian Forest also has lakes, mountain streams, pastures and areas of high moorland. The landscape is dotted with isolated little villages and farming communities. At its southern end is Germany's first national park, also called the Bavarian Forest, which in 2010 celebrated its 40th anniversary. Together with the Šumava National Park in the Czech Republic, it forms the largest area of protected forest in central Europe. With hundreds of kilometres of walking and cycling trails, the park is a nature-lover's paradise and one where you might be lucky enough to spot rare wildlife such as the lynx and the capercaillie (a type of grouse).

WHEN TO GO:
April–October (although if you like snow-walking or cross-country skiing, winter in the forest can also be very inviting).

WORTH A DETOUR:
The large wildlife enclosure in the national park will appeal particularly to children. You can walk all the way around its 7 km (4.3 mi) perimeter for great views of animals such as bison and wolves, which used to be natives of these forests.

LÖTSCHENTAL

Northern Europe/Switzerland

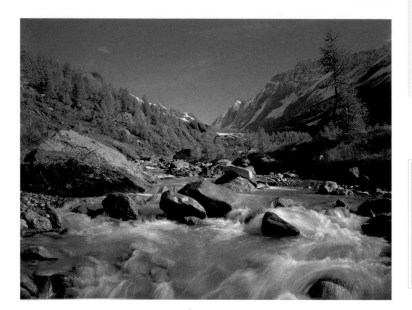

WHEN TO GO:
May–September
(December–April for winter
sports and snow-trekking).

WORTH A DETOUR:
The lovely old timber barns
and granaries in the village
of Kippel, many with richly
carved decoration.

YOU SHOULD KNOW
The Lötschental finishes at the
base of the Aletsch Glacier,
part of the massif containing
two of the country's most
celebrated peaks, the Eiger
and the Jungfrau.

Tucked into the southern fringes of the Bernese Oberland, the high alpine valley of Lötschental can lay claim more justly than most to its promotional tag as the 'hidden valley'. A mere 100 years ago it was still completely cut off from the outside world. It took the arrival of the railway and the engineering feat of a tunnel constructed through the Lötschberg in 1913 to begin the process of opening up the valley. The tunnel links Kandersteg to the north with Goppenstein at the western entrance to Lötschental. Ringed by steep-sided mountains, this is a classic glacial valley through which the River Lonza flows on its journey south to join the Rhône. Although the modern era has caught up with a vengeance and the valley is now a popular winter sports and summer hiking area with the high standard of facilities you expect of the Swiss, its isolation until relatively recently has meant that it has remained less developed than many other mountain resorts. This is wonderful walking terrain during the summer months. From the top of the Wiler cable car the Lötschentaler Höhenweg (high path) takes you high along the northern side of the valley, offering sweeping views before descending to the valley head at Fafleralp. Another classic walk starts from the Lauchernalp ski area and crosses the Lötschen pass into the Gasterntal and Kandersteg.

A further consequence of the valley's isolation has been the survival of old folk customs, including the carnival ritual of *Tschäggätta* in which local villagers parade through their communities wearing animal skins and fearsome wooden masks. The religious festival of Corpus Christi is marked with a colourful procession.

MURGTAL

Northern Europe/Switzerland

YOU SHOULD KNOW
This region is marketed as 'Heidiland' as it was the fictional setting for *Heidi*, Johanna Spyri's classic children's book.

HOW TO GET THERE:
The main railway line and motorway through the area runs along the south shore of the Walensee.

WORTH A DETOUR:
A cruise on the Walensee.

The Walensee in eastern Switzerland is one of the country's prettiest lakes. Lying close to the Liechtenstein border, this long and slender stretch of water is framed by dramatic mountain scenery that invites further exploration. The village of Murg on the lake's southern shore marks the entrance to the Murgtal, a valley which plunges into the southern massif. The mountains here may not be as immediately striking as the imposing Churfirsten range on the north shore but they still possess a wild and untamed air. Their unspoilt grandeur has been maintained thanks to a large part of the valley having been designated a nature reserve. The reason for the area's protected status is the mighty stone pine trees that grow in what are the largest such forests in the northern Alps. There are deciduous woods here too and, close to the lake, the unexpected sight of large stands of chestnut. The best way to appreciate the scenery is to trek through the chestnut forests and on up the valley from Murg. Alternatively, you can make your way to the head of the valley at Merlen from where a superb 14 km (8.75 mi) circular hike takes you right round the Hochmättli peak. Climbing up to 1,800 m (5,900 ft) the route takes you over moorland meadows, past bogs and waterfalls and yields outstanding views in every direction. It also passes a sequence of three classic little mountain lakes – sumptuous watery jewels in this remote fastness.

EISENWURZEN NATURE PARK

Northern Europe/Austria

DON'T MISS
There are some excellent white-water rafting opportunities in the park.

Tucked away in the far north of Styria, close to the provincial borders with Salzburg and Upper Austria, the beautiful alpine landscape that makes up the Eisenwurzen Nature Park looks entirely natural and unspoilt. But parts of this landscape would have looked very different 500 years ago when the mining of iron ore from the surrounding hills was a flourishing industry. Centred on the town of Eisenerz 25 km (15 mi) to the south, the mines were a major element in the livelihoods of the various small communities scattered throughout the Eisenwurzen region. Whether ferrying logs on wooden rafts down fast-flowing mountain rivers, or working in the area's many mills, the locals did well out of the industry until mining ceased in the 19th century. A few old mills still stand, including three flour mills close to the village of Gams. As well as its industrial heritage the park has the lovely valley of the River Enns and boasts many important geological features in the karst landscape, including caves, gorges and a lake which has no inlets (it is fed by water entering through natural springs in the lake bed). There are dramatic walkways along the narrow Noth and Water-Hole gorges; in the latter the waters originate from inside a huge limestone cave before dropping 300 m (984 ft) in a series of five falls into the Salza valley.

STUBAI ALPS

Northern Europe/Austria

DON'T MISS
Skiing on the Stubai glacier in high summer.

The Stubai Alps are a surprisingly quiet and unexplored section of the famous range. This wild and remote region is made up of a network of steep escarpments and criss-crossing ridges, with many summits topping 3,000 m (9,840 ft). The principal ridge in the range forms the border with Italy and includes the highest peak of the Stubai group, the Zuckerhüttl (literally, 'little sugar loaf') at 3,507 m (11,506 ft). The main access into these mountains is along the Stubaital, a long steep-sided valley which ends at the village of Mutterberg, from where a cable car whisks you up to high-level trekking or, if you are so minded, to skiing on the Stubai

glacier. Halfway down the valley the village of Neustift is the starting point for the Stubaier Höhenweg, one of the best long-distance hikes in the whole of the Alps. You need a good week for this challenging route and to ensure enough time to relish the stunning scenery, but it should be manageable by any adult who is reasonably fit. The route crosses several passes at around the 2,700 m (8,860 ft) mark, and paths can be rough and steep.

BOHEMIAN SWITZERLAND

Eastern Europe/Czech Republic

WHEN TO GO:
April–October.

Part of Bohemian Switzerland is now a national park of the same name, but this only accounts for a small proportion of the region which is bounded to the west by the Labe (Elbe) valley and extends eastwards from the German border at Hrensko to Ceská Kamenice. There are many well-marked trails to help you explore the area, of which the most popular is a 17 km (10.5 mi) round route from Hrensko which is manageable in a long day. This trail takes in the region's two most spectacular sights: the Pravcická brána, a huge stone arch that is the largest natural bridge in Europe, and the gorge of the Kamenice River which carves its way through Bohemian Switzerland before joining the Labe at Hrensko.

BROUMOV HIGHLANDS

Eastern Europe/Czech Republic

A special feature of the central European forests which cover the borderlands of the Czech Republic, Poland and Slovakia are the so-called 'rock towns' (*skalní mesta*). Several are to be found in the Broumov Highlands. Visiting these mysterious landscapes where plateaux, gorges, cliffs and caves are interspersed with strangely anthropomorphic rock formations, it is easy to believe you are walking through deserted settlements. Two of the best 'rock towns' are next to one another at Adršpach and Teplice in the north of the highlands. Trails lead to the most interesting rocks and the bizarre shapes which weathering has wrought in the soft sandstone. Grandmother's Armchair, Sugar Cone and the Hand are some of the names that have been applied to nature's work. And at a height of nearly 100 m (328 ft) the Courting Couple at Adršpach is the tallest sandstone pillar in the country.

WORTH A DETOUR:
The evocatively named Sibir (Siberia) Gorge at the Teplice rock town, which has its own microclimate where cool and damp prevail and towering tree-ferns thrive.

Another striking section of the highlands are the Broumov walls, a long thin sandstone ridge which effectively cuts off the town of Broumov from the rest of the country. Approaching from the west in this wooded region you would hardly know the 'walls' were there before coming to the edge of a precipice and being presented all of a sudden with a stupendous panorama of the plain below as it stretches away into Poland.

ŠUMAVA NATIONAL PARK

Eastern Europe/Czech Republic

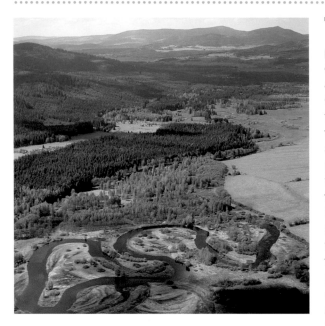

The Šumava is one of very few remaining parts of the crowded continent of Europe that can be legitimately described as a wilderness area. Situated on the southwestern fringe of the Czech Republic, this sparsely populated region forms part of the much larger Bohemian Forest which spills over into neighbouring Germany. It is a land of rolling hills, dark pine forests, meadows, peat bogs and low humpbacked mountains. With few gradients of serious consequence it is ideal terrain for cycling as well as offering magnificent hiking possibilities. A network of trails gives access to hidden valleys and tiny isolated villages which seem to have grown organically out of their natural surroundings. It may be a deservedly popular destination for lovers of the great outdoors, especially those from Germany and Austria, but the size of the Šumava means there's no problem in getting away from the crowds.

Established only after the collapse of communism in 1991, the Šumava National Park, together with its buffer zone which has the status of a Protected Landscape, covers an area of 1,630 sq km (630 sq mi). The country's most famous river, the mighty Vltava, has its source in the western hills and flows through the length of the park before turning north to Ceský Krumlov. Along the way a dam has created a large artificial lake at Lake Lipno, a popular recreation and watersports area in the summer months. The park becomes ever quieter and more remote and the woods ever thicker the further west you go. The area around Železná Ruda is particularly unspoilt, with two glacial lakes and the lovely Bilá Strž waterfall.

HOW TO GET THERE:
Šumava is four hours by bus and five hours by train from Prague. Local buses link the main towns and villages in the region but the scenic way to travel is on the two charming single-track railway lines that traverse the eastern and central areas of the park.

YOU SHOULD KNOW
The Šumava runs along what was once one of the most heavily fortified sections of the Iron Curtain, a factor which ironically has helped spare it subsequent over-development.

BESKIDY MOUNTAINS

Eastern Europe/Poland

WORTH A DETOUR:
The Poprad River running south from Nowy Sàcz is a particularly beautiful valley in the Beskid Sàdecki hills.

The Beskidy Mountains form part of the Carpathians, one of Europe's principal mountain chains. These gentle slopes and enticing valleys have an unpretentious and timeless appeal. Beech and fir are the main trees in these densely forested hills where you will have little difficulty escaping the crowds and communing with nature. You are sharing the woods with bears, wolves, lynx, and wildcats but you need not fret unduly about a close encounter with a predator since these are generally discreet and reclusive hunters who prefer not to be seen. What you will have no difficulty spotting are the wooden churches, some hundreds of years old, which are scattered across the landscape. These extraordinary edifices with their onion domes and richly decorated interiors stand as silent witnesses to a distinctive and almost vanished folk culture.

KASZUBY LAKES

Eastern Europe/Poland

DON'T MISS
The hand-carved snuffboxes Kashubians carry.

Kashubia extends for some 100 km (62 mi) southwest of Gdansk and is noted for its tranquil landscapes and serene beauty. This area is not one of nature's scene-stealers but one which wears its modest charms easily and appealingly to anyone seeking a less hurried pace of life and an insight into how the Polish peasantry lived 100 years ago. It is a world of low hills and quiet woodlands dotted with quaint villages containing many examples of traditional wooden and half-timbered buildings.

The area's most distinctive features are the many lakes scattered across the countryside – according to legend the footprints of giants who created the region. A local saying has it that 'wherever you throw

a stone in Kashubia, it will land in water'; not surprisingly, the area is a haven for canoeists and kayakers. The Radunia Circle is a particular favourite – a 60 km (37 mi) aquatic loop which takes in ten lakes, all connected by the Radunia River. The loop is in the countryside between Kartuzy and Koscierzyna, a landscape of hills and lakes known popularly as Kashub Switzerland.

You will still hear older Kashubians speaking a dialect of Polish that is thought to derive from an ancient Pomeranian tongue.

STOLOWE MOUNTAINS

Eastern Europe/Poland

HOW TO GET THERE:

The small town of Kudowa-Zdrój on the Czech border to the southwest is the best base for a visit to the Stolowe Mountains. The popular health resort lies on the main Warsaw to Prague highway.

WHEN TO GO:

April–October (but be advised that you may still find snow at the bottom of the Little Hell crevice as late as June).

WORTH A DETOUR:

If you are in the area you should certainly not miss the Chapel of Skulls in Czermna on the outskirts of Kudowa-Zdrój, a memento mori if ever there was one.

Part of the Sudetes Mountains which run for over 250 km (155 mi) along the Polish-Czech border, the Góry Stolowe or Stolowe Mountains have been attracting visitors to this corner of Lower Silesia for more than 200 years. The curious rock formations that are their particular fascination are certainly found nowhere else in Poland. When you look at the characteristic flat-topped profiles of these mountains it is not difficult to see why they are known as the Table Mountains (stolowe in Polish). These plateaus were formed as a result of deposits of soft sandstone building up in horizontal strata. Over time the forces of erosion have worn away the softer rock to leave the harder stuff exposed beneath. Inevitably the bizarre shapes thus created have been given names, such as Camel, Elephant, Hen and Pulpit, although it takes quite an effort of the imagination in some cases to appreciate the likeness.

The Góry Stolowe are now a national park. At 63 sq km (24 sq mi) it is relatively small by national park standards, which means you should be able to explore its principal sights in a couple of days. Numerous hiking trails and cycle paths lead through the spruce forests that constitute 90 per cent of the park area, including one that takes you on a large loop from the village of Karlów past various viewpoints and rock formations. After climbing nearly 700 stone steps to the Szczeliniec Wielki, at 919 m (3,015 ft) the highest outcrop in the range, you pass by other striking natural features, including a 20 m (66 ft) deep chasm in the rock appropriately named Little Hell. Elsewhere in the park there is a large group of scattered rocks known as the Petrified Mushrooms and the Bledne Skaly, a huge labyrinth composed of gigantic boulders.

YOU SHOULD KNOW

The waters from the area's natural springs have long been known for their curative and restorative properties. There are a number of elegant spa towns close to the Stolowe Mountains.

AUKŠTAITIJA NATIONAL PARK
Eastern Europe/Lithuania

Lithuania's Lake District has lots of lakes, including 126 in Aukštaitija National Park. They are scattered among wonderful country consisting of woods, meadows and gentle hills. The park is crossed by the River Žeimena, which is fed by numerous streams and occupies an area of around 400 sq km (154 sq mi) centred on the village of Palūšė, 100 km (62 mi) north of Vilnius beside Lake Lušiai. Although there are 115 traditional villages within the park, home to over 2,000 people, human presence does not detract from the area's outstanding natural beauty. Three-quarters of the terrain is wooded and much of the rest is water, ensuring great biodiversity undamaged by modern development. Indeed, some two per cent of Aukštaitija National Park is classified as 'strictly protected' and may be entered only if accompanied by a member of park staff.

The area has a long history – the park has 11 hill forts – and this heritage adds a pleasing dimension to any visit. Stripeikiai is the park's oldest village and hosts the quaintly named Lithuanian Museum of Ancient Beekeeping. Another worthwhile destination is Ginuciai, with its original watermill. But the lakes are magnetic and, since the park was established in 1974, water tourism has become the major leisure activity. Kayaks are easy to hire and a wonderful way of exploring this special landscape, with waterside campsites to encourage extended expeditions. Everyone who takes to the water should be sure to visit Baluošas Lake to explore the seven islands therein, one of which has a mini-lake of its own.

DON'T MISS
The ornate wooden 18th-century church of St Jezefa in Palūšė that appears on the Lithuanian 1 litas banknote.

GAUJA NATIONAL PARK

Eastern Europe/Latvia

Latvia's largest national park is one of four in the country and was established in 1973 in the region of Vidzeme. Running from northeast of Sigulda to southwest of Cesis, Gauja National Park occupies an area of 920 sq km (355 sq mi) along the Gauja River Valley – 60 km (37 mi) long and between 10 km (6 mi) and 30 km (17 mi) wide. Although it follows the river's course, the park also contains lakes – the largest being Lake Ungurs – and around half the terrain consists of dense forest, mainly spruce and pine. Spectacular sandstone cliffs along the Gauja River soar to 90 m (300 ft) in some places and feature strongly in the park's wilder northern sections around Sigulda, where strict preservation rules apply. There are many amazing rock formations and numerous caves carved from sandstone by wind, weather and water over many millennia. The southwestern parts of the park are more leisure orientated and a natural playground popular with the inhabitants of Riga, who enjoy rafting and canoeing on the river, or hiking, biking and horse riding. The forests provide a home for over 900 plant species, 150 types of bird and nearly 50 different wild animals. There are a number of campsites in the park, including some for river users. But quite apart from this carefully husbanded nature reserve, those who explore the park will find over 500 monuments testifying to the area's long and colourful history. There are overgrown castle mounds as well as real castles, archaeological sites, old churches, windmills and watermills, fortresses and ancient manors.

The town of Ligatne, which is within the park, has its own fascinating nature park, complete with trails.

YOU SHOULD KNOW

Birdwatchers flock to the Jonte Gorge for the rare opportunity to see three species of vulture circling (black, griffon and Egyptian vultures).

WHEN TO GO:

Any time. Winters are short and sharp (generally from January–March). Summers are usually mild but wet.

HIGHLIGHTS:

The beautifully reconstructed medieval Turaida Castle, right across the River Gauja from Sigulda. In addition to the original structure begun in 1214, the surrounding museum reserve includes an ancient wooden church and the Dainu Hill sculpture park.

WHEN TO GO: Any time. Matsalu is always filled with life, but spring and autumn bring the gigantic aerial armadas.

MATSALU NATIONAL PARK

Eastern Europe/Estonia

Every spring and autumn, most of the waterfowl which breed in the arctic tundra migrate along the southern coast of the Baltic Sea. Geese, swans, ducks and waders in their hundreds of thousands stop in western Estonia, on and around the Kasari River delta where it flows into Matsalu Bay and the Vainameri Sea. Protected by the brackish shallows of the Vainameri Sea from the full onslaught of the open Baltic, Matsalu Bay has no real tides to scour the rich silts that infuse the coastal meadows, reed beds, swamps, bogs, floodplains and slick mudflats that meld into the shoreline. The bay is 18 km (11 mi) long and 6 km (4 mi) wide, but barely 1.5 m (5 ft) deep, a sanctuary from everything except the wind and winter ice, which is thicker here, and lasts longer, because of its sheltered position. The 236 sq km (91 sq mi) of open sea within the reserve includes 40 islands which greatly extend the variety of nesting and rest sites available to the two million waterfowl which settle in Matsalu. It's hard to take in their magnificence. On the greyest day, to see 20,000 Bewick's swans materialize from a waterlogged horizon, and listen to the urgent thunder of 100,000 beating wings as greylag and barnacle geese slap down on the water, is to participate in some sort of homage to creation.

SOOMAA NATIONAL PARK

Eastern Europe/Estonia

Deep beneath the bogs and forests of Soomaa, the bedrock is inclined at an angle which causes its rivers and streams to drain into a single major river, the Halliste, which then flows into the Navesti River at 160 degrees against its stream. The almost head-on collision of water causes biblical floods every year. Over millennia the same sequence has created five huge bogs separated by thick swamp forests and enormous floodplains where the best way to get around is by dug-out log canoe, used here since the Stone Age. In the swamp forests (known also as 'carrs'), beaver and otter create river meanders with their building works; the alluvial meadows and river banks are coloured blue with wild iris, and harbour 200 other species including orchids; and in the fens and bogs you might see bear, wolves or lynx. Each of these geographic features is without direct parallel elsewhere in the world. Soomaa is an evolutionary laboratory on a colossal scale, and even its flora and fauna are adaptive. Its peculiar history of flooding makes it the most exciting wetland in Europe.

DON'T MISS
Bog-walking, with an expert guide to prevent disappearance without trace.

TEBERDINSKY NATURE RESERVE

Eastern Europe/Russian Federation

DON'T MISS
The gorgeous displays of wild flowers in the high meadows during the summer months.

In spite of these magnificent mountains being involuntary witnesses to many of the fiercest territorial disputes that have flared up in the aftermath of the break-up of the former Soviet Union (Chechnya is the most notorious), the mystique and rugged beauty of the Caucasus have been preserved remarkably intact.

The Teberdinsky Nature Reserve encompasses an area of 851 sq km (328 sq mi) on the northern spurs of the western Caucasus. With a vertical elevation of nearly 3,000 m (9,840 ft) within its boundaries the reserve displays an astonishing range of environments, from temperate mixed woodlands through dense conifer forests to high alpine meadows above the tree-line. Teberdinsky protects one of the most unspoilt and biodiverse ecosystems in Europe, a fact recognized internationally in 1997 when it was awarded biosphere reserve status by UNESCO.

The reserve offers splendid hiking opportunities but you should take a local guide with you, especially in the southern reaches which abut a sensitive national frontier (Abkhazia, a small breakaway republic from neighbouring Georgia, is on the other side). The forests are home to brown bears, bison, lynx and wild boars while on the rocky higher slopes you should have no difficulty spotting chamois and tur, the wild goats which with their large curved horns are found only in the Caucasus.

DON'T MISS
The autumn colours in the reserve are stunning.

KALUZHSKIE ZASEKI NATURE RESERVE

Eastern Europe/Russian Federation

In times past, city-states such as Novgorod and Muscovy relied on the impenetrability of the vast forests of the central Russian uplands. The use of felled trees stacked one on top of another was a further defensive measure; its Russian name, *zaseki*, has been given to one of Russia's newest nature reserves.

The Kaluzhskie Zaseki Nature Reserve is situated in the Kaluga region southwest of Moscow. Large parts of this region were formerly covered by mixed deciduous woodlands but, once the military threats from the south had diminished, the forests fell prey to logging and other forms of human exploitation and dwindled. However, as recently as the early 1990s, scientists came across an undisturbed tract of old-growth broadleaf forest. Considering the political turmoil of the times it was quite an achievement that they were able to safeguard this precious survival by establishing an area of 185 sq km (71 sq mi) as a nature reserve.

The reserve is criss-crossed by streams and wetlands but the vast majority of it is woodland and home to a remarkable proliferation of wildlife. Moose, deer, wild boar and wolves are the larger mammals that inhabit the forest; it is also home to over 160 different birds, including golden eagles, hawks and other birds of prey.

Right: Teberdinsky Nature Reserve

KOSTOMUKSHSKY FOREST

Eastern Europe/Russian Federation

The province of Karelia in Russia's far northwest has always been a land alive with legend and shrouded in romance. Inside the huge dark forest an air of mystery mingles with an almost oppressive stillness and, as you contemplate the serried rows of pines receding into the far distance, it becomes easy to imagine the spirits of the woodland that populate the rich folklore of the region. Indeed, it was on the banks of Lake Kamennoye that the poems and songs of the Kalevala had their probable origin (the great national epic of Finland which has proved such a fertile source of inspiration for the country's artists, most notably the composer Jean Sibelius).

The 10,500-ha (25,946-ac) Lake Kamennoye is the largest of some 250 lakes found in the Kostomukshsky Nature Reserve in northern Karelia. The reserve was established in 1983 to protect 476 sq km (184 sq mi) of virgin coniferous forest along Russia's border with Finland. This is a classic landscape of the boreal or northern taiga: dense pine and spruce forests interspersed with waterways, swamps and peat bogs.

WHEN TO GO:
June–August.

WORTH A DETOUR:
They may be an endangered species but you should be able to spot white-tailed sea eagles, either in their lofty bankside perches or circling and swooping over the rivers and lakes.

YOU SHOULD KNOW
Thanks to a special joint agreement, Kostomukshsky is now part of a much larger green belt which incorporates other reserves across the border in Finland.

It is home to large animals like the reindeer and brown bear, and to predators like the wolf and the lynx. Sadly, reindeer numbers in the reserve have halved over the past two decades, partly because of poaching but also because the barbed-wire border fence has impeded the creatures' natural east–west migrations. Among the birds to be found in Kostomukshsky are the capercaillie and black grouse.

YUGYD VA NATIONAL PARK

Eastern Europe/Russian Federation

WHEN TO GO:
May–September (the
spring snow melts offer the
best rafting conditions).

It is only fitting that a national park within the largest country on Earth should be on a similarly epic scale. Yugyd Va is practically the size of Wales and covers a 400 km (248 mi) length of the northern Urals. The park includes prime examples of taiga and Europe's largest remaining expanses of virgin spruce forest. In the foothills, the landscape changes to predominantly tundra. The Urals are not high – the highest peak, Mount Narodnaya, which is located within Yugyd Va, is less than 2,000 m (6,562 ft) – but the park lies just outside the Arctic Circle so there are glaciers and frozen lakes. If the Siberian spruce dominates the landscape of the lower slopes, the monotony of dark green is relieved occasionally by broad stands of that most evocative of Russian trees – the birch. There are established populations of elk, reindeer, sable and brown bears in the park, and you are likely to hear wolves even if you don't see them. Yugyd Va covers much of the basin of the River Pechora, one of Europe's longest, which flows north into the Barents Sea. Adventure rafting on its feeder rivers as they tumble down from the mountains is an increasingly popular activity but Yugyd Va is still seriously off the beaten track.

TSENTRALNO CHERNOZYOMNY NATURE RESERVE

Eastern Europe/Russian Federation

DON'T MISS
The flute-like song
of the golden oriole.

The city of Kursk lies 500 km (310 mi) south of Moscow on the northern fringes of Russia's fabled Chernozyom, or Black Earth belt. This region, much of it now in present-day Ukraine, was once known as the breadbasket of the Russian Empire, thanks to its deep, nutrient-rich soil. A well-drained humus layer, as much as 1 m (3 ft) deep, has provided one of the most fertile and productive agricultural landscapes anywhere on Earth. One 19th-century writer, indeed, called the Chernozyom 'the Tsar of soils, more valuable than oil, more precious than gold'. Unsurprisingly, it has been intensively farmed over the centuries, which makes the 130 sq km (50 sq mi, including buffer zone) of the Tsentralno Chernozyomny Nature Reserve outside Kursk all the more astonishing a survival.

The reserve is important because it protects a small but precious area of pristine steppe habitat that has never fallen under the plough. It marks the point where the wide open plains meet the belt of temperate forest to the north; roughly half its area consists of broadleaf woodlands. Fringed by the basins of two of Russia's mightiest rivers, the Don and the Dnieper, Tsentralno Chernozyomny also has its fair share of swamps and marshland. The forests are home to elk, roe deer and wild boar while smaller mammals include the Siberian polecat and the stone marten. Black kites are a common sight hovering overhead and the exotic hoopoe with its striking feathered crest and pinkish colouring can also be found here.

MOUNT ELBRUS

Eastern Europe/Russian Federation

YOU SHOULD KNOW
Walking on the southern slopes of the valley requires a border permit.

WHEN TO GO:
June–September (but note that there is also a skiing and winter sports season from December–May).

If you accept that the Caucasus Mountains are part of Europe (some people consider them to be in Asia), then Mount Elbrus is the highest peak in Europe at 5,642 m (18,510 ft) – significantly superior to Mont Blanc in France. Its distinctive twin peaks, under a permanent cover of snow, are an impressive sight at any time of year but, unless you are an experienced climber or a winter sports fanatic, you will need to come in the summer months if you want to see them. Elbrus is situated at the head of the Baksan River valley, on a spur projecting north from the central Caucasus range. The mountain forms the heart of the Prielbrusye National Park, a vast wilderness area comprising 1,000 sq km (386 sq mi) of alpine meadows and pine and birch forests in addition to the mountains themselves. Jagged ridges and lofty peaks flank the valley on both sides, offering spectacular panoramas in every direction.

Various trails lead off from the valley floor along smaller side valleys, presenting options for easy day-treks or longer, more strenuous hikes involving overnight stays in campsites or shelters. You cannot see the summit of Mount Elbrus itself from the Baksan valley, but a three-hour walk up the Terskol valley brings you to a dramatic hanging glacier (one of several in the park) where great shards of ice 'drip' over the cliff edge; from here there is a fine view of the twin peaks. The more popular and less effortful way of seeing the summit, though, is to take the cable car at the end of the valley to the Mir Bar station at 3,500 m (11,483 ft).

SHULGAN-TASH

Eastern Europe/Russian Federation

WHEN TO GO:
May–September.

WORTH A DETOUR:
Sample the product of those busy bees. The amber nectar may not come cheap but is rightly prized by the local population.

There are many reasons for protecting our precious natural environment but few can be stranger than the one which has given birth to Shulgan-Tash Nature Reserve in the rolling hills of the southern Urals. The reserve was established in 1990 in order to protect the natural habitat of the humble Burzyan honeybee. Renowned for the quality of the sweet golden honey they produce, these wild bees are able to survive very cold weather and Shulgan-Tash is the only place in the world where they are still found in the wild. The bees colonize hollows in trees and feed on nectar from linden trees and the fireweed plant (more popularly known in Britain as rosebay willowherb). The hives are now tended by rangers on the reserve, many of whom have inherited beekeeping skills passed down through generations of Bashkir families.

Bounded on its northern edge by the Nugush River and by the Belaya River to the south, Shulgan-Tash reserve is located in the autonomous republic of Bashkortostan, some 200 km (124 mi) south of the capital Ufa. The landscape is predominantly one of old-growth deciduous forests which cover the hills and low mountains, occasionally punctuated by clearings of meadow and grassland. Mountain tributaries of the main rivers wind their way through the terrain, creating dramatic canyons through the limestone ridges. Besides the bees, Shulgan-Tash's other claim to fame is the Kapov Caves, a huge underground complex of grottos and passages carved out of the karst by the Shulgan river. The caves, which can be visited on guided tours, contain some of Europe's most ancient rock paintings, estimated to be at least 15,000 years old.

YOU SHOULD KNOW
Conservationists are currently campaigning against a proposed hydro-electric dam on the Belaya River which they fear would flood important habitats in Shulgan-Tash.

DILIJAN NATIONAL PARK

Eastern Europe/Armenia

HOW TO GET THERE:

By minibus van from Yerevan to the upper Avtokayaran, then another to Ijevan that will stop at Dilijan. That said, a taxi from Yerevan is not expensive, even for budget travellers. Car hire offers freedom to see more of the park and its environs.

WHEN TO GO:

The Armenian climate varies considerably according to specific location, but the preferred time to explore Dilijan National Park is during the cool and moist summer. Autumn visitors will be delighted by the turning foliage, however.

HIGHLIGHTS:

The fabulous Haghartsin Monastery, in a beautiful wooded hillside setting near Dilijan. Constructed between the 10th and 14th centuries, it has many impressive buildings (some ruined) and the centrepiece is St Astvatsatsin Church with a wonderful dome that has no fewer than 16 facets.

It initially seems somewhat chaotic. Dilijan National Park in northeastern Armenia's Tavush Province – one of two national parks in the country – was created in 2002 to succeed a state nature reserve, itself the scene of forestry enterprises until the late 1950s.

Although it spreads across slopes of the Pembak, Areguni, Miapor, Ijevan and Halab mountains, all the high pastures are actually excluded from the park. There are numerous cultural monuments and settlements located within the park – including eponymous Dilijan town – and a railway line passes right through the middle. Tension between well-meaning nature conservation and commercial activity is endemic.

Sounds… unpromising? Actually, the largely forested Dilijan National Park is rather good, with plenty of unspoilt, wild terrain awaiting the adventurous traveller looking for an unusual destination. Dilijan itself is a charming old town nestling in the picturesque hills, and provides an ideal base for sallies into the surrounding countryside. This may remind visitors of Switzerland, as it has forests and alpine meadows very reminiscent of the land of alpenhorns and tinkling cowbells. Happily, this remote corner of Europe is gnome-free and anything but a tourist hotspot – seeming all the better for that.

The park cries out to be explored and is rich in flora and fauna. There are over a thousand plant species and a wide variety of trees, including oak, beech, hornbeam, lime, maple, ash, pine, juniper and many wild fruit trees.

Around 150 species of bird have been recorded, including real corkers like golden eagle, goshawk, black kite, honey buzzard, black grouse, Caspian snowcock and eagle owl. The animal population is scarcely less impressive, with the likes of brown bear, wolf, lynx, wild boar, wildcat and red deer among its 50 or so members.

YOU SHOULD KNOW

The resort of Dilijan is actually a modest spa town, renowned for its energizing mineral waters – although definitely not quite so grand as Bath or Buxton.

> **WORTH A DETOUR:** South of the main trail on Hoveria mountain is an impressive waterfall on the Prut River, a tributary of the Danube.

CHORNOHORA MOUNTAIN RIDGE
Eastern Europe/Ukraine

The western end of the Chornohora Mountain Ridge, the highest section of the mighty Carpathians, is jagged and the monolithic eastern massif contains the highest peaks, including Hoverla, Pip Ivan, Shpytsi and Tomnatyk. Postglacial depressions bottom out in lakes or peat bogs and narrow valleys slash the slopes of Chornohora. The lower elevations are heavily forested with beech and spruce trees, then there's a belt of alder and juniper brush before the alpine meadows and barren rock fields that make up the ridge. The local Hutsul people are mainly occupied with traditional animal herding on high pastures during a five-month season, although tourism is starting to play an increasingly important role in the regional economy. That said, the mountains are still isolated, lonely and potentially hazardous. So this is really one for an organized hiking tour led by a guide who knows the rugged terrain intimately. A number of treks are offered, lasting from one day to a week. Go-it-alone types should not be tempted to tackle the Chornohora Mountain Ridge unless their self-sufficiency skills and backcountry experience are well honed, although modest day hikes are comfortably within the reach of anyone who is reasonably fit and active.

SYNEVYR LAKE
Eastern Europe/Ukraine

> **WORTH A DETOUR:** The forest path from Lake Synevyr that climbs through the trees to a wonderful outlook offering a fabulous panoramic view across the lake and the wooded mountains beyond.

Ukraine's largest mountain lake sits in the picturesque heart of the Synevyr National Nature Park. It has an outflow into the Tereblya River and was formed when a landslide dammed the steep valley it occupies. It rejoices in the title 'Blue Eye of the Carpathians', encouraged by the presence of a tiny island in the centre that represents the pupil. This small but deep lake has recently been classified as a wetland of international importance. Although the surrounding mountains are wild and lonely – an ideal challenge for the hardy hiker who loves self-sufficient wilderness exploration – the lake is a popular destination.

The drive to the lake is an experience in itself, as the road winds up the steep Synevyrskiy Pass, far above the white dwellings of Svnevry village which are scattered around the silver thread of the Tereblya River. To see the lake in its marvellous setting from afar before actually going there, continue to the summit of nearby Ozirna Mountain before returning to the lake (road open in summer only). A word to the wise – Synevyr Lake's crystal-clear waters may look tempting, and often attract hardy swimmers, but think carefully before joining them. The water temperature rarely rises above 5°C (41°F), which makes the average cold shower seem, well, warm.

GRAND CANYON

Eastern Europe/Ukraine

DON'T MISS
A short day-hike along the canyon floor to Blue Pond and Bath of Youth pools.

Ukraine's very own Grand Canyon is found on the peninsula of Crimea, which juts into the Black Sea and is an autonomous republic within Ukraine. In no way does it measure up to its cousin in Arizona when it comes to the awesome natural wonder stakes – but is still a sublimely beautiful wild place.

The canyon walls tower up to an impressive height of 320 m (1,050 ft) and – amazingly – it is a mere 3 m (10 ft) wide at the narrowest point. The fast-flowing Kuru-Uzen races along the canyon's rocky floor, creating dynamic small waterfalls, pools and white-water rapids before joining the Auzun-Uzen River towards the canyon exit. Despite those dizzying rock faces, much of the canyon has shallower sides. They – along with the canyon surrounds and floor – are densely wooded.

There are two routes for hikers who want to travel along the Grand Canyon and enjoy its astonishing rock formations close up. One route follows the canyon floor beside the water, another passes along the right flank of the canyon. The former is impassable in winter and spring, when a raging torrent invariably overwhelms the path, but the latter may be used all year round. The favoured direction for hiking is from the upper to the lower end. This through-trek can be done in a day but is anything but a casual stroll. A good level of fitness is essential, for either route is demanding physically. In addition, there are side paths that lead nowhere and anyone tempted to follow one can end up hopelessly lost amidst tangled vegetation.

WORTH A DETOUR: Golden eagles nest in these mountains; you may be lucky to see these majestic birds circling high overhead on the thermals.

MALÁ FATRA NATIONAL PARK

Eastern Europe/Slovakia

The focus of Malá Fatra National Park is the beautiful valley formed by the Vrátna River as it carves its way into the mountains. The village of Terchová stands at the entrance to the valley but the real gateway comes a little way south as you enter the dramatic rockscape of the Tiesñavy gorge, with sheer cliffs and towering limestone pinnacles on every side. Further up the valley, exciting vistas open up of mountain rising above slopes which are covered in pine and beech forests.

The valley is completely encircled by brooding peaks which leave you in no doubt that nature holds sway here. From Chatna Vrátna at the head of the valley, 7 km (4.3 mi) south of Terchová, you can take a cable car up the mountain to the Snilovské saddle from where it is a 40-minute hike to the summit of Velký Kriváñ, at 1,709 m (5,607 ft) the highest peak in the park. If the weather holds, you will be rewarded with panoramic views of the Vrátna valley.

Right: Grand Canyon

PIENINY MOUNTAINS

Eastern Europe/Slovakia

HOW TO GET THERE: The Pieniny Mountains are 120 km (75 mi) from Košice, the main city in East Slovakia. Buses are infrequent so it is best if you have your own transport.

This small national park, together with a sister park on the north bank in Poland, exists primarily to protect the lovely valley of the Dunajec River, which forms the actual frontier between Poland and Slovakia. Jagged limestone peaks rise above the thick forests which cover nearly half of the park's 21 sq km (8 sq mi). Much of the rest is given over to small fields and richly grassed meadows, testimony to a traditional way of farming largely untouched by the modern age.

The best way to appreciate the mountains is from the river. You should not miss the trip downriver on one of the large wooden rafts. Starting at the 14th-century Red Monastery, the 90-minute journey takes you down a jaw-dropping 8.5 km (5.3 mi) gorge past cliffs which rise sheer from the water and tower over you.

This is no white-water trip so you have plenty of time to admire the dramatic scenery as you are poled along by rafters in their traditional embroidered waistcoats. The views change constantly as the river winds its way through the limestone hills. Your guide will point out the main features, such as the three rocks known as the Stone Monks and the Tri Koruny (Three Crowns); these are the highest peaks in the range, but Poland claims them as they are on the north bank.

WORTH A DETOUR: The traditional wooden churches of the area, a curious blend of western Catholicism and eastern Orthodoxy and the most visible reminder of the local Rusyn culture.

VIHORLAT HIGHLANDS

Eastern Europe/Slovakia

In the easternmost part of Slovakia the Vihorlat Highlands are a range of tree-covered volcanic hills which provide some of the country's best walking. The woodlands of the Vihorlat are composed mainly of mixed deciduous trees, with beech being the predominant species. In 2007 parts of these woods, along with counterparts in Ukraine, were inscribed on UNESCO's World Heritage List as Primeval Beech Forests. A hidden gem in the Vihorlat Highlands is the Morské oko lake, perhaps the most beautiful and unspoilt in the whole of Slovakia. This glacial lake owes its unusual name (*morské oko* means 'sea eye') to its distinctive blue-green colour. If you sit quietly on the shore you may see the black storks which nest in these parts and honey buzzards and eagles as they circle high overhead. From the northern lake shore it is a two-hour hike to another natural marvel of the region, the Snina stone, a great slab of rock which rises precipitously above the tree line. The strenuous climb to the top is up steep iron ladders attached to the cliff face but the outstanding views from the table-top summit, 1,005 m (3,297 ft) high, make the effort eminently worthwhile. On a clear day you can see all the way over the eastern border into Ukraine.

HORTOBÁGY NATIONAL PARK

Eastern Europe/Hungary

Rather like the Prairie in North America, the Steppes in Russia or the Veldt in South Africa, the Puszta not only indicates a vast flat grassy area, but also carries with it a meaning that portrays a way of life. The great Hungarian Plain is not only the largest natural grassland in Europe but is also a place of special harmony between humans and nature. On the Puszta herdsmen on horseback tend their grey cattle and Racka sheep, while oxen haul trailers brim full with bales of hay. It is a traditional place little changed since before the birth of Christ. Within this great plain lies Hortobágy National Park. Created in 1973, it was the first to acquire national park status in Hungary and its unique ecosystem was further recognized and protected when it was afforded World Heritage status in 1999. The park covers 800 sq km (309 sq mi) of meadows, low-lying scrub, bogs and lakes which provide a diverse range of habitats for a wide array of flora and fauna. Over 300 bird species have been identified in the park. One in particular provides one of the most spectacular avian displays in the world when, in the late autumn (October) evenings, cranes gather in numbers as great as 80,000 to rest on the park's lakes – in flight they almost block out the sky. The neoclassical white Nine Span Bridge, completed in 1833, is the most famous man-made landmark in the Hortobágy and at 170 m (558 ft) is the longest stone bridge in Europe.

WHEN TO GO:
It's best between April–October.

WORTH A DETOUR:
The Tisza Lake Water Trail –
a 1.6 km (1 mi) boardwalk
into the lake's wetlands,
complete with watch towers
and hides.

BICAZ CANYON AND RED LAKE
Eastern Europe/Romania

WHEN TO GO: It's beautiful all year round but clear of snow from April–October. The area is most beautiful in autumn (September and October) when the trees change colour.

Located in the northeast of Romania, Bicaz Canyon (Cheile Bicazulu) is a deep gorge burrowed out by the fast-flowing Bicaz River. The canyon is not only a destination in itself but also acts as a corridor linking the regions of Transylvania and Moldavia via a precipitous snaking road. Within the limestone walls of this most imposing canyon are hidden two remarkable caverns: the Black Cave and Waterfall Cave. As well as offering

ample opportunity for a spot of *spelunking* (cave exploration), the canyon is a favourite among rock climbers. Huge walls up to 300 m (984 ft) high rise to fantastic hanging ceilings, with deep scars in the rocks and huge clear spaces providing an adrenalin-filled climb.

Upstream from the canyon lies a spectacular lake. Sometime in the summer of 1837, after a huge storm system hit the area, an enormous chunk of Killer Mountain became dislodged and blocked three creeks, producing a natural dam which flooded the valley. The result was Red Lake (Lacu Rosu) – made red by alluvial deposits and the reflection from the purple flanks of Suhardu Mic Mountain in the water. The lake has an eerie appearance as stumps of pine trees poke out from beneath its surface.

DON'T MISS
The views of the Barsa Valley from the Crapaturii Saddle.

PIATRA CRAIULUI
Eastern Europe/Romania

Piatra Craiului (pronounced Cry-ooh-loo-e) is a 150 sq km (58 sq mi) national park in the Carpathian Mountains of Romania dominated by a mountainous ridge from which it takes its name. The north of the park, near the Barsa River, is made up of sloping intense-green pastureland which in spring and summer is dappled with wild blue orchids and yellow buttercups. But it is the spectacularly stark 25 km (15.5 mi) long black ridge, marbled with snow, that is the main attraction in the park. Hiking along the sharp-crested serrated ridge takes two to three days and, as well as offering spectacular panoramic views, takes the walker into the domain of the northern brown bear. Chamois (a goat-like antelope) forage along the precipitous mountain slopes, nimble and fleet of foot so as to elude the wolves and lynx that prowl the area. Falcons soar on the thermals thrown up by the sun-warmed scree, scouring the ground for the slightest movement that might indicate a meal. An area's environmental wellbeing can be measured by the number and diversity of its bird and butterfly populations, and Piatra Craiului triumphs on both counts as 120 species of birds have been identified in the park.

RETEZAT MOUNTAINS

Eastern Europe/Romania

Sometimes called the Transylvanian Alps, Retezat is the highest section of the Southern Carpathian range in Romania and covers around 500 sq km (193 sq mi). The range has a distinct 'H' shape with two parallel rims (Retezat and Little Retezat) connected by a short ridge.

The spectacular scenery of the area was carved out by glaciers of the Pleistocene epoch and the range, which has an average elevation of more than 1,500 m (4,920 ft), comprises spectacular granite and limestone massifs speckled with numerous turquoise tarns.

Although starkly beautiful when covered by snow in winter, the mountains gradually come to life after the spring melt. Alpine meadows blossom on the middle elevations in an area that boasts over 1,000 different plant species, with around 100 being unique to the region. The melting ice gives added force to the many waterfalls that cascade down the mountainsides, as bears and marmots slowly shake off their winter sleep. Lynx, otters, chamois and wolves all add to the remarkable diversity of life, while salamanders and vipers seek out sun-warmed rocks to raise their body temperatures.

The most spectacular scenery is to be found on the route between Mount Peleaga and Mount Judele, where a series of stunning lakes on the southern slope of Judele culminates in Lake Bucura, Romania's largest glacial lake. The area is ideal for hiking and in late summer the smaller mountain lakes warm up enough to provide pleasant conditions for swimming. However, frost-cracking means that the higher elevations are formed of unstable scree which can make progress difficult.

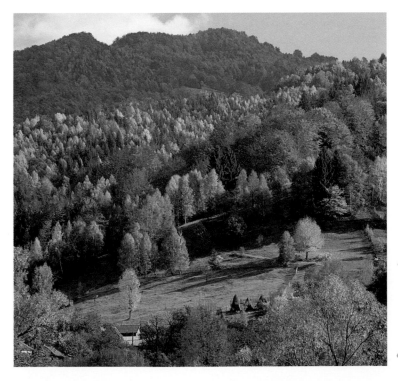

DON'T MISS
The view of the chain of mountain lakes from the higher elevations of Mount Peleaga.

CAPE KALIAKRA

Eastern Europe/Bulgaria

YOU SHOULD KNOW
Of all the legends associated with Kaliakra, perhaps the most poignant is that of the 40 maidens...

WORTH A DETOUR:
The museum, which as well as being a treasure trove, has the bonus of being housed inside a cave.

Located on Bulgaria's Black Sea coast near the border with Romania, Cape Kaliakra is a formidable place – so formidable that even the colour of its rocks is said to come from the blood of those who have defended it (although iron oxide in the soil provides a more prosaic explanation). It is where East meets West and where history and legend meld into one story. Dragons have been slain, great treasure lost in its caves and maidens have leapt to their deaths to avoid religious conversion.

The word *kaliakra* is of Medieval Greek origin and can be translated as 'Beautiful Fortress' – a fitting description of the cape on both counts.

Formed of limestone created beneath the prehistoric Sarmat Sea, it stretches 2 km (1.25 mi) into the sea and is protected by 70 m (230 ft) high sheer cliffs. The inaccessibility of the place made it ideal for the construction of a citadel – named Tirisis – which was successively used by Thracians, Romans and Byzantines. A small yet informative museum houses relics left behind by the ancient settlers.

In 1941 Kaliakra was declared a nature reserve which encompasses not only the land of the cape but also the waters around it. It has healthy populations of bird species all year round. Grebes and cormorants flourish in winter while eagle owls, alpine swifts and black-headed bunting breed here. Dolphins are a common sight out to sea, but the plight of the monk seal has brought into sharp focus the fragility of the cape's ecosystem. Once a common sight, they are now rarely seen.

Hiking along the top of the cape is popular, but great care should be taken as its rocks are subject to constant erosion. The Black Sea can be accessed via steep steps.

WORTH A DETOUR: Djendemite (Hell's) rock – an area that combines mature forest, sheer rock faces and a mighty natural obelisk.

CENTRAL BALKAN NATIONAL PARK

Eastern Europe/Bulgaria

The Central Balkan National Park is one of the largest and most important protected areas in Eastern Europe. Established in 1991, the park covers 720 sq km (278 sq mi) and encompasses nine distinct nature reserves. The park's topography includes alpine meadows, sheer rock faces, deep gorges, waterfalls and rapids, as well as 20 peaks above 2,000 m (6,562 ft). Old-growth forest of beech, spruce, fir, hornbeam and sessile oak cover over half of the park, and the reserves contain many astounding geological features. The granite and sandstone bedrock has been sculpted by erosion into weirdly wonderful shapes, most notably the fragile vertical stone pillars of Kalchovi Kamani and the rock bridge, Skalniya Most. Another breathtaking formation is a chain of ravines in the valleys of the Stara Reka and Cherni Osam Rivers. Underwater springs feed fast-flowing rivers and at many points their passage is interrupted by impermeable bedrock, thus creating many impressive cascades and waterfalls.

RHODOPE MOUNTAINS

Eastern Europe/Bulgaria

The Rhodope Mountains start south of the Bulgarian capital, Sofia, and run for about 240 km (150 mi) across the border into Greece. The western section is classic karst terrain – limestone bedrock cut by deep gorges and pitted with caves. To the east, the younger igneous rocks have been eroded to leave rock mushrooms and sharp peaks. The western section has the more spectacular scenery, most notably at Trigrad Gorge – a deep canyon bounded by sheer marble rocks. It is here that the Trigradska River is diverted underground into the Dyavolskoto Garlo (Devil's Throat) Cave, one of the highest underground waterfalls in Europe. About 8 km (5 mi) from Trigrad is the Yagodina cave, which is on five levels. Tours take the visitor into a subterranean wonderland of illuminated stalactites and stalagmites which was home to a troglodyte clan in prehistoric times.

DON'T MISS
Orlovi Skali (Eagle's Rocks) – a relic of ancient Thracian culture.

DADIA FOREST

Southern Europe/Greece

HOW TO GET THERE:

Buses run daily to Dadia from Alexandroupoli, which has good bus, train and air links with the rest of Greece.

WHEN TO GO:

The reserve is open year-round. Raptors may be spotted all day from October–March, and young vultures leave the nest in autumn. In May, many migratory birds are preparing to fly.

WORTH A DETOUR:

The Evros Delta, south of Dadia, is an atmospheric landscape of wetlands and dunes, and an interesting ornithological contrast. The visitor centre offers minibus and boat trips to see migrating waterfowl such as purple herons, little egrets and pelicans.

Towards the end of the 20th century, the black vulture faced extinction in Europe. The Dadia Forest in northeastern Greece was still home to a few pairs and, with active support from the World Wildlife Fund, an inner zone was set up – a protected reserve where black vultures and griffon vultures (also very rare in Europe) are now well established. The forest reserve covers a succession of volcanic ridges and its diverse habitats are home to a huge variety of flora and fauna, but it is most famous for birds. Its position on major migration routes attracts countless visiting species, but its prime importance is as a refuge for birds of prey. Of Europe's 38 diurnal raptors, 36 are seen here, including imperial and golden eagles, falcons and hawks.

A visit to Dadia Forest begins at the Ecotourist Centre, with informative displays and videos on the birds and on the work of the reserve. This includes augmenting the vultures' food as the greatest threat to their health comes from eating carrion picked up outside the reserve, which may be poisoned. A van takes visitors up to the well-designed observation area where binoculars, telescopes and knowledgeable staff help birdwatchers identify species.

There is a very good chance of seeing vultures feeding in the canyon below the hide. Marked trails through the sunlit clearings and the shady, hushed depths of the forest allow silent walkers the sight of rare birds among the trees, or silhouetted high above. Birds of prey can be seen at closer quarters as they take to the air, and a night in the Ecotourist Hostel gives a marvellous early-morning opportunity to watch them soar and take advantage of the first thermals.

YOU SHOULD KNOW

The only other nesting colony of black vultures in Europe is in Spain. The Dadia Forest Reserve does valuable work with local communities, encouraging the understanding of and participation in conservation. The municipality of Dadia runs the Ecotourist Centre and Hostel, and shares profits with the reserve.

PINDOS MOUNTAINS

Southern Europe/Greece

The magnificent Pindos Mountains stretch south of Metsovo and Ioannina from the Albanian border. Logging, road building and ski slopes have partly denuded the range but two national parks safeguard large areas of diverse, unspoilt landscapes and endangered wildlife. With deep river valleys, thick conifer and broadleaf forests, and sweeping alpine pastures, both are superb trekking country.

The remote northern Pindos National Park is home to some of Greece's rarest large animals. Lynx, jackals, wolves and brown bears are not often seen, but at dawn and dusk deserted hillsides echo with the howling of wolves. Zagori, south of the Aoos River, is more accessible but no less wildly beautiful. The Vikos–Aoos National Park covers part of a region which is remarkable not only for its dramatic, rugged landscape but also for the Zagorohoria – its numerous, traditional villages. Built on mountain ledges – level ground is used for cultivation – these were winter settlements for the shepherds, who traditionally spent summers on the mountains with their flocks. Greek-speaking Sarakatsani, and Vlachs, who speak an ancient Romance language, still make up most of the settled population, although many abandoned the harsh seasonal life. The almost deserted villages are now being restored and some of the traditional stone houses and the surprisingly grand 18th- and 19th-century mansions are guest houses.

The towering peaks of the Pindos, including Smolikas, the highest in the range at 2,640 m (8,660 ft), and Gamila, whose sheer face drops hundreds of metres to the river below, are long and challenging ascents even for experienced climbers. But the whole area is crossed by tracks – many used by shepherds for centuries – through ravines and forests, over uplands and ridges, to isolated villages and high lakes.

WHEN TO GO:
May, June, September, October.

WORTH A DETOUR:
The Vikos Gorge is a truly great walk. In one of the world's deepest ravines the foaming river twists and tumbles through narrow defiles and shaded valleys. From Monodendri to Papingo, the hike is 14 km (9 mi).

PETRIFIED FOREST, LESVOS

Southern Europe/Greece

WHEN TO GO:
Although the forest is open all year, it is very bleak in winter and parched in summer.

WORTH A DETOUR:
The Byzantine monastery of Ipsilou, close to the Petrified Forest, is dedicated to St John the Theologian. It is surrounded by a fittingly apocalyptic wasteland, scattered with a few fossilized tree trunks. Yet the courtyard is filled with flowers, the interior sumptuous and the small museum excellent.

Lesvos is a large island and most of its hilly terrain is very fertile, with fields of grain, orchards and olive groves interspersed by dense forests of oak and pine. For the Romans, this was a holiday island and for the Ottoman Turks, a productive larder. But the landscape of the far west is, in surprising contrast, almost desert, with spectacularly bare hills and stony, barren plains. A massive prehistoric eruption buried and transformed — completely and forever — the forested countryside around the volcano. A thick layer of volcanic ash and the action of heavily mineralized water turned all living things to stone, making this strange part of Lesvos a treasury of fossils.

Sigri, the little west-coast harbour town, has an excellent museum with permanent exhibitions on the primeval landscape and the geology and evolution of the Aegean which will enhance a later visit to the Petrified Forest with vivid images of this ancient world. On display are the fossilized trunks, twigs and leaves of the trees and plants which grew here between 15 and 20 million years ago, and a few fossils of creatures that inhabited the forests. Although sequoia and palm have disappeared from Lesvos, a surprisingly large number of the fossilized

trees — which include beech, oak, cypress, walnut and plane — still grow here, and examples are planted around the museum alongside the standing stumps of petrified trees. To the east of Sigri, the Petrified Forest covers the sun-baked eastern face of the extinct volcano, Ordhymnos. About 3 km (2 mi) of walks are laid out for visitors around the strange scattered logs and stumps. There is an evocative ancient and lonely atmosphere in this place of eerie, almost lunar, beauty.

DON'T MISS

The *dhrakospita*, or dragon houses, massive stone arches standing north of the village of Syra.

ISLAND OF EVIA

Southern Europe/Greece

Although in some places less than 50 m (165 ft) from the mainland, Evia, which is more than 150 km (93 mi) long, is Greece's second largest island. Particularly popular with Athenians are the picturesque fishing villages and beaches and the world-famous spa, Loutro Edipsou, on the sheltered coasts.

Most of inland and eastern Evia is remote, with forested mountains, shady hillside villages and unspoilt beaches. In spring, the countryside becomes a flower garden and, in autumn, open slopes are bright with cyclamen and autumn crocuses. Resident and migratory birds of prey include falcons, eagles and buzzards, while coastal wetlands and Lake Dystos are home to large numbers of waders and waterfowl. From the delightful village of Steni there are good treks around the forested foothills of Mount Dirfys and to some lovely, deserted beaches on the central east coast; but the peak itself is a very difficult climb. Mount Ohi is also demanding, although the walk up limestone slopes above the village of Myli is an easier approach. This route passes ancient quarries scattered with chunks of marble and unfinished columns.

LOUSIOS GORGE

Southern Europe/Greece

WORTH A DETOUR: At ancient Gortys a sunken excavation near the river contains the remains of the *Asklepieion* (therapeutic centre), including a bath, a circular portico and a temple.

Central Arcadia, with its green hillsides, beautiful old villages, fertile valleys, olive groves, orchards and flowery meadows sweet with herbs and tinkling with sheep bells, seems touched by ancient, idyllic magic. The narrow, serpentine road between Dimitsana and Stemnitsa allows glimpses of the Lousios Gorge, one of Greece's loveliest and most interesting hikes.

The trail from Dimitsana — a fascinating little town with fine 18th-century mansions and glorious views into the valley — descends through garden plots to the deep, wooded valley whose flanks narrow into sheer rock faces which, in places, reach almost 300 m (985 ft). Marked hiking trails cross the river at several points and, hidden among the trees, a clutch of monasteries cling to the crags. On the west side of the narrows, Nea Filosofou monastery has some fascinating 17th-century frescoes and the remains of the 10th-century Palea Filosofou monastery seem to merge into the surrounding stone. The remarkable Prodromou monastery clasps the eastern face of the gorge; it is built into the rocks, tucked away like a martin's nest, and occupied by about a dozen young monks. A long track zigzags to the road above.

The path up to the charming village of Stemnitsa, once an important metalworking town and now home to a school for gold and silversmiths, branches off a little further downstream. It is also worth walking along the valley to the Kokkoras Bridge — a high, arched medieval structure, once a major road link for Arcadia.

TAYGETOS MOUNTAINS AND THE MANI

Southern Europe/Greece

DON'T MISS
The spectacular road
from Sparta to Kalamata.

From the olive groves of Kalamata to the very south of mainland Greece, the middle 'finger' of the Peloponnese is dominated by the Taygetos Mountains, which divide the Mani east–west into 'Sunward' and 'Shadowed' coasts.

Fishing villages are scattered along the rocky and rather inaccessible east coast, while in the west, stony tracks over the austerely beautiful ochre and tan landscapes lead to villages of towers, sprouting from the hillsides, and tiny, richly frescoed and isolated Byzantine churches. To the north is Gytheio. This attractive, friendly port provides a comfortable base on the east coast; on the west coast there are two popular resorts – Stoupa with its fine sand beaches and Kardamyli, where the highest point in the Taygetos, 2404 m (7887 ft) Mount Profitis Ilias, soars above the coast. The peak can be attempted by experienced climbers from the Vyros or Rindoma Gorges, along steep, rocky escarpments and knife-edged ridges, or by hikers via the saddle between the sharp, pyramidal summit and a summer settlement reached by a dirt road. Around Kardamyli, *kalderimi* (cobbled mule tracks) fan out into the foothills and offer a number of excellent hikes, including a short walk to a pair of burial chambers known as the tombs of the Dioskouri – the Gemini twins. One of the tracks from Exohorio, a hamlet high above the Vyros Gorge, descends into a ravine.

WHEN TO GO:
The gorge is open all year, but in early spring snowmelt and rain may swell the stream dangerously.

IMBROS GORGE

Southern Europe/Greece

Hora Sfakion, squeezed between steep mountains and the sea, is the chief town of Sfakia, Crete's stoniest and most independent region. The little port is regularly packed with crowds making their way to and from the Samaria Gorge, but the White Mountains are carved by a dozen or so other deep canyons, and 'local' gorge hikes include the delightful Imbros to the east. The distance from Imbros to Komitades is about 10 km (6 mi); before the road was built, the ravine was the main route towards the coast and it is generally well cobbled and undemanding. For years, Imbros was something of a secret, but it is now on the coach-tour itinerary. The first bus up from Hora Sfakion, or a tranquil night staying in Imbros village, ensures a head start and a peaceful and lovely walk down a path following the stream through steep green valleys, under a rock bridge and into narrow, sheer canyons. In this gaunt landscape, only plants inaccessible to hungry goats thrive, and in spring these steep cliffs are a flower-decked, vertical rock garden and the air is sweet with oregano, thyme and dittany, a favourite Cretan hangover cure. Green lizards scuttle, butterflies dance and songbirds chirp in the thick vegetation which shades much of the gorge. High overhead, huge birds of prey hang motionless in the bright day.

Right: Taygetos Mountains

GAVDOS
Southern Europe/Greece

WHEN TO GO: May, June, late September or October. In early September, popular beaches display the aftermath of the summer crowds.

In recent years, the island of Gavdos has changed. In summer Cretans and mainland Greeks occupy ramshackle beach houses at Sarakiniko and Korfos. But, off-season, the little island retains its magic. The few 'villages' and even the 'capital', Kastri, are no more than clusters of simple cottages, mostly deserted. The island's archaeological remains are fragments of Neolithic and Minoan pottery.

The island is about 10 km (6 mi) long and there are good tracks over the undemanding terrain. The longest hike is to rocky Tripiti, the southernmost point of Europe, where swimmers in the crystal-clear waters

find themselves surrounded by small fish. The many beaches – sand or pebble, rocky or dune-backed and tamarisk-shaded – are often deserted. Tents can be pitched anywhere, and driftwood fires, the slap of wavelets, and a star-jewelled inky sky, are alluring options. But it is the small permanent population (about 50 residents from six families) that makes a long stay feasible and enjoyable. With friendly tavernas, barbecued fish, boat trips, even beer en route to Tripiti, Gavdos is a desert island without tears and offers a delightful, illusory isolation.

WORTH A DETOUR: One of the southern lakes is named the Lake of Flowers because it is covered with water lilies. When they bloom, the water is invisible beneath the overlapping leaves and white flowers.

LURA NATIONAL PARK
Southern Europe/Albania

Until 1990 Albania was a closed communist country and it remains somewhat mysterious. Much of its rural interior is unspoilt and now industrial activity is monitored and national parks preserve landscape and wildlife. On the eastern slopes of the mountain massif known as Lura's Crown, Lura National Park protects a wide belt of forest and a glacial landscape of ridges, ravines and high lakes.

The beautiful, cool forest consists chiefly of beech, fir and pine, and is home to many animals and birds. Pine marten, roe deer and capercaillie may be spotted, while the remote and inaccessible parts of the forest are said to shelter rare and elusive animals, such as brown bears, lynxes and wolves. Amphibians, including newts, live in the chilly waters. The Lura Lakes are well known to Albanians, but little visited by tourists. Numbering about a dozen, they lie like jewels among the trees; some are inky dark, reflecting the conifers, others bright with the blue of the open sky.

A large swathe of alpine pasture in the south of the park, the 'Field of Mares' is a popular place to relax. In spring and summer it is absolutely radiant, a glorious tapestry of wild flowers.

DJAVOLJA VAROS

Southern Europe/Serbia

WHEN TO GO:
May–September.

WORTH A DETOUR:
A detour from the Path of Health. After the last hamlet, the main path turns downhill, but an uphill track between two ancient oaks (one is roughly carved with Dj. Varos) leads to the edge of a precipitous gorge, high above the 'devils'. Looking down on the bristling throng as the light changes with the scudding clouds, the colours shift and seem to flicker, like infernal firelight.

Devil's Town (Djavolja Varos) occupies the watershed of two steep ravines – Devil's Valley and Infernal Valley – on the slopes of Mount Radan in southern Serbia. About 200 elongated cones, many over 15 m (49 ft) high, topped by flat dark stone caps stand crowded together like a multitude of tall, silent, sinister giants. Thousands of years of water erosion carved them from the soft red stone and their evolution continues – old towers change shape and crumble away, others grow slowly from the ground. When the wind blows, they seem to shriek, sigh, groan and wail. Close by, traces of habitation can be seen, as well as the ruins of a church, still visited despite the oak tree which has grown up through the altar. Those who once lived here invented stories about the place and named it – and the two highly mineralized springs – the Devil's Water and the Devil's Well.

Similar geological oddities exist worldwide, but these 'devils' are unusually tall and closely packed – it is almost impossible to squeeze between them – and Devil's Town was recently nominated for the new 'Seven Natural Wonders' list. Although it was not placed, visitor numbers have increased and current development projects will provide amenities and floodlighting for night tours. Independent travellers who want the place to themselves can walk there from Prolom Spa. The enjoyable 9 km (5.5 mi) hike, the Path of Health, crosses fertile farmland and climbs past isolated hamlets before descending through thick woods to the site.

YOU SHOULD KNOW
The most colourful of the folk tales about the Devil's Town concerns a wedding party making its way to church. God, wishing to prevent extreme wickedness of some sort – the precise details vary – turned them all to stone.

KRKA NATIONAL PARK

Southern Europe/Croatia

The Dinaric Alps extend down the Adriatic coast from Slovenia to Albania. Rugged parallel ranges of porous karstic limestone, broken and riddled by ravines, underground rivers and caverns, form most of mainland Croatia, while its myriad islands are the summits of a long-submerged western chain. The mountains are scattered with ruined fortresses – the daunting peaks have been a stronghold against invaders from early times – but the landscape is sparsely populated. The geology and wildlife of several areas are now protected as national parks.

The Krka River rises in the mountains near Knin and Mount Dinara and descends, through a typical karstic landscape of gorges, lakes and cascades of 'steps' built up from tufa to the fine old city of Sibenik, and the sea. The riverside scenery of the Krka National Park is diverse and dramatic – cliffs and caves, woods and marshes – with a remarkable range of plants and wildlife and some interesting architectural features. Entry to the park is from either side of the river, at Skradin or Lozovac. It can be explored on foot by paths and walkways, or by boat. Deserted watermills stand by the waterfalls, the Orthodox Krka Monastery at the head of the valley and the Franciscan Samostan Visovac is picturesquely sited on an island.

This wonderful patchwork of natural habitats is particularly important for birds. Resident and migratory species range from raptors, including osprey and eagle owls, to tinybrilliant bee-eaters. The river flows swiftly all year and there are two very dramatic cascades – Roski Slap, at the end of a deep canyon, and Skradinski Buk, a flight of 17 ever-widening steps, with fierce torrents gushing around rocks and surging down into the large lower lake.

HOW TO GET THERE:
Several buses run daily from Sibenik to both entrances.

WHEN TO GO:
April–October.

WORTH A DETOUR:
A boat trip. Walkers and birdwatchers may relish the peace of the land, but the voyage between the towering cliffs of the narrow gorge is thrilling, and the view of the monastery on its tiny island in the tranquil lake is quite magical.

YOU SHOULD KNOW

Its position near one of the few passes through the high Alps has always given Knin strategic importance. When Croatia became independent in 1990, Serbs from the region made the town capital of an independent state. It was re-taken in 1995; the Serbs left and now the Croatian flag flies over what is almost a ghost town.

Left: Roski Slap, Krka National Park

CERKNICA LAKE

Southern Europe/Slovenia

WORTH A DETOUR:
The Museum of Lake Cerknica, in a café-bar in Dolenje Jezero, is a family museum. Its displays include objects connected with life by the lake and a slide show, but the star attraction is the owner's working scale model of the area, which demonstrates how the lake fills and empties.

In the beautiful, unspoilt countryside south of Ljubljana, wooded hills, upland and valley farms, streams and isolated villages seem scarcely touched by the modern world. Between the Bloke Plateau and the Rakov Škocjan Regional Park lies an area which on some maps appears as an expanse of water, on others as wetland. This is Lake Cerknica, famous from ancient times for its mystifying periodic disappearances. Full, it measures about 10 x 5 km (6 x 3 mi) and is Slovenia's largest lake; empty, it is a low-lying area of lush hayfields. In 1689, the Slovenian scholar Valvasor proposed an explanation which so impressed the Royal Society that he was made an honorary member. The limestone of this region is perforated by caves and channels and when autumn rains swell streams above and below ground, water bubbles up into a depression which rapidly – often in a few days – becomes a lake. When the subterranean waters eventually recede, the lake empties through karstic sinkholes over a period of several weeks.

Activities on the lake include boating, windsurfing and skating as well as fishing. Its reed beds, an important habitat for huge numbers of nesting and migrating birds, including storks, reed warblers, corncrakes and lapwings, are a great draw for birdwatchers. The area's other attractions are grouped around the lake. There are good hikes into the hills (the views from the top of Velika Slivnica are superb); picturesque villages, including Otok which is, seasonally, Slovenia's only inhabited island; and, to the east, the little visited Krizna Water Cave, a remarkable network of tunnels and caverns, rivers and lakes.

KAMNIK-SAVINJA ALPS

Southern Europe/Slovenia

WORTH A DETOUR: Longer hikes into the cirque of high mountains around the Rinka Falls or to peaceful, road-less alpine valleys.

The Kamnik-Savinja Alps are part of the long chain of the Southern Alps. Although relatively low by alpine standards, they are dramatically steep and rugged and their sheer north faces are very challenging – mountaineering skills are essential. The gentler southern slopes, though, can be climbed by energetic hikers with good boots, maps and common sense. One group of peaks, which includes 2,558 m (8,392 ft) Grintovec, the highest in the range, can be reached from Jezersko, an alpine resort near the Austrian border. Winter activities – cross-country skiing and waterfall ice climbing – also take place in this area.
Pretty Kamniska Bistrika, deep in a wooded river valley north of the pleasant old town of Kamnik, is the

starting place for several walks – long tough hikes up into the mountains and more leisurely rambles around forest, ravines and waterfalls. About 10 km (6 mi) from Kamnik, a combination of cable car and chairlift runs to the top of the high limestone plateau, Velika Planina. In winter, this is a popular skiing and snowboarding area, while in summer its rolling pastures are home to herdsmen and their cattle, and walkers. Hikes up to the plateau and around its scattered settlements, over a gloriously open landscape with views north to the jagged peaks, make a wonderfully gentle introduction to alpine walking.

WHEN TO GO: May–October for walking, December–March for skiing.

POHORJE

Southern Europe/Slovenia

The Pohorje massif is geologically part of the central Eastern Alps. There are no towering peaks, but this is Slovenia's favourite winter sports location. From the outskirts of the town, a cable car whizzes skiers and snowboarders up to Maribor Pohorje for miles of uncrowded cross-country ski tracks and pistes. Pohorje is a year-round destination and, when the snow melts, ski tracks become routes for hikers and cyclists. This is a lovely 'big sky' area of rolling, undemanding terrain – thickly forested hills, high moorland and marsh, lakes and waterfalls. It is dotted with isolated farms and tiny churches and criss-crossed by long and short walks over unmade roads and forest tracks from both resorts. A particularly enjoyable hike from Rogla meanders through ancient forest to the Lovrenc Marsh Lakes, where walkers should be careful not to disturb the pools – the resident goblin brings bad weather if angered.
Trails from Maribor start at the Bolfenk cable car terminus. Several of the longer routes pass through Areh; a popular walk continues along a high path with stunning views to the Sunik waterfalls, deep in one of Europe's few tracts of virgin forest.

VAL GRANDE NATIONAL PARK

Southern Europe/Italy

At 120 sq km (46 sq mi), Val Grande National Park is the largest wild area in Italy and lies 100 km (62 mi) north of Milan, in the Italian Alps. The heart-shaped park, which is surrounded by mountains, is centred on two valleys: Val Pogallo and Val Grande. Trekking here is exacting and hikers are advised to take extreme care. The spectacular view from the top of Monte Faié includes the Pedum peaks, Lake Mergozzo and the valley itself.

WORTH A DETOUR:
The Villa Cigogna Mozzoni, near Varese, a lovely example of Lombardy's Renaissance architecture.

The valley floor and lower slopes are largely pasture and stands of birch, linden, willow and, most importantly, chestnut. Higher up are ancient beech woods as well as firs that segue into green alder, ferns and moss, then rhododendron and bilberry and, finally, alpine meadows and wild flowers such as gentian, columbine and arnica. The ravines are full of maple, lime, yew and alder. Many small mammals live here as well as chamois, roe deer, foxes, stone martens and badgers.

MAREMMA REGIONAL PARK

Southern Europe/Italy

DON'T MISS
The scuba diving at Argentario and the islands of Giglio and Giannutri.

Located in the southwestern corner of Tuscany, Maremma Regional Park extends from the mouth of the Ombrone River to Talamone, a 25 km (15 mi) stretch bordered inland by the Aurelia highway. The woods within Maremma are dominated by huge holm oaks, maples and myrtle, and both aromatic and flowering plants such as lavender, rosemary, juniper, clematis and broom bring bright splashes of colour. The park descends gently from the hills across the marshes and dunes close to the estuary, through farmland and pasture to the coastline. To the south, steep cliffs are evidence of coastal erosion. Sandy beaches, protected by indigenous Italian pine forests, are perfect for looking for shells and swimming. The Ombrone estuary offers splendid birdwatching opportunities; waders, ducks and herons are common. Inland, woodpeckers, finches, bunting, owls, buzzards and kestrels may be seen. Mammals include wild boar, skunks, stone martens, foxes, deer, and many smaller species such as rabbits and hedgehogs.

Right: Maremma Regional Park

GRAN SASSO E MONTI DELLA LAGA NATIONAL PARK

Southern Europe/Italy

YOU SHOULD KNOW

The Calderone glacier is the southernmost glacier in Europe. Glaciologists believe that it may completely disappear by 2020, due to climate change.

HOW TO GET THERE:
By train, car or bus.

WHEN TO GO:
At any time of year, depending on your particular interest.

HIGHLIGHTS:
The fabulous local food available in all the villages and towns in the area, including regional specialities such as *virtù teramane* (a sort of hotpot), *scamorze* (a type of cheese), truffles, and much more.

Encompassing three mountain groups, the Gran Sasso e Monti della Laga National Park is one of the largest protected areas in Europe. Formed in 1991 and part of the Appenines, the park includes both their highest peak, Corno Grande, at 2,912 m (9,554 ft), as well their only glacier, the Calderone. Within its territory are hundreds of villages and 44 towns.

The protected area is so vast and covers such diverse landscape and habitat that it is rich with rare flora and fauna, some of which are unique. Over 2,000 different species of plant are found here and mammals include the Abruzzo chamois, red and roe deer, wild cats, wild boar, foxes, polecats, martens, porcupines, small packs of Appenine wolves and many smaller species.

Birdwatchers often make for the Forca di Penne and Campotosto Lake where thousands of migrating birds rest by the shore, although birds can be seen throughout the area. At lower levels, where there are fields and pasture, Ortolan buntings, crested larks and red-backed shrikes may be found. At higher altitudes there are snowfinches, pipits, alpine accentors and choughs. This is also great country for raptors: golden eagles, lanners, goshawks and peregrine falcons are all at home here.

There are many activities to enjoy in the park and wonderful opportunities exist for exploring on foot, horseback, mountain-bike or by canoe. Rivers and streams rush down into the valleys and there are some spectacular waterfalls which, in winter, form an extraordinary sight when they sometimes freeze. Campo Imperatore, a high plateau, is one of Italy's oldest and most popular ski resorts. With guaranteed snow during winter, the park is a magnet for advanced skiers, with off-piste descents attracting free-riders from across Europe. Cross-country skiing is also popular, as is mountaineering and ice-cascade climbing.

DON'T MISS
The historic town of
Fondi with its palazzo,
cathedral and churches.

AUSONI AND AURUNCI MOUNTAINS

Southern Europe/Italy

YOU SHOULD KNOW
The Abbey of Montecassino
was founded by St Benedict
in AD 529. In February 1944 it
was destroyed during fighting
between Allied and German
forces. Paid for by the Italian
government, reconstruction
took ten years.

The Ausoni and Aurunci Mountains, located in central Italy, run from the Appenines to the promontory of Gaeta on the Mediterranean coast. Part of the Antiappenini, and also sometimes known as the Volsci, derived from their Roman name, there is no official dividing line between them. The highest peak in the range, Monte Petrella, stands at 1,533 m (5,030 ft).

In 1997, the Monti Aurunci Natural Park was created. If time is limited, this offers an excellent overview of these mountain ranges, from the plain to the top of Monte Petrella with its glorious vistas across the mountains to the sea. Magnificent beech trees cloak the northern slopes, and there are oaks, maples, hornbeams and chestnuts, too. In spring wild flowers are abundant. Meadows cover the valley, where brooms, Judas trees and 50 species of orchid thrive. The southern sector is on the route of many migratory birds, but there are also owls, nightjars and nightingales to be seen.

The rainfall in the mountains, which have typical karst topography, sinks through the limestone to reappear as springs and vernal pools on the lower slopes. This is good habitat for amphibians, and four types of salamander as well as four types of frog can be seen here.

A network of trails for both hikers and mountain-bikes runs throughout the park, and both inside and outside its boundaries the mountains are criss-crossed with small roads linking little medieval villages. Many of the inhabitants still raise cattle and work on the land and in the forests. The villages, with their ancient squares, cobbled streets and churches, are well worth visiting.

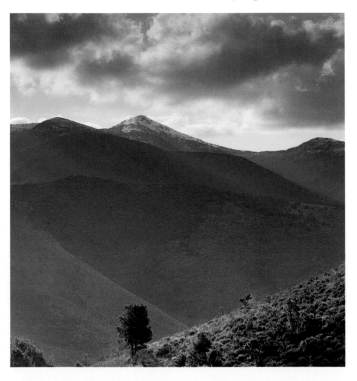

POLLINO NATIONAL PARK

Southern Europe/Italy

DON'T MISS
The Valle del Mercuri,
a beautiful, pristine,
natural site.

One of the largest national parks in Italy, Pollino National Park straddles the boundary of Basilicata and Calabria in southern Italy. Its highest peak, Monte Pollino, rises to 2,267 m (7,438 ft). Serra Dolcedorme is a major attraction, but there are other lovely ranges, too, including Serra di Crispo where the palebark pine grows right to the peaks – all twisted trunks

and branches shaped by the wind. From higher altitudes a view of both coasts may be enjoyed and, with luck, a golden eagle might be soaring through the blue sky above. As well as mountains there are never-ending upland plains dotted with peacefully grazing sheep, rolling hills and lush valleys, and a profusion of flowering plants and bushes, particularly during spring. Cave systems, too, are numerous and rich in prehistoric sites, such as Romito. There are castles and monasteries, ancient villages where the older inhabitants still wear traditional dress, and ethnic Albanians who maintain their traditional culture and speak their own dialect.

SUPRAMONTE PLATEAU

Southern Europe/Italy

WHEN TO GO:
April–June, September
and October

Found inland from the Gulf of Orosei, eastern Sardinia, close to Orgosolo, is the high plateau of Supramonte in a mountain range of the same name. Reminiscent of the Dolomites, this limestone massif is covered with forest and is a wonderful region for walking and trekking. The plateau's north faces are well known for their difficult and lengthy climbing routes.

Supramonte is weird and wonderful, its typical karst formation laced with drainage gullies and virtually no trails other than the route up Monte Corrasi. This is the highest peak in the area at 1,391 m (4,564 ft). The terrain is bleak, stony and harshly beautiful, with long views across the plateau to the Barumini Mountains. Visit the region of the Flumineddu River, which is surrounded by a thick forest of holm oak, yew, juniper, holly and oleander. Here the Flumineddu has cut the mountain in two and formed the Gorropu Gorge – one of Sardinia's most impressive natural sites. It is possible for experienced canyoneers to negotiate it with the correct equipment, but part of it is accessible anyway via a pretty path from the valley.

GARGANO NATIONAL PARK

Southern Europe/Italy

WORTH A DETOUR:
The Sanctuary of Monte Sat'Angelo sul Gargano. Dedicated to Archangel Michael, this is the oldest shrine in Europe.

The Gargano Peninsula sticks out into the Adriatic Sea like a spur above the heel of the Italian boot. This mountainous massif, comprising several peaks, is situated in the province of Foggia. Almost all of it is part of the Gargano National Park, and the heart of the park is the Umbra Forest. Once covering the entire peninsula, the 15 per cent that remains is glorious — broad-leafed trees such as beech, maple, hornbeam, oak and chestnut grow to enormous heights and, beneath them, anemones, violets and cyclamen grow in profusion. Some 35 per cent of all species of flora found in Italy are here, including an extraordinary number of orchids: 61 varieties and still counting.

Mammals include about 100 rare roe deer, martens, badgers, wildcats and numerous smaller species, while forest birds include raptors and four types of woodpecker — again, very rare in Italy. Another reason the area is protected is because of its wetlands. There are lagoons, marshes, lakes, vernal pools and springs, as well as the sea. These provide habitat for numerous amphibians and water birds, some of which arrive during their migration to and from Africa and central and eastern Europe. Between the forest and the sea are large stands of Aleppo pines, olive trees, and typical Mediterranean shrubland. On the coast itself the sea and wind have sculpted wonderful shapes into the limestone cliffs.

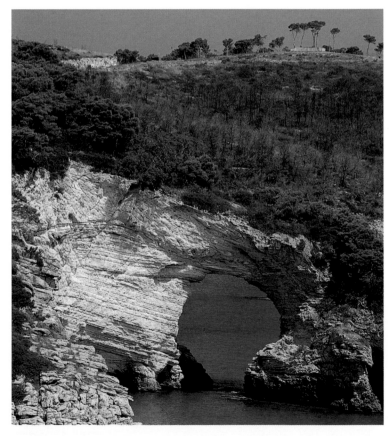

CIES ISLANDS

Southern Europe/Spain

HOW TO GET THERE: From June–September, travel by boat from Vigo, Baiona or Cangas to Monte Agudo, or join a tourist cruise.

The Cies is a group of three granite islands off the northwest coast of Galicia, northern Spain. They have been a nature reserve since 1980 and, with six other islands and archipelagos, in the year 2000 they were declared part of the National Land-Marine Park of the Atlantic Islands of Galicia. Once mountains, their cliffs on the Atlantic Ocean side rear sharply from the water and are riddled with caves formed by the action of wind and waves. The eastern aspect is far less severe; here trees and shrubs abound and rare plants grow in the sand dunes.

Although inhabited for centuries, the Cies suffered so many invasions that by 1700 they were deserted and re-populated only when a lighthouse was built on the island in the 19th century. Today, Las Islas Cies are best known for Playa de Rodas, a superb beach of fine, white sand that links Isla de Monte Agudo to Isla do Faro. At high tide the sea covers the area nearest the rocky shoreline, forming a lagoon but leaving a curved sand 'road' linking the two islands.

WORTH A DETOUR: The village of Bulnes, with its hardy, independent inhabitants, whose way of life is so completely different from that of most Europeans.

PICOS DE EUROPA

Southern Europe/Spain

The highest peak in Picos de Europa, Torre de Cerredo, reaches 2,648 m (8,688 ft), though many more are almost as high. It is also popular with cavers, as some of the country's deepest caves are found here. Its proximity to the sea means there is often snow, regardless of the season. The western massif boasts the Lakes of Covadonga – two perfect glacial lakes. Covadonga is accessible by car and there is an easy and beautiful hike round the shores of both lakes, winding through beech woods and across swathes of green pasture where shepherds guard flocks of sheep and goats, and delicious cheeses are produced. Cantabrian brown bears, Iberian lynx, wolves, wild boar, wild horses, roe deer, chamois and ibex are all found here, and birds include buzzards, vultures, golden and short-toed eagles and hundreds of smaller species.

DON'T MISS
The lighthouse, with its remarkable views over the Mediterranean.

CAP DE CREUS

Southern Europe/Spain

Situated at the northern end of the Costa Brava, close to the border with France, the Cap de Creus juts out into the Mediterranean. A nature reserve since 1998, protecting both land and sea, the peninsula is the largest uninhabited area of the Spanish Mediterranean.

The coastline rises stark and rugged from the deep-blue sea, indented with tiny bays and rocky islets, many of which are only accessible by boat. The rocks, scoured by centuries of high winds and waves, are notable for their bizarre shapes, some of which resemble birds and animals – for example, the eagle of Tudela. This is prime birdwatching territory, partly because, as the easternmost point of the Iberian peninsula, it is a magnet for migratory birds. From the highest point at Sant Salvador, several types of swift, black-eared wheatear, rock thrush and crag martins can been seen during summer. Thekla lark, blue rock thrush and black wheatear are permanent inhabitants. Peregrine falcons breed here and Bonelli's eagles hover overhead. Different species, such as Dartford and Sardinian warblers, inhabit the shrub land that forms most of the landscape – mainly cistus, broom, lavender, gorse and several Mediterranean herbs. Lupins and orchids also thrive, but the most interesting flora, including several endemic species, cling to the narrow coastal strip. In spring and autumn both Cory's and Mediterranean shearwater fly past, and kittiwakes, skuas, razorbills and gulls arrive for the winter. The clear, unpolluted sea contains a mass of fauna, including precious red coral, as well as spiny lobsters, scorpion fish and sunfish, among others.

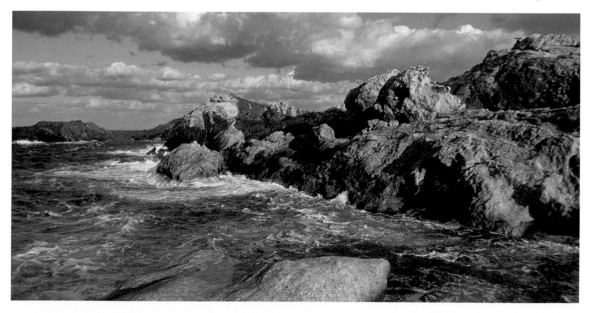

SIERRA DE GREDOS

Southern Europe/Spain

YOU SHOULD KNOW

The Sierra is snow-covered during winter, and cross-country skiing, mountain skiing and snowshoeing are all possible activities.

The Sierra de Gredos, part of Spain's central mountain range, is within reach of Toledo, Ávila, Cáceres and Madrid. Popular with climbers, it also offers great opportunities for hiking, walking, horse riding, mountain-biking and paragliding. A Special Bird Protection Zone, this regional park is home to a wealth of flora and fauna, including over 20 species of raptor.

The highest peak in the largely snow-capped Sierra de Gredos is Pico Almanzor. At 2,592 m (8,504 ft), it is also the highest peak in central Spain. Below the mountain's north face is the Laguna de Gredos, a glacial lake with paths to five other lakes. The scenery is glorious, changing from Mediterranean to alpine – depending on elevation. At lower levels, on the southern side, walk beside clear, sparkling rivers and along old Roman roads or stop to relish a picnic in valleys full of wild flowers, lemon and almond trees, and olive groves. Oak, pine, mountain ash, poplar and birch trees grow in quantity. Thyme, rosemary and oregano scent the air. Experts should look out for endemic species of sedum, saxifrage and antirrhinum.

Higher up, the landscape changes to alpine meadows with swathes of yellow broom and, finally, bare rock face decorated with lichen. Mammals in these mountains include elusive wild cats and beech martens, but Gredos ibex may be seen and otters slip and slide in the many rivers; there are also several endemic amphibians to be spotted. Raptors include golden eagles and several other eagle species.

WORTH A DETOUR:
The traditional villages, monasteries, and fortresses that can be found within the mountains or the Neolithic cave paintings called El Collado Braguillas, close to El Raso.

SIERRA DE GUADARRAMA

Southern Europe/Spain

Within easy striking distance of Madrid and Segovia, the Sierra de Guadarrama offers a great escape from the stress of city living. A continuation of the central mountain chain that runs from Spain to Portugal, this range is somewhat lower and gentler than the Sierra de Gredos, its principal peak, Peñalara, reaching 2,428 m (7,966 ft). Running from southwest to northeast, Guadarrama contains many interesting features, including the Peñalara Natural Park and the unusual granite range of La Pedriza.

Many rivers have their source in this region, noted for its high annual rainfall, and there are many small dams in the mountains. The natural park, on the southern slope of Peñalara mountain, contains many small glacial lakes which, during spring, produce small waterfalls and streams from meltwater. At the highest elevations, rock roses, lavender, juniper and ferns abound. Below 2,000 m (6,562 ft) are, firstly, pine forests – in autumn bursting with delicious fungi such as morels and chanterelles; and, secondly, Pyrenean oak – a protected species. A certain amount of logging is permitted here each year to provide the mountain villages with supplies of firewood.

La Pedriza, on the southern slopes of the Sierra de Guadarrama, is one of the largest granite ranges in Europe. Its peaks and cliffs are intersected with valleys and rivers as well as great boulders – some smoothly rounded, others weirdly eroded – which look as though giants have been playing bowls. There must be a thousand different routes for rock climbers, some easy enough for children to manage. Much of the rock is bare, but there are areas of scrub. Raptors are numerous, including over 100 pairs of griffon vultures. The river flows through the valley, cascading into several delightful pools in which to cool off after hiking in the heat.

HOW TO GET THERE:
By train, bus or car from Madrid.

WHEN TO GO:
All year round, if you don't mind the snow and ice between December–February.

WORTH A DETOUR:
The Royal Monastery of San Lorenzo de El Escorial. Full of world-class art and ancient manuscripts, it is a UNESCO World Heritage Site.

YOU SHOULD KNOW

Because of its proximity to Madrid, the Sierra de Guadarrama is criss-crossed by road passes and railway routes and caters well for tourists. It can get busy during the summer months but, even so, it is relatively easy to find a peaceful and beautiful spot in which to relax.

SIERRA DE ESPUNA NATIONAL PARK

Southern Europe/Spain

HIGHLIGHTS: The 'badlands', Los Barrancos de Gebas, in the eastern part of the Sierra de Espuna. The Walls of Layva – an area of limestone walls that attracts climbers.

Situated about 40 km (25 mi) from the coast, between Mucia and Lorca, is the National Park of Sierra de Espuna. A forested area rising to 1,585 m (5,200 ft), the park is a pleasant retreat in which to enjoy both hiking and numerous other outdoor activities. In summer it is cooler and offers more shade than the rest of this flat, dry region.

While there are no rivers in the park, there are many springs and streams, enabling it to remain verdant throughout the year. The highest peak, El Morron de Espuna, reaches 1,583 m (5,194 ft) and is often snow-covered during the winter. Pines are plentiful, although oak, cottonwood, elm, poplar and maple also grow on these hills. Forest footpaths and well-maintained tracks make for pleasant walking, horse riding and mountain-biking. On the slopes, hawthorn, juniper and shrubs such as thyme, rock rose and honeysuckle thrive. Towards the summit of El Morron is a group of 26 curious, circular domed wells called the Las Pozos de Nieve. The remains of snow pits, they were used from the 16th century until the 1920s when new refrigeration techniques took over. During winter, snow was collected and packed into these wells, to be cut into ice blocks and sold to businesses and individuals in nearby towns during the rest of the year. Wild boar, Barbary sheep, genet, wild cats, foxes, red squirrels, rabbits and hares enjoy this habitat, along with many species of birds – including raptors such as golden eagles, goshawks, sparrowhawks and owls.

DON'T MISS
The local handicrafts – particularly the rugs and blankets of Nijar.

CABO DE GATA-NIJAR NATURAL PARK

Southern Europe/Spain

The first terrestrial and maritime Protected Area in Andalusia is located east of Almeria, in southeastern Spain. The park is Europe's driest area and contains a wide variety of habitats, including semi-desert steppe, saltmarsh, beaches, dunes, cliffs and a large marine area. This is a wild and rugged landscape. The mountains are craggy and ochre coloured, white sand beaches and secret coves are backed by steep, 100 m (328 ft) cliffs, and lookout towers along the coast are testament to a history of incursions by Berber pirates. The terrestrial area of the natural park is home to low-growing vegetation that has adapted to drought conditions, such as cacti, dwarf fan palms and jujube, or red date. Most of the 1,100 species of fauna here are birds, although genets, wild boar and weasels can be seen. The Salinas de Cabo de Gata, a saltwater lagoon separated from the beach by a wide sandbar, is home to many resident birds such as flamingoes, herons, cranes and storks, as well as thousands of migratory birds that rest here during their lengthy biannual journeys. Seabirds include terns, shearwaters, shags and gulls, and the quantity of prey attracts raptors such as ospreys and peregrine falcons.

YOU SHOULD KNOW

There is prehistoric cave art in the caves of La Pileta, as well as Bronze Age megaliths.

SIERRA DE GRAZALEMA NATURAL PARK

Southern Europe/Spain

A UNESCO Biosphere Reserve since 1977, the Sierra de Grazalema is a magnificent area of karst landscape in which cliffs, gorges, caverns and valleys spread across the province of Cadiz and part of the province of Malaga, in southern Spain. Its 517 sq km (200 sq mi) is scenically spectacular, bursting with flora and fauna, and encompasses 13 pretty white towns and villages, or *pueblos blancos*, within its boundaries. Grazalema itself is one of the most attractive villages and lies between two mountain peaks. Notoriously, the region receives the most rain in Spain, but the upside of this is that 1,300-plus species of plant, including endemics, thrive here. Part of the park is a special reserve area within which grows the best-preserved forests of Spanish fir in the country. Native to southern Spain, this species is very rare, despite having been in existence since the Tertiary Era (1.6–65 million years BC). Other species that grow well are juniper, maple, Portuguese oak and ash, while willows and poplars flourish alongside the streams and rivers.

DON'T MISS

The Virgen del Carmen fiesta in Grazalema, held annually in mid-July.

Fauna include mountain goats, deer, genets, foxes and mongoose, and naturally there is a wealth of birds – including many raptors. The most renowned bird in the Sierra de Grazalema is the griffon vulture. The cliffs in the special reserve host Europe's largest colony.

The Sierra is a superb place to hike through, with many routes of varying degrees of difficulty to be explored. Other activities include exploring the Hundidero-Gato – Andalucia's largest cave system – which can be tackled by experienced cavers, plus mountain-biking, horse riding, climbing and canoeing. And for those who love adventure, there are also some excellent spots within the park for hang-gliding.

SIERRA DE TRAMUNTANA

Southern Europe/Spain

WHEN TO GO: To avoid crowds, go during the winter months. During summer the region is busier, but the area is cooler and fresher than staying by the coast.

The island of Mallorca, off Spain's eastern coast, is usually thought of as a holiday destination catering for mass tourism. While this is partially true, life inland is calmer and the scenery a delight. The Sierra de Tramuntana is a mountain range in the northwest, stretching from Andratx to the Formentor Peninsula. Many ancient trails and cobbled pilgrims' routes weave through the mountains, connecting the little medieval villages of the interior. Here, too, are Mallorca's highest peaks: Puig Major, at 1,445 m (4,741 ft) and Massanella, at 1,352 m (4,436 ft). The former is decorated with military installations, but Massanella is a beautiful hike of some three hours, ending with a superb view over the entire island, with Menorca in the distance on a good day.

Walk through the almond groves and gnarled olive trees of this timeless landscape; wild rosemary and other herbs scent the air and the hillsides glow with clumps of yellow broom – during January, February and March, almond and citrus blossom is an added bonus. Higher up, the vegetation changes to Spanish oak forest, carob and pine. Goats and sheep graze the hillsides, while black vultures hang in the sky above, keeping watch for a potential meal.

DON'T MISS

La Calera – a lovely white town perched precariously on a mountainside.

GARAJONAY NATIONAL PARK

Southern Europe/Spain

The Canary Islands are all that remain of a volcanic mountain range. La Gomera, the least heavily populated island, is relatively untouched by tourism and contains the Garajonay National Park. Located in the centre of the island, the 40 sq km (15 sq mi) of Garajonay is one of the best-preserved laurel forests still in existence. Made up of several laurels and laurel-type species, the largest variety reaches up to 40 m (130 ft). The park is usually wreathed in cloud and mist and the many small streams and springs ensure extraordinarily lush vegetation. Huge rocks lie scattered about and trees grow in bizarre, twisted shapes. Large ferns form dripping clumps, and the forest floor is rich with undergrowth providing cover for birds, invertebrates and bats. The Garajonay National Park comprises mountains and valleys, cliffs and ravines, and there are several routes through and across this unusual landscape. Make for the highest point on the island – 1,487 m (4,880 ft) – which is the summit of the eponymous peak.

DON'T MISS
The traditional
villages, such as
Lamas d'Ôlo.

ALVÃO NATURAL PARK

Southern Europe/Portugal

Formed in 1983, Portugal's smallest Natural Park reaches the height of 1,330 m (4,364 ft) and the Nature Conservation Institute works hard to promote conservation of species as well as the traditional culture of the small villages within its boundaries.

The park bestrides the transition area between the humid coast and the arid interior, and thus falls naturally into two separate components. At its highest altitude, in a rugged, rock-strewn region, the source of the River Ôlo springs from a large granite basin; at its lowest, the river runs through narrow valleys. Much of the park consists of green, leafy mixed-species forest that includes black and English oak, silver birch, hazel, holly, bay, chestnut and wild pear. The heathland is mainly covered in heather, gorse, broom and bilberry. Some of the valleys are terraced and planted with rye or with vines, and fruit and olive trees are also grown. There are still wild-flower-rich meadows in which cattle and goats graze. This mixed environment is home to diverse species of fauna; amphibians and reptiles thrive here, and it is a perfect habitat for bats. Mammals are mainly small – field mice, rabbits, wild goats, wildcats and, very occasionally, wolves. Several types of raptor can be seen, including round-winged eagles and peregrine falcons, as well as many smaller species such as choughs, bullfinches, flycatchers and water pipits.

WHEN TO GO: Try to see the summer festivals, when many of those who have left to work overseas or elsewhere in Portugal return home for a break.

MONTESINHO MOUNTAINS NATURAL PARK

Southern Europe/Portugal

One of the least visited and wildest regions in Portugal, Montesinho Mountains Natural Park was formed to protect not only the rare fauna that survives there, but also the unusually traditional way of life still led by its approximately 9,000 inhabitants. The villages, such as Montesinho and Franca, have cobbled streets and stone houses that are traditional to the region. Scattered across the slopes are *pombal* – round, medieval dovecotes with horseshoe-shaped roofs. These were built for rearing doves to be eaten.

This is a region of curved mountains separated by valleys, some of which are very steep, others gently sloped. The altitude ranges from 438 m (1,437 ft) at the Mente River to 1,481 m (4,859 ft) at the peak of Montesinho. The eastern section is the most easily accessible, but paths run throughout the park, enabling the visitor to explore the more remote and lush western section.

Along the edges of the streams and rivers running through the park are ash, alder, black poplar, wild cherry trees, willow and hazel, mixed with herbs such as apple mint, and honeysuckle, jasmine and peonies. Meadows are bursting with scented herbs and wild flowers, including orchids and several endemic species.

CAPE ST VINCENT NATIONAL PARK

Southern Europe/Portugal

DON'T MISS
The excellent surfing.

Cape St Vincent National Park runs for 150 km (93 mi) down the Atlantic coast to the southwestern tip of Portugal, from Porto Covo in Alentejo to Burgau in the Algarve. Truly a national treasure, the park has been protected since 1995 and could not be more different from the popular tourist destinations of the Algarve, being possibly the last genuinely wild coastal area in Europe.

Varying in width, 2–20 km (1.2–12.4 mi), the park is sparsely populated, but rich in flora and fauna – including rare and endangered species. Because of its location and long months of sunshine and very little rain, the flora is mostly formed of thorny shrubs and bushes, bulbs and annuals. Including seaweeds, there are at least 750 species here, 12 of which are unique to the area. Silene rothmaleri, a charming little white flower that was believed extinct since 1984, was re-discovered at Cape St Vincent in 2000.

The Cape itself is the most southwesterly point of Europe. The cliffs here rise almost vertically from the ocean, on the edge of which stands a lighthouse, built in the 1840s on the ruins of a 16th-century Franciscan monastery. A myriad of birds nest along this coast, many building precariously perched nests on the rocky cliffs. There are kites, peregrine falcons and Bonelli's eagles, as well as rock thrushes and pigeons. This is the only place in the world where white storks nest on rocks. Another unlikely creature to be found is the otter – rarely found in a marine habitat.

This is a coastline of towering – often ochre – cliffs, small, rocky coves and pristine beaches, backed by rolling hills, pine forests and almond groves. The best way to see it is slowly: walk, cycle or travel on horseback to truly appreciate the area.

SERRA DA MALCATA NATURE RESERVE

Southern Europe/Portugal

The Serra da Malcata lies on the Spanish border at the eastern edge of central Portugal and was created in 1981 in order to preserve the critically endangered Iberian lynx. Their preferred habitat consists of Mediterranean scrub with open forest that includes old trees and dense thickets, as well as meadows in which to hunt. The nature reserve is perfect country for wildlife of all sorts. Rising to just 1,078 m (3,537 ft), the rolling hills are covered with heather and there is plenty of old oak forest with chestnut and wild cherry trees. At higher levels rare strawberry trees can be seen and, during spring, white and yellow broom provides brilliant splashes of colour. Some of the land just within the reserve's boundaries is used for agriculture, including fruit orchards that look beautiful when in full blossom. Rivers and streams run through the area, beside which grow stands of willow, ash and alder. Small riverside beaches provide opportunities for paddling, swimming or canoeing.

The Serra da Malcata Nature Reserve is an important region for breeding pairs of various birds of prey, including short-toed and booted eagles and Montagu's harrier. Black vultures also nest here. Mammals include foxes, wildcats, wild boars, badgers, genets, as well as smaller creatures such as hares and rabbits. Otters hunt and play in the rivers, which are full of fish, and every species of amphibian in mainland Portugal has a presence here. It is thought that the Iberian lynx may have become extinct in the reserve, but as they are extremely hard to see, and hunt at night, this is a matter of debate. To be on the safe side, a captive breeding programme is being run across the border in Spain and in due course some of these animals will be introduced to Serra da Malcata.

HOW TO GET THERE:
By road from Castello Branco. The main information office is in Penemacor.

WHEN TO GO:
April–October.

WORTH A DETOUR:
If you are in central Portugal, don't miss the opportunity of visiting the historic city of Coimbra.

YOU SHOULD KNOW

The Iberian lynx is about twice the size of a domestic cat, but it has longer legs, a bobtail and pointed ears topped with black tufts. The main reason for its drastic decline is a shortage of rabbits – its favourite food.

EASTERN MED & MIDDLE EAST

AKAMAS PENINSULA

Eastern Mediterranean/Cyprus

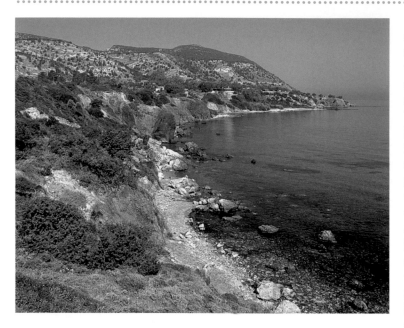

Jutting into the sea at the northwestern tip of Cyprus is the Akamas Peninsula, named after one of the sons of Theseus and his second wife, Phaedra. The third largest island in the Mediterranean, Cyprus has Turkey lying just 75 km (47 mi) to the north and Syria and Lebanon roughly 106 km (66 mi) to the east.

Covering about 230 sq km (90 sq mi), the Akamas Peninsula is the island's most wildly beautiful area. During the 1980s and 1990s, the British used Akamas for military exercises which, ironically, kept it free of the kind of development that was occurring elsewhere on Cyprus. Thus it remains a superb place in which to walk, mountain-bike, or even explore in a 4x4. On this mountainous peninsula discover perfect sandy bays, deep gorges, and forested heights. Thanks to its physical location between Europe, Asia and Africa, an unusually high number of plant species thrive here – 530, of which 33 are endemic – as well as 168 bird, 20 reptile, 16 butterfly and 12 mammal species. The headland is forested with pine, juniper, oak, laurel and myrtle and there are large areas of Mediterranean scrubland, gorges, cliffs and dunes, thus providing several diverse habitats. The most important natural site on Akamas is Lara Bay, where both endangered green and vulnerable loggerhead turtles come to lay their eggs in peace.

Trails snake around the peninsula – one of the loveliest is named after the goddess Aphrodite, who emerged from the sea just off the Cyprus coast and is the island's patron. Starting from the Baths of Aphrodite, it ascends to her sanctuary, noted for a resplendent oak tree that is over 800 years old. Climb higher still to reach a flat, rocky area from which the view is magnificent.

WHEN TO GO:
February–November, but between early March and the end of April for the marvellous show of wild flowers, including orchids. Take plenty of water with you if you are there during the height of summer.

DON'T MISS
The ancient ruins
of Salamis.

KARPAS PENINSULA

Eastern Mediterranean/Cyprus

The Karpas Peninsula, otherwise known as 'the Panhandle', lies in the northeast of Cyprus. It is an area of small villages, where the inhabitants either farm in the traditional style, or fish for their living. The hills, which reach 1,000 m (3,280 ft), are blanketed with pine, cypress and the trees of the Mediterranean scrubland. Golden Sands Beach is thought to be the best beach on the entire island, and is a nesting site for rare green and loggerhead sea turtles. Offshore, Mediterranean dolphins are frequently seen dashing and leaping through the sea.

The rare Andouin's gull can be spotted here, too. These fish eaters nest on the Klidhes Isles, just off the tip of the peninsula. Cyprus is good for birdwatching. The Karpas Peninsula is also rich in wildflowers and from February until June the region is bursting with species, including yellow crowfoot and purple iris. While there are no rivers running through the peninsula, there are 15 springs and many underground reservoirs that enable fruit trees, olives and tobacco to be farmed.

KACKAR MOUNTAINS

Eastern Mediterranean/Turkey

The Kackar range, whose densely clustered peaks soar dramatically above the Black Sea coast, is increasingly popular with walkers. On the southern foothills, villages amid cherry orchards cling to a deeply fissured, wildly rocky landscape, famous for white-water rafting. The walking here is tough, but the weather is excellent. The northern slopes are extravagantly lush. This is the wettest place in Turkey.
Experienced climbers head for the Kackar's precipitous alpine peaks but the network of fine walking tracks attracts most visitors. From villages in the lower highlands, long and short treks – with or without

guides – make use of the paths which link the *yaylas*, the stone-and-wood summer settlements. The walking is glorious: the views are breathtaking, the steep meadows are brilliant with flowers and butterflies, the hundreds of glacial lakes reflect the immense blue, light-filled sky. Grazing cattle, often pompom-bedecked, may be accompanied by Hemsin women, splendid in traditional black-and-orange headdresses.

WHEN TO GO: Late May–late September for walking, July and August for climbing the peaks.

KAZ DAGLARI

Eastern Mediterranean/Turkey

WHEN TO GO:
May, June, September, or
October. Avoid weekends:
Turkish town-dwellers visit.

Kaz Daglari (Goose Mountain), or Mount Ida of Greek classical
antiquity, is a conglomeration of peaks above the northern shore of the Gulf of Edremit. The summits are
windswept and bare. The highest, Kirklar – 1,774 m (5,820 ft) – is a fairly easy climb and the views in all
directions are superb. The thickly forested slopes are home to a remarkable abundance of indigenous flora.
A number of pleasant villages in the fertile northern foothills are linked by narrow roads and tracks.
Attractions for visitors include treks, rides, plane-shaded riverside restaurants and some excellent local
produce, including herbal teas, cheeses and tobacco. Higher slopes are thickly clad with pine and beech,
threaded by streams, dotted with lakes and waterfalls and criss-crossed by paths.
Above the coast, precipitous southern hillsides are fractured by cliffs and canyons. These are challenging hikes
and experience and specialized equipment are essential. Walks from Gure and Zeytinli, pretty little towns at
the eastern end of the gulf, are delightful. Good tracks lead through the woods to an impressive waterfall, to
some hot springs and up into the hills. In spring, streams race and flowers cover the meadows; in autumn the
mountains are clothed in gold and scarlet and visitors gather chestnuts alongside the locals.
To walk along the quiet trails, away from popular villages and picnic areas, is to experience a landscape rich in
ancient legend and traditional rural life.

DON'T MISS
Ancient Aspendos is
very close to the route
to Koprulu.

KOPRULU CANYON

Eastern Mediterranean/Turkey

The Koprulu National Park covers a large area of rugged forested
mountains through which the Kupru Irmagi (Bridge River) flows between the
towering cliffs of the Koprulu Canyon. The road from the coast meanders
through wooded hills and past isolated settlements, becoming increasingly
steep and serpentine, with views of distant misty peaks and the silvery river.
After Beskonak, a track leads to a narrow Roman bridge, still used to cross
the river to the park's other attractions. Near a second bridge (an elegant
Ottoman structure) the river forms still blue pools; upstream, for about
14 km (8.5 mi), it flows deep and calm between tree-clad cliffs, or white
and turbulent through narrow, towering ravines. The forest around the gorge
comprises huge swathes of dark cypress and mixed woodlands and is home
to wild animals which include deer, wolves and wild boar.

WHEN TO GO:
May, June, September, October.

MOUNT LATMOS

Eastern Mediterranean/Turkey

Mount Latmos is actually a ridge of many spurs and its modern Turkish name, Besparmak, means five-fingered. It looms above the northern shore of Lake Bafa, once the Latmian Gulf. The serrated crest reaches 1,500 m (4,921 ft); it is wild and formidable, littered with huge boulders and strange rock formations, pierced by caves, and eroded by streams into steep ridges. Guides are recommended for longer climbs – even the redoubtable Freya Stark found herself 'curiously uncertain as to where the confines of reality end or begin' on Latmos. The ancient Carian town of Latmus was a sizeable port before the gulf silted. The Romans built Herakleia ad Latmus along the western ridge of the mountain, and modern Kapikiri lies among its remains. This traditional Turkish village is a delightful community of small farmers and fishermen, a refuge from mass tourism and the starting point for some excellent walks. The Roman ruins, surrounded by a remarkably well-preserved wall, cover a large area along the lake and up into the foothills. Long hikes (which can be arranged in the village) involve climbing up the stony slopes and through hushed ancient forests, ascending to the caves which from the 8th-century sheltered Christian hermits, and to their monasteries, higher in the peaks. These long walks usually include a night under the stars.

YOU SHOULD KNOW
Another cave dweller was the legendary Endymion, locked into eternal sleep by jealous Zeus and visited nightly by the infatuated moon goddess, Selene.

SAKLIKENT GORGE

Eastern Mediterranean/Turkey

YOU SHOULD KNOW

Tlos was inhabited from the Bronze Age until the 19th century. There are remains of the important Lycian city and of Roman, Byzantine and Ottoman buildings.

Inland Lycia, despite coastal development, is a region of barren mountains, dark forests, rushing streams and precipitous valleys, and intensively cultivated fertile areas. The route to Saklikent Gorge is along narrow country roads, through fields of cotton, tobacco, wheat and vegetables; women in traditional dress walk goats, and old men play backgammon in shaded village cafés.

With a total length of about 18 km (11 mi) and cliffs soaring to 300 m (985 ft), this is Turkey's longest and deepest gorge and it is truly spectacular. The gorge proper begins after a long wooden walkway. About 4 km (2.5 mi) can be walked – the steep upper reaches are accessible only to fully equipped climbers and cavers. Water gushes and bubbles from the rocks and cascades in waterfalls; in some places the terrain is muddy or slippery over pebbles and rocks, while in others walkers must paddle or wade through fast-flowing water. The massive rock walls are awe-inspiring, closing in until the roof of the gorge is no more than a crack through which little sun and no warmth penetrate. Far below in the dim chill, with icy water surging between stupendous cliffs, the landscape is thrillingly Gothic.

YEDIGOLLER NATIONAL PARK

Eastern Mediterranean/Turkey

WHEN TO GO:
The park is open all year. The road from Bolu is closed in winter and three of the lakes dry up in summer.

The region of Bolu, about halfway between Ankara and Istanbul, is one of Turkey's greenest with about 60 per cent of the countryside forested. The area is very popular with hunters – some of the local wild boar are as big as small cows. One of Bolu's most tranquil and beautiful spots, the Yedigoller National Park, is reached by a drive through a wonderful, unspoilt, almost alpine landscape.

The park's seven lakes were formed when mudslides blocked the small, steep valleys; they lie on an upper and lower plateau and are fed by mountain streams. Around them grows some of Turkey's loveliest forest, much of it dense, native mixed woodland, with fir and pine, towering beeches and monumental ancient oaks. Birds and animals live safely here and bears and wolves are among the many creatures found deep in the forest. A section has been designated a deer park – set up to protect the endangered Caspian red deer, a large animal which, like other red deer, roars and has huge antlers.

YOU SHOULD KNOW
The Lebanese cedar feature in the 3,000-year-old Epic of Gilgamesh, one of the world's earliest pieces of literature.

AL-SHOUF CEDAR NATURE RESERVE

Eastern Mediterranean/Lebanon

Lying between Dahr al-Baidar to the north and Jezzine in the south, the Al-Shouf Cedar Nature Reserve lies draped across the ridge of Mount Lebanon's western chain, with views to the Shouf area to the west and the beautiful Bekaa valley to the east. The largest of Lebanon's nature reserves, covering perhaps 5 per cent of the country, it was declared a UNESCO Biosphere Reserve in 2005. Oak forests carpet Al-Shouf's northeastern slopes, and mixed oak and juniper cloak its southeastern slopes. But the jewels in the reserve's crown are the three superb cedar forests preserved within its boundaries – Al Barouk, Ma'aser Al-Shouf and Ain Zhalta/ Bmohray. Some of these cedars are believed to be 2,000 years old, and this is the southernmost area in the world in which they can be found.

The altitude varies from about 1,000 m (3,280 ft) to 2,000 m (6,560 ft) and thus far 500 species of flora have been identified here, including 48 that are endemic to Lebanon, Syria and Turkey, as well as 24 species of tree, although the main work is to re-forest areas that were previously logged. Al-Shouf is known for its regenerative powers – trees here spread naturally and provide habitat for 32 mammals, including grey wolves, golden jackals, striped hyenas, wild cats, mountain gazelles and Cape hares.

Birds are also plentiful, with some 200 species to be spotted – although many are migratory. Birds of prey, in particular, do well and the pheasants and partridges that were introduced to Al-Shouf for hunting have successfully colonized the area.

The Al-Shouf reserve is a wonderful place in which to hike, and trails for different levels of difficulty are available. It is also good for mountain-biking and, in winter, snowshoeing. Visit the Barouk information centre for details of cultural sites in the reserve, as well as hiking routes and other activities.

HOW TO GET THERE:
By car from Beirut or the Bekaa Valley.

WHEN TO GO:
Spring, summer or autumn, unless you want to enjoy the winter snowfall.

WORTH A DETOUR:
The cave castle Qalaat Niha, the last remains of a stronghold once used by Arabs, Crusaders and princes of Mount Lebanon, including Prince Fakhr-al-Din.

JEITA GROTTO

Eastern Mediterranean/Lebanon

YOU SHOULD KNOW

The engineers wrote down their names and sealed them in a bottle they left on top of a stalagmite. Limestone has since covered the bottle and joined it to the stalagmite.

Some 18 km (11 mi) north of Beirut lies the longest cave ever found in the Middle East. Inhabited by prehistoric man, the lower cave was explored in the 1870s, when engineers from the Beirut Water Company made their way deep inside. The caves were known as the Grottoes of Nahr al-Kalb, after the underground river whose source the engineers found here and which supplies much of Beirut with fresh water. Subsequent exploration continues to this day. A tour of the lower galleries involves an electric boat trip along a black underground lake. Modern lighting spotlights incredible shapes, columns and stone draperies carved by water across millennia, all within vast, vaulted caverns. The upper galleries, opened in 1969, can be visited on foot. The Red Chamber, so called because of its colour, towers to 106 m (348 ft), although the third chamber is even higher. The White Chamber has the best formations, including the world's longest stalactite at 8.2 m (27 ft).

AJLOUN FOREST RESERVE

Middle East/Jordan

WHEN TO GO:
Mid March–mid November.

Only one per cent of Jordan is forested, of which the Ajloun Forest Reserve is a significant part. Established in 1988 by Jordan's Royal Society for the Conservation of Nature, the 13 sq km (5 sq mi) area, located north of Amman in the Ajloun highlands, shelters many rare animals and plants. This is perfect habitat for forest animals such as wild boar, red fox, striped hyena, stone marten, golden jackal, wolves, Indian crested porcupine and Persian squirrel. It was once home to roe deer; the RSCN has introduced a captive breeding programme here, bringing the animals from Turkey, and has now added a similar programme for Persian fallow deer. Five trails run through, designed not only to show the visitor different environments but also to intersect with local communities with whom the reserve authorities have established some co-operative initiatives through raising public awareness. The Rockrose Trail, which takes four or five hours to complete, takes hikers through olive groves, for which the area is famous, across forested ridges and valleys to Lebanon's snow-capped Jebel Sheik, Syria and the West Bank.

DANA NATURE RESERVE

Middle East/Jordan

WHEN TO GO:
March–end of November.

Dana Nature Reserve extends across a long chain of mountains and valleys that are remote, stunningly beautiful and packed with both natural and archaeological treasures.

The landscape of Dana, which covers 308 sq km (1,209 sq mi), varies from wooded mountains and red rock slopes to stony plains, majestic sandstone cliffs and classic sand dune desert, and therefore supports a variety of flora and fauna. This is home to Phoenician juniper, pine, evergreen oak and the world's southernmost areas of Mediterranean cypress, as well as acacia and desert shrubs. Mammals include wolves, sand cats, red foxes, hyenas, jackals, porcupines, hares and rabbits. Captive breeding programmes have saved the Nubian ibex and three species of gazelle that were almost extinct here. Birds include Palestinian sunbirds, white-throated kingfishers and Syrian serins – their largest breeding colony is in the reserve. Many raptors make their homes here, including houbara bustards, saker falcons and migratory species such honey buzzards and steppe eagles.

WADI MUJIB

Middle East/Jordan

DON'T MISS
The hot springs
and waterfall of
Hammamat Ma'in.

A genuinely remote and wild place, Wadi Mujib, part of the Mujib Nature Reserve, is a gorge that extends to the eastern shore of the Dead Sea some 90 km (56 mi) south of Amman. Established in 1987, the reserve protects 220 sq km (85 sq mi) of the mountainous hinterland and, at 410 m (1,345 ft) below sea level, is the lowest nature reserve on Earth.

The mountains in the reserve reach to 900 m (2,953 ft) above sea level, and the large variation in elevation, combined with constantly flowing water from seven tributaries, ensure unusual biodiversity of flora, fauna and, especially, birds. The landscape of harsh sandstone mountains, desert and plateaux, is intersected by steep cliffs and gorges, with a lake at the bottom of the wadi where a dam has been built.

There are several terrific hikes to undertake, all but one of which must be guided. In part this is because of the sensitive nature of the reserve, but it is also because this is dangerous terrain. Highly experienced hikers can easily become lost and, as with all wadis, flash floods can suddenly appear. The Siq trail is straightforward but the rest are tough, requiring a good degree of fitness, the ability to swim and no fear of heights.

Scientists continue to explore and document Mujib and thus far ten species of carnivore have been found, including Arabian leopards, caracals, wolves, jackals and hyenas. Mujib is a haven for birds, and not simply because it is a resting place for migratory species. Raptors include griffon vultures and Bonelli's eagle.

DASHT-E LUT

Middle East/Iran

DON'T MISS
The UNESCO World
Heritage Site of
Persepolis.

YOU SHOULD KNOW

Iran is a troubled country and
there are areas where it is
unwise to visit.

Iran's mountains provide a protective barrier that virtually encircles the whole country, within which is a large central plateau, divided into drainage basins. At 480 km (300 mi) long and 320 km (200 mi) wide, Dasht-e Lut is one of the largest of these basins and is a bleak place. The eastern region of the Central Plateau is formed of two deserts: Dasht-e Kavir, the Great Salt Desert, and Dasht-e Lut, the Desert of Emptiness, which extends southwards. The former, which is even larger, is named after its many salt marshes. Virtually uninhabited, the marshes, apparently covered by a solid crust of salt, behave like quicksand – drive onto it and sink. Few oases exist in Dasht-e Kavir, where people eke a living from breeding camels and sheep, and a little agriculture. Dasht-e Lut iis a place utterly hostile to man. Totally covered with black volcanic lava, it absorbs the extreme heat of the sun, becoming a wind tunnel due to the difference of temperature between it and its surroundings, which are at a higher elevation and a lower temperature.

DON'T MISS
The thermal springs at
Abe Garm Larijan
at the base of the volcano.

MOUNT DAMAVAND

Middle East/Iran

Mount Damavand is not only Iran's highest peak at 5,671 m (18,606 ft) but also the highest peak in the Middle East. Long dormant, it produced a large new vent in its crater in 2007 that continues to belch sulphuric gases, smoke and steam. The crater itself has a huge diameter surrounded by yellow, sulphuric rocks, and is about 30 m (100 ft) deep. The summit lake is usually frozen, although at the height of summer it may disappear completely.

Although there are 16 known ascent routes on the volcano, most are for experienced climbers only and it is the south-face route that is normally used. This is often compared to the route up Mount Kilimanjaro, in Tanzania, because although it is not technically difficult, it is a long, hard slog. Climbers not only have to be fit and strong, but they must also acclimatize themselves.

The volcano's flanks are particularly beautiful in spring, when vast poppy fields come into flower, along with wild tulips, iris and other species of flora. The best climbing time, however, is during summer when much of the snow has melted.

GOLESTAN NATIONAL PARK

Middle East/Iran

Golestan National Park is situated in the north of Iran, stretching across a thickly forested area of the Caspian highlands and the steppes of Khorasan province. The very varied terrain includes temperate rainforest, high cliffs, rivers, springs, marshes and grassland plains. Protected since 1957, this lovely area is the oldest national park in the country.

The variety of habitats in Golestan has made it an important sanctuary for wildlife, and mammals include the Persian leopard, brown bear, wild cat, wild boar, Persian ibex and mountain goat, all of which survive happily in the hot summers and snowy winters of the park. Over 150 species of bird also live here, including lammergeiers, three other types of vulture and golden eagles. The lammergeier, unlike other vultures, does not have a bald head and is sometimes mistaken for an eagle. It is a symbol of luck and happiness in Iran. Golestan is also on the route of many migratory birds.

As well as the forested hills and rocky crags, the park is home to many wild fruit trees and bushes, such as mulberry, wild pear, fig, barberry and raspberry, and many of the smaller plants are used as traditional remedies.

Sadly, Golestan is under threat for a variety of reasons. One of these is hunting, but worse still is the construction of a road right through the forest, allegedly with the welfare of local inhabitants in mind. Despite numerous pleas to put the road around the area instead, the authorities have so far refused to budge. Just an hour's drive from the Caspian Sea, Golestan is very popular with Iranian tourists during the summer months.

WORTH A DETOUR:
The town and beautiful beach of Bandar Gaz; and don't forget that the Caspian Sea is the main source of Beluga caviar.

BU TINAH

Middle East/United Arab Emirates

WORTH A DETOUR:
The archaeological sites – Stone Age, Bronze Age, Iron Age, pre-Islamic and Islamic – on Marawah.

Bu Tinah is a tiny horseshoe-shaped group of islands and shoals some 25 km (15 mi) from Zirku Island, the oil-exporting terminal for Abu Dhabi's vast Zakum oil fields. Part of the UNESCO designated Marawah Marine Biosphere Reserve, the largest protected area of the UAE, Bu Tinah is so low lying – its highest point is perhaps 3 m (10 ft) above sea level – that at low tide the islands and shoals are more or less joined.

The main island has a sheltered, mangrove-lined lagoon to the south and the shoals are surrounded by seagrass beds and coral reefs. These reefs fascinate marine scientists because the conditions in which they thrive are very hard. The Persian Gulf is both extremely salty and very warm. In the height of summer the water temperature can reach up to 35°C (95°F), which would kill most corals in the world. Here, at least 16 species survive happily and are rich with marine life.

The Persian Gulf is home to the world's second-largest population of dugong, 60 per cent of which – some 600 individuals – live in the waters around Bu Tinah. Dugong is the only sea mammal that is entirely herbivorous, hence its common name: sea cow. It is a critically endangered species, still illegally hunted by man, and the seagrass which is its main diet is under threat from oil and chemical pollution. Other marine creatures, including three species of dolphin, abound.

DON'T MISS
Taking a boat safari – not only will you see whales, but you may also be able to swim with dolphins.

SOCOTRA

Middle East/Yemen

Socotra, a small archipelago lying 380 km (240 mi) southeast of the Arabian Peninsula, is part of the Republic of Yemen. Its extreme isolation, together with the fact that the archipelago was originally part of a continental landmass, and not volcanic, makes Socotra unique – one-third of its flora is endemic – and it is often described as being the most alien looking place on Earth. Most of the inhabitants live on Socotra Island, with a few hundred living on two other islands, leaving the remainder uninhabited. Until recently, Socotrans have survived by fishing, rearing animals and cultivating dates. Now, however, ecotourism is becoming an important new source of revenue.

There are only two species of mammal – bats and civet cats – native to the islands, but there are plenty of camels, donkeys and goats to be seen. The great strength of Socotra is its insects, reptiles, marine biodiversity and birds. The most extraordinary tree on Socotra is the Dragon's Blood tree. It looks like an umbrella, and its name comes from the red resin exuded from the bark. Dorstenia gigas, the Socotran cucumber tree and Socotran pomegranate are all highly visible, strange looking, endemics.

HOW TO GET THERE: Drive from Dubai to Khasab – ensuring you have all the correct visa entries; fly from Muscat or take the world's fastest diesel-driven catamaran.

MUSANDAM PENINSULA

Middle East/Oman

Often referred to as the 'Norway of Arabia', the Musandam Peninsula has an extraordinary coastline of rugged mountains cut with fjords or channels, hidden bays and villages that cling like limpets to towering walls of rock that reach to more than 2,000 m (6,560 ft) and where traditional customs of dhow building and fishing remain unchanged. This is the Ru'us al Jabal, the dramatic finish of the Hajar Mountains and an important eco-region. Explore remote villages by 4x4; hike in the mountains among wild olive, fig and juniper; or wander the valleys lush with pomegranates and apricots. Arabian tahrs, an endemic, goat-like animal, thrive here. The warm waters contain one of the richest marine environments in the world, with coral gardens and an immense variety of marine life. Rent a boat, cruise on a dhow, or join a dive boat and swim, snorkel or scuba dive to your heart's content. Fishing trips are also popular – there are more than 900 species of fish in these waters – or rent a kayak, relax and take it easy.

RUB' AL KHALI

Middle East/Oman

DON'T MISS
The horse and camel racing between September and June.

The notion of a vast expanse of sand desert is, for some reason, wildly romantic. The Rub' al Khali covers most of the southern third of the Arabian Peninsula, including parts of Yemen, Oman, UAE and all of southern Saudi Arabia, and is some 1,000 km (620 mi) long and 500 km (310 mi) wide. Far from being romantic, this desert is a harsh, unforgiving environment.

Rub' al Khali was inhabited by prehistoric man before the region was desertified and there is much evidence of the presence of both man and animals, especially around what were once lakes. Stone tools, fossilized clam shells and the fossilized bones of various mammals, including goats and hippopotami, have been found. There are also traces of camel caravans that carried frankincense across areas now almost impassable and

home to no one. The dunes can reach over 300 m (985 ft) and, in summer, temperatures may soar to 55°C (131°F) in the middle of the day and sink to below 0°C (32°F) at night. Rub' al Khali slopes from 1,006 m (3,300 ft) in the north, where a long, narrow corridor joins it to the Nafud desert, down to sea level in the east. Salt marshes exist in the southeast and, around the edges of this inhospitable region, a few Bedouin feed their camels on the sparse vegetation living in the sand.

ASIA

UVS NUUR BASIN

Central Asia/Mongolia

DON'T MISS
Altan Els, the world's
northernmost dune
desert ecosystem.

The World Heritage Site and Biosphere Reserve of Uvs Nuur Basin covers 10,689 sq km (4,125 sq mi) of northwestern Mongolia. Set at just 759 m (2,490 ft) above sea level, the lake itself is Mongolia's lowest point, but its waters are five times saltier than the ocean and it has no edible fish. It has no outlet either. The 38 rivers that flow into it evaporate in the enormous wetlands on its shores – the feeding, nesting and breeding grounds of some 362 bird species including cranes, spoonbills, geese, swans, snow herons, egrets, steppe hazel grouse and gull species which fly thousands of miles from the South China Sea for a brief northern summer.

The 'closed' system of Uvs Nuur Basin makes it as fascinating to scientists as it is to travellers. In fact it is usually uncomfortable for both. It is one of the hottest places, and always the coldest, in Mongolia, with temperatures ranging from over 40 to −57°C (104 to −70.6°F), and these extremes make it an ideal subject for studying climate change.

WORTH A DETOUR: The Yolyn Am Natural History Museum, which displays dinosaur bones and eggs and describes the desert flora and fauna to look for nearby.

YOLYN AM

Central Asia/Mongolia

Yolyn Am is a long, deep and narrow gash set high in the Gurvan Saikhan Mountains. The jagged gorge winds for miles, almost concealed by the overhang of sheer rock walls that block out the sunlight, deflect the winds and trap winter in the canyon's depths. Where sunlight falls, the rock is burning hot, and the combination of extremes produces a unique desert ecosystem. There is a small spring in the valley's depths. Even in the 45°C (113°F) air temperatures of high summer it barely flows, because the valley floor hardly ever warms sufficiently to melt the constricting ice that builds for nine months of the year, every year, over millions of years.

Summer releases pockets of ice in the canyon walls, but the hundreds of dripping waterfalls only feed the ice field, which becomes several metres thick by the end of winter and several kilometres long. Sunlight reflects from on high onto the cracked slabs of ice, flashing prisms of colour across the defile and a spectacular abstract of blues and greens deep into the hollows. The 'Gobi Glacier' feels like a dream world, a Gobi myth that evaporates where the gorge opens out into a wide mountain valley.

BAYANZAG FLAMING CLIFFS

Central Asia/Mongolia

Aromantic mystique clings to the Gobi Desert. It is a desert with many faces – Mongolians can distinguish 33 separate kinds of 'Gobi' to describe a vast territory of high mountains, springs, forests and rolling steppe grasslands as well as the arid semi-deserts and wind-whipped dune systems of popular imagination – and every one more than matches its mythology. Partly it's a matter of scale. Where there are sand dunes, for example, they are the highest, longest, and most bizarre. The dunes of Khongoryn Els rise in a sand massif 20 km (12 mi) wide, 100 km (62 mi) long and some 800 m (2,625 ft) high, with individual dune peaks over 30 m (100 ft). Travellers can hear the dunes 'sing' from miles away, a musical drone similar to a light aircraft caused by the grating of billions of grains of sand in the sighing wind. The dunes are in Gobi Gurvansaikhan in Mongolia's south, a national park that protects some of the Gobi's most spectacular features. There is an escarpment that rises out of a forest of desert-hardy saxaul trees, a ragged wall of reddish sedimentary rock eroded over millions of years that blocks the horizon. At sunrise and sunset the cliffs of Bayanzag radiate orange, scarlet and crimson against an arc of cerulean sky. Seen from a short distance, it's as though the horizon itself is exploding in flames. Close-to, visitors bathed in the fiery reflections feel a primal rush, as though nature itself claimed sacrifices for its spectacular furnace. That's not all. The Flaming Cliffs were named by explorer Roy Chapman Andrews, who excavated the first dinosaur eggs on this very spot. The terrain has yielded whole skeletons of various dinosaur species and many mammals; and Andrews himself found the skeletal remains of a hornless rhinoceros, the largest mammal known in the world.

WHEN TO GO:
May–September.

YOU SHOULD KNOW

At nearby Tugrugiin Shiree, excavations revealed the skeletons of two dinosaur species still locked in combat. Fossils are very easy to spot – but remember that removing even a tiny memento is one of the greatest crimes you can commit in Mongolia.

KHANGAI MOUNTAINS

Central Asia/Mongolia

These are the sacred hills of Chinggis Khaan, the epic highlands he chose as the centre of his Mongol Empire and the site of his capital, KaraKorum. The Khangai Mountains stretch northwest from central Mongolia to the Russian border, parallel with the longer Altai range to the south, and reach their highest peak on 3,905 m (12,812 ft) Mount Otgontenger, east of Uliastai where Zavkhan meets the Aimags of Arkhangai and Bayankhongor. Otgontenger is popular with serious mountaineers but, for ancient religious reasons, women are not allowed to climb it. In any case, this central section of the Khangai Mountains is a famously beautiful configuration of thick forests dotted with snow-capped peaks, lakes, white-water mountain rivers, hot and cold springs, and alpine meadows full of musk deer, antelope, lynx, bear, curly-horned wild sheep, ibex, bustards, golden eagles, black vultures, storks and Dalmatian pelicans. The spectacular landscapes spread a huge distance southwest, where the Khangai Nuruu National Park also includes the eight descending freshwater lakes of Khuisyn Naiman in Ovorkhangai Aimag. Connected by an underground system of channels, they are one of Mongolia's most intriguing geological sites, and one of the loveliest panoramas in the country.

> **HOW TO GET THERE:**
> By 4x4 from Ulaanbaatar to regional centres like Tsetserleg, Bayankhongor and Uliastai. Horses and camels are available locally.

> **WORTH A DETOUR:** The Buurug Dune, covering 4,000 sq km (1,545 sq mi) and the biggest single dune in Mongolia; rafting on the Tes or one of the many brilliant rivers.

UVS AIMAG

Central Asia/Mongolia

Mongolia's Uvs Aimag (province) occupies the great lakes depression of the country's northwest, between the high mountain extension of the Khangai range to the east, and the 4,000 m (13,120 ft) peaks of the northern Altai Mountains to the west. Even disregarding Uvs Nuur, the province's biggest lakee, Uvs Aimag is a remote wonderland of mountains, dune deserts, salt and freshwater lakes, tearing rivers and swampy meadows.

Tsagaan Shuvuut is a Strictly Protected Area in Uvs' extreme north, by the Russian border. Steep elevations up to 3,000 m (9,840 ft) guarantee an amazing variety of mammals and birds in their different ranges, guaranteed to flourish. It's the same at Turgen Uul, where the 4,000 m (13,120 ft) Kharkhiraa and Khankhukhii peaks dominate one of Mongolia's most beautiful regions, a meld of glaciers, stark cliffs, white-water rivers in forested canyons, waterfalls and flower-carpeted forest glades.

LAKE SONG-KUL

Central Asia/Kyrgyzstan

HOW TO GET THERE:
By 4×4 from Bishkek –
300 km (186 mi) or Naryn –
150 km (93 mi).

WHEN TO GO:
June–September.

WORTH A DETOUR:
The ride over 32 Parrots
Pass to where the Song-Kul
River meets the lake and
where herds of semi-wild
horses come to bathe;
the Tyulek River ride to a
village where women weave
traditional carpets invested
with coded folklore; the water
birds in the marshes of the
lake's nature reserve; any
chance to eat and drink with
nomadic shepherds and lake
fishermen.

The nomadic culture of Kyrgyzstan is written into the spectacular landscapes of Song-Kul, an alpine lake shimmering in a 3,000 m (9,840 ft) high plateau of steppe grassland. Every year, herders bring their livestock up from the Kochkor Valley to graze on the lush pastures stretching out from the lake to the surrounding ring of mountains, yet centuries of repetitious custom have left no blemish on its tranquil serenity. Instead, travellers are greeted by a creation scene of almost biblical drama. Untethered horses graze freely among yak and sheep all along the lakeshore, watched over by enthusiastic children chasing each other on scraggy ponies at breakneck speed to the apparent indifference of the adults doing chores by the felt yurts erected for the duration. This timeless scene of human domesticity – in unselfconscious harmony with the natural order – has the power to move even stony hearts, and it sets the tone for travelling in the region.

Nearly 30 km (19 mi) long and 18 km (11 mi) wide, the lake is small enough to feel like a self-contained world, and big enough to change colour from blue to pink to violet with the time of day and the weather. It is alive with movement and sound – songs and shouting and laughter as well as the cackle of thousands of wild geese, ducks and waterfowl. Only at night does the clamour fade to the rise and fall of conversations round crackling open fires, and an occasional solitary hooting over the lapping water. Some travellers can spend weeks drinking in the fragile simplicity of the idyll – but all around the lake there are fantastic trails to ride or trek, like the descent to the Tyulek River over the Aktash Pass, or the Moldaashu ravine. Many visitors swear that, however many times they come, Lake Song-Kul is where Kyrgyzstan makes them feel at one with nature's family.

YOU SHOULD KNOW

Lake Song-Kul is the place to go native. This means not only camping in yurts, but helping to pitch and repair them as part of the trek. Most of all it means responding to extremely friendly – and wholly genuine – overtures of hospitality with the same warmth, even if it feels a little uncomfortable for urbanized city folk on an exotic break. Song-Kul is all beauty and no artifice – natural or human – at all.

FAN MOUNTAINS

Central Asia/Kyrgyzstan

WORTH A DETOUR:
The Achik Tash meadows with the Big Peaks in the distance; any of dozens of local festivals featuring Kyrgyz bareback horse racing and oiled wrestling; drinking fermented mare's milk in a felt yurt with Kyrgyz mountain shepherds.

The western border of Kyrgyzstan is shaped like giant pincers, squeezing the meeting point of Uzbekistan, Kazakhstan and Tajikistan. Politically and geographically, it's a confused area. The pincer's upper joint follows the most northerly spur of the Tien Shan Mountains to its western end. The southern arm runs back eastwards on a parallel ridge, gaining serious altitude between the Turkestanskiy sub-range and Pamir-Alai Mountains, which form the northern limit of the famous 'Pamir Knot' and the mountain corridor linking it to the Tien Shan. These southerly hills are an integral part of the giant mountain system of Pamir and Tien Shan, but distinctive enough to retain their own name – the Fan Mountains.

Within Kyrgyzstan, the Fan Mountains are seventh heaven for trekking on foot and on horseback. Most of the 11 summits over 5,000 m (16,400 ft) and 30 above 4,000 m (13,120 ft), including 5,489 m (18,008 ft) Chimtarga, the highest, lie over or on the border with Tajikistan; and the very highest 7,000 m (22,966 ft) peaks, like Pik Lenin (now officially called Koh-i-Garmo) far to the east, are in or shared with Gorno-Badakhshan. Apart from the staggering experience of driving the Pamir Highway from Khorog to Osh – clean across the region – only serious mountaineers want to risk the encounters with armed personnel that are a feature of

trekking the trophy peaks. The high peaks are impressive, but the Kyrgyz Fan Mountains are beautiful. They are heavily forested, with sapphires for lakes, alpine meadows, canyons terraced with rocky bluffs, wild orchards in pretty river valleys and, above the tree line, glacial moonscapes and just enough snow-capped bare rock for cheerful self-congratulation. Blessedly empty of 'altitude tourists', the Fan Mountains in Kyrgyzstan are a revelation awaiting the kind of experienced trekkers who see and understand the magnificence in the smallest as well as the greatest manifestations of nature.

SARYARKA

Central Asia/Kyrgyzstan

WORTH A DETOUR: Lake Balkhash, now the largest lake in Central Asia since the dramatic shrinkage of the Aral Sea.

Saryarka – Steppe and Lakes of Northern Kazakhstan is a UNESCO World Heritage Site. The reserves are situated in a wide band of steppe grassland which extends from Ukraine in the west to China in the east. Bounded by evergreen forest to the north and an arid area to the south, they are a fertile oasis of wetlands, lakes and open grassland. More than 15 million migratory birds, many rare and endangered, use the area's precious saturated lowlands as a hub on their journeys from Europe, Africa and East Asia to breeding grounds in Siberia. Birdwatchers from around the world flock to the reserves at news of sightings, including the imperilled Siberian white crane as well as the more common Dalmatian pelican and pink flamingo. The reserves are also crucial to the survival of *Saiga tatarica*, an antelope which once roamed the plains in vast herds but is now on the verge of extinction through hunting and illegal poaching. Travel within these golden grasslands is easy and the recent growth in ecotourism has rewarded the efforts of the reserves' authorities, even though tourism was only a secondary consideration when they sought to preserve this area of immense ecological importance.

In this land of big skies there are numerous hilltop mausoleums, built by nomadic peoples to honour their ancestors and to mark out grazing rights. These round-roofed structures, although now in a state of disrepair, are a reminder that the area has long been a place where humans have lived in harmony with nature.

SAYRAM-UGAM NATIONAL PARK

Central Asia/Kazakhstan

DON'T MISS
The crystal-clear
waters of the River Sairamsu.

Located in the Kaskasu River valley in the Tole Bi District of southern Kazakhstan, Sayram-Ugam National Park is a wildlife sanctuary. The Ugam Mountains offer unspoilt beauty, characterized by huge glacial valleys, turquoise morainal lakes and steep-sided ravines covered in birch and juniper forest. A road takes the traveller into the heart of the mountains, but stops abruptly near the lower slopes. It is then time for a change of pace as the impressive sight of Sayram Peak, at 4,238 m (13,904 ft) the park's highest point, dominates the skyline.

The area has a rich history and was once a strategically important section of the Great Silk Road route that carried goods from east to west. There are also numerous ancient monuments, mausoleums and burial mounds scattered across the park which bear witness to its ancient cultural history.

The best climbing is to be found on Kizil-bush and Druzhba which are both over 4,000 m (13,120 ft). Less demanding but still challenging, the most scenic trail is along the slopes of the scree-lined Kaskasu ravine. Sayram-Ugam is a place of rare splendour, a tranquil place far removed from the bustle of modern life.

PAMIRO-ALAI MOUNTAINS

Central Asia/Tajikistan

Pamiro-Alai is a mountain system of central Asia stretching 800 km (500 mi) from the region of Pamir towards the Sino-Tajikistan border. It is made up of five mountain ranges – Alaiskiy, Zeravshanskiy Turkestanskiy, Karateginskiy and Gissarskiy. In Persian, Pamiro-Alai translates as 'paradise at the roof of the world'. While its exceptionally harsh environment and extreme remoteness may not be everyone's idea of paradise, it fits well with the local Sunni Muslim belief that paradise should be hard to reach. The ranges are composed of a succession of huge sheer rock faces with over 30 peaks above 5,000 m (16,400 ft). Roads are few and far between, particularly in the west of the area where access is only really possible by helicopter. Where roads do exist, such as the one near Chimtarga Peak, they are often so narrow and steep that traffic has to be tightly controlled and it is customary to drive up in the morning and down in the afternoon. The area was often chosen to host the all-Russian climbing championships during the Soviet era and it presents some of the most challenging rock climbing anywhere in the world. The season is short, with only August being dry and warm enough to allow full access. Progress on the precipitous rocks can be slow, with advances of only a few hundred metres per day possible on the toughest stretches.

The most accessible and perhaps the most beautiful climb in Pamiro-Alai is a route that links Lake Alaudinskie with Lake Kulikalon. A full day's hike along the scree-lined Shogun-Aga pass takes the walker into an area surrounded by towering peaks, while the descent offers incredible views over Lake Kulikalon and across the lavishly green Laudan river valley.

HOW TO GET THERE:
By helicopter from Samarkand or Dushanbe. It is possible to reach the area by road, but this involves an arduous journey and it is very easy to get lost.

WHEN TO GO:
August is the only time when the weather is likely to be benign.

WORTH A DETOUR:
The view of the northwestern face of Mount Chapdara from the Shogun-Aga pass.

CHITRAL GOL

South Asia/Pakistan

DON'T MISS
The historic city of
Peshawar, the centre of
Pashtun culture and arts.

Situated in the Hindu Kush, a sub-range of the Himalayas in Pakistan's
North-West Frontier province, Chitral Gol is a remote region of valleys encircled by snow-covered peaks.
Within this area, the Chitral Gol National Park may be found alongside the Chitral River. It used to be the
private game reserve of His Highness Sir Shuja ul Mulk, and is still owned by the family, although the Wildlife
Department is now responsible for the wildlife. This is a stunning area of ancient deodar cedar trees, pine
oaks, junipers and birch. The park is renowned for its markhor goats. The national animal of Pakistan, the
markhor is a large and endangered type of wild goat with superb spiral horns. Siberian ibex and Ladakh

urial can also be found here in small numbers, along with
carnivores such as the yellow-throated marten, red foxes,
jackals, wolves and visiting snow leopards. The birds that may
be seen include golden eagles, Lammergeier's and peregrine
falcons, snowcocks, Monal pheasants, and many ducks and
other waterfowl which pass through en route to India.
Hunting is a popular pastime here and unfortunately ducks, in
particular, make an easy target.

WORTH A DETOUR: The spectacular Hunza Valley,
supposed to be the inspiration for Shangri-la in James
Hilton's book, *Lost Horizon*.

KHUNJERAB NATIONAL PARK

South Asia/Pakistan

One of the highest national parks in the world – more than 50 per cent is over 4,000 m (13,120 ft) –
Khunjerab is situated in the Karakoram mountain range and was set up in 1975 to protect the magnificent
display of alpine flora and increase the population of snow leopards and Marco Polo sheep.
Starting 30 km (19 mi) from Sost, the valley is at first narrow, with mountains forming high walls to either
side, but soon it widens out into broad and beautiful alpine meadows where 66 species of bird live, including
kestrels, falcons, sparrow hawks, marsh harriers, Himalayan griffon vultures, golden eagles and Lammergeiers.
But Marco Polo sheep and snow leopards are the stars of the area. Marco Polo rams have the longest horns
of any sheep, averaging about 140 cm (55 in) and spiral in shape, with the tips pointing outwards.
It is thought that the highest density of snow leopards in the Himalayan ecosystem live in this region. These
beautiful solitary and secretive cats, active at dawn and dusk and very well camouflaged, are difficult to count
but the Snow Leopard Trust is conducting studies at several sites. Within the boundaries of the park are the
Ghuzerav mountains, at the heart of which rises the perfect pyramid of Sonia Peak.

ROYAL BARDIA NATIONAL PARK

South Asia/Nepal

YOU SHOULD KNOW

An exciting way to reach the park is by organized rafting down the Karnali River.

WHEN TO GO:
From October–early April.

WORTH A DETOUR:
What may be the largest Asian elephant in the world, named Rajah Gaj, lives in Bardia. He stands 3.4 m (11 ft) at the shoulder.

Previously a royal hunting reserve, Royal Bardia National Park became a wildlife reserve in 1976, and in 1988, after being extended to encompass the Babai River Valley, it was established as a national park. Remote and undisturbed, the wilderness covers an area of almost 1,000 sq km (386 sq mi). Located in Western Terai, much of Bardia lies on the slopes of the Shiwalik hills that form its northern border. The land slopes gently down to rivers in the south and west, while in the east a section of highway bisects the park.

More than 70 per cent of the park is covered with forest, mostly sal trees, but the grassland, savannah and riverine forests forming the remainder provides wonderful habitat in which many endangered animals live and breed.

Bardia is bursting with wildlife. Greater one-horned rhinos were successfully relocated here from Chitwan National Park, and now there are 100 of these rare animals. One of the last known herds of wild elephants often pass through as they tramp these remote western Nepalese jungles and six species of deer, gaur, nilgai, Himalayan tahr, serow, and jackal can be seen. In pride of place are Royal Bengal tigers, of which there are thought to be over 50 individuals. Around the rivers, gharial and marsh mugger crocodiles snooze, otters and water birds splash and play, and Ganges river dolphins leap through the blue waters.

Take a guided tour by foot, 4x4, or elephant. These magnificent animals carry their passengers deep into the park through tall, whispering grasses and past vast termite mounds, picking their way delicately through streams en route. With luck, many birds and animals will be seen, and even a glimpse of a tiger is a possibility.

PIN VALLEY NATIONAL PARK

South Asia/India

DON'T MISS
The Dhankar
monastery, built almost
1,000 years ago.

Located in the north of Himal Pradesh, right up by the Tibetan border, Pin Valley National Park, in the valley of the Pin River, is cold, high and remote. Its elevation varies from 3,500 m (11,500 ft) to something over 6,000 m (20,000 ft). Declared a National Park in 1987, it covers 650 sq km (250 sq mi) and has a buffer zone of 1,150 km (715 mi).

The Pin Valley is an astonishing place. Austere, beautiful and other-worldly, it has a distinctly Buddhist atmosphere, due in part to the monasteries and culture of Tibet which is all-encompassing here. Because of the altitude, vegetation is sparse, dominated by alpine trees, stands of Himalayan cedar and rare medicinal plants. By mid-June the snow has melted and the vegetation begins to grow. Rapidly, the lunar landscape is transformed by a carpet of wild flowers, and some of the park's rare animals descend to lower levels to feed.

The park was largely formed to protect the endangered snow leopard, the grey ghost of the Himalayas, but these animals are notoriously hard to spot. However, it is home to many other animals including ibex, Tibetan gazelle, blue sheep, woolly hare, fox, wolf and bear. As vegetation is thin, it is easy to view wildlife here and it's wonderful for twitchers, who may spot Himalayan snowcock, chukor, snow partridge, several species of finch and wagtail, pigeon, red-billed chough, golden eagle and Himalayan griffon.

There are several paths to trek, of varying difficulty and all over 3,000 m (9,840 ft), and huts in which to stay overnight. Porters and local guides are available to help, and there are even Chhumurthi horses for hire. It is impossible to drive in the park, so for those who are not so fit, horse trekking is an option.

PINDARI GLACIER

South Asia/India

DON'T MISS
Views of
Nanda Devi.

The Pindari glacier, in the Kumaon Himalayas, is situated between Nanda Kot, 6,861 m (22,510 ft), and Nanda Devi, 7,817 m (25,646 ft). A steep, imposing glacier, Pindari measures 3 km (1.9 mi) in length and 250 m (820 ft) in width. A trek here is an adventure for anyone who is fit and the reward is worth the climb. Starting at Song, on the banks of the Revati Ganga River, the route is via Loharkhet, where the forest begins. This dense forest is at a relatively low altitude and is bursting with ferns, rhododendrons, wild flowers, berries and moss. Troops of langurs, India's sacred monkey, swing through the trees above.

At Dhakuri Khal pass, a small detour brings the valiant trekker to a small, beautifully situated temple. This is the hardest day, but as the misty dawn reveals the first snow-clad mountains, anticipation grows for what is yet to come. The path runs beside the pristine Pindari River, the source of which rises at the glacier, before reaching Dwali and the treeline.

The climb from here to Phurkiya is tough: the air is thin and cold, with frozen streams to cross, even in midsummer. The river, too, is frozen, but water can still be seen, flowing beneath a thick slab of ice. Skirting the edge of a deep valley, the views are stunning and there is even a slender waterfall to admire. Phurkiya is the last stop before the final ascent to Zero Point.

WHEN TO GO:
May 1–June 30, or
September 1–October 15.

Pure white, with touches of blue and brown, Pindari glacier gleams in the sunshine and is an exhilarating sight. Although this is an arbitrary place to stop, only serious mountaineers continue – ordinary mortals can only sit and stare at what must be one of the grandest views in the world.

WHEN TO GO:
May–September, but July and August for the best of the wild flowers.

CHOPTA VALLEY

South Asia/India

The Chopta Valley is located in north Sikkim, at an elevation of 4,023 m (13,200 ft). India's second-smallest and least-populated state, Sikkim is bordered by Nepal, Tibet and West Bengal, and has long attracted tourists to its biodiversity, culture and outstanding natural beauty. Set in the Himalayas, Sikkim boasts the world's third-highest mountain, Kangchenjunga, which can be found on its border with Nepal. Chopta Valley is pristine and magnificent, surrounded by snowy mountains, whose peaks are always frozen, and deep green forest. The valley floor is crossed by lovely meandering rivers and in June and July, when the snow has melted, the streams and rivulets run free. But for much of the year they are frozen, enabling visitors to walk over or along them. This is an uninhabited area but, during the summer months, nomadic Tibetans bring their yaks up to graze on the lush alpine pasture. At this time of year, Chopta Valley is like the Garden of Eden, smothered with glorious wild flowers of many species and hues, including gentians, saxifrage, violas, busy lizzies, primulas and anemones. On the higher slopes, low grasses and cushion plants succeed in growing among the scree and boulders.

RANTHAMBORE NATIONAL PARK

South Asia/India

WORTH A DETOUR: Visit the fort, built in AD 944, for nature spotting and atmospheric architecture. This area was the scene of endless battles until it became part of the kingdom of Jaipur in 1569.

Ranthambore is an expanse of jungle scrub, grassland and dense, dry forest, hemmed in by rocky ridges. Hilly southeastern Rajasthan is relatively green, and the reserve, bounded to the north and south by rivers, is well watered and dotted with small lakes. It is named after a ruined fort which stands on an isolated rock. Ranthambore is one of the best places in this part of India to see tigers in the wild; their numbers have become quite healthy after a recent, distressing decline. Although the reserve is part of India's Project

Tiger, it was government officials who were, eventually, implicated in poaching tigers. At the time of the tigers' disappearance, the decrease in population was blamed on villagers and farmers. Tiger-spotting trips around the park are in six-seater 'Gypsies' – open-topped Jeeps – or in 'Canters', trucks with seating for 20 people. There is of course plenty of other wildlife in Ranthambore and good walks to various observation points – the lakes, near one of which stands an enormous banyan tree, are particularly rewarding for birdwatchers. Also resident in the lakes is a large population of marsh crocodiles.

GANGOTRI NATIONAL PARK

South Asia/India

Northwest of Nanda Devi, in Uttarakhand and on the border with China, is the huge Gangotri National Park. An enormous expanse of 2,390 sq km (920 sq mi), the park is characterized by high ridges, mountains, glaciers, gorges, narrow valleys and alpine meadows.

Gangotri's forested areas are made up of Himalayan cedar, fir, spruce and, at lower elevations, oaks and wonderful stretches of colourful rhododendrons. But major landslides have caused areas of irreversible isolation between some of the forested areas. This may prove hazardous in the long run for the welfare of some of the wildlife, which thus far includes 15 species of mammal and 150 species of bird. Mammals such as black and brown bears, musk deer, tahr, Nepalese Bengal tigers and the mysterious snow leopard live in the forests and high crags.

This is a park for those seeking adventure. Here visitors can raft on the rivers, paraglide, hang glide and ski as well as climb, trek or take a Jeep safari. The mountains themselves are a magnet for climbers and form a magnificent, snow-clad background. The Gangotri glacier, which flows from Chaukhamba – at 7,138 m (23,419 ft) the highest peak of the Gangotri group – is the source of the River Ganges and is one of the holy Hindu shrines. Pilgrims travel here to bathe in the icy waters before visiting the three other sites of the Himalayan Chhota Char Dham, representing all three major Hindu denominations.

HIGHLIGHTS:

Rishikesh, another sacred site about one day away from Gangotri. Nicknamed the 'world capital of yoga' for its many yoga centres, there are also many ashrams here, including the now-closed ashram of Maharishi Mahesh Yogi, where the Beatles wrote much of the White Album.

HIGHLIGHTS:
A boat trip. Regular trips are run by a co-operative and tour the whole lake area for birdwatching. They also visit the temple, the sandbar and its pristine beach, and head out to sea to look for Irawaddy dolphins – the only known population of this critically endangered species in India.

CHILIKA LAKE

South Asia/India

The world's second-largest lagoon, Chilika Lake, is separated from the Bay of Bengal by a long sandbar with a mouth that allows saltwater into the lagoon. It then mingles with the outflow of several rivers and this brackish habitat and its unique marine ecosystem is the largest wintering ground for migrating birds in the whole of India. Late in the dry season the lake measures about 600 sq km (230 sq mi); with the monsoon, it almost doubles. Recent silting resulted in decreased salinity, the invasion of freshwater species such as water hyacinth and a reduction of fish stocks, on which villagers from around the lagoon depend. The Chilika Development Authority cut a new mouth in the sandbar, and the delicate balance was restored. The CDA has received awards for its conservation work.

On one of many tiny islands in the lagoon stands Kalijai temple, where Hindu pilgrims flock every January to worship the sun god, Suraya, at the Makar Mela. Another island, Nalabana, is central to the bird sanctuary. After the monsoon, as the mudflats re-emerge from nutrient-rich waters, over a million birds fly in from as far away as Siberia. The whole lake, its wetlands and marshes, shallows and sandbars, is alive with birds. Among the hundreds of species are heron, flamingo, stork, spoonbill, kingfisher and osprey.

On the mainland shore some villages have accommodation, often with lake views, and regular ferries run to Nalabana and to Satapada, a headland settlement with an excellent visitor centre complete with upstairs observatory and bird-identification charts. From here, boat trips tour the lake and sandbar.

KANHA NATIONAL PARK

South Asia/India

Covering 1,945 sq km (750 sq mi) of southeastern Madhya Pradesh, Kanha is one of India's largest national parks and has, since 1955, dedicated itself to preserving a variety of animal species. Today, it is one of the most beautiful reserves in Asia. The Surpan River meanders through a central area of undulating grasslands, jewelled in the dry season with flowering trees such as laburnum with its scented yellow cascades, and brilliant flame trees. To the east and west grow thickets of bamboo and ancient forests of deciduous and evergreen trees, while rocky escarpments north and south provide panoramic views.

The forests are home to troops of monkeys and numerous shy, nocturnal animals; the grasslands are grazed by herds, ranging from tiny mouse deer to enormous gaur. Kanha is particularly proud of its large population of barasingha, a rare swamp deer saved from extinction by excellent conservation work. The herbivores provide prey for the 80 or so tigers (and the smaller carnivores) in Kanha. Jeep safaris tour the whole park, and some parts can also be visited on foot. Well-established nature trails lead from the visitor centres at Khatiya, Kisli and Mukki gates. The varied habitats are a joy for birdwatchers; birds of woodland, plain and the numerous small lakes include hoopoe, bee-eater, parakeet, pond heron and stork.

Kanha is one of several places claiming to be the setting for Kipling's *The Jungle Book* and there is indeed a real magic here in a vast, ancient landscape that is still home to two tribal groups. The Gonds are farmers and herders and the Baiga live by cutting firewood and gathering wild honey in the depths of the forest.

WHEN TO GO:
February–June. The park is closed between July and October. May and June are very hot and night temperatures drop to freezing point in winter.

WORTH A DETOUR:
Glimpsing a tiger in the wild is spin-chillingly exciting. Kanha arranges link-ups between jeeps and elephants, so that tracking can continue on elephant-back in places where scouts have spotted evidence of tiger – pugmarks, signs of fresh prey and so on.

BHAGWAN MAHAVIR WILDLIFE SANCTUARY
South Asia/India

WHEN TO GO:
November–March.

WORTH A DETOUR:
Dudhsagar Falls – the name means 'Ocean of Milk' – is south of Colem and can be reached by a dirt road and a rocky scramble. It is a tiered waterfall, one of India's highest and absolutely spectacular after the monsoon. The railway runs very close to it, over a viaduct; some local trains slow to allow passengers a good view.

Even those tourists for whom Goa is synonymous with beaches and bars will notice the exotic butterflies and birds in their hotel gardens. This tiny state has a lush interior of rivers and wetlands and forested mountains and a wealth of wildlife. The Bhagwan Mahavir Sanctuary was founded in 1969; it now includes Mollem National Park and is the largest of Goa's protected areas, and one of the most tranquil. The Western Ghats, in whose foothills it lies, are a formidable barrier for man – very few roads cross the mountains – and a route for animals to travel unmolested. Herds of elephant regularly make their way through the park and tigers are occasional visitors.

Macaque and langur monkeys, sloth bears and porcupines, leopards and wild dogs (considered by the locals more dangerous than tigers) are among the inhabitants of the well-watered, moist deciduous forest and evergreen canopy trees. Venomous snakes include Russell's viper, the deadly 'speckled band' of the Sherlock Holmes story. A rainbow of small birds with names as pretty as their plumage – golden oriole, emerald dove, fairy bluebird, paradise flycatcher – are just a few of hundreds of species found here, and many more, unseen in the depths of the forest, can by identified by their calls. Many of Goa's glorious resident butterflies are also seen here, including the large, slow-flying malabar tree nymph and, during and after the monsoon, India's largest butterfly, the southern birdwing, whose wingspan reaches 250 mm (10 in).

Most animals in the sanctuary are nocturnal and avoid people; even birds are more visible at dawn and dusk. Visitors who spend a night in Mollem's pleasant forest accommodation have a better chance of seeing them and will enjoy not only the glorious scenery but also the enchanting atmosphere and evocative sounds of nightfall and sunrise.

BILIGIRIRANGAN HILLS

South Asia/India

WORTH A DETOUR:
The temple can be reached by road, tracks and steps and makes a fine walk.

The Biligirirangan Hills in Karnataka are part of a protected area, the Biligiri Rangaswamy Temple Wildlife Sanctuary. The hills form a biological bridge between the Western and Eastern Ghats, allowing animal migration throughout the Deccan plateau.

Since early studies by a British coffee planter, the region has been of great interest to naturalists. Temperature and rainfall differ markedly between lower and higher altitudes in the sanctuary, resulting in a fine mosaic of habitats from grassland, scrub and thick deciduous forest to stunted trees and montane grassland. The average height of the hills is around 1,500 m (5,000 ft); one of the rocky peaks is the site of the temple to Lord Rangaswamy around which the sanctuary was originally created in 1974. Jeep safaris and elephant rides can be arranged from the Wilderness Camp, where most visitors stay, and there is a good network of hiking tracks. Walkers will spot some of the smaller animals and large numbers of birds. Among hundreds of species seen here are the crested eagle, the racquet-tailed drongo, with its trailing feathers, and the tiny, multicoloured purple-rumped sunbird, which flits between flowers, sipping nectar.

DON'T MISS
The blue-winged parakeet and the great pied hornbill are two of the most spectacular birds in the forest.

PERIYAR WILDLIFE SANCTUARY

South Asia/India

One of Kerala's principal animal reserves, Periyar lies in hill country in the south of the state close to the border with Tamil Nadu. An extensive plateau forms the west of the reserve, while peaks rising to over 1,700 m (5,600 ft) predominate to north and east. A small portion only of the reserve (7 per cent) is accessible to visitors; this is centred around the large artificial lake in the western section, which was created by the British when they dammed the Periyar River in 1895 to improve the water supply to Tamil Nadu.

Boat trips on the lake are a popular activity here; you will boost your chances of seeing wildlife greatly if you take one early in the morning when animals such as elephants and sambar deer come down to drink at the lakeside in the relative cool of dawn. Better still is to take a three-hour guided trek through the jungle; leading groups no larger than five, a local guide (who may once have been a poacher) will use his trained eyes to introduce visitors to the rich activity of the forest. With more than 260 recorded bird species, you should not come away disappointed.

HOW TO GET THERE: By train.
WHEN TO GO: May–July and September–November (July and August are the rainy season).

KALKA TO SHIMLA ON THE 'TOY TRAIN'
South Asia/India

An air of excitement builds audibly as the train pulls in to Kalka Station. Railway enthusiasts crowd round to examine the powerful little engine, as street food sellers jostle for your attention. A piercing whistle announces that it's time to board the train and head towards the 'Queen of the Hill Stations' – Shimla. This important rail link was built in 1924 and its 'toy trains' still do a roaring trade running on an improbably small 760 mm (2 ft 6 in) narrow gauge set of rails. The construction was an incredible feat of engineering – the track passes through more than 100 tunnels and over 960 bridges, up into the Himalayan foothills. Immaculately maintained stations line the route and the arrival of the train elicits intense interest from locals at every stop along the way. You are carried along the crests of rich green valleys, climbing inexorably at a sedate 25 kph (16 mph). The charming station at Solan marks the halfway point on this stately excursion, and it is from here that you catch the first sight of Shimla high in the distance. The snow-capped peaks of the Himalayas appear in all their majestic beauty as the forest thins to reveal ever more spectacular vistas. When the train draws serenely in to Shimla at an altitude of 2,420 m (7,940 ft), it becomes immediately apparent why the British chose the town as their summer capital. While Delhi swelters in the summer sun, Shimla delights in a near perfect 20 °C (68 °F). The town itself is worthy of a day or two's exploration – with its striking Victorian architecture surrounded by magnificent mountain scenery.

ANAMUDI PEAK
South Asia/India

HOW TO GET THERE:
The park and peak can be reached by autorickshaw from Munnar.

The Western Ghats range extends from Mumbai (Bombay) almost to the southern tip of India. These mountains are exceptionally verdant – forests cover the rugged heights, while foothills, cloaked in tea or coffee bushes, billow like emerald eiderdowns. Just north of Munnar in Kerala, Anamudi Peak – 2,695 m (8,842 ft) – is the highest in the range, and in the whole of southern India.

Nowadays, with its rivers and streams, rolling hills and lush forest, the park is a beautiful place and very good trekking country. A wealth of plants and flowers grow here, from rare mountain orchids to blankets of rhododendron. One shrub, the kurinji, grows only in the Western Ghats and blooms only once every 12 years, covering the hillsides with a mist of purplish-blue. Pine, bamboo and teak forests shelter innumerable animals and the grasslands are home to species including the Nilgiri tahr, one of the world's rarest mountain goats. Anamudi means 'elephant's forehead' and the peak is a blunt, hunched mass. Walkers can climb to the summit up technically easy slopes to the north and south, starting from a base elevation of about 2,000 m (6,560 ft). To the west and east it is much steeper, with challenging rock faces and deep gorges.

ROYAL MANAS NATIONAL PARK

South Asia/India

YOU SHOULD KNOW

Although the Royal Manas is once again on the itinerary for tour groups, obtain official travel advice if you are contemplating a visit.

The Royal Manas is the crown jewel among Bhutan's national parks. The first area of the country to be given protected status – in 1966 – as a wildlife sanctuary, the Royal Manas was declared a national park in 1993. Today it encompasses an area of 1,023 sq km (395 sq mi) in the south of the ancient mountain kingdom.

Along with the Black Mountains National Park to the north and India's Manas National Park over the border to the south, it forms a 5,000-sq km (1,930-sq mi) highland fastness covering a huge diversity of habitats, from tropical grasslands and temperate moist forests to alpine meadows and scrublands.

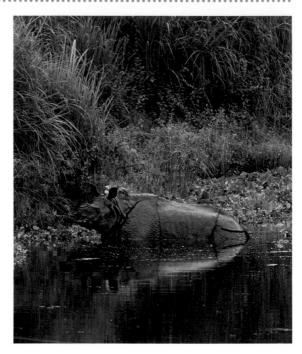

Over 90 per cent of the park itself is still forested, making it one of the best examples of an undisturbed ecosystem in the eastern Himalayas.

The border here used to be a dangerous one and for many years the region was off-limits to travellers because of the activities of separatist groups in India. The absence of visitor numbers in recent times has contributed to the pristine, unspoilt nature of the Royal Manas and for the past 15 years the World Wildlife Fund has been working with the local authorities to keep it that way. A comprehensive conservation management plan has recently been agreed, designed to enable the park to meet future challenges, especially those associated with tourism development and climate change.

All the big players on the wildlife scene of the Indian sub-continent can be found in the Royal Manas National Park: rhino, elephant, buffalo, bear, the ox-like gaur and several species of deer. Tigers and leopards also make their home here, although they are rarely seen.

HOW TO GET THERE:
Travelling independently in Bhutan is still difficult. The easiest way to visit the Royal Manas sanctuary is on an organized tour from the capital, Thimphu.

WHEN TO GO:
November–February (the dry season).

HIGHLIGHTS:
There are no fewer than four types of hornbill among more than 350 species of bird that have been recorded in the park.

DON'T MISS
The jungle walk
from the hill station to
the Popokvil Falls.

BOKOR NATIONAL PARK

South Asia/Cambodia

On Cambodia's coastline southwest of the capital, Phnom Penh, Bokor National Park is one of the country's most important protected areas. Lying at the southern end of the Chuor Phnom Damrei, or Elephant Mountains, a wild region of impenetrable forests and sheer rock outcrops, Bokor encompasses 1,581 sq km (610 sq mi) of primary rainforest. Moist evergreens predominate on the lower slopes while mixed deciduous trees occupy the higher levels.

This area was formerly a stronghold of the Khmer Rouge and witnessed some of the fiercest fighting between their forces and the Vietnamese army. Built by the French in the early 1920s as a refuge from the oppressive heat of the coastal plain, a now-abandoned hill station sits at an altitude of 1,080 m (3,543 ft). Having fallen into disuse after the war, the colonial edifices are now in ruins; they include the Black Palace which was once Prince Sihanouk's summer retreat, a Catholic church and a huge hotel and casino complex. Wandering around these deserted buildings is a decidedly eerie experience, especially when the frequent mists close in over the hills. The cooler temperatures are definitely a boon, though.

CARDAMOM MOUNTAINS

South Asia/Cambodia

Following the Vietnamese victory in 1979 the defeated rump of the Khmer Rouge regime retreated to the Cardamom Mountains where they continued a sporadic guerrilla campaign for the next 20 years. The presence of these forces and the constant threat of landmines ensured that people stayed away. With few roads and little in the way of infrastructure, visiting the Cardamoms is really only for the intrepid traveller who reckons with a degree of inconvenience and discomfort in order to experience nature at its most rawly beautiful.

The dense virgin rainforest which covers the mountains is home to an astonishing profusion of wildlife, including elephants, bears and the rare Siamese crocodile – not a man-eater but probably best avoided as a swimming companion. The most accessible part of the Cardamoms is the Koh Kong Conservation Corridor which skirts the NH 48 road between Sihanoukville and the border town of Krong Koh Kong.

WHEN TO GO:
November–March.

SIHANOUKVILLE COASTAL ISLANDS
South East Asia/Cambodia

DON'T MISS
Having a tropical beach all to yourself.

If you want to see what Thailand's Ko Samui looked like 30 years ago, then the islands off Cambodia's coast are the place to go. Although development is slowly getting under way, many islands remain gloriously unspoilt and largely untouched by the tourist dollar. White sand beaches fringed by palm trees present a picture of a tropical paradise that really is as perfect as it looks. Apart from a few picturesque fishing villages, the islands are for the most part uninhabited, offering the ideal refuge from the rat race. They lie mostly off the coast surrounding the once fashionable seaside resort of Sihanoukville. Situated on a peninsula at the mouth of Kompong Som Bay, Sihanoukville has lots of operators offering boat trips to the islands.

The islands form three distinct groups: the Kompong Som Islands are due west of Sihanoukville and, being the easiest to reach, are popular for day trips, while the Ream Islands are scattered offshore to the east. The Koh Tang Islands, meanwhile, are further out to sea and best visited with an overnight stay in mind.

All the islands provide good swimming, snorkelling and diving opportunities, although Koh Rong Samloem in the Kompong Som group and the more isolated Koh Tang Islands are particularly favoured. The seas here are rich in marine life, with large fish, excellent visibility and sunken wrecks that can be explored with local guides. If you like to catch your own food, there are plenty of game fishing opportunities here, too, including the chance to bag the prized barracuda.

WHEN TO GO: October–February (although if you are prepared to brave the heat and wet of April you will be able to catch the spectacular New Year festivities).

KHAMMOUANE PROVINCE
South East Asia/Laos

Khammouane is situated at the narrowest point of Laos where its long heel begins. Sandwiched between Thailand and Vietnam, the province is predominantly rural, the majority of the population living in the riverside settlements along the Mekong which marks the Thai border. Covering some 6,300 sq km (2,430 sq mi) in all, the three National Protected Areas here are typical examples of a karst landscape: limestone plateaus, cliffs, bluffs and steep escarpments, dissected by flat-bottomed valleys. Many of the rivers flow underground and there are numerous caves, the most spectacular of which is the Kong Lor cavern, a 7.5 km (4.7 mi) long underground tunnel which you can travel through by boat. The semi-evergreen and mixed deciduous forests which cover much of the land are home to elephants, bears and several types of monkey, including gibbons and macaques.

WORTH A DETOUR:
The rivers of Luang Nam Tha provide some of the best white-water rafting in the country.

LUANG NAM THA

South East Asia/Laos

The northwestern province of Luang Nam Tha has been an important crossroads on human migration routes for centuries, and more than 20 distinct ethnic groups make up the population. A common border with Myanmar (Burma) and China adds to the diversity; the Tai, the cultural and ethnic ancestors of the Lao people, originated over the border in China's Yunnan province. Most of the province comprises mountainous terrain covered in evergreen and deciduous forests interspersed with lush valleys. The omnipresent rice fields are the clearest indicators of human activity, although a less happy reminder are the areas which have suffered heavy deforestation as a result of commercial logging and slash-and-burn agricultural practices. Yet the scenery is still captivating, nowhere more so than in the Nam Ha National Protected Area. Ecotourism is key here and the Laos government, with support from various international agencies, is committed to developing tourism along environmentally responsible lines. A range of trekking tours is available taking you into the hills and forests, often involving overnight stays in remote ethnic villages. It is illegal to trek in Nam Ha without a licensed guide.

PLAIN OF JARS

South East Asia/Laos

WORTH A DETOUR:
The best of the jar sites is at Hai Hin Laat Khai, 35 km (22 mi) south of Phonsavan, where around 150 jars are scattered over a small hill with a good view of the plains.

The Plain of Jars in central Laos harbours one of archaeology's great unsolved riddles. On the Xieng Khuang plateau, a place scarred by unexploded ordnance from the Vietnam War, thousands of huge jar-shaped vessels fashioned out of the local sandstone lie scattered across the grasslands and hillsides around Phonsavan. The jars have an average diameter and height of 1.5 m (5 ft), although some are up to 3 m (10 ft) tall and weigh around 15 tonnes.

No one knows for certain who built them, their date of construction, or what they were used for. The most comprehensive investigation to date was conducted by a French archaeologist in the 1930s who concluded that the jars were funerary monuments of a Bronze Age culture which flourished some 2,000 years ago. More recent research has cast doubt on this theory, suggesting instead that the jars may have had a more prosaic function as storage vessels for rice and wine. Whatever the explanation, they present a singularly bizarre and impressive sight.

WATERFALLS OF BOLAVEN PLATEAU

South East Asia/Laos

YOU SHOULD KNOW
On the far bank of the Mekong west of the Bolaven Plateau stands Wat Phu, a Hindu and Buddhist temple complex which predates the temples of Angkor.

WHEN TO GO:
Any time of year (although if you visit November–February you should be prepared for temperatures to drop significantly at night).

WORTH A DETOUR:
The bustling market at Paksong, where the region's farmers gather to sell their coffee crop and tribespeople come down from mountain villages to sell their wares.

With an average elevation of 1,200 m (3,940 ft) the Bolaven Plateau in the far south of Laos boasts a surprisingly temperate climate. Rising high above the Mekong Valley to the west, Bolaven is 10,000 sq km (3,860 sq mi) of fertile uplands spread over four different provinces. The lion's share belongs to Champasak Province and most visits to the Bolaven Plateau start from the provincial capital, Pakse. The plateau is a lovely patchwork of rivers, forests, grasslands and fields where the crop is grown for which the area is famed. It was the French who introduced coffee plantations; after a considerable hiatus caused by the Vietnam War, coffee production has been revived by local farmers and is flourishing again. Inevitably perhaps, the success of the business has generated intense pressures to clear land for further cultivation; this has now become the greatest threat to the local environment.

The Bolaven Plateau is also noted for its many waterfalls. These are no show-stealers but, with temperatures rarely rising above 30 °C and plenty of shade afforded by the lush surrounding vegetation, they provide wonderful places for relaxation and tuning in to the sounds of nature. At Taat Lo on the Seset River northeast of Pakse you can swim

beneath the broad, 10 m (33 ft) high falls, while Taat Fan and Katamtok demand a more respectful distance as their waters crash down more than 100 m (330 ft). A particular delight of exploring this area is to trek to remote waterfalls and believe that you really could be the first people to have discovered them. One of the best places to go trekking is in Dong Hua Sao, a national protected area of dense forests which rise up the steep western slopes of the plateau.

DONG PHAYAYEN MOUNTAINS

South East Asia/Thailand

DON'T MISS

The wreathed hornbill, one of four types of hornbill found in the national park.

Once entirely covered in forest, the Dong Phayayen Mountains have been largely stripped bare as a consequence of intensive agriculture and logging. The most well-known of the parks protecting what forest remains is Khao Yai at the southern end of the range. Most of the park is covered by dense primary evergreen forest, with small areas of secondary-growth scrub and savannah, the result of cultivation by villagers and poachers who have long since been evicted from the park. These man-made open grasslands provide important grazing areas for many large mammals and thus offer some of the best wildlife-viewing opportunities. Evening is the time for observing sambar deer, gaurs, wild pigs and bears. Khao Yai is the best place in Thailand for seeing elephants in the wild; there is a population of around 200.

KHAO LUANG NATIONAL PARK

South East Asia/Thailand

DON'T MISS

Stunning views of wooded slopes from the summit of Khao Luang.

The mountain of Khao Luang is the highest point on the Thai peninsula. Rising to 1,835 m (6,020 ft) it stands at the heart of the national park to which the peak gives its name. The park encompasses 570 sq km (220 sq mi) of mountains, valleys and tropical forests. The variation in elevation creates a range of habitats, from moist evergreen forest in the lowlands to cloud and montane forest at the higher levels. Khao Luang is particularly noted for a number of beautiful waterfalls located throughout the park which are at their most impressive at the end of the rainy season in December and January. Nature trails lead to two of the best falls, at Karom and at Krung Ching, both of which are good half-day walks.

For a more challenging trek the summit of Khao Luang itself beckons. The ascent is best undertaken as a three-day trek starting in Khiriwong village, where you can arrange the services of a local guide. The ascent takes you up through dense rainforest and some of the world's largest tree ferns. Over 300 types of orchid thrive in the humid environment of the lower levels; your guide will enlighten you on the varieties. Although tigers, clouded leopards, elephants and macaques are all found in Khao Luang you are unlikely to see them. What you will undoubtedly see, however, are some of the dazzling birds that are resident here, including sunbirds, eagles and three species of hornbill. You will also come across evidence of an unusual form of agriculture practised by local farmers: fruit orchards which grow using the shade from indigenous trees.

PHA DAENG NATIONAL PARK
South East Asia/Thailand

WHEN TO GO: Winter (December–February) is the time to come for the wild flowers and cherry blossom. The forest is at its greenest and most luxuriant during the rainy season (June–September).

In the far north of Thailand the small town of Chiang Dao is the gateway to the Pha Daeng National Park which covers an area of 1,155 sq km (446 sq mi), extending north and west to the border with Myanmar (Burma). The park comprises two mountain ranges divided by a central lowland area.

The western ranges are covered by lush tropical forest while the more exposed limestone mountains to the east include peaks with dramatic profiles such as Doi Pha Tang and Doi Pha Daeng itself. Both summits offer superb views of the surrounding landscape. The park is studded with secluded valleys and waterfalls; the sparkling streams that originate in these mountains feed into one of northern Thailand's principal rivers, the Ping. The hot springs at Pong Ang are an unusual feature which are well worth visiting for the variety of birdlife they attract throughout the year.

Limestone means caves and underground rivers. While none are as grand and extensive as the famous complex outside Chiang Dao, caves such as Chaeng-Pa Hok and Rom in the north of the park offer spectacular stalactites and stalagmites and an absence of the crowds you find at Chiang Dao. In the cave at Krab ancient human remains have been found deposited in coffin-like niches.

Pha Daeng National Park is contiguous with the Chiang Dao Wildlife Reserve which has been a sanctuary for the region's animals and birds since 1978.

DON'T MISS
2 m (6.5 ft) long water monitor lizards (don't worry, they aren't crocs!).

PHANG NGA BAY
South East Asia/Thailand

In Phang Nga Bay in southern Thailand, long-buried layers of limestone were exposed and fractured, then subjected to steady erosion by monsoon rains. Plant roots split open the rocks and water seeped into the cracks, eventually creating underground streams and enormous cave systems. Drowned karstland is the term geologists use to describe this environment of towering limestone crags and pinnacles which plunge dramatically into an azure sea. Boat tours take visitors on cruises around the bay and include landings at some of the larger islands for a closer look at their natural highlights, including some striking caves. A more ecologically friendly way to explore the bay and its islands is to rent a canoe. Provided you heed local guidance, these smaller, lighter vessels should enable you to penetrate to the mysterious hongs within several of the more isolated islands – secret sea chambers that are completely enclosed by cliffs.

PHU KRADUNG

South East Asia/Thailand

YOU SHOULD KNOW

Legend has it that lovers who help each other to reach the top of Phu Kradung will stay together forever, but if they quarrel along the way they are fated to separate.

The imposing sandstone plateau of Phu Kradung in northeastern Thailand is visible from a huge distance. Covering an area of 348 sq km (134 sq mi) – the plateau itself comprises 60 sq km (23 sq mi) – it has been a national park for nearly 50 years. The classic table-top mountain looms more than 1,200 m (4,000 ft) above the surrounding forests, which once covered the summit as well; regular fires and the thin soils have turned the plateau into rolling grassland, dotted with pines. Small patches of the original evergreen forest do still survive on the plateau; because of the cooler temperatures, these 'relic' forests abound with tree species more usually associated with temperate zones, such as oak, hornbeam and birch. Indeed, the park generally is a haven for plant species that prefer a cooler climate. The only way to the summit of Phu Kradung is on foot. It is a tough 9 km (6 mi) trek to the edge of the plateau, including some very steep sections; from there it is a further 4 km (2.5 mi) to the upper park headquarters. The relative isolation of the plateau gives it a 'lost world' atmosphere. Once on top you have a choice of over 50 km (31 mi) of marked trails which lead to waterfalls, flower meadows and cliffs with stunning viewpoints. The park is noted for the diversity of its plant life, including many rare and unusual orchids and several carnivorous plants, such as pitchers and sundews, which compensate for the poor soil on the plateau by absorbing the nutrients they need from the insects which they trap and digest.

HOW TO GET THERE:
Phu Kradung is 70 km (44 mi) south of the provincial capital Loei. The journey takes 90 minutes by bus.

WHEN TO GO:
October–February.

WORTH A DETOUR:
Seek out the crimson leaves of the maple tree which add a splash of brilliant colour to the forest floor when they fall.

THUNG SALAENG LUANG NATIONAL PARK

South East Asia/Thailand

DON'T MISS

Sit on one of the ledges of Poi Waterfall and feel the invigorating spray.

Established in 1972, Thung Salaeng Luang National Park is an area of vast open fields surrounded by statuesque pines and dry oak forest. Within it are limestone caves, thundering waterfalls, cascading rapids, salt deposits and beautiful wildflower meadows. Situated in the Phitsanulok and Phetchabun Provinces of Thailand, near the Laotian border, the park covers 1,262 sq km (490 sq mi). It is home to elephants, civets, wild pigs and the occasional visiting tiger. Birds flourish in the area with around 200 species being identified, including herons, eagles, woodpeckers and the majestic Siamese fireback pheasant.

The best places to start for those inexperienced in tracking are any of the park's many salt licks. These natural deposits of sodium, calcium and zinc attract animals from miles around and the minerals are a vital part of their diet, facilitating the development of bone and muscle.

The area is blessed with three spectacular waterfalls, with Namtok Kaeng Sopha being the most impressive. Dubbed 'Thailand's Niagara Falls', it is a many-layered staircase cascade and, in the rainy season (July to October), it throws up such a volume of spray that the valley is shrouded in a cloak of mist. The area is also popular with cavers and two classic karst caves can be found there in the shape of Wang Daeng and Dao Duan, while the Kaeng Wang Nam Yen Rapids (scene of an annual inter-village boat race) is great for white-water rafting.

WORTH A DETOUR: Ao Vua Waterfall: a three-tiered cascade that flows into an emerald-green lake that is best viewed from above.

BA VI NATIONAL PARK

South East Asia/Vietnam

An isolated triple-peaked limestone mountain, Ba Vi is some 50 km (30 mi) west of the Vietnamese capital Hanoi and forms the centrepiece of the national park to which it gives its name. The mountain rises suddenly out of a flat, densely forested plain and at the higher elevations the gradients reach one in three. Although the national park is relatively small at a little over 74 sq km (29 sq mi), it is considered by locals to be the 'lungs of Hanoi' and its lush greenness is certainly striking. The unique ecosystem is home to over 1,000 rare plant species (many with medicinal properties), 45 species of mammal, 25 kinds of reptiles and amphibians and over 100 species of bird.

The mountain is more often than not shrouded in mist, offering only tantalizing glimpses of its peaks. Access to the peaks is straightforward as, during the colonial period, the French built a hill station at Ba Vi which included a road that takes the traveller to an altitude of 1,100 m (3,610 ft). Once at the top, if the weather is kind, the views of the forest below are stunning. If it is not, then an 11th-century shrine to Saint Tan Vien, one of the four immortal founders of Vietnam, makes the climb worthwhile.

HALONG BAY

South East Asia/Vietnam

YOU SHOULD KNOW

The junks that transport visitors around the bay may look basic, but many are quite luxurious.

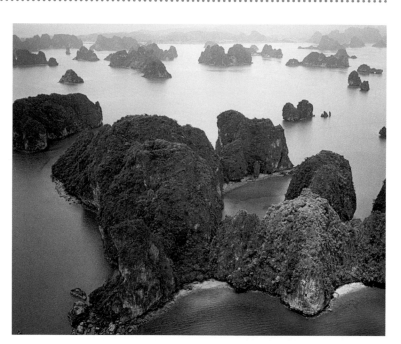

Legend has it that, soon after the Viet people founded their country, invaders came from the sea. As the raiders approached the shore the Jade Emperor sent Mother Dragon and her children down to Earth to aid the people in their resistance. The dragons opened their mouths and spat out a shower of pearls which turned into thousands of islands. Unable to stop, the attackers crashed into the rocks and the boats were smashed to smithereens. After the battle the dragons stayed on Earth in the place that is now known as Halong Bay, with their tails forming a long sandy beach called Long Vi.

Whatever its true origin, Halong Bay, located in Vietnam's Quang Ninh Province near the border with China, is a place of remarkable beauty. Travel around the bay is best undertaken aboard a junk, the iconic Indo-Chinese mode of transport. The boats cut their way through crystal-clear water, weaving in and out of the numerous limestone pillars that fill the bay. The islands and islets are sprinkled with countless beaches and grottoes created by the combined power of wind and waves. The shallow waters are home to over 600 species of fish and mollusc, but it is the islands that steal the show. This surreal seascape has been moulded by 500 million years of erosive forces into astonishing shapes. Ga Choi islet looks like a pair of fighting cocks (a popular sport in Vietnam), while Voi islet resembles an elephant. Another looks like a sail and one is even perceived to take the shape of an incense burner. Aside from its outstanding natural beauty, the bay has a wide diversity of ecosystems. These include sandy beaches, swamp and mangrove forest, coral reefs and small rainwater lakes. These eerily beautiful habitats are home to numerous mammals, birds and reptiles – including monkeys and iguanas.

WORTH A DETOUR:
Bo Nau (pelican) Cave – a wide-mouthed classic limestone cave bristling with stalactites and stalagmites. It is so called because pelicans often take shelter there.

MOUNT FANSIPAN

South East Asia/Vietnam

DON'T MISS
Thac Bac
(Silver Waterfall),
just outside Sapa.

Vietnam's recent increase in food production has been of great benefit to its economy, but unsustainable farming methods have seen a rise in habitat destruction, pollution, soil leeching and water degradation. However, there is a growing number of fledgling projects that seek to marry the changing needs of local people with preservation of the area's pristine rainforest environment. One such community-based project is centred on the Hoang Lien Mountains, a 100-million-year-old range in Northern Vietnam. The Community-based Conservation of the Hoang Lien Mountain Ecosystem Project is seeking to arrest the fragmentation of the rainforest and so protect the area's threatened flora and fauna. Ecotourism is an integral part of this. The range's biggest draw is its tallest peak. At 3,143 m (10,312 ft), Mount Fansipan is also the highest point on the South East Asian Mainland. The most popular route up the mountain starts in Sapa, which is reachable by road. The beginning of the hike takes the traveller through terraced paddy fields and hill-tribe villages, before crossing the Muong Hoa River near the village of Cat Cat, which gives the route its name. Above 2,000 m (6,600 ft) the vegetation changes to arrowroot plantations and then to thick bamboo, which has been used to construct a basecamp at 2,300 m (7,550 ft). The last stretch of the climb is the most challenging as the trail passes through primary forest of giant pine trees as well as dense bamboo. At the summit of Fansipan, the 'roof of Indochina', the air is wonderfully pure and the panoramic views are stunning.

WORTH A DETOUR: Ma Nhai Stele – an historical site commemorating the Tran Dynasty army's victory over Mongol invaders around 700 years ago.

PU MAT NATIONAL PARK

South East Asia/Vietnam

Pu Mat National Park is situated in Vietnam's Nghe An province, around 140 km (90 mi) from Vinh. The park covers three districts – Tuong Duong, Anh Son and Con Cuong – with an area of 910 sq km (350 sq mi). It takes its name from the Thai Pù Mát, which translates as 'high slope' and this is an accurate description of this densely forested section of the Annamite Mountains.

The true value of Pu Mat, however, is as a sanctuary for the region's unique and increasingly endangered plants and animals. The park is home to around 900 flora species, 240 different types of mammal, 140 bird species, 25 types of reptile and 15 kinds of amphibian.

This ancient forested landscape has many beautiful geological features. Among the attractions are the 150 m (500 ft) high Kem Waterfall, which verges on the torrential during the rainy season, and the wide Giang River, perfect for exploration in a traditional wooden boat. The park is also home to several ethnic minority communities and visits to their villages are a must for those interested in traditional arts and crafts, such as tho cam, a colourful highly prized woven fabric.

JAVA'S BEACHES

South East Asia/Indonesia

WORTH A DETOUR: Langse cave (east of Parangtritis beach). Situated 400 m (1,310 ft) up a cliff, it contains a sulphur spring said to cure skin ailments.

Java is blessed with many fine beaches where the waters of the Indian Ocean and the Java Sea take the edge off the humid heat. The most popular beach, Parangtritis, is only 30 minutes by car from the ancient capital, Yogyakarta. This long, snaking piece of shoreline is famous for the variety of its scenery. The beach is framed by mountains on its eastern side and the dark, volcanic sand contrasts wonderfully with the crests of the giant rollers that pound the shore. A graceful way to explore the area is aboard a bendi – a local horse-drawn carriage. The beach does, however, have it drawbacks as the ocean at this point on the coast is turbulent and unpredictable and swimming is banned.

Thankfully the Javanese 'Riviera' offers a wide variety of beaches for all tastes: divers should head for Drini and Kukup beaches for their beautiful coral reefs, lying just offshore; at Baron beach there is an underground river perfect for bathing in the shade; Wediombo beach is ideal for swimming as it has a shallow bay flanked by gleaming white sands; at Ngrenehan beach traditional fishing methods are fascinating to watch and provide some of the island's freshest and finest seafood, while Sundak beach is favoured by the young.

KARIMUNJAWA ISLANDS

South East Asia/Indonesia

WORTH A DETOUR: Karang Kapal – a huge submerged reef, home to large bumphead parrotfish and the whitetip reef shark.

Karimunjawa is a 27-island archipelago that runs in a northwesterly direction in the Java Sea 80 km (50 mi) from Jepara. The islands are characterized by rainforest plain, fringed by seagrass and mangrove swamps. Each island is edged with long golden strands, but the real treasure of Karimunjawa is to be found just out to sea in the form of coral reefs. The main island is Karimun and a further six are inhabited. Others are in private hands, are nature reserves or are used by the Indonesian Navy. The islands and the seas immediately around them are protected, according to a system of four different grades; this works well to preserve these island and underwater gems.

Many of the reefs have grown up around shipwrecks. The waters off the archipelago support 90 types of hard, soft and red corals as well as sponges and sea fans. Over 240 species of brightly coloured fish live in the reefs, including the rare crocodile fish and leafy scorpion fish. Larger creatures patrol the waters near the islands and the majestic whale shark is a year-round resident.

MOUNT MERAPI AND THE DIENG PLATEAU

South East Asia/Indonesia

DON'T MISS
The view of Merapi at sunrise – best seen from the resort of Plawangan.

Located in central Java, Mount Merapi is a very active stratovolcano 25 km (15.5 mi) north of Yogyakarta. Its steep ash-covered slopes rise to a height of 2,970 m (9,740 ft). Dense vegetation clothes its flanks as the volcanic ash nourishes the soil, making the area attractive to both wildlife and local farmers. But living in the shadow of such a raging monster can be a perilous existence. Merapi erupts on a regular basis with small eruptions every couple of years, larger ones every decade or so and devastating eruption at roughly half-century intervals. Known as the Sacred Mountain of Fire, Merapi provides a breathtaking spectacle when viewed from afar, as constant plumes of white smoke can be seen emerging from its many craters. When docile, it is safe to climb and this can be done in about five hours.

Travelling northwest from Merapi a less volatile but equally striking landscape can be found in the form of the Dieng Plateau. The Dieng, which translates as 'Home of the Gods', is an ancient volcanic caldera plateau 2,000 m (6,560 ft) above sea level. It is an astonishing landscape and, although the volcano is now dormant, there is still a great deal of thermal activity. Steam vents send clouds of gas high into the sky, turquoise lakes fizz with sulphurous fumes and craters filled with boiling mud gurgle.

All this is taken for granted as a backdrop to the everyday lives of farmers who tend their potato fields – an unusual crop for the region made possible by the combination of volcanic-ash-enriched soil and the plateau's altitude. In the heart of the Dieng lies the Candi Arjuna complex, a collection of ancient Hindu temples now in a state of semi-ruin. These relics are among the most important remnants of the island's religious past.

DON'T MISS
The sweetest, juiciest, chemical-free pineapples in the world!

GUNUNG MURUD

South East Asia/Malaysia

Gunung Murud is in the isolated Kelabit Highlands of Borneo. There, a traditional way of life is still the norm in settlements reached with difficulty by taking a ride on one of the MasWings Twin Otters that fly in to all sorts of simple airstrips, weather permitting. Failing that, it's a matter of travelling rough tracks in a 4×4, hitching a ride on a logging truck or slogging into the backcountry on foot. Worth it? You bet!

The Kelabit Highlands is an extensive upland plateau with scattered villages in the valleys. There are few roads and rivers have rapids that make boat travel impossible, so the only way to explore one of the world's last great wilderness areas is to go afoot, ideally with the help of a local guide.

Gunung Murud is an excellent objective, starting from the regional centre of Bario (basic airfield, no mains electricity). The trail goes through Pa Ukat and on to the summit of Sarawak's highest mountain, first ascended by a European as recently as 1922. Along the way will be a fascinating glimpse of life in local longhouses, lush tropical foliage, leeches galore, lots of uphill slogging – and breathtaking scenery (if anyone has any breath left, that is) reaching a dramatic climax at the summit of Gunung Murud.

KINABATANGAN RIVER

South East Asia/Malaysia

WHEN TO GO: The northeast monsoon occurs November–January; outside of these months expect high daytime temperatures and exceptionally high overnight temperatures.

Situated in the Sabah region of the Malaysian section of Borneo, the Kingabatangan is the country's second-longest river. From its source in Banjaran Crocker, it travels 560 km (350 mi) down to a wide saltwater mangrove swamp estuary and finally into the Sula Sea. It is one of only two places in the world where ten species of primate live, including the solitary Bornean orang-utan, the more social proboscis monkey, the maroon leaf monkey and the Bornean gibbon. The river cuts right through otherwise impenetrable rainforest, where Bornean pygmy elephants can be seen emerging from the dense growth to feed on its banks.

The area is best explored by a combined boating and hiking trip. There are a small number of chalets dotted along the river and there is much to see in its basin, most notably at the Gomantong Caves. These are home to several species of swiftlets – small birds that nest in their millions inside the caves. The birds' nests are highly prized for food and medicine in China and at various times throughout the year a perilous harvest takes place. Using rattan ladders and bamboo sticks collectors climb the 60 m (200 ft) high walls of the caves to scrape the tiny nests from the roofs using a tool called a jalok.

SEMENGGOH NATURE RESERVE

South East Asia/Malaysia

YOU SHOULD KNOW
Animals must never be fed by visitors, and the picking of plants is also forbidden.

WORTH A DETOUR:
Orang-utan feeding time at Semenggoh's rehab centre. But sightings are not guaranteed as the adult animals forage in the forest as part of their rewilding programme, and sometimes only show up later to collect the free bounty.

For those seeking to cram in as many of Borneo's natural wonders as possible into a relatively short time, a trip to Sarawak's Semenggoh Nature Reserve should be high on the must-visit list. At just 650 ha (1,600 ac) it's not vast, but still offers a great variety of rewarding things to see and do in a single day. This former forest reserve is now an important facility for conservation and a showcase for Borneo's incredible biodiversity. The Sarawak Forestry Department has an experimental station at Semenggoh that houses a botanical research centre, wildlife centre and arboretum. These provide a great start to the visit, before getting out into the reserve. The wildlife rehabilitation centre is the place to see strictly protected orang-utans, for here animals that have been incapacitated or confiscated from poachers are readied for release to boost Borneo's shrinking wild population of these endearing primates. The centre has a number of large mammal and bird enclosures, plus animal and bird captive-breeding programmes.

Interesting though these attractions may be, Semenggoh is a place to wander at will through mixed lowland dipterocarp forest consisting of primary jungle, well-established second-growth trees and patches of kerangas forest. The primary jungle contains incredibly rich flora – watch out for the world's largest flower, the 1 m (3 ft) spotted red bloom of the parasitic *Rafflesia arnoldii*, but enjoy this phenomenon from afar. It's also the world's worst-smelling plant, emitting a truly noxious odour that smells like rotting meat, to attract pollinating insects. There are waymarked trails complete with informative notices explaining the flora, but it's quite possible to step off the paths and imagine that this beautiful place is the remotest of rainforests.

DON'T MISS
Exploring on camel
or horseback.

LAKE KARAKUL
Far East/China

The clarity of the air at an elevation of 3,600 m (11,810 ft) intensifies colour and perspective, but Lake Karakul doesn't need sunshine. Weather changes foster the illusion of the lake as a living creature of infinite moods. It is equally beautiful in summer sun, or covered in roiling black clouds. Karakul is dwarfed by 7,546 m (24,757 ft) Muztagh Ata, closest to it, and by the even higher peaks of Kongur Tagh and Kongur Tiube in their distant splendor. Their contribution is strictly scenic. Several trails explore the grass and scrub pastures between the lakeshore and the shale foothills – worthwhile if only to avoid being near the road at lunchtime. Improvements to the Karakoram Highway have increased traffic, and now it is usual to share Karakul's harsh alpine beauty with tour buses stopping for a photocall and yak-milk tea. Karakul is one of the great natural sights of Western China.

TAKLAMAKAN DESERT
Far East/China

WHEN TO GO: Any time, subject to biting winds and frequent winter lows of more than −20°C (−4°F). It's more fun frying in the midday sun from May–October.

One of the world's biggest sandy deserts, the Taklamakan Desert has been horrifying and fascinating travellers for centuries. Over 1,000 km (620 mi) long and 400 km (250 mi) wide, it straddles central Asia between the Tien Shan and Kunlun mountain ranges. The centre is a waterless death trap that a recent traveller described as 'like walking into a hairdryer'. But for those who dare, the Taklamakan is a rare and beautiful wilderness, dotted with the ruins and remnants of vanished cultures. Taklamakan is a 'moving' desert.

Its shifting sands have buried Turkic, Mongol and Uygur fiefdoms as well as Chinese; and even obliterated some of the handful of oases which make crossing the desert possible.

The futility of recent attempts to build artificial oases has only emphasized the desert's real treasures, like the enormous alluvial fan of the Molcha River spreading meltwater from the Kunlun glaciers into springtime wetlands full of rare birds, and the moonlit 'waves' of the dunes in the Tarim Basin sand ocean. So close to the freezer of Siberia, Taklamakan's flora and fauna are uniquely adapted to its special demands.

KUNLUN MOUNTAINS

Far East/China

HOW TO GET THERE:
By 4×4 cross-country, then extended treks on (domestic) camel with yak porterage, and on foot.

The Kunlun Mountains form the northern rim of the Tibetan Plateau. The hundreds of miles of dun-coloured mountain steppe and interminable rolling hills of sun- and frost-shattered rock shale may conjure a certain poetic beauty, but little in the way of comfort. The mountains' historic isolation, and changes in political and environmental thinking, have between them rejuvenated endemic wildlife in several gigantic reserves in the central and eastern Kunlun, and on the north Tibetan Plateau and the north slopes facing the Tarim Basin. It's the only place in the world travellers can expect to see large herds of big hoofed animals in the wild. It is heart-stopping. The Arjin Shan Reserve may be vast, but there's no hiding 10,000 wild yak, 30,000 wild asses (kiang), 75,000 Tibetan antelope (chiru), gazelle, Argali sheep, blue sheep, lynx, wolves, leopards and steppe cats; nor even family groups of up to 50 wild Bactrian camels or the originals of the endemic wild horses later named by the explorer Przewalski. The Kunlun Mountains are their Great Plains.

DON'T MISS
The hides and watchtowers in the different habitats around the shore.

LAKE XINGKAI/KHANKA INTERNATIONAL NATURE RESERVE

Far East/China

Xingkai's complex wetlands include marshes, grasslands, swampy meadows, some forest, beach and even cliffs on the northwest shore, as well as the water itself. For centuries it has been famous for its luscious fish, the fare of Chinese emperors in the Middle Ages. The 74 species include black carp, black Amur bream, Soldatov catfish, Chinese soft-shelled turtles and enormous 600 kg (1,320 lb) Kaluga fish. The area is also a biogeographic crossroad attracting both Indian and Chinese species – and more than three quarters of all the bird species protected as migratory or endangered pass through, overwinter, or breed within it. They also attract predators to the margins of the shallow waters.

The spit between the two lakes provides just enough cover for Amur wildcats, raccoon dogs, Siberian weasels, and even bears, wild boars, wolves and (regularly seen) Amur tigers to stalk unwary prey. In a relatively small area, the biodiversity is astonishing and extremely exciting. Xingkai is certainly difficult to reach, and travellers need to remain conscious of being in a sensitive border area – but the rewards are astronomical, and completely justify the effort.

LAKE MANASAROVAR

Far East/China

In Tibet, geographical beauty is inextricably linked to the spiritual life of the human community. Lake Manasarovar, Mapam Yumco in Tibetan, is the 'eternal and invincible jade lake' that honours the triumph of 11th-century Buddhism over contemporary Bon beliefs, but for at least 1,000 years before that it was already the most sacred lake in Tibet. Small wonder, since it lies just to the south of Mount Kailash, the 6,714 m (22,027 ft) diamond-shaped peak of black rock that is both the source of the Indus, Sutlej and Brahmaputra Rivers, and the sacred centre of the spiritual world of the Buddhist, Jain, Bon and Hindu faiths. Pilgrims come in their thousands to make the Kailash kora – a 53 km (33 mi) circumambulation from the little town of Darchen. The act cancels a pilgrim's bad karma (evil deeds). And if the pilgrim continues, and walks around Manasarovar, the further benefit of salvation is guaranteed. The lake is the second half of the pilgrimage. It's quite beautiful. In the clarity of the air at 4,556 m (15,000 ft), it often glows the intense, deep blue of outer space, or mirrors the surrounding Olympian drama of mountain wilderness and vast bowl of sky. Manasarovar is the highest freshwater lake in the world, and important monasteries line its 88 km (55 mi) shore. The monks officiate at the many rituals specifically associated with the lake pilgrimage, like the annual Manasarovar Yatra ceremonial bathing.

HIGHLIGHTS:

The nine monasteries around the lake. Each plays a different role in the complex rituals that re-enact key stories from Buddhist scriptures, Hindu mythologies and Jain and Bon legends. Gyiwu and Curgu monasteries are especially well known: the shore next to Curgu is the holiest and purest bathing place of all.

YARLUNG ZANGBO CANYON

Far East/China

WORTH A DETOUR: The Hidden Falls are the biggest of dozens of cascades along the gorge, and so sacred that Monba shamans concealed their existence for years.

The Yarlung Zangbo is a sacred river, running 2,057 km (1,280 mi) along the northern slope of the Tibetan Himalayas from its glacial source on Mount Kailash before flowing south to India, where it is called the Brahmaputra. At the great bend the river hard-turns 130 degrees to squeeze between the two 7,500 m (24,606 ft) peaks of Namchak Bawa and Jialabailei, cutting the Himalayas in two and carving a gorge with an average depth of 5,000 m (16,500 ft) throughout its 496 km (310 mi) length. Incredibly, it was only in 1994 that Chinese scientists discovered – by accident – that it was longer and deeper than Colorado's Grand Canyon.

Its revelation to the world is almost a pity. The superlatives of its size, splendour and dramatic features pale beside those of its biodiversity. It is not the bleak and stony Tibet that the world knows, but an ocean of forest green nourished by warm monsoon winds sucked through the gap in the Himalayas and constricted by the steep canyon walls. Even so, that altitude means that every ecological zone from polar to tropical rainforest is represented distinctly within the canyon itself. And it is pure, primeval, untouched. Only a handful of indigenous Monba and Lhoba have ever shared the lush forests and rushing rivers, the waterfalls literally pushing through fairytale trains of hanging orchids, or the stands of giant dragon spruce higher up, teeming with golden monkeys and birds.

HOW TO GET THERE: Car or bus from Chengdu (ten hours), or by air to Huanglong and a one-and-a-half-hour bus ride.

JIUZHAIGOU

Far East/China

Jiuzhaigou lies at the southern end of the Minshan Mountains that dominate northwest Sichuan, some 340 km (206 mi) north of Chengdu. It is a giant picture-book fairytale fantasy of nature, with added giant pandas. The word 'picturesque' could have been created for the achingly pretty waterfalls, the rainbow of jewelled lakes, the bird-filled forests, flower-choked glades, rocky bluffs and distant, snow-capped peaks that smite the traveller's eye at every turn. No picture or even series of pictures or film can do justice to the magnificent profligacy of nature in carelessly cramming together so much pristine beauty into a mere 1,320 sq km (510 sq mi) of reserve and buffer zone.

Each feature also tells a story drawn from the massive body of Chinese folklore and faith-based legend and mythology: a whirlwind life of princesses in gold chariots plunging from the skies and 108 dropped pearls that became Jiuzhaigou's 108 lakes.

DON'T MISS
Trekking the wildlife
watchtowers up the Zheng
He River to Zheng He Lake.

WOLONG NATURE RESERVE

Far East/China

The giant panda sanctuaries of northwestern Sichuan are the Last Chance Saloon for the world's favourite species of bear. Wolong is the centre of China's giant panda research and breeding programme. It protects over 150 giant pandas (roughly half of them in captivity) on the maxim of what's good for pandas is good for lots of other species of fauna and flora. The spectrum of broadleaf, mixed and coniferous woods, with alpine marsh and grassland, bare rock and the snow line above them, guarantees that visitors enjoy Wolong's floral fairyland of diverse habitats as much as the aesthetics of rare creatures like red panda, golden monkey, white-lipped deer, and gnu. Most visitors come to see Hetao Village, where they are encouraged to coo over baby pandas. Pandas can be 'adopted', and bulletins on their progress sent out by email; and because so many of Wolong's pandas are tagged, visitors with a guide and a GPS can find them even in the depths of the vast bamboo stands on which they feed.

QINLING MOUNTAINS

Far East/China

WORTH A DETOUR: Practise tracking pandas from their droppings, broken bamboo shoots and paw prints – most likely they will be feeding in the umbrella bamboo at Sanguanmiao or Xihe in Foping Reserve.

Giant pandas are now found in just 20 or so isolated habitats in the margins of Gansu, Sichuan and Shaanxi provinces, in the Minshan and Qinling mountain ranges. With peaks over 3,700 m (12,140 ft) the Qinling mountains are the watershed between the Yellow River and the Yangtze. They form a natural barrier between north and south China, blocking cold northern winds and soaking up the warm southern rains which make it rival Minshan as a biodiversity hotspot. Inevitably, Qinling's rich forests are threatened by legal and illegal logging, but thousands of years of encroachment in the region have left intact a core area full of endemic flora and fauna.

Protecting the Qinling wild pandas means protecting their habitats rather than introducing breeding programmes. The success of the four panda reserves at Foping, Changqing, Taibai and Zhouzhi led in late 2009 to the opening of two more at Sangyuan and Qingmuchuan, both almost completely forested and rich in arrow bamboo, giant pandas' favourite food. Foping is the best-established, and it has a higher density of wild giant pandas than anywhere else on Earth. The first sighting in the wild makes your pulse race – but gradually you realize that Qinling pandas have smaller skeletal frames, bigger side teeth, and traces of brown in the familiar black-and-white fur livery. Only very recently scientists discovered that they are indeed a distinct subspecies of China's other giant pandas – and Foping has between 110 and 130 of them.

YUNNAN STONE FOREST

Far East/China

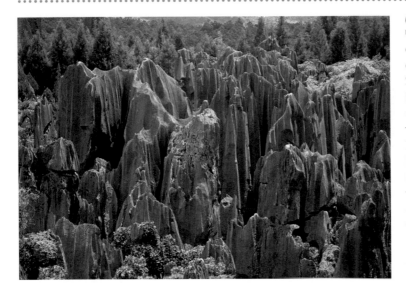

Southeast of Kunming, capital of China's Yunnan Province on the border with Laos, the Shilin (Stone Forest) National Park proclaims a 350 sq km (135 sq mi) area of ancient karst, the spectacular remnants of a 270-million-year-old seabed of limestone sediment. Concertinaed by tectonics into a ridged plateau, then whittled by 200 million years of water and weather into other-worldly rock formations, Shilin's sculpted contortions are like a giant's fantasy playground petrified into shards of jagged rock; and like everywhere else in China, each major formation, and the individual rocks, pillars, air bridges, streams, waterfalls, caves, stalagmites, stalactites, cliffs and ravines that contribute to them, are integrated into the sacred mythologies of local culture.

The park consists of seven distinct Scenic Areas. Zhiyun Cave is 400 m (1,310 ft) long, and has caves within caves big enough to hold 1,000 people. The cave walls are hollow where stalactites once hung, and ring musically when struck. Small formations resemble pagodas, old men with walking sticks, beds and other things deemed to have been abandoned by 'celestial beings'. It's typical of Shilin that Zhiyun's highlights should have names like Jade Elephant Propping Up Sky, Hanging Golden Chickens Upside Down or White Dragon Sacrificing. The mental images are very effective at making the shock of each natural spectacle manageable.

WORTH A DETOUR:
Strange Wind Cave, a complex formation where, every half-hour between August–November, a gale-force gust blows out of the cave for two minutes.

The Stone Forest itself is so far beyond usual human experience it needs mythologizing. Thousands of razor-sharp pinnacles rear up like a skyscraper megalopolis, emanating danger but inviting close examination. When it was a wilderness, it must have been terrifying to enter, but now manicured grass walks make visiting an exotic promenade, a curiosity instead of an adventure. It's unmissable, but imaginative travellers will understand more about Shilin's revered place in ethnic culture from the less-visited but equally amazing scenic outposts like the Dadieshui Waterfall, Moon Lake, Bushaoshan and Liziyuanqing.

DON'T MISS
The magnificent
sprawl of 1679
Songzanling Monastery.

SHANGRI-LA, ZHONGDIAN

Far East/China

Zhongdian's local culture, an unusual ethnic mix of Tibetan, Lisu, Naxi and Yi, is hallmarked by traditions of ancient harmony, tranquillity and faith in living nature. The county is itself made up of a series of smaller reserves protecting the snowbound ridges and high peaks, sweeping alpine prairie meadows, gorges deep enough to harbour subtropical forests, limpid blue lakes and crystal mountain torrents. Every feature is named, illuminating every landscape with the extra dimension of its religious significance. Aeons of calcium deposits transformed the Baishui Terraces below the Haba Snow Mountains southeast of Zhongdian town into a sculpted masterpiece of descending, overlapping pools. To the Naxi, whose Dongba culture was born on the magnificent Bashui Tableland, the terracing is like a huge, white jade representation of the most holy spirits of nature, set off by the surrounding mantle of green; and every year they assemble to sing and dance in celebration of them.

ZHANGJIAJIE NATIONAL FOREST

Far East/China

WORTH A DETOUR: See the 'Imperial Brushes' of the ultra-slim, forested sandstone spikes emerging from the mists on Tianzishan (Emperor Mountain).

Zhangjiajie National Forest in northwest Hunan Province is as geologically weird as anything on Earth, and as beautiful – for real – as any dream you can remember enjoying. Its most memorable landscapes are the sandstone and limestone karst formations that make it a convoluted rocky labyrinth of sky-high pillars, needle-sharp mesas, Rubik's Cubes of four-level cave systems, towering, multi-peaked mountains and plunging valleys that seem to twist impossibly on their axes between high and low. With morning mists wisping through its serried peaks, or veiled by imperceptible drizzle, it is the reality of what the West regards as 'classic' Chinese art. Zhangjiajie forest's relatively sudden rise to international prominence has brought a colossal influx of Chinese and foreign visitors, and it's not yet clear if the numbers can be controlled without damaging the extraordinary features that make it so special. The Bailong Elevator catapults people 326 m (1,070 ft) vertically up a mountain for the panorama over some of the forest's 3,000 200–300 m (650–1,000 ft) rock columns and sky bridges; and there is a cable car to Huangshizhai for perhaps the best overview of all. Ask a guide for help with Zhangjiajie's cultural significance – the aesthetics and geology speak for themselves.

SANQINGSHAN NATIONAL PARK

Far East/China

WORTH A DETOUR: The mountain's luminosity, reflected in named phenomena like Cloud Sea, Cloud Waterfall or Five Colours Road in the Clouds.

Sanqin Mountain is a geological marvel of extremely rare granite landforms, and of exquisitely subtle beauty. Every tree, column, rock formation, hillside, spring and peak is incorporated into a schemata of essential Taoist philosophy first noticed and ordered over 1,600 years ago by the great Taoist Master Ge Hong (284–364). Although nothing has been physically altered – other than by wind and rain – in the landscape, the infrastructure available to visitors makes it impossible to view the mountain in any other way. Sanqingshan has triple peaks, equated with the three divine spirits. It is also exceptionally steep, and its position high above the coastal plain of the China Sea means it attracts heavy mists for 200 days of each year. With thick fog or wispy tendrils spiralling through the crags and parting suddenly so that sunshine seems to focus on one or another feature, it's easy to appreciate how the faithful might interpret this randomness as divine.

Modern visitors have the advantage of the 'east' and 'west' 'plank roads', each over 3 km (2 mi) long and rising to 1,600 m (5,250 ft) on either side of the peaks, with a forested mountain on one side and a deep canyon on the other, with views to what feels like infinity. From them it's possible to see most of the 48 granite peaks and 89 granite pillars worked into a grand design that includes 230 cultural relics – pagodas, temples, pavilions, pools and bridges – still acknowledged as the ideal blueprint for a Taoist layout.

DON'T MISS
A trip in a glass-bottomed boat in Ashizuri Marine Park.

CAPE ASHIZURI

Far East/Japan

Cape Ashizuri is a famous beauty spot, much appreciated by the Japanese as a place where the exquisite harmony of the azure Pacific Ocean crashing against towering 80 m (265 ft) granite cliffs is complemented by the clean white pencil of Japan's tallest lighthouse, built in 1914 and visible 40 km (25 mi) out to sea. There are two observation decks that offer stupendous maritime views and a 2 km (1 mi) nature trail takes visitors through a spectacular tunnel of camellia plants to the gaping mouth of Hakusan sea cave. A star attraction is Kameyobiba ('Place to summon turtles') where there's every chance of spotting these magnificent sea creatures.

The Ashizuri Observatory and the Tengu-Nose Observatory stand high above the waters of the powerful north-flowing Japan Current where it makes its nearest approach to land, carving out dramatic features like the Hakusan Do-mon, a wonderfully dramatic rock arch.

WHEN TO GO: Serious forays into the mountains are best undertaken between June–September. Alpine wild flowers put on a great show from mid May–July.

KAMIKOCHI

Far East/Japan

Kamikochi in the Hida Mountains is a stunning setting. It's not the wildest of places, and plenty of people arrive in high summer. But this 15 km (10 mi) river valley has plenty of room for everyone, and those seeking solitude can quickly find it in the surrounding mountains, with Mount Hotaka at the northern end and the active volcano Mount Yake to the south. There's excellent day-hiking along the Azusa River, starting with a crossing of the Kappa-bashi suspension bridge near the bus terminal. Trails lead up and down the valley. Highlights include the attractive Takezawa Marsh, tranquil Myojin Pond with nearby Hotaka Shrine, Tashiro Pond and the extraordinary Lake Taisho, formed by a volcanic eruption that dammed the river in 1915, which still has skeletal dead trees standing in the water. Preserved in its natural state, Kamikochi has been designated as one of Japan's National Cultural Assets. Those lucky enough to see this special place will understand why.

LAKE BIWA

Far East/Japan

WHEN TO GO: Any time. The temperate climate is subject to sudden weather changes and the more accessible areas of the lake get crowded in summer.

Japan's largest freshwater lake is in Honshu's Shinga Prefecture, close to the former Japanese capital of Kyoto. Lake Biwa's characteristic shore consists of extensive reed beds, but despite protective ordnances, development has inexorably encroached. However, this beautiful expanse of water is large enough to ensure that considerable unspoilt stretches remain to satisfy those who like to appreciate Mother Nature's spectacular creativity, untrammelled by the intrusive contributions of humankind. The sunsets over the mountains to the west of the lake, viewed from the opposite shore, are as good as they get.

The sternwheeler *Michigan* plies the lake, lake cruises are available and workaday ferries operate, connecting Chickuba, Hikone, Okishima and Otsu. The islands of Chikubu and Okishima are popular destinations for visitors and pilgrims. Boats and bicycles can be rented in many places and there is an excellent network of cycle paths around the lake. Fishing is a popular pastime, along with birdwatching and the usual watersports. For those hankering after lonely places, there are some splendid hikes in the Hira-san Mountains on the west side of the lake.

TOWADA-HACHIMANTAI NATIONAL PARK

Far East/Japan

DON'T MISS
The Hakkoda Mountains, south of the coastal town of Aomori.

At the northern tip of Honshu is a national park largely unsullied by the insensitive hand of man. The northern section of Towada-Hachimantai National Park surrounds Lake Towada, while the southern section encompasses the Hachimantai Plateau and the surrounding peaks of Iwate, Koma and Nyuto. The area is one of Japan's most precious scenic gems with a wealth of sylvan vistas, waterfalls, crystal-clear lakes, swamps, primeval forests and alpine plants set within rugged landscape dominated by volcanic cones.

Lake Towada is a large crater lake with a surface area of 60 sq km (23 sq mi). The shores are crowded by trees, and the road around the lake skirts two promontories at the southern end that reach out and enclose three delightful bays, imaginatively named West, Middle and East Lakes. These may be viewed from the water by taking a trip on one of the pleasure boats that ply the lake between Yasumiya and Nenokuchi (April–October only). The whole emphasis is on allowing visitors to get close to nature, and sensitively developed areas like Yasumiya at the base of the Nakayama Peninsula offer facilities like campsites, lodgings and nature trails with free guided walks. There is a lakeside promontory and a nearby observatory with wonderful lake views.

To the south is the Hachimantai Plateau, a dramatic upland shaped by volcanic activity that hasn't ceased, as boiling mud pools and assorted vents emitting steam or smoke soon testify. This is great hiking country with stunning views from summits such as that of Mount Hachimantai in the centre of the plateau. This is high moorland at its scenic best, with wetland ponds like Hachiman-numa providing aquatic punctuation. There are various nature trails – Goshogake and Onuma being good examples – while notable peaks include Yake with the impressive Onigaja lava dome and Mount Nyuto with its sweeping distant views.

SEORAK-SAN NATIONAL PARK

Far East/South Korea

WHEN TO GO:
Autumn is prime time, when the stunning reds and yellows of foliage against the rocky landscape are mightily impressive.

Seorak-san National Park consists of rugged forested landscape with many rushing streams. For many, the first valley they see upon arrival is quite enough to satisfy their love of wild places, offering almost too much to see and do in a day. This valley houses the main entrance and contains several natural wonders and man-made ones in the form of historic Buddhist temples.

Two waterfalls – Biryong (Flying Dragon) and Yukdam – may be seen on the left side of the valley, less than an hour's walk from the car park. The Biseondae is a rock platform above a stream, from whence a cave with stunning views may be reached by those of athletic bent. Further from the entrance lies the Valley of a Thousand Buddhas, where the rock formations look like a legion of timeless statues.

TAROKO GORGE

Far East/Taiwan

DON'T MISS
Rafting on the Sanjhan North River through the waterfalls of Golden Canyon.

One of Taiwan's Eight Scenic Wonders, Taroko Gorge is a marble-and-granite canyon with 3,800 m (12,467 ft) Mount Nanhu at one end and the Pacific Ocean a mere 20 km (12 mi) away at the other. Drivers benefit from the Cross Central Highway, which runs from coast to coast but is specifically designed to give them stunning views of the dramatic scenery in Taroko Gorge. Hikers can choose from several trails either alongside the milky green, swirling water of the Liwu River which carved out the whole unlikely creation, or tributaries like the Shakadang, a secondary chasm marked by gleaming scars where fresh slabs of marble have splintered from the rock face.

The most sensational section of any of the trails is Jiucyudong (Tunnel of Nine Turns), where several sheer 900 m (3,000 ft) cliffs angle into each other in a sequence that resembles a coiled dragon.

Taroko Gorge is a national park as well as a world-class geological masterpiece. Away from the waterside trail (in fact, the original single-track road of tunnels and ledges) the occasionally maddening crowds melt away. Hikers starting above Tienhsiang, the ethnic village at the upper end of Taroko Gorge itself, can head through a 380 m (415-yd), pitch-black marble tunnel, high up a dizzying ledge to the Baiyang Waterfall and a whole series of curtain waterfalls beyond. Serious trekkers will prefer the solitude of the high peaks and alpine grasslands of Hehuanshan on the park's western edge.

THE PILLARS OF LENA

Far East/Russian Federation

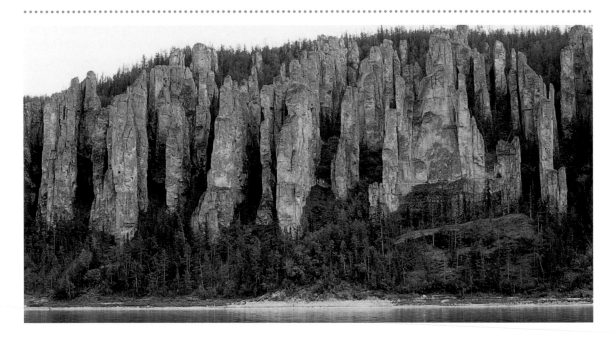

The extraordinary Pillars of the Lena River are a geological freak – a serrated edge of limestone and dolomite rock spikes carved along an 80 km (50 mi) section of the edge of the Prilenskoye plateau by the mighty Lena River, halfway along its epic 4,472 km (2,780 mi) course from Lake Baikal to the Arctic Ocean. Formed from an 80-million-year-old Cambrian-era sea-basin, the pillars owe their vertical stability, their 150–300 m (490–985 ft) height and their bizarre shapes to specifically Cambrian-era geological conditions. The Lena Pillars, and the 485-sq km (187-sq mi) nature park that contains them, are a geological capsule of a vital stage in the development of life on Earth. The area is rich in all kinds of fossils of the Cambrian biodiversity boom, and of later fossils including mammoth, fleecy rhinoceros and Lena horse. The land itself is stamped with frozen ground reliefs like frozen karsts, silt pinnacles and geographical oddities like the 'fluttering sands' called *tukulans* – miniature desert dune systems punctuating the forests on the river bank opposite the pillars. The pillars are best seen by boat, or even raft, with a tour company – arranging the correct permits to go it alone on the weekly ferry from Ust'-Kut to Yakutsk is a nightmare.

HOW TO GET THERE:
By tour agency boat, raft or helicopter from Yakutsk (any other way isn't worth the bureaucracy).

DON'T MISS
The spectacularly
intimidating 10 km (6 mi)
long Rytoye Gorge.

LAKE BAIKAL
Far East/Russian Federation

Lake Baikal is a mighty, 11-million-year-old gash in the Earth's fabric, a V-shaped rift nearly 11 km (7 mi) deep stopped up by roughly 9 km (5.6 mi) of silts from the 336 rivers that feed it, and still deep enough to hold 20 per cent of all the fresh water on the planet. At (400 mi) long and as much as 79 km (49 mi) wide, the lake is a jewel of aquatic purity with 1,000 species of specialized flora, 29 endemic variations of a single kind of fish, and the nerpa (endemic Baikal) seal. There are warm, shallow coastal lakes, boggy river deltas, alpine meadows, boreal forests carpeted with moss, huge mountains cut with ravines and river valleys, and windswept taiga.

Travellers seeking more than the summertime beach life on Olkhon Island offered by many tour agencies might head instead to Baikalo-Lensky Zapovednik on the lake's northwestern rim. It sings with 240 species of birds, and in spring numerous brown bears come to the shore to feed on the caddis flies swarming on the rocks.

KRONOTSKY BIOSPHERE RESERVE

Far East/Russian Federation

WHEN TO GO: July–August is best for trekking – but the drama of volcanic activity is sensational against the white-out of winter.

Sited on the transition zone between tundra and boreal ecosystems, the Kronotsky Reserve on the Pacific coast of Russia's Kamchatka Peninsular turns nature on its head. Geothermal heat meets glaciers; active volcanoes and Pacific storms constantly remodel a multicoloured universe of mineral-rich bogs and swamps, silicon-blue lakes and huge dark-green valleys. Nights flicker with the hellish red glow of volcanic eruptions; and morning can reveal whole mountain-sides flensed of forest and vegetation by lava flows. The dynamic geology of the 11,421-sq km (4,410-sq mi) reserve transforms the sullen pallor of the glacial north into a primary-coloured catalogue of the world's most magnificent landscapes. Eleven active volcanoes and the hydrothermal anomalies of as many extinct cones double the ecosystems represented within it, concentrating the highest biodiversity in Kamchatka into a relatively small area. Visitors can only gaze in wonder at brown bear – by the dozen – grazing in berry-filled valleys or fishing the waterfalls for Pacific salmon against a background of sea eagles wheeling over a panorama of distant snow-capped mountains, glaciers and the red and yellow autumn lightshow of larch forests.

KEDROVAYA PAD BIOSPHERE RESERVE
Far East/Russian Federation

HIGHLIGHTS: The exotic warblers, nuthatches, flycatchers, buntings, buzzard-eagles, grey goshawks and 150 other species that nest in Kedrovaya.

A mere 20 km (12 mi) across Amur Bay from the ceaseless turmoil of the great port of Vladivostok on the Sea of Japan lies a sanctuary for one of the world's rarest creatures. Dependent on ecologically pure wilderness for its very survival, the Amur ('Far Eastern') leopard steadfastly resists the relentless encroachment of toxic urbanization on its shrinking habitat. Some 30 of these magnificent predators are regularly seen in Kedrovaya Pad, including two families known to breed and live permanently within the reserve. If a similar population exists elsewhere in the world, nobody knows of it.

In fact Kedrovaya Pad is crammed with as many rare birds, trees, flowers and vegetation as mammals. Although small – 179 sq km (69 sq mi) – it benefits from the collision of northern boreal forests with the dense deciduous jungles of subtropical forest ecology. Watered by dozens of streams spilling down the low ridges of the Manchurian (Black) Mountains' coastal spurs where they push into Russia from China and North Korea, the reserve is warmed by ocean currents and southern air coming up from the Phillipines. 'Islands' of pristine forest reflect its dual character. Manchurian oak, Siberian fir and yeddo spruce represent the Korean taiga; but elsewhere Mongolian maple, elm, birch and ash predominate. The warm summer monsoon encourages exuberant vines of trailing clematis and thick ropes of lianas in the canopy, and the dense undergrowth that provides habitats for deer, wild boar, raccoon and innumerable other creatures.

WORTH A DETOUR: See the birds in the wetland flood plains around Ak-kem Lake; the Katun Gorge, and rafting on the wild Katun River.

MOUNT BELUKHA
Far East/Russian Federation

As the highest peak in the Katunsky range of the 'Golden Mountains' of Altai, 4,506 m (14,783 ft) Mount Belukha is a trophy summit. Reaching the top needs at least the technical know-how of experienced trekkers, but for any reasonably fit person, the adventure of a lifetime is just getting there. Mount Belukha presides over the 'bandit country' of Russia's border with Kazakhstan and the ancient mountain passes to both China and Mongolia. Trekkers must travel 750 km (466 mi) by bus from the nearest big town, Barnaul, to the trailhead in the village of Tyungur. This is 'old' Russia, populated (thinly) by Staroveri (Old Believers) faithful to shamanistic traditions abandoned by the industrial world.

The foothills of Mount Belukha conceal a cross-section of the natural treasures of the Altai Mountains: steppes, dense taiga, alpine meadows filled with flowers, glacial lakes, mountain tundra, boggy river valleys, craggy ravines resounding to rushing streams, and the sky-borne ridge where clouds merge into snow caps.

SIKHOTE-ALIN MOUNTAINS

Far East/Russian Federation

DON'T MISS
Rafting on the
Ussuri headwaters.

The Primorye region is the southernmost part of Russia's far east. The Sikhote-Alin mountain range is its 900 km (560 mi) long coastal spine, an ocean of highland forests and plunging valleys home to the world's biggest feline, the Amur tiger. Some 30 tigers still survive in the wild here. Coupled with altitudinal hallmarks of the 1,500 m (4,920 ft) ascent from the valley floor, the Amur tigers' hunting grounds include mossy jungles of ferns, broadleaf woodlands, small lakes, waterfalls and bubbling rivers. A little higher, Manchurian walnut, Mongolian oak and cedar stand next to pine and evergreen forests, giving way to spruce and fir, with stone birch and upland shrubs nearest the alpine tundra of the highest peaks. Trekking here is a jaw-dropping botanical adventure of colourful lilies, orchids, irises, rhododendrons and hundreds of lichens, mosses and ferns. birds. The heart of Sikhote-Alin is near-uninhabited and barely explored. It is a labyrinth of forests, radiant with colour and the music of living nature. The glow it engenders in every visitor is intensified by knowledge that, somewhere, an Amur tiger is enjoying the view, too; and the view could be you.

DALNEVOSTOCHNY MORSKOY

Far East/Russian Federation

HOW TO GET THERE:
By public ferry or private
boat from Vladivostok.

Much of Khasan's coast falls within Dalnevostochny Morskoy (Far East Marine) Nature Reserve, which protects 643 sq km (248 sq mi) of rocky coast, islands, outcrops and open water in the Sea of Japan. Peter the Great Gulf is the biologically richest part of the Sea of Japan. The convergence of warm and cold ocean currents and colliding air masses attracts plants, trees, fish, marine mammals and hundreds of species of marine, coastal and forest birds at their northern and southern limits. Even the topography helps: rocky islets support big colonies of egrets, cormorants, loons, puffins and murrelet; while shallow coves are ideal for breeding fish which serve a local food chain extending to whales, sea lions, dolphins and the seal rookeries on the islands. Underwater reefs, caves and shallow ravines harbour giant octopus, Kamchatka king crab, sea urchins, starfish and a living carpet of warm- and cold-water species. Although only two per cent of the reserve is terrestrial, it includes meadows, marshes, brackish wetlands and sculpted cliffs, enhanced by the anomaly of both temperate and subtropical forest cover.

AUSTRALASIA & OCEANIA

CAPE ARID

Australia

DON'T MISS
From July–October
migrating whales can
often be seen from the shore.

At the far western end of the Great Australian Bight stands Cape Arid, a wilderness that has an isolated beauty all of its own. The area is now a national park, its 2,800 sq km (1,080 sq mi) covering an extensive stretch of shoreline as well as a large rugged interior. The coast here is one of rocky promontories and sweeping beaches with excellent swimming, especially at Mount Tagon bay, around the mouth of the Thomas River and at Yokinup Bay (also a good location for windsurfing).

Further back, young sand dune systems support coastal heathlands with patches of banksia and paperbark stands. From the top of Mount Arid on the cape itself there are fine views of the varied coastal scenery and the many little offshore islands which make up the eastern end of the Recherche Archipelago. As you move inland sandy plains give way to low granite hills and more arid vegetation. The terrain is dominated by mallee scrub and small eucalypt woodlands. The main feature of the north of the park are the hills of the Russell Range which include the highest point in the park, the aptly named Mount Ragged – 594 m (1,949 ft). More than 160 species bird have been recorded here, including several that are rare and threatened. Oystercatchers and terns are among the waterfowl and waders to be seen in the Thomas estuary, while Cape Arid is one of the few remaining habitats of the Cape Barren goose and the western ground parrot.

WHEN TO GO:
In April and May many
people come to Ningaloo for
the awesome experience of
swimming with the world's
largest fish, the whale shark.

NINGALOO REEF

Australia

For those in the know, Ningaloo Reef on Australia's northwestern coast surpasses the Great Barrier Reef itself. It cannot, of course, compete in terms of sheer scale and variety but Ningaloo has so far managed to escape the worst effects of mass tourism and the other commercial pressures which bedevil its renowned eastern counterpart. The country's largest fringing coral reef, Ningaloo harbours a marine environment of global importance; its entire 300 km (186 mi) length is now protected as a marine park. Proximity to the continental shelf is what gives the reef its stunning diversity of marine life. With some 250 different types of coral and over 500 species of fish recorded, the reef is a diver's paradise, although it also provides exceptional scope for ordinary snorkellers owing to the fact that, in contrast to the Barrier Reef, it lies so close to the coast. Indeed, Ningaloo is the world's only large reef found so close to a continental landmass. Never more than 7 km (4 mi) from the coastline, in some places it is barely 100 m (330 ft) offshore; from the beach at Coral Bay, for example, you can clearly see the white swell breaking over the reef.

PERON PENINSULA

Australia

The Peron Peninsula forms the middle prong of the W-shaped landmass enfolding Shark Bay, the westernmost point of the Australian mainland. It is a wild realm of sandy plains covered with mulga scrub and acacias which have adapted to the mercilessly dry conditions. The dramatic red cliffs of the bluffs and headlands around the coast present a vivid contrast with the blue waters and white beaches below. The far north end of the peninsula is now the Francois Peron National Park, named after a pioneering French zoologist. The area now covered by the park, 525 sq km (203 sq mi), was formerly a sheep station; you can see the old homestead to get an idea of what life must have been like.

YOU SHOULD KNOW

The national park is part of Project Eden, a state government initiative to re-establish native wildlife species by eradicating feral and imported animals.

One unusual feature of the landscape is the gypsum claypans that were once saline lakes; in some places, such as Big Lagoon, the sea has broken through into the claypans to form a shallow inland bay. Shark Bay is a protected marine park and its shallow, clear waters are rich in marine life. The cliff tops of the Peron Peninsula provide good viewpoints for spotting dolphins and rays; even the threatened dugong, a gentle giant, can sometimes be seen grazing in these waters. But the most remarkable feature of all is what thrives in the shallow waters of Hamelin Pool on the eastern side of the peninsula: colonies of sediment-trapping algae, known as stromatolites, which are direct descendants of the Earth's earliest life forms, dating back over three billion years.

KALBARRI NATIONAL PARK

Australia

DON'T MISS

Displays of colour when the wild flowers of the heathlands and sandplains burst into bloom in the spring.

Rock formations and colours are the main attractions of Kalbarri National Park which lies on Australia's west coast some 600 km (375 mi) north of Perth. The spectacular red-and-white banded gorges which the Murchison River has carved out of the rock as it winds its serpentine way to the sea are definitely not to be missed. They are best seen from two sites on the upper Murchison. The cliff top of Z Bend offers the most dramatic viewpoint where you can gaze down to the river far below; you can also walk around the Loop, a wide horseshoe bend in the river, in two to three hours, depending on how many times you are tempted by swimming spots (best to do the walk in the early morning). On the way you will come across a natural rock arch known as Nature's Window. There are similarly spectacular cliffs south of Kalbarri town. Tidal inlets and creeks have created coastal gorges at sites with evocative names like Rainbow Valley, Mushroom Rock and Red Bluff.

PURNULULU NATIONAL PARK

Australia

Purnululu National Park is much better known as the Bungle Bungles. This mighty sandstone massif (*purnululu* means sandstone in the local tribal language) burst on to the world stage as recently as the early 1980s; until then, its remote location had ensured it was known only to the nomadic Aboriginal peoples whose ancestral land this was and to the odd cattle drover and pilots of the outback. Now this landscape of hundreds of weather-beaten rock domes is a standard feature of Australian tourist brochures, as iconic an image of the country as Uluru.

The terrain is the result of millions of years of erosion and uplift, in the course of which the soft sandstone has worn away to form these curious beehive shapes. The colouring of the rocks is equally remarkable. It is now thought that sediments from two different sources were deposited in alternating strata to create the orange-and-black banding which is such a distinctive feature of the domes. The colouration is caused by the different minerals present: iron and manganese in the case of the orange, while the darker bands are composed of more permeable material where water has supported algal growth.

The stripes are only a fragile crust over a soft and powdery interior that is all too easily eroded. The best way to appreciate the contours of this exceptional landscape is from the air. If you want to reduce your carbon footprint (although probably not by much), the alternative is to take a 4x4 into the park.

WORTH A DETOUR:
The awe-inspiring walk along Cathedral Gorge with its ever-narrowing ravine and sheer, towering cliffs.

WATARRKA NATIONAL PARK

Australia

Deep in the Red Centre of Australia the Watarrka National Park is as rugged and isolated a location as you could wish for from the Outback. It comes as a surprise, then, to discover just what a range of environments the park encompasses; as well as the expected desert plains and rocky spurs, you also find plateaux, gorges, red sandhills covered with desert oaks and spinifex, and hidden springs with delicate ferns and cycads growing in profusion around them. It is a surprise, too, to learn that the park is home to more than 600 different types of plant; its name, indeed, refers to the unmistakable umbrella bush which is a common feature of the area.

Watarrka National Park includes the western end of the George Gill Range, itself an extension of the MacDonnell Ranges that frame Alice Springs. At its heart lies Kings Canyon, the natural feature that most people come to Watarrka to see. The sight of the canyon's sheer sandstone walls, rising to 100 m (330 ft) in places, is breathtaking, especially in the early morning sunlight. This is definitely the best time to undertake the 6 km (3.75 mi) walk around the canyon rim, before the day's temperatures become too punishing. The route takes you through a curious maze of little sandstone domes – miniature Bungles – and past a lookout offering a fine view of the imposing southern wall. At the head of the canyon, and roughly halfway along the walk, a surprise awaits you: a sheltered chasm filled with palms and ferns. This haven of greenery is known as the Garden of Eden and it comes complete with a shady pool where you can take a refreshing dip.

HOW TO GET THERE:
Watarrka is 450 km (280 mi) southwest of Alice Springs on sealed roads, so it is accessible in a conventional vehicle.

WHEN TO GO:
April–September.

WORTH A DETOUR:
See the early morning sunlight on the red rocks and cliff faces.

COBOURG PENINSULA

Australia

DON'T MISS

Wild populations of animals introduced to the peninsula by the British, including Indonesian banteng cattle.

Places don't come much more remote than the Cobourg Peninsula on Australia's northern coast. The overland approach involves an epic 4x4 journey across Kakadu and Arnhem Land. Arnhem Land is a huge wilderness that has remained in Aboriginal hands; access by non-indigenous visitors is carefully managed. Camping is possible, however, within the bounds of the Garig Gunak Barlu National Park which covers the entire peninsula. The land area of 2,200 sq km (850 sq mi) is more than doubled by the waters of Van Diemen Gulf and the Arafura Sea, along with islands which form a marine reserve; extensive coral reefs and seagrass meadows support a rich array of marine life. The Cobourg Peninsula is a wild and beautiful mosaic of coastal grasslands, dunes, beaches, mangrove swamps, lagoons and patches of rainforest. There are magnificent white sand beaches and good birdwatching opportunities, too, as this is an important habitat for waterfowl and migratory birds. If you absolutely have to go on an expedition, then the ruins of Victoria Settlement, a failed attempt in the 1840s to establish a British colony and trading post, await exploration; as they lie on the other side of the Port Essington inlet, however, you need a boat to reach them.

ELSEY NATIONAL PARK

Australia

DON'T MISS

The old wartime Aboriginal army camp.

The Roper River is one of the principal rivers of the area around Darwin, popularly known as the Top End. Flowing into the Gulf of Carpentaria to the east, the river is a green lung in the arid plains and grasslands south of Katherine. Its upper reaches are protected within the Elsey National Park, which also

includes a number of springs that feed the river. During the dry season the Roper presents a picture of calm serenity as it courses its gentle way through large waterholes and over rocks and tufa dams. In the wet season, however, it is an entirely different proposition and you would be hard pushed to believe the raging torrent before you was the same river.

This is a world which encourages a slower, simpler way of life. Fishing and canoeing are popular activities here, as is swimming, although as with anywhere in the Top End you should heed local advice about where it is safe to enter the water. Cruises along the Roper River are the best way of appreciating the scenery, taking you into an extensive area of freshwater wetlands.

KAKADU

Australia

HOW TO GET THERE:

The western boundary of Kakadu National Park is 150 km (93 mi) east of Darwin. From there it is a further 100 km (62 mi) to the park headquarters at Jabiru. You can also enter Kakadu from the south by turning off the Stuart Highway at Pine Creek.

WHEN TO GO:

Any time of year. Most visitors arrive during the dry season months of May–August when the temperatures are at their most tolerable; but connoisseurs reckon the true spirit of the place is revealed only in the wet season, when nature bursts forth in all its verdant profusion.

WORTH A DETOUR:

A boat trip on the Yellow Water billabong, preferably in the early morning or late afternoon. These wetlands provide exceptional opportunities for spotting wildlife.

Everything about Kakadu draws you to superlatives. The facts about Australia's greatest national park are staggering for a start: an area the size of Wales – nearly 20,000 sq km (7,720 sq mi); more different reptile species than are found in the whole of Europe; five out of the world's seven types of turtle; one third of the entire bird species of Australia; over 5,000 rock-art sites.

It can all seem rather overwhelming on a first visit, and you wonder whether it is possible ever to get the full measure of the park. The truth is, the most you can hope for is a flavour of this extraordinary place, but what a flavour it is! A huge variety of land forms and habitats are featured in Kakadu, an area large enough to encompass the entire catchment area of a river. As the South Alligator River flows north into Van Diemen Gulf, the landscape changes from sandstone plateaux and heathlands in the south through savannah woodlands and paperbark swamps to the coastal belt, which is made up of tidal wetlands and mangrove forests. Presiding over all is the imposing Arnhem escarpment running down the eastern side of the park.

Kakadu is jointly managed by the Australian government and the local Aboriginal groups who still live in the park and are the traditional owners of the land, much of which remains sacred to them and is consequently inaccessible to the casual visitor. Other sites are only for serious off-road types; at certain times of the year they are not even reached by 4x4s. Places which everyone can get to on sealed roads include the incredible sites at Ubirr and Nourlangie, outdoor galleries of rock art depicting animals, birds, humans and ancestral spirits in paintings, some of which are 20,000 years old.

Right: Kakadu National Park

KATA TJUTA

Australia

DON'T MISS
Uluru seen from the
road to Kata Tjuta at sunset.

The stunning assemblage of giant sandstone rocks known as Kata Tjuta seem happy enough to cede star billing to Uluru, the monolith that has become for many people the defining image of the country. They are just 50 km (31 mi) apart and are both contained within the same national park, which is managed jointly by the local Aboriginal community, who own the land, and the federal government. *Kata tjuta* means 'many heads' in the Aboriginal language, an entirely apt description for this cluster of 36 domed rocks divided by narrow chasms and broader valleys. Whether or not you climb Uluru is a controversial subject these days, but there is no such dilemma here as you are not allowed to climb on the Kata Tjuta rocks. Their

smooth, rounded tops may look inviting but the sheer sides of many of the rocks make it an unfeasible prospect. The eastern part of the complex is completely off-limits to visitors since this is a sacred site to the Anangu Aborigines under their law. You can still get an outstanding impression of the site, though, by doing the Valley of the Winds walk, a 7 km (4.4 mi) loop trail through a desert landscape of sand hills covered in spinifex and small stands of desert oak.

WORTH A DETOUR: The remarkable magnetic termite mounds found on the plains. These mounds can be as tall as 2 m (6.5 ft) and get their name from their north–south orientation.

LITCHFIELD NATIONAL PARK

Australia

A couple of hours' drive south from Darwin brings you to the boundary of Litchfield National Park. The park encloses much of the Tabletop Range, a rugged sandstone plateau with eroded cliffs which drop away to black-soil plains covered in spear grass. The dominant trees of the forest here are the Darwin woollybutt and the stringybark, while sand palms, acacias and banksias proliferate closer to the ground. Litchfield's most famous features are the waterfalls which tumble off the plateau at various points throughout the park. Often set in pockets of dense rainforest, they come with deep plunge pools at their bases, perfect for a refreshing dip following a walk. Wangi Falls are easily the most popular and can get very crowded. Tjaynera Falls are just as attractive and much quieter, as befits their more isolated location. Tolmer Falls are the most impressive, although you can only view them from the cliffs opposite.

DON'T MISS
The cliff-top lookout over the river near the visitor centre. It's a stiff climb but the views are superb.

NITMILUK NATIONAL PARK
Australia

The big attraction at Nitmiluk is the Katherine Gorge, where the Katherine River has carved a spectacular 12 km (7.5 mi) course through the Arnhem Land plateau. Although described as 13 separate gorges, which are separated from each other by rapids of varying length, this is really one continuous canyon which turns first this way then that, depending on the prevailing fault lines. The sheer gorge walls may not be especially tall, but when bathed in sunlight their orange hues present a gorgeous spectacle.

The best way to appreciate the gorge is from the water. If you are an intrepid spirit and possess the requisite energy you can explore the gorge under your own power in a canoe. But most visitors take one of the cruises on offer which travel upstream as far as the second, third or sixth gorge, depending on the length of the trip. It's not all plain sailing, though; there are places where you have to disembark for a scramble over rocks in order to board another boat further upriver. This adds to the sense of adventure.

ORMISTON GORGE
Australia

HOW TO GET THERE:
Ormiston Gorge is 135 km (84 mi) west of Alice Springs.

The West MacDonnell Ranges in the heart of Australia boast a number of striking gorges and chasms. The deep shadows cast by their towering walls have made them important refuges for a rich variety of flora and fauna, including several relict plant species surviving from an ancient tropical past. Ormiston Gorge is perhaps the most impressive of all. The presence here of a permanent waterhole, up to 14 m (46 ft) deep, has generated a slopes covered in spinifex, mulga woodland, rocky plains and stands of lofty red river gums.

The Ormiston Pound circular walk is particularly worthwhile. Starting at the information centre the route traverses rocky slopes before crossing the flat expanse of remote Ormiston Pound and returning down the gorge itself and past the waterhole – perfectly placed for a refreshing dip. The best time to do the walk is in the early morning when the sun lights up the mighty cliffs. The small campground at Ormiston Gorge is a good base for a longer exploration of the western half of the West MacDonnells. From here it is a good day's walk to Bowmans Gap, or two days to Mount Giles. Spending a night on the mountain is recommended for the stunning view at sunrise over Ormiston Pound to Mount Sonder and its surroundings.

SIMPSON DESERT

Australia

YOU SHOULD KNOW

Don't be too surprised to see camels in the desert. They are the wild descendants of the original beasts brought here by Afghan cameleers before the Ghan railway reached Alice in 1928.

WHEN TO GO:
April–September.

It doesn't come much bleaker than the Simpson Desert, 150,000 sq km (58,000 sq mi) of emptiness straddling the borders of the Northern Territory, South Australia and Queensland. Largely devoid of human activity and as inhospitable as it seems, anyone who has spent serious time in a desert will know that appearances are deceptive and that these environments possess a raw beauty all their own. Habitats you might expect to find, such as gibber plains and mulga scrub, are joined by more surprising ones like gidgee woodland and coolabah plains; these support a fragile but profuse ecosystem of some 800 plant species, 180 types of bird and over 90 different reptiles. If you are fortunate enough to visit immediately after a rare rainstorm you will find the Simpson transformed by carpets of wild flowers which emerge for a brief moment in the sun.

The reason most people come to the Simpson Desert, however, is the sand dunes; rows upon rows of them stretching to the horizon. The Simpson is one of the world's outstanding sand-ridge deserts; the dunes run parallel to one another in a direction dictated by prevailing winds. Crossing the Simpson Desert is one of the outback's great adventures but it is strictly for the experienced and well-equipped 4x4 traveller.

The most direct route, the so-called French Line, is also the toughest since it strikes straight across the dunes in a punishing succession of climbs and descents, some as high as 40 m (130 ft).

You do not have to be an adrenalin junkie, though, to get a taste of the Simpson's endless expanses. There are 4x4 day tours from Alice Springs that follow the line of the original Ghan railway, taking you deep into the desert to sights like Rainbow Valley and the mighty sandstone column of Chambers Pillar.

WORTH A DETOUR: The park's beautifully marked yellow-footed wallabies. After being hunted to near extinction for its fur, this delightful rock-hopper is still around, if in smaller numbers.

MOUNT REMARKABLE NATIONAL PARK

Australia

Mount Remarkable National Park – named after the 960 m (3,150 ft) summit of the same name – offers splendid scenery in diverse terrain that stretches up from coastal plains west of the Flinders Ranges to foothills above the town of Wilmington. Native vegetation includes assorted woodland containing trees such as eucalyptus, northern cypress pine, acacia, peppermint box, sugar gum and blue gum. Imposing river red gums line watercourses and there's a brilliant display of wildflowers in springtime. A diversity of wildlife ranges from kangaroos through over 100 bird species to numerous amphibians and reptiles such as the rare carpet python.

The variety of animals and plants adds interest to a rugged landscape that's a star in its own right. The eroded sandstone Mount Remarkable range dominates the park's eastern side. This massive hogsback has impressive outcrops, like Cathedral Rock, with vertical rock faces. To the west, the Alligator Syncline features Mount Cavern and Alligator Gorge. The latter is the top natural attraction in the South Flinders Ranges – a spectacular gorge between ragged quartzite walls, cut over countless millennia by Alligator Creek.

BLACK MOUNTAIN (KALKAJAKA) NATIONAL PARK

Australia

DON'T MISS
The James Cook Museum in Cooktown.

Black Mountain National Park is at the top of the UNESCO Wet Tropics of Queensland World Heritage Site in northeastern Queensland's section of the Great Dividing Range, where it meets drier savannah woodlands. The resulting 'Black Mountain' environment has a unique combination of flora and fauna, supporting at least three species – the rock-haunting frog, Black-Mountain gecko and Black-Mountain skink – these are found nowhere else in Australia. Other interesting creatures include ghost bats and Godman's rock wallabies.

There are excellent observation points for those who simply want to stroll and look (binoculars essential), but anyone getting in among the park's intriguing landscape of monolithic boulders – many the size of houses and stacked in a way that apparently defies gravity – should take sensible backcountry precautions.

There are age-old Aboriginal legends and a number of sacred sites, but white incomers soon added their own tales of horses, cattle and even prospectors who entered the Black Mountains in the 19th century… never to be seen again.

CARNARVON GORGE

Australia

WORTH A DETOUR:
The Amphitheatre, behind
the ancient rock wall of
Carnarvon Gorge. Entered
through a narrow vertical
crack, this incredible crevice
can only be described as
awe-inspiring – and anyone
who raises their voice will
find that it has the most
amazing acoustics, too.

In southern-central Queensland, Carnarvon Gorge is the centrepiece of the national park that bears its name. Hidden in rugged uplands of the Great Dividing Range, this 2,900-sq km (1,120-sq mi) preserve not only encompasses the mountains but also the inaccessible and heavily vegetated Consuelo Tableland. This is a place where truly awesome landscape vistas roll away in every direction, although most visitors hurry to the enclosed world of Carnarvon Gorge – and what a wonderful world it is for those sufficiently determined to get there. This requires effort but around 65,000 people make the pilgrimage every year and are well rewarded.

The gorge is 30 km (19 mi) long and 600 m (2,000 ft) deep at the mouth, carved into sandstone by the passage of water and time.

Most visitors get no further than the first 10 km (6 mi), as this stretch offers a wonderful variety of natural and cultural features that would require weeks of extended travel and exploration to experience anywhere else in the state, if they could be found at all. The main trail follows the limpid creek where platypus may be seen diving into pools, while an extensive network of graded side trails perambulates through tall eucalyptus trees and lush greenery that includes palms and giant ferns. Side gorges and waterfalls abound, offering exciting voyages of discovery. More remote tracks, including Devil's Signpost and Battleship Spur, are for experienced hikers only.

GREAT BARRIER REEF

Australia

WORTH A DETOUR:
Mon Repos Conservation Park near Bundaberg, which has the largest concentration of nesting marine turtles in eastern Australia, including the most important nesting population of loggerheads. Laying season is November –March, but the best period to observe nesting turtles is from mid November to February. Hatchlings emerge and head for the sea between mid January–late March.

Queensland's Great Barrier Reef in the appropriately named Coral Sea is in fact a conglomeration of nearly 3,000 individual reefs and 900 islands stretching for more than 2,600 km (1,600 mi). This vast natural treasure house supports a huge variety of life including headliners like whales, dolphins, porpoises, dugongs, sea turtles, sharks, stingrays, seahorses and over 1,500 fish species, plus 200 types of bird that visit or breed on the reef's islands. The majority of the reef is protected by the Great Barrier Reef Marine Park, which seeks to ensure that human intrusion becomes neither excessive nor damaging. Even so, tourism is of major importance to the local economy, with a large number of visitors drawn to the Queensland coast by the opportunity to experience a little piece of this magical marine masterpiece. The most popular activity by far is getting up close and personal by snorkelling or scuba diving, often from live-aboard dive boats. Although tourism is economically vital, it is carefully policed to protect the reef for posterity.

KANANGRA-BOYD NATIONAL PARK

Australia

WORTH A DETOUR: Jenolan Caves. Australia's best can-be-viewed cave system is close to the park and has 11 impressive show caves featuring underground rivers and amazing rock formations.

Some of the most inaccessible terrain in New South Wales can be found in Kanangra-Boyd National Park. It has two sections. The gently undulating Boyd Plateau is relatively accessible, has stunning views and offers everything from gentle strolls to stimulating day hikes. An unmade road leads to a campground at Boyd River and on to the Kanangra Walls area. These are ideal bases for bushwalking or simply enjoying stunning distant views from the rim of the plateau. Some of those views roll away across the labyrinthine Kanangra wilderness area, a broken jumble of thickly vegetated valleys, overgrown streams and sandstone cliffs that stretches for 60 km (37 mi). This empty backcountry should be tackled only by the most experienced and self-reliant of bushwalkers – ideally those also possessing climbing skills.

The park's best-known features are Kanangra Walls – spectacular orange-and-grey sandstone cliffs that tower above the shadowed Kanangra Creek Gorge below – and the 225 m (740 ft) Kanangra Falls, a scenic cascade that spills down an angled rock face. The car park at Kanangra Walls is the starting point for most of the park's established walks, including the wheelchair-friendly path to the first lookout or a stroll down to the nearby falls. The established Plateau Walk is longer, delivering awesome views of Kanangra Walls, Falls and surrounding cliffs. Longer hikes lead out along the Gangerang Range to Mount Cloudmaker and on as far as Kaloomba, or south to the Gingra Range and thence to the Kowmung River. It's all wild and wonderful, and the views alone are worth the effort needed to reach this remote place.

WORTH A DETOUR: The track along Coombadjha Creek has signs that provide an informative introduction to the park's features. There's a delightful shallow pool where swimming is allowed.

WASHPOOL NATIONAL PARK

Australia

Washpool National Park in Australia's New England protects some of the most varied rainforest in New South Wales, including Australian red cedars and the world's largest stand of coachwood trees. A dramatic landscape of steep gorges, broad ridges, pristine waters and forested escarpments is a haven for threatened animals like the koala, parma wallaby and spotted-tailed quoll, a beautiful cat-like marsupial. It is also a rich habitat for birds, with nearly 150 different species recorded. The park's true beauty can only be appreciated fully by those willing to venture away from the immediate environs of the highway. The inspiring four-hour Washpool Walk takes visitors along twisting paths beside rushing boulder-filled streams and through awesome rainforest beneath canopies of tree ferns, accompanied by the distinctive call of bellbirds. The Gibraltar-Washpool World Heritage Walk encompasses an 80 km (50 mi) network of hiking tracks that can occupy up to five days of rewarding exploration in rugged mountain country above the Clarence River Valley.

YENGO WILDERNESS

Australia

WHEN TO GO: Take your pick – summers are very hot, winters are cooler. The heaviest rainfall occurs between December–January.

As part of the Greater Blue Mountains World Heritage Site, the newly established Yengo National Park stretches for over 70 km (45 mi) from Wisemans Ferry to the Hunter Valley, much of it remote wilderness characterized by predominantly sandstone gorges and rocky ridges. The park is rich in cultural heritage and Mount Yengo, in particular, is sacred to local Aboriginal communities who co-manage the park. The area is still criss-crossed with their traditional routes, established over thousands of years. The habitat is mainly eucalypt forest – dry on ridge tops and northern slopes, wet in gullies and on southern slopes. There are smaller areas of wet and dry rainforest and some open woodland. Wildlife to watch out for includes koalas, wombats, gliding possums, geckoes and endangered brush-tailed rock-wallabies. Numerous opportunities for short walks exist and there are overnight hiking routes for experienced walkers. Scenic car tours for those disinclined to go by foot, such as the Finchley-Yango-Boree loop that starts near Laguna and gives an excellent overview of the dry sandstone terrain, are well worthwhile. Another scenic drive goes from St Albans via Mogo Creek Road to Bucketty, taking in extensive wetlands and historic Deans Quarry, plus the pleasant must-stop-for-lunch Mogo Creek Picnic Area. Tough types can do the 4x4/trailbike/mountain-bike Big Yango Loop Trail that circles Mount Yengo, with great views over the wilderness area, or tackle the Howes-Yango Trail across the northern section of the park – a five-hour return trip.

MURRAY-SUNSET NATIONAL PARK

Australia

YOU SHOULD KNOW
River red gum trees can and quite often do drop heavy branches without warning.

DON'T MISS
Red kangaroos. The park is one of the few areas in Victoria where these iconic creatures can be seen .

Close to South Australia and New South Wales in northwestern Victoria is the state's second-largest national park. This protects one of the last semi-arid regions in Australia that has almost (but not entirely) escaped human interference – there was once a salt production industry and residual evidence of gypsum mining remains. But that's a pinprick set against Murray-Sunset National Park's impressive 6,300-sq km (2,430-sq mi) expanse of untouched wilderness. The flattish landscape is filled with grasslands, mallee eucalypts, porcupine grass, saltbush and buloke, broken by stands of native cypress-pine and belah woodlands. River red gums line creeks and black boxwoods surround floodplains. The park has four salt lakes – the Pink Lakes, so called because of their colour in late summer when they've dried out to leave a crust of carotene-tinted salt.

There are first-class walking trails in the Pink Lakes area, but Murray-Sunset National Park deserves a longer stay. The campground on the shore of Lake Crosbie has good facilities, including a supply of scarce-in-the-park clean drinking water. There are alternative campgrounds at Rocket Lake, Lake Becking, Mount Crozier and Mopoke Hut. Accommodation can also be booked at an old shearer's hut. There are remote campgrounds with primitive facilities in the wilderness. Those are the very best places to truly appreciate the park's vast isolation and enjoy its wide-open landscapes, incredible sunsets and brilliantly lit starry night skies.

WILSONS PROMONTORY

Australia

Perhaps appropriately for such a vast and relatively empty continent, the southernmost point on the Australian mainland is the largest remaining coastal wilderness in the state of Victoria. Colloquially known as 'The Prom' by Victorians, Wilsons Promontory is an unspoiled peninsula jutting into the Bass Strait that boasts a stunning 130 km (80 mi) girdle of inspiring coastline consisting of bold granite headlands, tumbled boulders, sheltered coves, intertidal mudflats, dunes, swamps … and beautiful beaches. It has been protected since the late 19th century and is now a national park.

One Tidal River is just what the name suggests, swelling with each tide as it discharges into Norman Bay. The river water has a strange purple-yellow colour as a result of tannin emanating from the large number of tea trees in the area. The other Tidal River is the immediately adjacent settlement that serves as a focal point for visitors, not least because it has one of the park's finest sandy beaches. Also, the drive from Yanakie to Tidal River is super-scenic (don't hurry, abundant local wildlife that includes assorted marsupials, kangaroos, wallabies, koalas and emus is liable to stray onto the road).

The park's information centre at Tidal River has a wealth of information on the park's history – from Aboriginal occupation going back at least 6,500 years to the activities of rough-and-ready sealers in the early 19th century – plus general displays on the park's geology, flora and fauna. This is also the place to learn about disabled access to nearby sites such as Squeaky Beach (named for the sound made when tramping the fine white quartz sand) and the Lilly Pilly nature walk.

> **WORTH A DETOUR:**
> The view from the top of Mount Oberon for a wonderful panoramic outlook over Tidal River, rugged coastline and the green interior with its rainforest, woodlands and heathlands. Happily, the uphill hike isn't too hard.

WORTH A DETOUR: Take the opportunity while on this light-pollution-free island to observe the magnificent Aurora Australis, the Southern Lights. Prime months are April and October but the lights can switch on at any time.

BAY OF FIRES
Australia

The wild and wonderful coastline known as the Bay of Fires offers fascinating opportunities to explore an unspoilt wilderness coastline and experience the rich diversity of backing woodlands. This is a place of white beaches that glint in the sun, intense blue water and orange-splashed granite (the colour comes from lichen). The northern section is from Eddystone Point to the Ansons Bay outlet, which cannot be crossed. This is in the national park and can be accessed from Eddystone Road, just before the lighthouse. There's a brisk walk across dunes to the shore and visitors should take all necessary supplies, especially drinking water. This is for day use only but Deep Creek campground is close to Eddystone Point.
The middle section encompasses Ansons Bay and is the destination of choice for those who want to spend time communing with nature. The primitive Policemans Point campground offers numerous sites scattered among the trees, many with direct beach access, but happy campers will become unhappy unless they bring everything necessary for their stay – there are no on-site toilets, no water or firewood. The southern section stretches from The Gardens to Binalong Bay and has several campgrounds: again, pitches only.

NINETY MILE BEACH

New Zealand

WHEN TO GO: Any time, although winter (June, July and August) occasionally sees the main road closed owing to floods or landslips.

This stunning expanse of white sand arches faces the Tasman Sea and is backed by dunes up to 6.5 km (4 mi) wide and up to 140 m (460 ft) tall. They are higher at the northern end, where they resemble nothing so much as the Sahara Desert when approached from the landward side. The dunes steadily decrease in height towards the south where they are stabilized by marram grass and lupins, but elsewhere they are bare but for occasional patches of scrub and are constantly being reshaped by the wind. This austere 260-sq km (100-mi-sq) sea of sand is a lonely wilderness that may soon become pine forests.

There are beachside campgrounds and motels at the southern end, but as a whole Ninety Mile Beach is a wild and lonely natural wonder. Getting onto the beach isn't actually that easy, with few access roads. The best way to see it is to drive. Warning signs suggest that Ninety Mile Beach is a potentially hazardous place for anything with four wheels, particularly for a couple of hours either side of high tide, but it was used as a runway for early airmail flights in the 1930s and provides a perfectly usable scenic highway.

Left: Bay of Fire

BAY OF ISLANDS

New Zealand

WHEN TO GO:
The bay area often experiences fairly heavy summer rainfall in December. It's best to avoid mid December–early February anyway, as school holidays see a serious influx of camper vans, tourists and noisy children. The winter months (June, July and August) are much quieter.

Close to the northern tip of New Zealand's North Island, in the appropriately named Northland Region, lies the beautiful natural feature that seduced the first European settlers to arrive in the country. Captain Cook named the Bay of Islands after coming upon this natural harbour in 1769. Whalers soon followed, whose profane ways attracted missionaries. The first European child to be born in New Zealand was delivered there in 1815 and the towns around the bay are rich in national heritage sites.

The bay area is as attractive to people today as it was then. This irregular inlet on the northeastern coast is 16 km (10 mi) wide with several arms that extend inland. It is a special destination and its pristine environment attracts plenty of visitors all year round, drawn by wonderful coastal scenery and the opportunity to enjoy a variety of activities from simply romping on

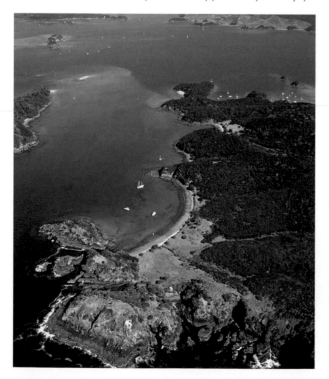

white sand beaches to cruising, boating, sailing, sea kayaking, swimming with dolphins and whale-watching. Other popular possibilities are paragliding, jet boating, big-game fishing, scuba diving, snorkelling, cycling, bushwalking, horseback trekking and camping.

But despite the plethora of recreational temptations, the Bay of Islands Marine Park has 144 islands that remain a natural wonderland of native forests, secluded bays and subtropical beaches. This ensures that there are always lonely corners to be found, where those who value solitude can escape the tourist zone. This is particularly true for anyone who goes afloat, exploring the islands until finding a suitably remote spot to land, like an early pioneer stepping ashore for the first time.

In addition to abundant natural charms, the bay is something of a cultural centre, with pleasant towns like Paihia, Russell, Opua, Kerikeri and Waitangi offering craft galleries, museums and heritage trails. There are numerous opportunities to explore Maori culture, too.

DON'T MISS
The Kauri Coast,
where the forest
touches the sea.

WAIPOUA FOREST

New Zealand

Almost all native kauri forests have been lost to logging or fire, with only around four per cent of the original stock of these noble trees remaining, mostly in small pockets. They are not necessarily the most abundant species in the forests that bear their name but that merely encourages the huge variety of flora that flourishes beneath spreading crowns. The best opportunity to roam original kauri woodlands with their lush undergrowth – and appreciate what so much of New Zealand was once like – is at Waipoua Forest, although happily around three quarters of Warawara to the north survived after logging was stopped in 1972. A road through the forest passes impressive kauri stands and provides a wonderful feel for the place. Beyond that, there are plenty of established walks and tramping tracks, ranging from short scenic strolls to long hikes that require overnight bush camping. Full details of these may be obtained at the information centre in Dargaville, where the Waipoua Forest Visitor Centre is also located.

COROMANDEL PENINSULA

New Zealand

The inhabitants of the happy-go-lucky Coromandel Peninsula are concentrated in relatively small settlements, with only Thames having a population of more than 5,000. What's more, these historic communities are clustered along the southwestern and southeastern coasts, with population density decreasing rapidly towards the northern tip of the peninsula.

The hilly interior is almost completely undeveloped, with steep slopes largely covered in rainforest. Much of the Coromandel range is protected as a lush forest park, providing a challenging opportunity for adventurous bushwalking. But those who prefer to be beside the sea will be gratified to discover long stretches of dramatic coastline where rocky headlands punctuate deserted beaches, with the added bonus of many scenic offshore islands. One highlight should be digging (and relaxing in) a natural spa bath on aptly named Hot Water Beach.

DON'T MISS
The Cathedral Cove
recreational reserve
with its famous
rock arch.

WAIMANGU VOLCANIC VALLEY

New Zealand

WORTH A DETOUR:
The valley's stunning Champagne Pool, a hot spring with large and impressive terraces. It's an ideal spot to linger and enjoy an al fresco meal.

Stand by to be wowed by another world superlative – the globe's youngest geothermal system, the Waimangu Volcanic Valley to the south of Rotorua. As a bonus, the world's largest hot-water spring also awaits (the sizzling Frying Pan) beside the ominously titled Inferno Crater. This protected scenic reserve and wildlife refuge is set in pristine bush country. An extraordinary new landscape was shaped by the eruption of Mount Tarawera in 1886 and the valley now consists of seven craters. Tarawera split in half, opening up a 16 km (10 mi) rift valley and reshaping the landscape into a weird and colourful volcanic wonderland soon to be colonized by verdant vegetation and wildlife, notably wallabies and black swans normally found only in Australia, introduced with help from 19th-century governor and premier of New Zealand, Sir George Grey.

This geothermal masterpiece was named for the Waimangu Geyser, first seen in 1900. It was another top dog, namely the world's most powerful geyser. But four years later it stopped as suddenly as it had started, although not before claiming the lives of two over-curious couples who wanted a closer look and thought they knew better than their guide. It's perfectly possible to make unassisted visits to Waimangu, but local companies offer assorted guided tours for those who prefer not to go it alone.

A paid-for outing usually includes a fascinating cruise on Lake Rotomahana, notable for exotic birdlife and smoking geothermal features of its own. The lake consists of 15 interlinked craters and is the deepest on the North Island. Serious hikers should take the Mount Hazard Trail from the Inferno Crater. This elevated route offers fabulous views down onto the valley floor and across a wider landscape that includes Rainbow Mountain, Mount Tarawera and Lake Rotomahana.

DON'T MISS
Honeycomb Hill Caves at
Karamea, famous for finds of
bones from extinct bird species.

KAHURANGI NATIONAL PARK

New Zealand

Kahurangi National Park is a vast wilderness area offering a huge variety of landscapes from rocky coastline to wild rivers, and glaciated mountains to deep valley floors. Many spectacular landforms include areas of marble and granite sculpted into tortured shapes, arches and caves by the relentless action of water. Wonderfully diverse terrain provides an ideal habitat for more than half of New Zealand's 2,400 native plant species. Palms on the coast impart a tropical look, while the vegetation changes from podocarp forest with lush undergrowth in the west to beech forest in the east. There's a thriving bird population that includes iconic species such as the great-spotted kiwi and blue duck. Among the less appealing wildlife are giant cave spiders and carnivorous giant snails that luckily prefer worms to people.

This is a place where those who revel in outdoor recreational activities will be well served, as will self-sufficiency types who have the opportunity to heft a backpack into the Tasman Wilderness Area and get away from the stresses and strains of modern life. Demanding caving, kayaking and rafting are popular, while the Karamea River is renowned for trout fishing.

MARLBOROUGH SOUNDS

New Zealand

WORTH A DETOUR: Ship Cove, where Captain Cook made his base in the 1770s, proclaiming British sovereignty over the South Island.

Although the Marlborough Sounds occupy no more than the northeastern tip of the South Island, this jumbled assembly of sea-drowned valleys between Tasman and Cloudy Bays accounts for one-fifth of New Zealand's entire coastline. The DOC (Department of Conservation) manages over 50 reserves in the area, indicating how important this marine marvel is in ecological terms.

The hauntingly beautiful Marlborough Sounds remain a sparsely populated jigsaw of winding sounds, craggy islands, peninsulas, quiet bays and steep wooded hills where many small and isolated communities or individual homesteads can only be reached by boat. This makes exploration difficult, but transport may be hired in the form of launches, yachts, motor boats and sea kayaks. Although some visitors go afloat simply to explore, sailing and sea kayaking are popular pastimes in their own right. There are passenger boats offering cruises for those who like their scenery to come with minimal effort, while water taxis ply from Picton and Havelock to D'Urville Island.

PAPAROA NATIONAL PARK

New Zealand

WORTH A DETOUR:
The famous Pancake Rocks near Punakaiki. This awesome maze of blow holes and eroded rock formations are named for their layered appearance.

This national park covers an area on or near the coast of the northern Westland and rises up to the top of the Paparoa Ranges. There are many geological variations, but the most important is karst landscape – the only lowland karst in New Zealand with undisturbed forest cover, featuring gorges, caves and streams.

Much of the park is covered in contiguous lowland and montane forest with diversity unmatched anywhere else in the country – wonderful habitat that supports an abundant bird population. It is a vital refuge for the endangered great-spotted kiwi and supports the only known breeding colony of black Westland petrel. The park is also perfect for dedicated backcountry trampers. There are pleasing possibilities for anything from short strolls to day walks and one longer route – the Inland Pack Track cut through the forest in the 1860s to bypass coastal cliffs – but beyond that it's a lonely wilderness crying out to be explored. Other outdoor activities include caving and kayaking.

WHEN TO GO:
Those not interested in snow should make it any time but winter (when there's lots of it).

YOU SHOULD KNOW
Gold was discovered on the West Coast in the 1860s.

ARTHUR'S PASS NATIONAL PARK

New Zealand

In the heart of Ka Tiritiri o te Moana lies Arthur's Pass National Park. It consists of high country that features tall mountains, extensive scree slopes, plunging gorges and wide rivers. A historic railway and road 'pass' through the middle en route from Canterbury to the West Coast.

The pass sits on the South Island's backbone and there is a marked difference between western and eastern slopes. To the west, luxuriant podocarp rainforest and red-flowering rata boasts a lush understorey of shrubs, ferns and mosses. To the east is dry beech and tawhai forest. Snow tussock and alpine meadows may be seen (and visited) from the summit of Arthur's Pass itself. Birdwatching is a popular pastime, with many species to be found in and around Arthur's Pass village. Good 'twitches' include kea, blue duck, rock wren, South Island robin, bellbird and fantail. The endangered great-spotted kiwi may be heard whistling away. More demanding activities include mountaineering (Mount Rollaston is a popular target), mountain-biking (formed tracks only) and 4x4 driving (approved roads only). But this is really a place in which to walk, walk, walk. Gentle strolls from the road allow sedentary types to enjoy champagne mountain air with great views.

RANGITATA RIVER

New Zealand

WORTH A DETOUR:
Rafters can enjoy the sheer thrill of white-water swimming and a daring leap into the river from the famous Jump Rock halfway down Rangitata Gorge. It's the 10 m (33.8 ft) rock for the ambitious, and the 4 m (14 ft) rock for everyone else willing to take the plunge!

A liquid rollercoaster drains the eastern side of the Southern Alps between the Lyell and Godley Glaciers and rushes 120 km (75 mi) to the sea near Temuka. The Rangitata River is formed by the confluence of two major tributaries and its most spectacular stretch is in the mountains. Once on the fertile Canterbury Plains it becomes a typical-for-these-parts braided river – a network of small, shifting channels divided by sandbars – before splitting and forming a large island delta, then discharging into the Pacific.

But the gentle pastoral beauty of the Canterbury Plains is not what attracts adventurous types to the swift Rangitata River. Jet boats whizz hither and thither, fishermen exercise their skills (it has some of the best salmon fishing in New Zealand), kayakers test their abilities. If that isn't enough, white-water rafting on the upper river is surely the most exciting way to view the stunning mountain scenery, with various companies offering three-hour white-water, white-knuckle rides that are nonetheless suitable for beginners, with a period of relative calm for safety instruction and familiarization before finally hitting fearsome Grade 5 rapids swirling between monster boulders – the infamous 'Pinch' in the rocky Rangitata Gorge that conducts the racing river out of the mountains.

Those interested in savouring the stunning scenery of the Upper Rangitata Valley as opposed to running the river can drive up either side of the gorge from Arundel, past Mount Peel and on to Erewhon sheep station (right bank) where the Clyde and Havelock rivers merge to form the Rangitata. This was named by Samuel Butler, the first white settler to own nearby Mesopotamia station and author of a famous satire on Victorian life also called Erewhon, which almost but not quite spells 'nowhere' backwards. That's how Butler intended it to be read and the name seems entirely appropriate in these back-of-beyond mountains.

MOUNT ASPIRING NATIONAL PARK

New Zealand

WORTH A DETOUR: The Upper Wilkin Valley – one of the most picturesque in the whole of New Zealand, which is saying something.

Nothing beckons lovers of remote places more seductively than Mount Aspiring National Park. This vast area is an unspoilt land of stunning views, mountains, glaciers, alpine lakes, valleys and white-water rivers. Beech forests predominate below the bush line, while higher up the vegetation consists of snow-tussock grassland and herb fields bright with wild flowers in spring and early summer.

The park extends to an impressive 3,500 sq km (1,350 sq mi). The awesome spike of Mount Aspiring is a great reference point, proving an irresistible challenge to experienced alpinists. However, the main activity in the park is walking. As ever, there are countless short walks for those content to soak up the awesome scenery without straying too far from folding chairs and picnic lunch.

But serious visitors head for one of the long-distance hiking routes that lead into the interior and often link to adjacent areas. These include the Greenstone and Caples tracks (two fabulous valleys, moderate five-day round trip), Rees-Dart Track (a four-day circuit taking in two rivers and some of the park's best scenery) and the ever-popular three-day Routeburn Track (linking Mount Aspiring and Fiordland National Parks). There are campgrounds and numerous huts within the park (pre-booking advisable in summer), plus plenty of primitive campgrounds along the various tracks. Peace and quiet are not absolutely guaranteed. This being New Zealand, the sound of jet boats may be heard in the vicinity of the park's larger rivers.

HALEAKALA NATIONAL PARK

Hawaii

In the southeast of Maui, Haleakala National Park is a wilderness of two halves stretching from brooding volcanic heights at Mount Haleakala down through the clouds (often literally) to verdant coastline at Kipahulu. The island's highest peak often delivers dramatic views across a sea of clouds and this island in the sky is a starkly sculpted landscape of contrasting colours unlike any other.
Haleakala's slopes and the surrounding wilderness offer backcountry hiking against a magnificent backdrop, with access to rare endemic plants and birdlife. It's one of the few accessible places in Hawaii where native species thrive in abundance. This dramatic area on top of the world offers many contrasts, from the dry, cold air of the mountain with its towering cindercones to moist cloud forest rich in ferns at lower altitudes.

DON'T MISS
Seeing stars from the summit of Mount Haleakala on a clear night.

The wilderness can be accessed from two trailheads near the summit, Halemauu at 2,440 m (8,000 ft) and Keoneheehee (Sliding Sands) at 2,970 m (9,750 ft). The trails eventually merge and lead down to the park's coastal zone. Along the way there are primitive campgrounds and historic cabins that can be booked in advance by overnighters. The coastal part of the park is reached by road from Hanu along Maui's spectacular northeastern coast. There is a campground but this area is remote and there is no piped water supply. Ocean swimming can be dangerous but there are plunge pools on the stream that runs down the Oheo Gulch, where the short Pipiwai Trail is popular with day hikers enjoying verdant tropical greenery.

KEALAKEKUA BAY

Hawaii

WORTH A DETOUR:
The narrow road at the south end of the bay that leads to Pu'uhonua Honaunau National Historical Park, to see a complex of archaeological sites that includes temple platforms, royal fishponds and coastal village sites along with reconstructed vernacular building such as the Hale o Keawe Temple. The original pu'uhonua itself was a place of refuge where those who broke sacred laws could seek refuge from certain death and obtain forgiveness.

The Kona (leeward) Coast of the Big Island of Hawaii is an area of historic settlement with many heritage sites and stern natural beauty. One of the highlights is Kealakekua Bay, 19 km (12 mi) south of Kailu-Kona, the main town in West Hawaii.

Horseshoe-shaped Kealakekua is the largest sheltered bay on the island, measuring 2.5 km (1.5 mi) in length and 1.5 km (1 mi) in width. Access is to the south end, where a road winds down to a wharf and Napoopoo Beach.

This is no remote wilderness — just a beautifully unspoilt stretch of rugged coastline with volcanic cliffs rising above an inviting expanse of blue water. The bay offers some of the best snorkelling and scuba diving in the Hawaiian Islands. It's a Marine Life Conservation District and an extensive coral reef protects the bay, creating a calm haven where visibility can be as much as 30 m (100 ft) in water that is invitingly warm. The corals are stunning and host colourful arrays of tropical fish. A pod of Hawaiian spinner dolphins frequents the bay and turtles are frequently sighted. Those who wish to explore the shore must be prepared to do some serious scrambling down steep terrain and brave dense vegetation that crowds the water on gentler slopes.

Kealakekua Bay is famous as the spot where Captain James Cook was killed by indigenous Hawaiians in 1779, having estimated upon arrival that there were two thousand people living in two villages on the bay. A sheer cliff face was the burial site for Hawaiian kings and there were royal residences nearby, but by the early 20th century the once-thriving community had declined to the point where the bay was returned to nature's tender embrace, with abandoned village sites quickly invaded by kiawe trees.

YOU SHOULD KNOW

Molokai is famous for the work of the now-canonized Father Damien de Veuster, a Catholic priest who cared for leprosy sufferers at a colony on the island in the 19th century before himself dying of the disease aged 49.

MOLOKAI
Hawaii

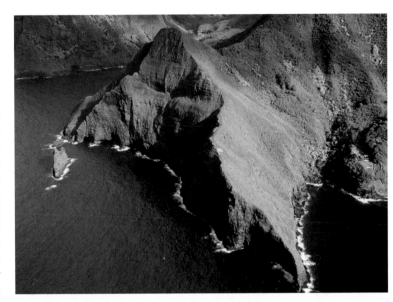

In the geographical centre of the Hawaiian Islands is Molokai, one of the least developed and most interesting parts of the USA's 50th state. The island lies on a westeast axis between Oahu and Maui, measuring 60 km (37 mi) by 16 km (10 mi). The few thousand inhabitants have fiercely resisted efforts to turn Molokai into a non-floating tourist barge. That said, the locals – with a higher percentage of native Hawaiians than any other island – are extremely friendly and their principled stand has preserved much of Molokai's natural beauty for the benefit of visitors more interested in wild places than lying on white sand beaches (although there are plenty of those, including Papohaku, Hawaii's longest and widest). The arid western end of the island with its scrubby grazing land and pineapple plantations is less interesting than the eastern half, although both northern and southern shores have some of the most remote and beautiful beaches in all Hawaii. Molokai was formed from two volcanoes. East Molokai's volcano split in half 1.5 million years ago, collapsing into the Pacific Ocean and leaving the world's highest sea cliffs behind (as featured in the movie *Jurassic Park III*). This is an area of breathtaking tropical landscape – a high plateau rising to 1,500 m (4,920 ft) at Kamakou's impressive peak with lush forests that form an extremely diverse ecosystem.

In addition to those awesome cliffs, there are numerous waterfalls – including the pounding 530 m (1,740 ft) Kahiwa Falls – deep gorges and rugged coastline. This is not tourist central – much of this marvellous terrain can only be reached by hard hiking, after access roads suitable only for 4×4 vehicles run out well short of the best sights, including those famous sea cliffs. In fact, the best way to appreciate their soaring grandeur is to take a sight-seeing helicopter ride from Maui.

WHEN TO GO:
Any time (but the weather in February can be volatile and unpredictable).

PALMYRA ATOLL

Palmyra Atoll

DON'T MISS
The world's largest land invertebrate, the rare coconut crab.

Halfway between Hawaii and American Samoa the true adventurer will find Palmyra Atoll, a tiny speck in the vast North Pacific administered by the USA that extends to 12 sq km (4.5 sq mi). The 14 km (9 mi) of coastline has just one safe anchorage, West Lagoon. An extensive reef system protects two shallow lagoons and 54 sandbars and reef-rock islets that are almost all connected.

Palmyra provides the only nesting site for seabirds in a huge expanse of ocean and attracts over one million birds in the breeding season. Resident species include red-footed boobies, brown boobies, masked boobies and sooty terns. The atoll is a haven for the endangered green turtle, while the surrounding reef and lagoons

are populated by an extraordinary diversity of hard corals – 125 different types, which is three times more than Hawaii or the whole Caribbean can boast. The reef fish are as brightly coloured as the corals they patrol and include various sharks. Whales are frequent visitors.

Palmyra is a stunning marine wilderness and has no indigenous population, although scientists have a base on Cooper Island from which to study the corals.

WESTERN HIGHLANDS

Papua New Guinea

The vast majority of Papua New Guinea's population still practises a traditional rural way of life, and this remote country – occupying the eastern half of the island of New Guinea – remains one of the world's least-developed nations. Only recently has access become possible for tourists, as opposed to the most determined of serious travellers.

The Western Highlands are typical of PNG. This is a dramatic landscape of rainforested mountains, fertile valleys, rushing streams, rivers and swamps in the Lower Jimi Valley. Mount Hagen is an excellent base for exploration of habitats that range from lowland forest to alpine grasslands, dotted with coffee plantations that produce the local cash crop. There are a few hotels and tourist lodges, but this is still a primitive destination not for the faint-hearted. The Wahgi Valley remains a lush green oasis that is intensely cultivated, but Mount Hagen is the gateway to the wild and undeveloped areas further west.

DON'T MISS
The annual Mount Hagen Cultural Show in August.

OFU ISLAND

American Samoa

HOW TO GET THERE:
Ofu can be reached by air (small planes, irregular service) from Pago Pago on Tutuila, itself served by twice-weekly flights from Honolulu.

WHEN TO GO:
Any time.

It doesn't represent much of a Pacific empire, but since quitting the Philippines American Samoa is as good as it gets for the USA – and very good indeed for get-away-from-it-allers. This alluring tropical destination is not as high on the must-visit-islands list as it deserves to be. First impressions are not favourable – the capital of Pago Pago on the main island of Tutuila is tattily commercialized – but that's just a visual glitch. The rest of the island is a natural paradise. Towering peaks surround the town's harbour, lonely roads crowded by dense forest switchback over isolated mountain passes and stunning palm-fringed beaches more than match up to the picture-postcard Pacific white-sand/turquoise-sea standard.

The most discerning travellers head for American Samoa's Manu'a Island group in general and Ofu Island in particular. This volcanic isle is completely uncommercial and unspoilt, while Ofu beach on the west coast must be one of the world's finest. This 3 km (2 mi) stretch of pink coral sand is stunningly beautiful, with a backdrop of swaying palm trees, jagged volcanic peaks and lush greenery. This is a place to swim and walk, often in complete solitude – enjoying the sun, sea and scenery of this dreamy hideaway. Snorkelling off the beach is first-rate, offering wonderful coral formations and vivid underwater life, but it's essential to take the necessary kit. Ofu is not a place where equipment can be rented.

The National Park of American Samoa encompasses 42 sq km (16 sq mi) of land and water on Manu'a islands of Tutuila, Ofu, its twin Olosega and Ta'u, protecting their wild locations from unseemly development. This hopefully precludes the sort of tourist pressure that often overwhelms unspoilt beauty that attracted visitors in the first place. American Samoa remains a dream destination for those willing to make the effort needed to plan a visit.

YOU SHOULD KNOW

As desert islands go, Ofu ticks all the boxes. But what makes it so very special – and allows it to remain that way – is an almost complete absence of tourist facilities. Accommodation is limited and eating out is not an option. The national park promotes a home-stay programme that encourages visitors to lodge with local Samoan families.

NAMENALALA ISLAND

Fiji

WORTH A DETOUR: The evidence of Namenalala's mysterious past – the intriguing remains of an ancient ring fortification at the island's highest point, dating back for at least two millennia.

Sometimes, getting away from it all requires a fat wallet and a little help from those who cater for people who can afford to get away from it all in singular style. A visit to the privately owned Fijian island of Namenalala offers just such an experience. Just six hexagonal *bures* (Polynesian-style houses on stilts made from timber and woven bamboo) have been built among tall native trees on the dragon's tail, accommodating no more than a dozen guests at any one time, who are treated to the ultimate in desert-island living.

Each *bure* overlooks beaches, reefs and a great sweep of sea from a vantage point on the cliff top, while the food is based around fresh produce grown on the island or caught from the surrounding ocean. The rest of

the island is completely undeveloped and provides the opportunity to explore a manageable stretch of original tropical rainforest. But for most visitors the main attraction will be snorkelling or scuba diving along the 30 km (18.5 mi) of Namenalala's pristine barrier reef, with its brilliant assortment of corals and tropical fish. Other possibilities include sport fishing outside the reef, canoeing, windsurfing or simply relaxing in this secluded paradise.

WHEN TO GO: Any time – but it has to be October–December to see the fabulous Tagimaucia flowers at their very best.

TAVEUNI

Fiji

Cigar-shaped Taveuni is the tip of a shield volcano that rises from the floor of the Pacific. The island is dotted with volcanic cones and has suffered less from land clearance than Fiji's other islands. Many visitors dive on the island's famed coral reefs but those who prefer to remain ashore will find plenty to explore. One of the most spectacular natural attractions is Lake Tagimaucia, a crater lake at a height of 800 m (2,625 ft), nestling beneath the impressive Des Voeux peak. This is the place to see Fiji's national flower, the red-and-white Tagimaucia. See this woody vine high in the forest canopy on the approaches to the lake, which is covered with floating vegetation. It's a healthy all-day hike to Lake Tagimaucia, but non-trampers can get most of the way there using a 4x4 vehicle.

DON'T MISS

The Isle of Pines, where the Kuto/Kanuméra area is a picture-perfect tropical paradise.

BARRIER REEF

New Caledonia

New Caledonia's Barrier Reef is the world's second longest at 1,500 km (930 mi), surrounding the main island of Grand Terre and various smaller isles. Despite damage to the reef's eastern section as a result of nickel mining effluent, this unique eco-region remains in rude good health and provides safe haven for a great variety of life, including endangered dugongs (sea cows) and green turtles. Such is the diversity of species that new fish and invertebrates are regularly discovered. So far, 1,000 types of fish, 5,000 different crustaceans, 5,500 molluscs, 600 sponges and 23 species of breeding bird, including the charming red-footed booby, have been recorded.
Coral formations are outstanding and can provide the experience of a lifetime for scuba divers and snorkellers who boat out to the reef, although non-water-babes can get a feel for the place by taking to glass-bottomed craft or indulging in numerous watersports.

ANTARCTIC PENINSULA

Antarctica

It's the end of the book, and the end of the world. The planet's last great uninhabited wilderness is covered by ice averaging 1.5 km (1 mi) in thickness, and if it all melted, sea levels around the world would rise by nearly 20 m (66 ft). Due to global warming, this is happening. The Antarctic Peninsula is the northernmost part of the mainland. Its coasts have the mildest climate in the continent and are snow-free in summer months. The peninsula is characterized by offshore islands connected to the mainland by ice and stand-alone ice shelves — many of the latter retreating or disintegrating at an alarming rate. Even so, the wildlife (penguins, seabirds, seals and whales), seascapes and mountainous interior remain spectacular. Antarctic cruise ships are small, rarely carrying more than 150 passengers. Expedition ships offer varying levels of luxury, while some with ice-strengthened hulls go where intrepid passengers can enjoy activities like sea kayaking. At the sharp end (literally) are icebreakers that go where no other ship can.

YOU SHOULD KNOW

Huts on Ross Island were used as bases by polar heroes Robert Falcon Scott and Ernest Shackleton.

INDEX

PICTURE CREDITS

123RF ammit 91; andreyshevchenko 257; bennymarty 364; Chad Zuber 76; David Martyn Hughes 184, 202; Denys Bilytskyi 243; designpics 199; efired 292; Filip Fuxa 118; Frank Bach 182; John Cameron 170; Konstantin Kalishko 278; lorcel 6 above, 36; Oliver Nowak 216; Pavel Timofeev 236; penta 255; Piotr Gatlik 353; Putt Sakdhnagool 35; Somchai Jongmeesuk 8; stevanzz 263; Steven Prorak 143; stocksolutions 184; Tanya Puntti 344; Wong Chun Wai 371. **Alamy Stock Photo** AA World Travel Library 283; Accent Alaska.com 29 below; Adam Burton 188, 200 above; Adam Eastland 267; Aditya "Dicky" Singh 309; Adrian Davies 189; AfriPics.com 7 below, 160; Alaska Stock LLC 30; Alistair Petrie 197; All Canada Photos/Barrett&MacKay Photo 24; allOver photography 179; Andrew Watson 330; Andria Patino 78 below; Andy Sutton 172 above; Angus McComiskey 291 above; A.P. 152; Arco Images GmbH./B. Fischer 273; Ariadne Van Zandbergen 122 below; Art Directors & TRIP/Martin Barlow 131 below; Arterra Picture Library/Arndt Sven-Erik 215; ArteSub 374; Atmotu Images 318, 320, 378 above; Aurora Photos/Ted Wood 300 above; Banana Pancake 82; Bill Bachman 350; Bill Gozansky 86; blickwinkel/Bala 221 above; blickwinkel/Kaufung 213; blickwinkel/Irlmeier 117 below; blickwinkel/McPHOTO/ZAD 129, 144 above; blickwinkel/Meyers 304; blickwinkel/Salminen 180; Bob Gibbons 67, 247; botanikfoto/Steffen Hauser 219; BrazilPhotos/Flavio Varricchio 84 below; Carol Dixon 284; Cephas Picture Library/Jeffery Drewitz 360; Chad Ehlers 7 centre, 178 above, 248; Charles O. Cecil 117 above; Craig Lovell 335; Chris Howarth/New Zealand 346; CuboImages srl/Bluered 262; Culliganphoto 238; Danita Delimont/Cindy Miller Hopkins 70; Danita Delimont/Gavriel Jecan 90; Danita Delimont/Greg Johnston 62; Danita Delimont/Scott T. Smith 81 below; David Buzzard 158; David Lyons 193; David Noton Photography 354 above; David R. Frazier Photolibrary, Inc. 105; David Robertson 175, 261, 281 above; David Shaw 92; David Wall 365; Dennis Cox 336; Derek Payne 186; Dinodia Images/India Images 308; Doug Steley B 357; Emil Enchev 249 above, 249 below; Emmanuel Lattes 206; Eric Nathan 141; Eugene Feygin 225; Eye Ubiquitous/David Forman 64; Fabienne Fossez 75 below; F1online digitale Bildagentur GmbH 246; First Light/Darwin Wiggett 18; First Light/ Ron Watts 27; Frans Lanting Studio 157, 295 below; Friedrichsmeier Archive/Bleyer 163; Friedrichsmeier

Archive/Burger 154, 156; Gary Cook 232; Hemis/Christophe Boisvieux 121; Hemis/Pawel Wysocki 168; Hemis/ Stéphane Frances 78 above, 79 below; Holger Mette 89; Iain Lowson 270; Iconotec/Sir Pengallan 80; imagebroker/ Christian Heinrich 104; imagebroker/ Guenter Fischer 161; imagebroker/ Konrad Wothe 258; imagebroker/ Martin Siepmann 61 above, 226; imagebroker/Michael Krabs 223; imagebroker/Oliver Gerhard 159; imagebroker/Stefan Auth 120, 300 below; imagebroker/Thomas Vinke 93 below; Images & Stories 281 below, 376; ImagesEurope 209; Images of Africa Photobank/Dominic Harcourt-Webster 133; Images of Africa Photobank/Lanz von Horsten 166; IML Image Group Ltd./Roberto Meazza 256; Indiapicture/P.S. Lahiri 306; INSADCO photography/Profimedia International s.r.o. 142; INTERFOTO 221 below; isifa Image Service s.r.o./ Berger Jiří 228; Ivan Vdovin 285; Janusz Gniadek 229 above; Jan Wlodarczyk 244; Javier Etcheverry 109; Joanna Szycik 229 above; JoeFox Argentina 110; Joel Day 348; John Sylvester 10; John T.L 311; John Warburton-Lee Photography 151; John Warburton-Lee Photography/Julian Love 149; John Warburton-Lee Photography/Mark Hannaford 96; John Warburton-Lee Photography/Nigel Pavitt 135; Jon Arnold Images Ltd 68 below, 134; Jon Arnold Images Ltd./Doug Pearson 210 below; Jon Arnold Images Ltd./Gavin Hellier 103; Jon Arnold Images Ltd./Paul Joynson Hicks 139; Jon Gibbs 191 below; Jon Massie 81 above; JTB Photo Communications, Inc. 339 above, 340, 341 below; Kaido Kärner 233; Kevin Ebi 42; Kevin Schafer 87, 95, 98, 99; Kurt Lackovic 363; Ladi Kim 313; Lee Beel 192 above; Lee Dalton 75 above, 85 above; Lonely Planet Images/Grant Dixon 101; Lonely Planet Images/Peter Hendrie 377; LOOK Die Bildagentur der Fotografen GmbH/Holger Leue 286 above; LOOK Die Bildagentur der Fotografen GmbH/Michael Boyny 93 above; LOOK Die Bildagentur der Fotografen GmbH/Rainer Martini 227; Marcin Mikolajczak 58; Marion Bull 207; Marion Kaplan 128, 136; mediacolor's 224; Michael Dwyer 126; Michele Falzone 342; Mikael Utterström 181; Mike P Shepherd 115; Mountain Light/ Galen Rowell 85 below; M.Timothy O'Keefe 71; Nancy Hoyt Belcher 48; Nejc Vesel 260; Nigel Hicks 331; Oyvind Martinsen 68 above; P.A. Lawrence, LLC. 29 above; Pavel Filatov 296; Pep Roig 310; Peter Arnold, Inc./ Ray Pfortner 77; Peter Bowater 208; Photos 12/Serge Sautereau 201 below; Photoshot Holdings Ltd. 84 above;

PVstock.com 45; RIA Novosti 235, 239; Robert Dziewulski 282; Robert Harding Picture Library Ltd. 314; Robert Harding Picture Library Ltd./ David C Poole 147, 148; Robert Harding Picture Library Ltd./Ethel Davis 83; Robert Mayne 198; Robert Morris 276; Robert Preston Photography 88; Rod Edwards 6 centre, 251; Ron Evans 190 below; Ron Niebrugge 39 above; Ron Yue 339 below; Rupert Hansen 265; Saman Bagheri 289; Scott Barclay 355 below; Scott Bowman 355 above; Scott Kemper 201 above; Sean Burke 183; Sergio Pitamitz 137; Shaughn F. Clements 14; Shisanu Tongchim 323; Spring Images 16 above; Stefano Paterna 72; Steve Stock 298; TAO Images Limited/Liu Kuanxin 333 below; tbkmedia.de 11, 218; The Africa Image Library 144 below, 145, 164, 165, 167; The National Trust Photo Library/Joe Cornish 191 above; Thierry Grun 122 above; T. Kopecny 242; Tom Bean 79 above; Top-Pics TBK 106; Travelscape Images 130; Trevor Booth Photography 21; United Archives GmbH/KPA/ Gerken&Ernst 252; Vince Li 333 above; Vladimir Medvedev 297; Vova Pomortzeff 295 above; WorldFoto 138; Zach Holmes 56 above. **Corbis** 274 below; All Canada Photos/Barrett & MacKay 7 above, 23, 25; All Canada Photos/Michael Wheatley 15; All Canada Photos/Rolf Hicker 20; All Canada Photos/Russ Heinl 19; All Canada Photos/Wayne Lynch 379 below; amanaimages/Satoru Imai 341 above; Ann Johansson 131 above; Arctic-Images 173; Atlantide Phototravel 132; Aurora Photos/Ian Shive 46 above; Bernd Kohlhas 274 above; Bob Krist 174; Catherine Karnow 325; Christophe Boisvieux 343; David Muench 47, 53 above, 54; Diego Lezama Orezzoli 347; DLILLC 337; Donohue Photography/Broudy 372; epa/Mike Nelson 114; Frank Krahmer 370; Frans Lanting 6 below, 169, 329, 369; Gallo Images/Anthony Bannister 150; George H.H. Huey 33, 38, 40, 43 above; George Steinmetz 153, 288 above, 291 below; Goodlook/Philippe Giraud 211; Hans Strand 177; Hemis/ Bruno Morandi 319; Herbert Spichtinger 162; Ivan Vdovin 302; Jack Fields 178 below; JAI/Alan Copson 37; JAI/Doug Pearson 280, 366; James Randklev 51; John and Lisa Merrill 322; John Harper 187; Jose Fuste Raga 39 below; Keren Su 334; Kerrick James 100; Loop Images/Marc Bedingfield 192 below; Macduff Everton 378 below; Martin Harvey 312; Momatiuk – Eastcott 41; O. Alamany & E. Vicens 268 above, 286 below; Paul A. Souders 367 above; Pete Saloutos 17; Photolibrary 356; PICIMPACT 268 below; Radius

Images 22, 358; Raymond Gehman 12, 16 below, 56 below; Reuters/Laszlo Balogh 245; Richard Glover 367 below; Robert Harding World Imagery/Luca Tettoni 359; Robert Harding World Imagery/Occidor Ltd. 338; Robin Weaver 190 above; Roger Antrobus 196; Roger Wood 288 below; Roland Gerth 269; Ron Watts 43 below; Sandro Vannini 266; Science Faction/Ed Darack 375; Science Faction/Louie Psihoyos 299; Scott T. Smith 52; Stuart Westmorland 31; Sygma/Zoko/Pierre Perrin 28; Theo Allofs 97, 107, 349; Tim Tadder 32; Tom Bean 46 below; Tony Roberts 373; Tribaleye Images/J Marshall 328; Ula Holigrad 231; Visions of America/Joseph Sohm 34; Yann Arthus-Bertrand 125. **Emma Hill** 172 below. **Getty Images** Andrea Pistolesi 332; Ian Shive 53 below; Jeff Foott 57; Luis Veiga 94; Mariana Eliano 108; Panoramic Images 61 below; Patrice Hauser 210 above; Patricio Robles Gil 316; Purestock 50. **Lonely Planet Images** Casey Mahaney 321; John Mock 305, 307; Richard I'Anson 351, 354 below. **National Geographic Stock** Michael Melford 26. **Photolibrary Group** CuboImages/ Marco Casiraghi 327; JTB Photo 294; Peter Arnold Images/Mark Carwardine 317; Photononstop/Alain Even 379 above; Rob Jung 361; Silvi Glattauer 362. **Pixabay** 66, 111, 112, 123, 214, 220, 264.

Every effort has been made to trace the copyright holders, and we apologise in advance for any unintentional omissions. We would be pleased to insert the appropriate acknowledgement in any subsequent edition of this publication.